THE ARAB WORLD
PERSONAL ENCOUNTERS

Books by Elizabeth Warnock Fernea

A STREET IN MARRAKECH

A VIEW OF THE NILE

GUESTS OF THE SHEIK

MIDDLE EASTERN MUSLIM WOMEN SPEAK
(with Basima Qattan Bezirgan)

Books by Robert A. Fernea

NUBIANS IN EGYPT: PEACEFUL PEOPLE

SHAYKH AND EFFENDI: CHANGING PATTERNS
OF AUTHORITY AMONG THE EL SHABANA
OF SOUTHERN IRAQ

SYMPOSIUM ON CONTEMPORARY EGYPTIAN NUBIA

The Arab World

PERSONAL ENCOUNTERS

by Elizabeth Warnock Fernea
and Robert A. Fernea

Photographs by Thomas Hartwell

ANCHOR PRESS / DOUBLEDAY
GARDEN CITY, NEW YORK
1985

Grateful acknowledgement is made for permission to quote copyrighted material, as follows:

Lines from Jabra Ibrahim Jabra, "A Poem Sequence"; Ahmad Abd al-Mu'ti Hijazi, "Caption to a Landscape"; Nizar Qabbani, "What Value Has the People Whose Tongue Is Tied?"; Badr Shakir al-Sayyab, "An Ode to Revolutionary Iraq," in *An Anthology of Modern Arabic Poetry* edited by Mounah A. Khouri and Hamid Algar. Published by University of California Press, 1974. Used by permission of the publishers.

Lines from Imru al-Qays, "The Muallaqa," and from Labid, "Mu'allaqa," translated by Basima Bezirgan and Elizabeth Fernea, in *Cultural Expression in Arab Society Today,* by Jacques Berque. Copyright © Editions Gallimard, 1974; translation copyright © University of Texas Press, 1978. By permission of the publishers.

Lines from "Sunday Morning," by Wallace Stevens. Copyright 1923 and renewed 1951, by Wallace Stevens. Reprinted from *The Collected Poems of Wallace Stevens,* by permission of Alfred A. Knopf, Inc.

Lines from Abid ibn al-Abras, "Lament for an Arab Encampment," and "Unknown, ninth century," translated by Omar Pound, from Omar Pound, *Arabic and Persian Poems.* Copyright © 1970 by Omar S. Pound. Reprinted by permission of New Directions Publishing Corporation.

Lines from C. P. Cavafy, "Sham el-Nessim." Copyright © 1959 by Rae Dalven. Reprinted from *The Complete Poems of Cavafy,* translated by Rae Dalven by permission of Harcourt Brace Jovanovich, Inc.

Lines from Rashid Hussein, "Tent 50 (Song of a Refugee)" in *Enemies of the Sun.* Published by Drum and Spear Press. Used by permission of the translators, Edmund Ghareeb and Naseer Aruri.

Book design by Beverley Woods Vawter Gallegos

Library of Congress Cataloging in Publication Data
Fernea, Elizabeth Warnock.
The Arab world.
1. Arab countries. I. Fernea, Robert A. (Robert Alan), 1932–   . II. Title.
DS36.7.F47   1985   909'.0974927082   82–45245
ISBN 0-385-17123-4

In Memory of

Malcolm H. Kerr
1931–1984
Beirut

Scholar, Colleague, Friend

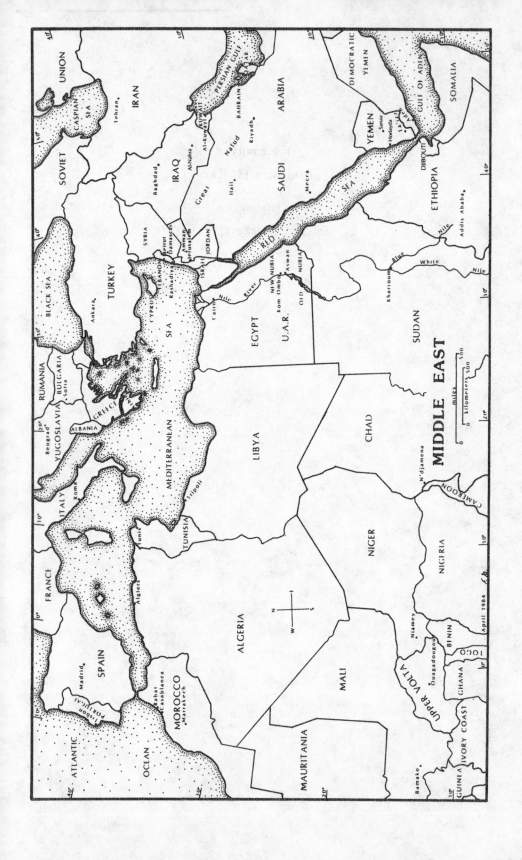

CONTENTS

PREFACE

W E WENT to the Arab world for the first time in 1956 and we have remained involved in the area ever since. We lived for two years in Iraq and for six years in Egypt, where our three children were born. We spent a year and a half in Morocco and have visited other parts of the region for briefer periods. Bob has written books about Iraq and Egyptian Nubia and done research in Afghanistan, Jordan, and Saudi Arabia. B.J. (Elizabeth) has written books about Iraq, Egypt, and Morocco and produced films about Arab women.

The incidents in the book which follows are all real, as are the people, although in almost all cases we have changed names and sometimes created composite characters so that people might not be embarrassed. It is impossible to name all our friends in the Arab world who have contributed to the making of this book, but we would like to thank them for their hospitality and friendship over the years.

We would also like to express our appreciation to Basima Bezirgan, Izzat Ghurani, Peter Gubser, Dagmar Hamilton, Salah-Dine Hammoud, Wm. Roger Louis, Safia Mohsen, Carol and Sidney Monas, Carolyn Osborn, Robert Stookey, and Heather Taylor for reading parts of the manuscript and making many important suggestions.

Our thanks go to the following institutions, which, from time to time over the past twenty-eight years, have made research in the Arab world possible: the National Science Foundation, the Oriental Institute of the University of Chicago, the Ford Foundation, the Fulbright-Hays Commission, and the National Endowment for the Humanities. Our trip to Libya was made possible by a grant from the Arab Development Institute.

The University of Texas at Austin has been our home since 1966. Bob teaches in the Department of Anthropology there, and B.J. in the Center for Middle Eastern Studies. We would like to thank the center for its assistance, including Daniel Goodwin, Ann Grabhorn, Marjorie Payne, and Jenny White. Cora Boyett, Joy Lough, James Taylor, and Suzanne Rodriguez have typed various drafts of the manuscript. We thank them all.

We have been fortunate in Sally Arteseros, our friend and editor at Doubleday. She encouraged us to write this book in the first place and has guided us patiently and thoughtfully through its various forms. But we do not hold her or anyone else responsible for our opinions, which are our own.

INTRODUCTION

THE ARAB WORLD, in recent years, has moved to the forefront of American attention. Events such as the oil blockade of the early seventies, the Iranian revolution and the subsequent hostage crisis, and the U.S. Marine Corps intervention in Lebanon have dominated the news. Americans have viewed the Arab world—and the entire Middle East—on their television screens and in their newspapers and magazines with a frequency unthinkable twenty-five years ago. Then the Middle East seemed remote and unapproachable. Today the average American is familiar with the sight of sheikhs in flowing white robes and headdresses signing oil agreements; with mothers grieving in the background for children or husbands killed in conflicts in Lebanon, Israel, Iran, Iraq; with young men in camouflage battle dress, shaking their machine guns aggressively at the screen. Yet despite this coverage, this continual series of images beamed into American homes, the Arab world still remains remote and strange. The people themselves, their hopes, fears, and dreams, remain distant from us, as they run for cover in Beirut or Jerusalem or Basra, turn away from the lens of the television camera, shield themselves behind veils, robes, sunglasses, tears. The very nearness of the television images, presented without explanation or background, accentuate the differences between "us" and "them"; "they" dress differently, look different, seem to worship a different God. Only Egyptian President Anwar Sadat seems to have crossed the barrier from stranger to familiar figure in the American media. But President Sadat is dead.

The images of the Arab peoples seen by millions of Americans every day are far removed from our own impressions, our own experiences in the Middle East over the last quarter of a century. We are aware of both the differences and the similarities between us. But we are also aware that none of these differences and similarities is fixed, and that life in the Arab world, like life everywhere else, is undergoing significant and constant change. Out of our concern over the incomplete image, even stereotype, which Americans have of the Arabs and out of our concern with ongoing change which is affecting us in America as well as in the Arab world, we have written this book.

Our friends and acquaintances are not representative of the entire area; but they are certainly part of it. And the changes over the past twenty-five years in the lives of the people we have known then and now seem indicative of larger transformations in the society, which are affecting the lives of everyone.

Our book is titled *The Arab World: Personal Encounters* with reason. Each chapter records different kinds of personal encounters, with people we have known for years, in Egypt, Iraq, Morocco, Lebanon, and with people we have met more recently, in Yemen, Jordan, Libya, Saudia Arabia. Encounters are meetings, but they are also forms of exchanges; experiences of daily life. We have learned much from our friends and have been altered by our experiences.

Change is often discussed in abstract terms, defined by statistics, surveys, and other quantitative data. Such an approach tends to see the situation not in terms of everyday life but in terms of one ideological position or another. Yet people do not live according to abstractions; few of us are galvanized by theory. Most live in terms of the problems of daily life: chores, pleasures, disappointments, meetings, duties, work, failures. To understand the texture of change, its effects on families and individuals, we must turn to the patterns of people's lives. Daily experience, whether in America or in the Arab world, often changes one's views, tears holes in the comfortable abstractions, causes one to question the generalities, to search for qualitative as well as quantitative data.

The book opens in Beirut, because it was in Beirut that we began our journey to the Arab world in 1956 and it was to Beirut that we returned in 1981. The book follows our journeying and records our observations and experiences in Jordan, Yemen, Libya, Egypt, Morocco, Saudi Arabia, and Iraq. But many of the changes in progress are common throughout the area. All Arab countries were affected by the Western colonial presence. France, Britain, Italy, and Spain occupied or ruled most countries of the area for shorter or longer periods from 1800 to 1962. By 1962, almost every country had gained its independence from the West. A series of new nations emerged, eager for development.

The Arab world is attempting to achieve in a generation or two the social and technological transformations which took more than two hundred years in the West. The pace of the effort has understandably left people breathless and hopeful, but also anxious and fearful about the possibilities which the future holds. "The sting of change lies not in change itself, but in change that has no meaning," E. H. Frankel has written. For the Arab world, change is inevitable, but its meaning and its long-term effects are still unclear. As with Americans, earning a living and raising a family occupy most of the people of the Middle East. As with Americans, the foundations of the old society their parents knew have been threatened, even destroyed. An agricultural region less than twenty-five years ago, the Arab world is now in the process of industrialization. With industrialization has come the growth of modern capitalism, of consumerism, of a new middle class, of urbanism.

Not all Arab countries are oil-rich, as the media might suggest. Those that are —Saudi Arabia, Kuwait, Libya, Iraq, the Gulf States—are changing more rapidly than the Sun Belt in the United States. They not only are expanding their own economies but are importing labor from other Arab nations and from the Third World. They are also investing their capital gains outside their own countries. Thus, the Arab oil wealth is in many ways spreading out to many people far from the refineries and the gushers—people in America, Europe, and Asia as well as the Middle East.

In Lebanon, the oil wealth which flowed into the banks increased enormously after 1948, when Arab nations withdrew their deposits from Jerusalem, following the declaration of the State of Israel; and from Cairo after the revolution in 1952. The revenues enriched some Lebanese, particularly the bankers, the majority of whom were Christian Arabs. But not all shared in the wealth. Lebanon and Jordan were further affected by the influx of thousands of Palestinian refugees, who poured across the borders in 1948, and again in 1967. Three hundred thousand refugees still live in Lebanon, two hundred thousand in Jordan; many compete for jobs with Lebanese and Jordanians. Such disturbances in the economic and social order of these small countries has led to revolts, civil wars, invasions, the effects of which have not yet ended.

On the surface, the situation in Egypt seems less dramatic. Although Egyptians have lost husbands, brothers, sons, and fathers in the wars of 1948, 1967, and 1973 with Israel, Egyptians have also signed a peace treaty with Israel. Egypt, with a population of 44 million, twice that of any other Arab country, has been struggling, more than any other nation in the area, to maximize its limited natural resources through industrialization. Thousands of men and women have migrated from the country to the city in the past twenty years in search of factory wage labor, much as Americans thronged to the cities from the farms in the early years of the twentieth century. Egypt is now more urban than rural, an abrupt shift that has caused much family concern and individual dislocation. The same was true in the United States, but Egyptians, unlike Americans, have been forced by rising inflation costs and population pressures to continue moving beyond the borders of their own country.

Labor migration has now become international, as men and women from Morocco, Algeria, Tunisia, and Yemen move within the Arab world to Saudi Arabia, Libya, Iraq, and abroad to America and to Europe, a movement of poor to rich countries in search of work. An estimated 4 million people are involved, which has had as yet unmeasured effects on individuals, on families, on the position of women. Women now find themselves managing households, farms, and businesses alone, often for the first time. Children are raised without fathers. For a society that twenty years ago was tied together by the close bonds of kinship within the extended family, such pressures are new—and disturbing. Yet work is essential, whether at home or abroad. And the remittances sent home by men (as much as $1 million per month from the Detroit auto workers to their Yemeni families) allows families to buy consumer goods that they could never have afforded in the past: television sets, washing machines, refrigerators, automobiles, houses. Consumerism, in other words, is on the rise all over the area.

And if this is the case in the poorer countries receiving remittances from abroad, it is doubly and triply so in the oil-rich countries of Saudi Arabia, Kuwait, the Gulf States, and Iraq (until the recent devastating war with Iran reduced the level of material prosperity). New kinds of consumer goods are available on a level which was not predicted by the Western economic forecasters of the fifties and sixties.

Affluence raises many issues. Does wealth destroy or reaffirm the traditional roles of men and women? Saudi Arabia seems to be a case where wealth is used to maintain traditional roles, to block (through the importation of outside foreign labor) the entry of women into the workplace, to provide separate but equal educational facilities for women and men. In Kuwait, affluence is said to have had the opposite effect, supposedly freeing women from traditional restrictions, both public and private.

In every country in which we have lived or have visited, the increase in free public education, from primary school through university, is remarkable. In Egypt alone, university education jumped from 33,000 students in 1950 to 196,000 in 1969. In 1974 it stood at 250,000. Rich states and poor states alike have enormously increased educational, health, and other social services for all their citizens, in line with promises made in the fifties during the rise of Arab nationalism and the subsequent declarations of independence by the new nations from Morocco to Yemen.

Education in the Middle East is proving to be the kind of catalyst John Kenneth Galbraith suggested might be true for all poor countries in his essay "On the Origins of Mass Poverty." Education has been the means, as it was in the United States, for men and women to break out of a cycle of poverty, out of a system where no options had existed other than the one they were born into. However, it has happened so fast that it has produced another unexpected problem: in Morocco, in Egypt, in Algeria, hundreds of thousands of young people are either unemployed or without the kinds of jobs they had been led to believe their education would bring them. This has been happening in the United States as well, but more gradually. In the Arab world, the situation is a major source of frustration for the young and newly educated, a situation which cannot be expected to improve unless local economies expand.

The growth of local media has added an important new element to the lives of millions of people. Nine daily papers are published in Cairo; six in Baghdad; five in Casablanca. More glossy weekly and monthly magazines are appearing (*Usratii* in Kuwait, *Musawwar* in Cairo). Book publishing, always valued in the area, is increasing; more books of poetry, fiction, philosophy, and religious essays, as well as technical scientific translations from European languages, are available in cheap paperback editions in every newspaper kiosk and bookstore. The Egyptian film industry now ranks third in the world in sheer output, just behind the United States and India. Video and tape cassettes are for sale in provincial towns and villages as well as large cities, and carry not only music and light amusement but also the sermons and addresses of influential leaders.

As in the United States, the real breakthrough over the last generation has been the widespread dissemination of television broadcasting. Fifty-five percent of all Egyptians own television sets, but nearly 70 percent have access to television. Morocco, Algeria, Libya, Iraq, Saudi Arabia, Lebanon, and Syria all have government-owned and -controlled television corporations.

Television in the Arab world, like television everywhere, is proving to be a mixed blessing. It provides inexpensive entertainment, but at the same time pictures upper-middle-class life-styles (as in "Dallas") and consumer goods (in Western-style commercials) which are beyond the pocketbooks of the average viewer. Consumer expectations are raised that cannot be fulfilled, and frustration results. This is especially true in Egypt. Television is also being used, for better or worse, as education and for the promotion of government policy. Kuwait has adapted "Sesame Street" for Arab audiences, and Egypt offers daily tutoring sessions in mathematics. In all Arab countries, regular religious instruction is offered. In Morocco, Libya, and the Gulf, the state not only controls the television but also restricts the amount of Western programming, in an effort to reduce local dependence on outside entertainment, and encourages indigenous programs instead. In these contexts, television becomes a powerful tool for effecting change.

National pride and positive self-image are increasingly important. Arabs are still recovering from what they view as the humiliation of the colonial presence, the defeat in the Arab-Israeli wars. For many, a new sense of common identity as Muslims is evident. Throughout the area, in Morocco, in Egypt, in Saudi Arabia, in Yemen, people spoke to us about the need to return to roots, to reaffirm the basics: family ties, parent-child relationships, religious beliefs. They said they wanted the convenience of modern technology, but not at the expense of their traditional values. The rise of movements urging a return to traditional male and female behavior roles (as in Saudi Arabia) and a restatement of belief in Islam (the religion of over 90 percent of the people) should not be too surprising to Americans, who are experiencing some of the same phenomena in their own lives. Thus, to deal with the sting of change, the new information, the new demands, the new pressures, Arab peoples are using old methods as well as new, arranging them in new combinations in order to give meaning to their radically changed lives.

Today the old romantic image of the Arab as a figure mounted on horse or camel is no more useful a contribution to American thinking than is the stereotypical media view of this group of more than 160 million people as fanatics and terrorists. The interdependence of our common well-being is too important to permit such fantasies. Americans share with Arabs common beliefs in monotheism and in ideas about family. Our science, our language, even our diet, have been influenced by discoveries made long ago by Arabs. Like friends who have drifted apart over the years, we are being brought back together by the force of circumstance: the world market, the needs of industrial societies, the struggle for peace.

For over a quarter of a century people in many countries of the Arab world have welcomed us, tolerated us, educated us. We hope our book may serve to illuminate for our fellow Americans some of the complex human dilemmas the people of the Arab world are facing today.

THE ARAB WORLD
PERSONAL ENCOUNTERS

CHAPTER I

Beirut, Lebanon

1956

At daybreak we come down to the harbor
Where ships have spread sails for departure.
And we cry, "O beloved sea,
As near as the eyelids of our eyes,
We are eager for the voyage. . . .
Shepherds have told us of those islands
Where people have challenged destiny,
Planted settlements like teeth in the desert
That have grown into cities of light, and of glory
To fill one's eyes with wonder.
Of such magical cities,
Men dream in childhood."

Yusuf al-Khal
The Voyage

IN THE COURTYARD of the French Archaeological Institute hostel, where we stayed on first arriving in Lebanon, a fine Alexander Calder mobile turned gently in the sunshine and sea breeze that marked the early Mediterranean fall. Red and black, it was obviously very modern and yet it seemed to fit perfectly with the old Lebanese house, its stone stairway and rooms built around the spacious, sunny, whitewashed courtyard. Within the institute library the high windows were bordered with pointed arches in the Islamic style; the stained glass was arranged within the windows so that the light formed shifting patterns of color upon the floor, upon the modern rush chairs, the dark, carved Druze chest, the shelves of old books and new scholarly publications from Europe and America.

Bob and I sat up on the balcony, reveling in our new adventure in this beautiful setting. We had docked in Alexandria a week before but had not been allowed to land because of rioting there. President Gamal Abdul Nasser, the new President of Egypt, who had ousted King Farouk in 1952, now had the audacity to nationalize the Suez Canal. Stockholders in France and Britain were incredulous and outraged. "The gyppies just can't do this to us," was the general European sentiment. Other authoritative voices were assuring it would only be a matter of days before the canal would be blocked; the Egyptians would soon come crawling back to London and Paris, begging for the European pilots to return, for the European engineers to run the locks. Meanwhile, our ship had sailed on to the friendlier shores of Lebanon. And here we sat, watching the scene outside, waiting for Bob Adams to arrive from the University of Chicago before we all set out across the desert to Baghdad. The Jewish school nearby was full of children, their chanting reverberating up and down the narrow lane. To our left, the local streetcar went binging along the rails. The passengers inside sat stiffly in baggy pants and turbans, all-enveloping cloaks, French-made skirts and sweaters, white body-fitting shirts and pants. An occasional embroidered hat, a patterned vest, signaled another representative of Lebanon's many ethnic and religious groups. From the balcony we saw people in turbans, skullcaps, flat pillboxes, fezzes, and veils both black and white climbing onto the streetcars, jumping off. These were exotic signs of a diversity of origins which we still could not decode.

We were enchanted with Beirut. Our ship had sailed into port two days before in bright sunshine, the houses gleaming white on the hills and the mountains rising behind the city, terraced green ridge upon ridge. The sky was blue, the sun warm but not hot. The next day we had climbed onto the streetcar in front of the French Institute and sat on the woven rush seats reminiscent of my childhood, when I had taken my aunt Rose's plump hand and gone with her on the Old State Street car into downtown Chicago.

It seemed incredible to be riding a streetcar in Beirut, ancient Phoenicia, where Greek sailors had caroused two thousand years before, and where today people walked about as though this were just another ordinary city.

"I don't like the ice cream, though," I said.

It was funny, the ice cream, sweet and stringy like taffy—long on sugar and short on milk, Bob said. "But that's just because we're prejudiced Americans," he carefully added.

I agreed, and we happily dined on other great specialties more to our taste: *shawarma* (sliced barbecued lamb), fresh tiny wild strawberries brought in from the mountains, and tabooli, a marvelous salad made from parsley and tomatoes and cracked wheat.

Downtown, we wandered into the Bourse, through the markets, looking at banks of scarlet flowers, yellow asters, and white roses. We looked at wine, at auto parts, at fine French furniture, head scarves, long Arab cloaks, plumbing fixtures, cement, perfumes, tiles. Goods from all over the world seemed to be laid out before our eyes on stands and counters, on small rugs and colorful lengths of cloth spread out on the ground. Occasionally someone would holler:

"Hey! This main drag. You American?"

"Here, George, good English cloth, see!"

"Brooklyn Bridge, ha ha! Good price!"

Each day we stayed at the French Archaeological Institute Bob went swimming in the sea, for the beach was within easy walking distance. He visited the grocery store across the street. "Every time I go," he said, "the proprietor wants to talk politics. Everyone I meet wants to talk politics." So it seemed.

I went to Sunday mass with an elderly French gentleman who was an authority on Syrian Christian art. The church seemed full of Europeans.

"That is because this is the Latin rite," the French gentleman explained. "If we went to the Nestorian church or the Armenian church or the Maronite cathedral, you would see a different congregation. And you are American?"

I nodded.

He smiled. "We usually think of Americans as Protestants. Like the Near Eastern School of Theology here, and the American University, of course." He paused. "Mission schools. Unlike the French." He smiled again, somewhat mischievously.

"But the French nuns were here, too," I burst out defensively. "Why, you told me yourself the French Institute used to be the headquarters of the Little Sisters of the Poor."

The French gentleman stroked his mustache. "No need to be upset, madame. All do good works. But the nuns, they do not proselytize, directly, that is, for our Lord Jesus Christ."

I was silent, but I was furious. And later I burst out to Bob about the self-satisfied attitude of the French, who were covert about their proselytizing, but were obviously just as much up to it as the Americans with schools and missions; why, this very building had been a convent, and—

"Okay, okay, B.J. No need to take it so personally. Besides, before the Little Sisters of the Poor, this building housed a great revolutionary leader, a Muslim leader at that. From revolution to religion and finally scholarship. All that within these four walls," he added, glancing around.

He was right. In the courtyard, beneath the shade of a sculptured overhang, a brass plate had been affixed to the wall commemorating the Emir Abd al-Kader, who fought against the first French settlements in Algeria, escaped to Morocco, and was eventually captured by the French.

Emir Abd al-Kader, leader of his people,
lived here in exile under French protection
for seven months in the year 1856.

French protection indeed, I thought indignantly.

Bob Adams arrived, our visas were duly stamped, and before we set off in the University of Chicago Jeep across the desert to Baghdad, we were invited to dine at the summer home of M. Henri Seyrig, the director of the institute, where we had been staying. Up in the mountains, he said. "A simple dinner of native dishes." His messenger offered to drive us to the retreat above Aley.

Dusk was coming down over the sea as we climbed, the setting sun staining the rock ridges pink as we wound around them in the Jeep, shading the oleanders, pink and white, muting the red tiled roofs of the stone houses in the mountain villages. We braked and paused for bleating sheep, for a few cows being chased by a boy in a skullcap and an embroidered shirt, for a procession of women in red dresses, with diaphanous colored veils that spread out behind them in the evening breeze, like haloes around their heads.

M. Seyrig greeted us on the terrace of his summer house, a man in late middle age, small and compact, dark, and with a gracious manner, an inquisitive eye. After aperitifs, dinner was served by a woman servant in bloomers and embroidered blouse, her hair tied up in one of those evanescent veils, this one purple. A simple meal of native foods—yes—delicious shawarma, rice, salad.

We sat with M. Seyrig, looking out over the dark valley dotted with rows of tiny flickering lights marking the houses along the terraces we had just climbed. The sea, studded with flecks of foam glimmering white on the black water, seemed scarcely distinguishable from the land. Behind us hung modern canvases by an unfamiliar Parisian painter, great strokes of orange, green, black, crimson, in unexpected combinations on the walls of the whitewashed summer house. To our right a Maronite cathedral loomed in the dusk, reflecting dim light among shrubs and trees.

The woman in the purple head scarf served dessert: fried bananas in rum. We had thick, strong coffee.

"Yes," murmured M. Seyrig. "This region is ageless in its beauty."

"It is very beautiful," I replied.

What else was there to be said? We were young and impressionable, full of ourselves and our new adventure, our new marriage, our new lives. The vista of hills stretched below us, darkly clotted with fig trees; some aromatic bush vied for sweetness in the dimness with the fumes of rum from our dessert. The sea washed and foamed far below. The evening posed the possibilities of sensual delights that were almost overwhelming. M. Seyrig seemed part of this setting, so relaxed, so knowledgeable. Perhaps it was the conjunction of ancient splendor, natural beauty, and the modern wall-high swaths of bravura color in the paintings behind us that left us speechless. We were from America, a new world, and all this mixing of old and new seemed unreal, strange, something to experience but hard to feel part of yet.

M. Seyrig was speaking, interrupting our reveries. He was describing his daughter. She was an actress on the stage in Paris, but she was thinking of taking part in what looked like an interesting new film. "What is her name?" I interposed politely.

"Delphine. Delphine Seyrig."

Years later, when we saw *Last Year at Marienbad,* with Delphine Seyrig, her hair cut short above her ears to set the fashion for a decade, I remembered the hills above Beirut. The fig trees. The cathedral and the modern paintings. The dark-haired woman and the bananas with rum.

Beirut. 1960. 1964.

During the years to come, when we lived in Iraq and Egypt, Beirut continued to be the closest thing to a visit home. In some ways, we felt a bit ashamed of the fact that we should enjoy the pleasures of Beirut when we were supposed to be involved in the patterns of another culture, not our own. We admitted to each other that Uncle Sam's hamburger restaurant and its American-style ice cream seemed awfully good—the first time around on each visit, at least.

But it was more than familiar sights and sounds. Beirut seemed to us a hopeful place, a sign of the future, where the church bells could ring on Sundays, the synagogues fill up on Saturdays, and the calls to prayer from the mosques sound throughout the week. Whenever doubt flickered like a shadow across our lantern-slide images of the great peaceful future of the Middle East, we thought about Lebanon and Beirut, Switzerland of the Middle East, ancient Phoenician port, where all races and religions mixed, talked, enjoyed a free press and a constitutional government, and made a great deal of money from banking and trade. We saw some hope in all of this. East and West seemed to combine here without perceptible strain.

Then there was the sense of freedom we felt when we arrived in Beirut on a direct flight from Cairo. Gone were the military uniforms seen everywhere in Nasser's Egypt. Gone were the watchful, punctilious customs officials, the careful scrutiny of visas, the strict rules and regulations governing money changing. Abdul Nasser had put tight controls on imports and exports, on the flow of foreign currency, on the travels of Egyptians and even of residents like ourselves. He was fighting to put Egypt in a better economic position. This was laudable and understandable, and from our academic point of view part of the necessary transformation of Egyptian society then in process. But it was hard on everyone, ourselves included, and we felt sometimes as if we were being treated as criminals rather than the helpful, tolerant, law-abiding, and underpaid types we thought ourselves to be. For the most part, the government seemed as distant in Beirut as it seemed close in Egypt. The sense of relief on arriving in Beirut in those days remains a vivid memory.

In 1960, when Laura Ann, our elder daughter, was not yet a year old, wonder of wonders, we could buy disposable diapers in Beirut, and prepared baby food from the States. While Laura Ann dined on Gerber's strained apricots, we could splurge at Ajami's, the honored old restaurant at the foot of the flower market, down from the banking center of the city, only a short walk with a baby stroller along the sea from the old St. George Hotel. Barbecued lamb, Lebanese white wine with its faintly resinous flavor, fresh pears, plums, peaches, baklava, pistachio nuts. And no one took any notice of us. Materialism, consumerism, anonymity, a certain kind of freedom.

Perhaps it is not surprising that we found, as did many fellow expatriates from the States, that Beirut was a familiar oasis in a changing, sometimes difficult Arab world. And what made it all so comfortable was that no one seemed particularly poor in downtown Beirut, no one made us feel a pang of guilt for such pleasures. The Palestinian refugee camps were out of sight, on the outskirts of town. Their occupants were not welcome in downtown Beirut.

"All Lebanese think first thing, when they get up in the morning, about what they'll put in their mouths that day," a friend's mother told me. "Then and only then, my dear, do they think about whether or not they can afford to buy it. Aren't Americans the same?"

Were we? Bob and I didn't accept the similarity precisely, though we certainly felt more at home with the consumer goods than with the churches and missions.

We said to ourselves that Lebanon felt like America because it shared many of our much vaunted freedoms. Was that true? There was freedom of speech, it seemed. College texts described the Lebanese constitution as a model of religious and ethnic accord. Political asylum was taken for granted. If we felt a sense of relief from just being in Beirut, so did hundreds of others with much better reasons, political exiles from throughout the region.

It was not unusual to find a former Iraqi government official of the old Nuri Sa'id government eating fresh sole at Faysal's restaurant while at a nearby table a well-known Communist unwelcome in Nasser's Egypt enjoyed the grilled marinated chicken with whipped garlic sauce. Beirut provided free trade and the appropriate political atmosphere for high-rolling international capitalism. The two were not unrelated, of course. Business was booming without hindrance; taxes and duties were low. Everyone seemed to carry on his or her affairs without bothering others. The focus was on living well and accumulating the means to do so. As the major trade center of the Middle East, home of international banking and of most foreign concerns who wanted a Middle East location free of government interference, Beirut was needed by all parties, friendly or otherwise.

And so life in this sea-blown oasis seemed assured through long sunny summers and long sunny winters. Foreign experts, exiles, businessmen, and educators came and went and the future looked bright and full of promise, at least in downtown Beirut.

CHAPTER II

Beirut, Lebanon

1981

The sun's valleys have no color. Children's nails
have no color.
    Bracelets of fire have no color.
    Screaming has no color.
    Beirut . . . you are screaming.

      Hoda Namani
      I Remember I Was a Point, I Was a Circle

AFTER AN ABSENCE of ten years, Bob and I had come back to live in the Arab world again. We were alone, like the first time: our children, Laura Ann, David, and Laila were far away in America, studying, we trusted, intellectually stimulating and perhaps even useful subjects in colleges and universities. This time we were supposedly able to look at the region with more experienced eyes. After talking about the Middle East in anthropology courses for fifteen years, Bob was setting out to revisit some of the countries of earlier research, to update his firsthand experience. I had a National Endowment for the Humanities grant to make an educational film about social change from a woman's perspective. A new experience for me.

We did not feel self-assured. We felt nervous, for we knew the Arab world had changed radically. But we also felt fortunate, for we had been given the opportunity to come back and see that change for ourselves.

As we peered out the window of our Middle East Airlines plane, now settling in to Beirut, once a brightly lighted San Francisco in the Middle East, there was nothing visible but the winking reflectors along the runway—and darkness.

The airport was nearly empty, and Bob's voice inquiring about taxis sounded very loud. No one was there to meet us, although we had sent telexes and cables. Obviously, the machinery was not working. We knew why, but we did not want to remind each other. Civil disorder. In beautiful Lebanon. Civil war.

The customs official in a crumpled khaki uniform looked vaguely at our luggage. We were waiting for him to stamp it, chalk it, pass it, but he did nothing.

Finally, realizing we were waiting for him, or perhaps deciding to take notice of us, he gestured us past. He was the last representative of state authority we would meet during our stay in Lebanon. The family in front of us, the only other passengers to deplane in Beirut, got into a waiting car outside the airport and drove off. We were left with a row of shouting drivers, all of them after our business. The only business.

"Here, George, over here!"

George? Echoes of the past. (Bob had once wondered if they knew that was his father's first name.)

Bob was already bargaining with a quieter, middle-aged man and our bags were stowed into the trunk of an old American Chevrolet, fifties style, fins and all. But the cab, after a roaring, revving start, stopped again. Out of gas already? The light inside the cab flashed on suddenly and we found ourselves blinking into the faces of two young men leaning into the car, wearing baseball caps and uniforms, not of the New York Yankees but of some military group. Pants, shirt, hat, all of camouflage cloth. The young men flicked their flashlights over us, in the way policemen do to suspects in B movies. We could see their faces. And then the flashlights moved upward, as a signal to go on, and we rolled slowly past the checkpoint. I looked back at it curiously, nervously, as the taxi picked up speed. It was a lean-to with a tin roof, banked by piles of sandbags. One of the men had already disappeared into the hut, but the other, his rifle slung casually over one shoulder (was it a machine gun?), was staring after us. For a panicky moment I wondered if he would run after us, *shoot* at us. Maybe we were guilty of something we didn't even know about?

But no, the taxi had moved straight out the airport road. I relaxed a bit. But— whoosh, the taxi came to a sudden halt again. Checkpoint two. Another lean-to, surrounded by sandbags. The cab light was flicked on again, and another man came to look us over. This one wore, instead of a baseball cap, a red beret with his army fatigues, but he had the same kind of gun over his shoulder. A cigarette was burning between his lips; the smoke came through the open window and filled the damp air of the cab.

Checkpoint-two man shifted his rifle and removed his cigarette. He waved us on without a word. Off went the overhead light. The taxi was roomy, as big American cars are, but its springs must have been recently installed—badly, for when the car moved, we moved back and forth with those springs, over the slippery plastic-covered seats.

"Four more to go!" cried the driver cheerfully, in excellent English. These were his first words to us. He had not spoken during the first two inspections.

"Four what?"

"Four more checks like that," he replied curtly and speeded ahead on the empty, silent route to town. In the darkness, little could be seen but dark blotches beside the road, marking hollows and holes where buildings had presumably once stood. The yellow glare of the headlights glinted off jagged trees and broken bricks, illuminated shadows which might or might not have been people, occasionally picked out piles of rubbish, twisted piping, car parts, chunks of cement that had been imperfectly swept so the road could remain open.

Could this be Beirut? No landmarks appeared to jog the mind and say, "Here I am. Remember me?"

Another jolt. Another stop. Another set of guards moved forward toward us as the cabdriver flicked on the light so we might be observed once again. These men sported green rather than red berets and they looked younger than our own children, now in their early twenties. One stroked a tentative mustache. The gun he carried was not tentative, however, and he seemed to be holding on to it in a way that suggested it could be aimed in our direction rather quickly. I tried to sit up straighter in the slippery taxi seat so as not to appear intimidated. Although we had been in Beirut for less than an hour, I found I was already thinking in clichés, about smelling fear everywhere, terror lurking in the streets. But I did smell fear. Bob sat up straight next to me and stared silently at our observers. Was I smelling our own fear?

"*Yallah!*" The wave of the arm. The taxi light clicking off. We lurched forward into the dark again.

A brand-new sign ahead on the left proclaimed in shocking-pink-and-white neon "Supermarché." The Supermarché was not open, however, so late at night: around it lay more piles of rubble, these more neatly stacked than the ones we had seen before. We speeded around an empty traffic circle where half an acacia tree still stood, the partially severed branches flapping about like incongruous tattered flags.

Beirut. Meeting place of East and West.

Two beautiful gray horses looming up in our headlights smartly trotted over to the side of the road. We both turned in our slippery seats to look at what seemed a curious sight on this dark, heavily guarded, nearly empty road. The gray horses were led by two uniformed riders, in boots so highly polished they gleamed in our headlights.

Checkpoint four. The men at this one were sleepy. They sat in their sandbagged bivouac, listening to the radio from which an old recording blared forth. It was Um Kulthum, Egypt's great beloved chanteuse, singing still in that rich full voice though she had been dead nearly a decade. The men preferred her music to us, obviously, for they waved us past with hardly a glance.

A jumbled group of buildings. We seemed to be heading away from Beirut to the sea, the long way around town. Bob leaned forward to ask why.

"This is the only way. Can't go the other way," the driver said cryptically. "Blocked by a raid."

We fell backward on the slippery seats again.

"We change the route depending on what's going on, what's been blown up recently, who's in charge," explained the driver.

"I understand. Just remembered from the last time we were here."

"When was that?"

"Nineteen sixty-four."

The driver snorted. Twice.

We drove in silence. Checkpoint five looked larger, more substantial. One of the three guards was reading a book by the light of a kerosene lantern. The old oil barrels edging the sandbags were smeared with slogans which had run in the rain. Paint? Blood? Martial music blared from the radio inside. We slowed to a stop and an old man with a heavyset face peered at us for a second and gestured us on. He held in his hand a *stikan* of tea, the little fluted gold-banded glass out of which we had drunk so many gallons of pleasant sweet tea over past years, the tea of traditional Arab hospitality. The first familiar sight.

"Why did you come back?" the driver asked.

"To see friends at the American University."

"American University." He laughed unpleasantly. "They call it PLO University these days."

We turned in from the sea near the British Embassy and stopped at a gate, a high gate, whose pointed spikes were wound about with barbed wire. Two guards emerged. The cab light flicked on.

"American University," announced the driver. "You're here."

Bob got out and went to the gate.

I watched from the taxi while he gestured, spoke, was given a telephone. The taxi motor continued to run, hiccuping at various speeds. Was our friend Jim not there? Would we be obliged to turn around and drive back to the airport, past the rubble and the five checkpoints, to wait for the next plane out? I sat up on the slippery seat, trying to look confident and hopeful.

"Sure your friend's here?" said the taxi driver.

"Oh yes," I said, more loudly than I intended. "Yes, he's here."

"You English or American?"

"American."

The taxi driver laughed and shook his head. "Americans at the PLO University. Would you believe it? You guys don't even talk to the PLO when you're at home."

Fortunately I did not have to reply, for something was happening at the gatehouse. Bob leaned into the open taxi window.

"Jim's here but we have to wait for him to come to the gatehouse to vouch for us. Security is pretty tight."

He nodded toward the American University guards. In their neat, dark blue suits, they looked very different from the armed men we had seen along the airport road. Their weapons were not carried carelessly either, in fact they were not even visible, I saw with satisfaction. But a second later I found myself looking wildly for their weapons. Surely they were armed, for the good of the university? Perhaps in that bulge at the side of their navy blue coats? The American University, unlike much of the city we had just passed through, looked well lit, a reassuring sign like the neat, well-dressed guards. Certainly they would be professional enough to be armed. Yet what could the driver mean, this was *PLO* University?

I sat in the taxi. The motor continued to hiccup. The guard looked pointedly at his watch. Bob leaned against the side of the taxi, appearing casual, but I could see his fists clenched in tension.

"Bob!" A familiar figure stepped from the darkness into the gatehouse light. I could barely restrain myself from saying triumphantly to the taxi driver, "See! We *do* have a friend here."

Jim slid in next to the driver as we drove through the gatehouse, past the reassured guards. We headed for the faculty apartment building where Jim lived at the far end of the campus. Even on the campus in the taxi with Jim, an ex-student of Bob's and an old friend, the alien atmosphere of the city seemed to prevail and we traveled the half mile in silence. There was relief but little joy in our meeting.

We woke in the morning to bright sunshine, but when I looked out across Jim's ground-floor terrace, the Mediterranean glittered through a screen of barbed wire, two feet high, that topped the stone campus wall and had, through time, become entwined with the crimson bougainvillea.

"That's the way it is," said Jim. "The whole campus is under strict security. It has to be. Every faction thinks that the American University at Beirut is full of its enemies: Maronites, Shi'as, Sunnis, Nasserites . . . and Palestinians, of course."

"And the PLO?" asked Bob.

"We don't discriminate on this campus," said Jim.

"What does that mean?" I asked.

"Exactly what I said," he replied.

The city seemed in a suspended state of siege. The American University had a rather special position; it could afford to lay expensive barbed wire, like jagged lengths of dangerous embroidery, along the tops of all the high walls that enclosed the campus: its beautiful old stone buildings and tennis courts had been built in an age when the colonial foreigners, even those who went to do good, expected to live well. Many of the new, expensive modern apartment buildings did likewise; some had installed complex lock systems, and one of the buildings leading up from the American University to Rue Hamra, commercial center of West Beirut, had its own antiaircraft gun on the roof, above the penthouse. I saw the black massive front of the emplacement on our second day in Beirut, and pointed it out in amazement to my friend Penny Williams, the artist.

She shrugged. "Of course," she replied. "Things that look amazing to you are now taken as a matter of course by everybody. Here, quick, B.J.," and she shoved me into the open door of a photo shop, where I found myself staring at a huge color enlargement of a fat, bare-bottomed baby smiling toothlessly and cheerfully at the camera from its recumbent position on the standard fur rug. High above us an ominous popping sounded, seemed to burst out, stop, then burst out again.

"What's that?"

"The Israeli planes are breaking the sound barrier," said Penny matter-of-factly. "They fly over every so often. Part of the war of nerves."

"But why are we in here? They're not bombing."

"No," the man behind the photo shop counter said, "but you never know when they might."

"And then," went on Penny, in a tone I associated with teachers trying to present difficult information to dull students, "the antiaircraft defense often fires, and bits of shrapnel from those shells fall down long afterward. Somebody my husband knows was hit by a stray piece of shrapnel just walking along Rue Hamra."

"Yes," said the shop owner. "Have to be careful these days."

Street smarts. Or, more accurately, war-in-the-street smarts. People went out jogging very early as Jim and Bob had done that morning, and they did their grocery shopping long before noon, for the militias were known to be late sleepers, and thus shelling usually did not seriously get going till afternoon.

The civil war had theoretically ended in 1976, but five years later many sorts of struggles continued. Various religious factions sometimes clashed briefly or shelled each other's positions across the city. An auto accident on a side street became the excuse for a pitched, armed battle. No one knew what the day would bring.

Life had, people said, returned more or less to normal, but the scars of the war were all around us. The whole center of the old city was gone, the Bourse, the flower market, Ajami's restaurant where we had dined with such pleasure twenty years ago. What was left was split in two between Christian sector and Muslim sector. The streetcars we had ridden long ago had disappeared. The split in the city was marked by what was euphemistically known as the Green Line, but far from being a strip of lawn and garden, the line was a no-man's-land, blasted and broken, over which two sets of militia guarded several sets of checkpoints.

Many people had to cross the line every day from home to work, and on bad days or threatened bad days absenteeism in offices and businesses was a major problem.

Yet schools remained open most of the time, and banks and stores continued to do business. Vegetable merchants wheeled their carts full of peppers and tomatoes, oranges and grapefruit, across the Green Line into the areas of Beirut that still functioned. Newspapers were published in Arabic and French, restaurants served meals, and the telephones worked occasionally. Night life, it was true, had ceased almost completely, for it was not safe to be out on the streets after dark. The old days of nightclubbing along the Corniche till daybreak or gambling in the casinos was over; Beirutis had retreated into their homes, or what was left of them. But the sidewalk cafés did a brisk business in the morning, and lunch was still a time to entertain friends and colleagues.

The media image of Beirut living in the face of constant anxiety and terror was further confused for us by the fact that many people looked so well dressed, so well fed, so well wined and dined, at least in West Beirut. It was not uncommon to see a bookstore owner setting out the newest French novels while next door, in a collection of rubble, the rubble's owner and proprietor was hawking Cacharel blouses, hung on a length of wire across the jagged stones and chunks of smashed cement.

"Oh yes," the bookstore owner would say cheerfully while we looked over the books. "A plane from Paris came in yesterday. Books and blouses," with a gesture to his business neighbor sitting in the rubble next door.

Stalls offered the best Courvoisier Cognac for ten dollars a bottle, Bass Weejuns from America for half price, German cameras, Japanese calculators, English tweed at unbelievable reductions.

"No taxes," our friends explained.

"Well, you know what no taxes means," said Bob. "No taxes equals no government equals anarchy."

"We already have that," answered Jim.

And Penny, when I asked her about a great hole in the front garden of their seaside apartment house, said no, it wasn't a shell, it was the first attempt to dig a well.

"A well?"

During the war, water supplies were often cut off, explained Penny, so the tenants had contributed toward the wages of a well driller. Not a success, she added, but they might have to try again if things worsened.

Individual persons were reported to have performed great acts of bravery during the troubles, but since the truce, the country "seemed to go nowhere," one of the professors at the American University (AUB) said. "Everybody's waiting for everyone else to settle down, stop fighting."

And, Bob pointed out to me, no outside forces had appeared, as in the past, when Greek, Roman, Ottoman, and French occupation forces had come in to "pacify" Lebanon. Even the U.S. Marines, who had appeared in 1958, had not turned up.

"Lebanon is a great trading post," someone said bitterly. "It didn't ask to be a model nation. The West—you—wanted to make us into a showpiece. But we're the ones who are stuck with it."

Frozen in strife. The image seemed contradictory, impossible. Yet it served, somehow, to convey the feeling of the city, where life went on, a kind of life anyway, but the old mechanisms of national government had wound down to a faint murmur, and even the street signs were gone. As we traveled through the city, visiting old friends, we had a confusing sense of déjà vu one minute, which would be rudely dispelled the next. "No," Bob would say. "This isn't right. There was a church here." But no more. From a distance we could see the famous Pigeon Rocks standing in the sea and the golden beach would begin to unfold as we approached; but before we reached the old scenic point the view disappeared, blocked by rows of makeshift shops that had sprung up, unzoned and unsupervised, along the seafront. The middle-class shopping center of the city had moved to the beach, where, presumably, one could see an enemy coming and take one's most valuable stock to shelter.

"I find it hard to see how people can go on living day after day with such confusion and insecurity," I said to Hind al-Sayed, a Lebanese sculptor who had invited me to tea. We had mutual friends in America.

"Some people have left," she replied, "but many people can't. All they own is here, and their families, or their business, or their health, keep them here. Some of those who left before came back to find everything gone."

"So now they are determined to stay?"

"Yes," said Hind, pouring out the tea in the old Lebanese house which she and her journalist husband had rebuilt into a studio and living quarters. The long, high living room had been cut into three levels. At the top was her studio, where the giant sculpted forms for which she was famous in Lebanon were created. The sleeping loft on the second level and the narrow staircase leading to the studio were visible from the ground-floor living room, where we sat. Old French furniture had been re-covered in gray corduroy. Books were stacked in corners. Brightly striped rugs covered the cold tile floors.

"But they don't stay just for these material reasons; you in the West always stress that, see it as the spring of all action. Materialism!"

I bridled. "Not really. There is a lot more to the quality of life in the West than just that. You know that. You yourself studied in Paris, Hind. Don't you miss it?"

"No," she said abruptly. "Oh, don't misunderstand. I learned a great deal, but I find these days I'm not much interested in the West anymore. It seems finished, over with."

"The West? Finished?" I returned. "We *are* still the center of the industrial world," I heard myself proclaiming, maybe a bit too loudly.

She smiled, a gentle softening of the angular features, the broad forehead and deepset eyes, "There you go again, off on materialism. . . ."

"I didn't mean just that," I protested.

"I know," she said. "Let's look at it another way. You asked me how people can bear to stay here. It's often terrible. Of course many can't leave, but still whatever is going on here, it's alive. We are beginning things, changing things our own way. It is painful, this birthing process, but it is alive. The West does seem dead, or at least in decline. Look at your television programs, your drug problems."

I protested, talked about changes in America, movements for women's rights, desegregation, issues that didn't receive much coverage in the Arab world because of stereotypes about the West. "Soaps like 'Dallas' are what a lot of you would *like* to think about us," I exclaimed forcefully.

Hind smiled that gentle smile again. "You sound like *we* did ten years ago. We thought the Western way would solve all our problems. *We* know better now. The West is no answer for us."

"Well . . ." I rose to defend my country. Always critical when at home, Bob and I had to admit that we were full of patriotism when abroad. *We* could say those things about ourselves at home, but *they* shouldn't say them over here, went our argument to ourselves. *They* must see the full picture, grasp the subtleties, before jumping to conclusions, we felt rather defensively.

Hind listened politely, partly, I am sure, out of deference to the mutual friends who had brought us together. We drank our tea and sat quietly, but without the ease of friends. Our knowledge of each other was too slight, too new. Hind pulled down a book she had edited—children's drawings of the Arab-Israeli conflict. I shuddered at the overall effects, but found, too, that I was interested in some of the images: childish drawings of apples cut in half, people cut in half, objects which could be either crooked trees or automatic rifles or both. Then she invited me to the gallery where she would have a show soon, the first since the truce. I promised to come.

"Goodbye," she said. "Be careful."

"Be careful, B.J. Be careful, Bob."

Those admonitions, recited like a litany, followed us each time we left Jim's apartment, arrived in another friend's house, left the friend's house. Be careful.

We were careful. It didn't take long to learn some basic street smarts. Sheer instinct for survival taught us that if caught on the streets when afternoon shelling began, one ran close to the sides of the buildings and ducked into the nearest open bookstore or hotel lobby or restaurant to stay until the raid, or the "exchange," as some people called it, was over. The sight of the money changers pulling down their iron shutters was a signal that something more serious than a mere "exchange" might be on the way. Hence one ducked into a place where one could stay for a while. Restaurants were the best.

Once safe inside a restaurant, we felt liberated, freed, safe from oblivion, and, like everyone else in the restaurant, laughed louder than usual, told many jokes, ordered the best wines and the specialties of the house—*shish taouk* at La Pasha, kibbe at Maarouche, and the fish catch of the day at Faysal's. During these times, the waiters always seemed to fly around, giving especially good service, and the music poured out of the stereo: Arabic music with pipes and drums and violins, French love songs, old Beatles hits.

Music of several cultures. Wine from France, wine from Lebanon. Meat. Fruit. Tangible pleasures. Reassuring laughter. With a sense of fin-de-siècle, repressing thoughts of present dangers, we watched it all, strangers, outsiders, caught up and held, like flies in amber, in a kind of suspended life that bore no relation whatsoever to those old halcyon days of the fifties. We were lucky. We could always leave, we said to ourselves. Didn't we have American passports? The people of Beirut, descendants of the quiet, pleasant people we had watched going up and down on the old streetcar years before, dressed in the garments that were signs of their group, their religious belief, their sex—these people were trying to survive in an incomprehensible, totally changed world. They went to school, they shopped, they worked, they ate lunch, they made love, and then fighting broke out and things stopped dead . . . for a moment.

Beginnings and endings. We walked down streets that ended in the middle, like life in Beirut, which seemed periodically to come to a dead stop. Traffic would be suddenly blocked by broken pieces of buildings, and yet after a ten-minute detour around total desolation, traffic would be resumed. Life went on. It seemed as though Beirut was holding on, waiting for a savior. But none came.

What had Hind said? "It is painful." The same could be said of both living and dying. Which was it?

We were invited to lunch by our old friends Mona and Abdul Latif al-Shafei. I would go early in a taxi, we decided, and have some time by myself with Mona; Bob would come on his own, as he had appointments at the university before-hand. It sounded like a logical program, but of course we had not counted on the realities of trying to get from one part of Beirut to another, especially to an apartment house like the al-Shafeis', which was close to the Green Line.

The morning was damp and cold, not auspicious for a reunion: low clouds and a steady misting drizzle curtained off the sea. Street signs were gone in East Beirut, but to make matters worse that day, several "incidents" had taken place and the taxi driver had been detoured a dozen times. When I objected mildly, he cried out, "Lady, believe me, I'm not trying to cheat you. Most drivers won't even *go* to this area. It's not *worth* the money." I had to agree as he left the main road to cut through narrow streets and was turned back twice by new piles of sandbags being set up on street corners. An hour and a half after I had set out from AUB, the taxi deposited me in front of the al-Shafeis' apartment house.

As she embraced me, Mona burst into tears. We had not seen each other for fifteen years, but her tears were not totally nostalgia for past friendship.

"I was so worried, I was so worried, thank God you arrived safely," she cried, wiping her tears with a lace-edged handkerchief. "You haven't been here for ages, you don't know the problems."

She led me into the spacious living room and sat me down in a rose-colored velvet armchair. I set my purse on the side table covered with bibelots and immediately managed to knock over a Persian miniature in a tiny black display easel. A Damascene carved box went with it.

"Oh, I'm sorry, Mona. I'm so clumsy!"

"No, no, it's nothing."

"My mother always used to say that if I knocked over a glass of water at the beginning of the dinner party, then there wouldn't be any more accidents. But at the end—"

"Oh, B.J.," said Mona, "stop it, just stop it. It's good to see you." She wept again. "I'm sorry to be so emotional—we Arabs are supposed to be overly emotional, I guess—but you never know these days what's going to happen from one minute to the next. I mean, from the time I talked to you this morning on the phone until now, the whole route from AUB to here could have been changed by a shelling, or a shifting of the militia checkpoint. You just never know. And with Abdul Latif ill—"

"Yes, I heard. I am so sorry."

"He is better and will be at lunch," said Mona firmly. "I'll take you back to see him in a moment, but he is resting now."

"Mona, I've heard about you over the years." I smiled, blinking my own wet eyes and finally finding a tissue in my overstuffed purse, now set firmly on the room-size Persian rug, out of harm's way. "Not just the poetry—you're famous enough for that in many parts of the Arab world—no, about your political activities."

"My *political* activities?" Mona all but whooped.

Mona's laugh was the same. I remembered that laugh well, a well-bred giggle that had first endeared her to me, long ago in Cairo, when she was the extremely beautiful, extremely fashionable wife of the dean at the American University in Cairo. She had organized a baby shower for me twenty-two years ago, before Laura Ann was born. Abdul Latif, who was also a professor of physics, was Mona's first cousin and husband, a good twenty years her senior, gentle in his dry humor, respected for his fair judgments, Bob said. But it was Mona one remembered in the receiving lines we passed down in the old days of formal receptions and cross-cultural dinner parties, when we felt that the American University in Cairo was a living example of the American spirit of liberty and academic freedom, an island in the military regime. Lugubrious occasions, usually, but Mona lightened them, partly by her beauty, but also because she could not maintain a serious mien. She tried, but she was an ebullient person and she could not help laughing. The laugh was irrepressible in the face of pomposity, pedantry, or even heavy-handed gallantry—whether German, French, Swiss, Egyptian, American, or British. She took each formal remark addressed to her with a grain of salt and a giggle and charmed everyone.

Mona had been born in Damascus; her great-grandfather was an illustrious Sufi poet, her distant ancestor a renowned historian of Islam. Her generous-spirited amusement was perhaps a product of her background, her knowledge of her own ancestry, her sense of her place in the world. Western pomposity was no different from Egyptian pomposity, after all; over the centuries Damascene sophistication and humor had absorbed such peccadilloes, though not without a certain sense of cultural superiority, it was true. Mona had none of that arrogance; instead she had a secret life: she wrote poetry. I had once asked Professor Muhammad al-Nuwaihi, one of the reigning kings of Arabic belles lettres at the time, about Mona's poetry.

"Very nice little verses," he had replied in a patronizing tone. "Very nice. But not important. Mona is so pretty; she should be satisfied with that and occupy herself by bringing up her sons."

"How are the children?" Mona interrupted my thoughts.

I described them, showed pictures of Laura Ann, David, and Laila, all at different levels of college. "They're all grown up," I said.

"My boys are, too," said Mona. "Amr and Hassan will be here for lunch; they are *men.*" She giggled then. "How old we seem to have become, my friend."

I nodded. "But how *little* we've changed," I said. We both giggled.

"Mona." I stopped. "You are a famous poet now. I wonder what Professor Nuwaihi would think if he read your work today." Mona leaned forward in the crimson velvet sofa. Her black dress, the yoke cross-stitched red in Palestinian embroidery, was very attractive, it suited her, but the ethnic quality of the garment, though charming, was a far cry from the Parisian couturier fashions she had worn so marvelously in Cairo.

"You know, B.J., my work wasn't Nuwaihi's style. He thought he was a Renaissance man, a thoroughly modern man of the new day, or something like that. But you know he had two wives at the same time, one Egyptian, one English, so how modern was *that?* Anyway, he considered my sort of Sufi poetry archaic, a thing of the past—"

"But—"

"It wasn't that I was a woman—that's what you Americans always thought—no, it was my *work* he considered old-fashioned, not in tune with the new poetry."

"Your political activities," I prompted.

"Shhh," said Mona lightly, but her eyes sparkled. "Not before Mama, please."

"Your mother's here from Damascus?"

"Come in, Mama, you remember B.J., she and Dorothy Shane came to us in Damascus a long time ago—"

"In the big house, Mona dear?" A small woman, somewhat stooped, took hold of the arm of my chair and peered around into my face. Yes, it *was* Mona's mother, twenty years older, dressed in black, her hair henna-colored and a bit gray at the roots, but her bright eyes clear; and she was wearing the most exotic carpet slippers I had ever seen, all brocade, with tassels fore and aft. That was indeed Mona's mother, whom I remembered vividly from my 1964 visit to Mona's house in Damascus, a brief vacation when Laila, our youngest child, had just turned two.

"No, Mama," Mona corrected her. "B.J. came to see us when we were in the new apartment, after we sold the big house in the old city."

"Ah yes." The old lady sat in a matching rose velvet chair nearby and looked me up and down. "Ah yes, I took you to the souk to buy brocade, didn't I, while Mona and your other friend were too tired! Yes, yes." She nodded her head as the memory came back, and she took a cigarette, very deliberately, from the Damascene box on the table and lit it, eyeing her daughter.

"Mama, you know what the doctor said about smoking."

"I know." She inhaled and a smile of great voluptuous enjoyment came over the wrinkled face with the bright eyes. "Ah yes. I know." The old lady put one hand up to her hair, to adjust it, a coquettish gesture that did not look ridiculous, despite the imperfectly dyed hair, the stooped back. Mona's mother, Aida, was still a presence.

"You have very nice shoes, B.J.," she said suddenly, and I felt as though I had been given the fashion award of the month, for Mme. Aida had worn clothes of great distinction at home in Damascus. She had changed for every meal, and also for tea every afternoon. Tea was the time when her brother had come for his daily call, and Mona, Dorothy, and I had been banished to the bedroom like immature schoolgirls.

"All these years," Mona had explained to Dorothy and me, sitting on our beds in the guest room, "and he still comes every day."

"But why?" asked Dorothy.

"To ask her advice," said Mona. "My uncle is the Minister of Defense. Who else can he trust to give him advice in these troubled times?"

"Your mother, as his older sister, can manipulate the foreign affairs of the entire country of Syria," I suggested, laughing.

"No, no, of course not," Mona replied. "But he talks things over with her. Everybody needs a trusted confidant. Mama knows more about what's going on in the government than I ever will."

"As, for instance . . ."

"Well, she told me he was worried about a friend of ours, a young colonel in the army who was getting very ambitious and wanted to launch an attack on the Golan Heights. My uncle felt that was ridiculous, suicidal at the time, but our young friend was stirring up his fellow officers. What is your advice, dear sister? he asked, and Mama pointed out that his wife was not too well, so why not offer the colonel and his wife a nice mission to Paris? That sort of thing."

"Power behind the throne . . ." murmured Dorothy.

"No," said Mona. "Not that, not that cliché. We are talking about the power of *family* ties, men and women. It takes different forms in response to different needs."

Dorothy and I did not pursue the argument. It was obvious, however, that Mme. Aida was a force to be reckoned with, even as she changed her clothes five times a day, wrote a little in her journal, thought about menus, knitted for her grandchildren, and attended to her role as chief daily adviser to the Minister of Defense.

Now she sat beside me, smoking a forbidden cigarette, past eighty, and still noticing the cut of my shoes. "Appearance," she might have said, as my mother and grandmother used to say, "has a great deal to do with one's effectiveness." Mme. Aida, obviously, would have agreed with them.

"So how is your husband?" she asked, leaning forward again, the forbidden cigarette burning down slowly in the old wrinkled hand, its nails tipped with a matte rose polish.

"He is fine, thank you. He is coming to lunch and is looking forward to meeting you."

She smiled enigmatically, finished the cigarette, and said to Mona, "I will wait in the other room for the little boys to come from the park."

"Okay, Mama," and to me, "She slips in and out of the past these days, but as you can see she was right in the present when she was talking to you."

"Yes," I said. "Iron hand in velvet glove, I see, still."

"What?"

"A cliché, my dear, used to describe strong women."

"Oh yes, I see." Mona thought about it. "Yes, that is Mama exactly."

"Now, Mona, tell me, what are you doing these days?"

"Let us greet Abdul Latif first," she said and smiled. "Isn't that the polite thing to do, B.J.?"

Ah yes. The gentle critic was what we had called her, Dorothy and I, in the years we wrote together, the three of us, in Cairo, Mona, Dorothy, myself—meeting every other week at each other's homes and reading aloud our newest "pearls" of prose and poetry.

"The thing about Americans," she was saying, as we rose and moved down the long, carpeted hall, hung with tapestries and Bokhara embroideries, "is that they are unpredicted."

"The word is really *unpredictable*," I corrected, "but why *not* unpredicted? Why couldn't that be an unpredicted quality, since Americans are unpredictable?"

Mona clapped her hands with pleasure. "Words! Words! Yes, it's the same. I was afraid you would have changed and gotten dull, B.J."

"Girls!" The stern voice was that of Mme. Aida at the door of her bedroom. "Can't you be quiet? Your husband, Mona, is ill."

The closed door was on our left. Mona took a deep breath. "He may not know you, B.J. His last stroke was bad; he is recovering very slowly. . . ."

The square bedroom was simply furnished. In the large mahogany bed lay Abdul Latif, a long waxen figure covered by starched white sheets and a green plaid afghan with fringes. Mona came up close beside him.

"Abd, here is B.J., remember B.J. from Cairo? She had her first baby there, remember, and then—"

"It was a girl." The words came slowly but distinctly from the ashen lips of Abdul Latif, and he tried to raise his head from his single pillow and look at me.

I went over and took his hand. It was long and cool, bony and waxen yellow like his face. "How are you, Abdul Latif?"

He nodded, slowly, twice. Then his eyes wandered a little. "W-where is—"

"Bob? My husband?"

A nod.

"He is coming for lunch."

Another nod. A faint stretching of the ashy lips, the preparation for a smile.

"We will get you some lunch, my dear, don't worry." Mona bent over, kissed him, and smoothed the pillow, unnecessarily, since the pillow had scarcely a wrinkle. "Come, B.J."

His eyes followed her, in the red-embroidered black dress, her black hair tied back with a narrow red silk ribbon.

"We'll see you in a few minutes, when Bob comes," I said.

In the hall, Mona cried, "He spoke! He spoke! It doesn't happen every day, it has been really bad, trying to regain the speech. . . ."

"Do you have a speech therapist?"

Mona stared. "Speech therapist? Where are we going to find a speech therapist in Beirut today? People like that who could earn a living anywhere have all left."

She led me back to the living room, saying, "Other people are coming to lunch to meet you and Bob. It might be fun. Is Bob bringing your friend Jim from AUB?"

"Yes. Can I help?"

"Thank you." We made our way into the kitchen. "We don't have servants anymore, they won't come here, we're too close to the line. You can see the museum from here"—she pointed out the window a few blocks down—"there, see the checkpoint? Those soldiers are just boys, B.J., they sit there all day." She sighed. "Do you wonder they sometimes just shoot off their guns—I mean, they don't read, they don't do anything except just sit there. . . ."

"And that," I said firmly, as I chopped parsley to go on top of the tahina, around the eggplant casserole, "brings us to your political activities. There's no escape. Tell me, famous Mona al-Shafei, what you've been doing. I've heard about you even in faraway America!"

"Your friends exaggerate, I'm sure," demurred Mona, moving back and forth from the kitchen, while I did as I was told and laid out the heavy silver forks and knives and spoons on the lace-covered mahogany dining room table. Salads, *baba ghanooj,* tahina, cucumbers in yogurt, a great epergne of red apples and oranges; glasses for wine and juice. On the sideboard, below the dark canvas of an academically presented still life, stood bottles of wine (French, Lebanese), a cake with chocolate icing. "Yes, yes," said Mona. "I will tell you, I promise. Let's just get the food ready; Amr will bring the kibbe and kebab when he comes from the office, the rice and the aubergines will stay warm in the oven, with the meatballs—"

"Mona, you have enough for twenty people, not twelve. Will Abdul Latif come to the table?"

"No, no," absently. "I will feed him." Then, in a different tone, "You know us, my dear, we cook like mad, have a lot of things, and then we eat it for days afterward, us Arabs, we Arabs, that is. . . ." Smiling as she corrected herself.

"I thought the idea was to give the leftovers to the poor," I said mischievously.

She laughed. "You've read too many books about us, B.J., it's about time you came back here to live for a while. The world has changed; *our* world has changed. It's not like it was. . . ."

"Well, I can *see* that. . . ." And I looked out the window at the militia point near the museum, a point along the scarred line that split the city in two.

"Yes, you can see it, B.J., but you can't *feel* what it means," replied Mona shortly. "That feeling fills us all days and all nights, the anxiety, the worry when the shells go over whistling, the worry when they don't. While Abdul Latif lay there with his first stroke, they cut off the water, the boys brought it in pails from the bank where Amr works, they came in the car with pails of water on the floor. We felt lucky to have those pails of water. Some people were not so lucky—"

"But—"

She held up her hand. "And that is how my so-called political activities began," she said. "One night someone banged on our door, crying please help me, please help me, my son is very sick, on the other side, and has to go to the hospital, I know you are the poet, they might listen to you and let me cross, please, please. . . .

"It was after the curfew, so theoretically no crossing was allowed," went on Mona, "and I thought what if it were me and Abdul Latif were dying, so I got dressed and I went out on the street and I explained to the soldiers at the checkpoint about the woman's son, and they let her across. One of the soldiers said are you really Mona al-Shafei, and I said yes, and he said I've read your poems. Next time it was easier to help somebody across. That's all."

"That's *all?*"

"Well, you know poets are respected here, we're able to do these things because poetry is . . . what it is . . . it has *honor* in the Arab world."

"Weren't you afraid to go out there in the middle of the night, knowing they might just shoot?"

Mona stared. "Of course. Wouldn't you be? I was scared to death."

"I think your family must be proud. You're fulfilling the Arabic poetic tradition, after all, fighting beside the armies, speaking up in political rallies."

"Proud?" Mona turned. "No, not proud. Not even Abdul Latif is proud, nor the boys, I think, though they don't talk about it. They don't like me to go out, they're afraid for me, now especially because people are saying that my poetry, my *Sufi mystical* poetry, is becoming political. Look at this." She broke off arranging lettuce leaves artfully around the tabooli salad to get a scrapbook and show me a long interview in Arabic. "This one says I'm with the Palestinians, another one says I'm with the Sunni Muslims. The point is I am a *poet.*" She fairly shouted the word. "Poets are political always, because they are concerned with *life* and what is reality and all that . . . but I have to confess I hate all this nonsense"—she struck the page in the scrapbook—"and I say so. What is happening to us? Oh God, what has *already* happened to us?

"Guests." She patted her hair in the hall mirror before she opened the door. Mme. Aida was behind her, looking expectant. "Here they are, to meet you and Bob and your friend Jim," she called back. "Where *is* Bob?

"Nadia Twainey, my friend, the poet, Muhammad Hallaj, you know his work, maybe, he is a Palestinian sculptor; this is B.J., my friend from America . . . her husband will be here soon. . . . Where is your husband, Nadia? . . . Oh, I'm sorry, the flu is everywhere this winter. . . . Oh yes, Sonia, I believe we did meet in the newspaper office one day, you are with Muhammad, welcome and this is your sister Jihan, *ahlan wusahlan, enchantée.* . . ."

We moved forward into the living room, followed by Mona's mother, who looked carefully at everyone, out of those bright old eyes, admiring the chic clothes of the women, a black suit, a lilac silk dress, gold glittering at ears and wrists.

"Where is your husband?" Mme. Aida asked me.

"He hasn't come yet."

"Tell me when. I want to see him."

I promised I would.

Now Amr and Hassan had come. "Amr, did you bring the kibbe?" called Mona. "Thank you, my dear, here is B.J. Guess what, your father recognized and spoke to B.J. this morning, yes, he did."

Two young men, tall, good-looking, in three-piece business suits, smiled at me.

"They *are* grown up," I said foolishly, remembering the two little boys in short pants that used to come in and shake hands politely when we dined at the al-Shafeis' in Cairo.

"What did you think?" Mona smiled. "Of course they are grown up. Here, Amr, put the kibbe right on the table, no, not on the Spanish platter, there, that's right. Bob is late, why is he so late?"

"Oh, Mama," said Amr. "You know what the traffic is like. Hello, Grandma," and he bent down to kiss the tiny old woman. She smiled beatifically.

She grabbed his sleeve, dark blue pinstripe, a banker's suit, and looked at me. "Isn't he handsome?" she said in Arabic, smiling once more.

I nodded, and Amr rushed away to make the drinks. He was still young enough to be embarrassed by his loving grandmother, I thought. But Hassan was older, more reserved. He simply smiled and said hello, stuttering slightly.

"We are trying to catch your attention, Mona," called the Palestinian, Hallaj, from the living room. "How do we do it? Maybe if I begin to say your poems, you will listen to us. Hmmm? They tell me all the poets in America, madame, are either superrealists or they teach in the universities and write so obscurely that no one reads them. Is that true?"

"Oh, I don't really think so—" I began.

Mona interrupted. "Be careful, Muhammad. Americans are *unpredictable*"— she looked at me—"isn't that so? You never know what she might do—or her husband either. Here she is making films; the last time we met we were raising babies."

Hallaj was not to be put off by pleasantries. He wore a heavy dark turtleneck sweater, jeans, and cowboy boots, and his beard was flecked with gray.

"Art and politics don't mix in America, isn't that right, madame?" he persisted. "The artist is outside his society, isn't that a contradiction, a negating of the artist's purpose? He has a responsibility to speak."

"Like you," I answered. "Yes, I have heard about your work. Hind al-Sayed says you have been compared with Orozco, Diego Rivera."

Hallaj inclined his head. "I am honored. They were great artists. They *assumed* their artistic responsibility. What American artist has done the same?"

"America has different problems. . . ." I found myself passionately defending the position of the artist in America.

Mona's mother had moved her chair closer to him; he was speaking English, which she did not understand, but the look the old lady gave him was withering. Was he not handsome enough for her taste? Did she disapprove of the cowboy boots? Or did she just not like being left out of the conversation? I suspected the latter, for at that moment she took out another cigarette and leaned across to him: he could not avoid that standard coquettish gesture, and he carefully lit her cigarette. She smiled radiantly back. "Thank you so much," she said in French.

When Bob walked in with Jim we were drinking juice, wine, beer, and Perrier water and conversing in a mixture of French, Arabic, and English.

"You're late!" cried Mona. "But we are glad to see you. You were always late in Cairo, too, but you blamed B.J. Abdul Latif used to do that to me; why does everyone blame the *ladies?*" She giggled again and made introductions, slightly flustered, I thought. Jim was looking appreciatively at the journalist's sister, Jihan. Her hair, à la Farrah Fawcett, floated about a pointed lively face.

"Sonia is a journalist at *Nahar.* I think Jihan is a singer. Really, I never did meet her before, but she is pretty. Maybe they want to be in your film," whispered Mona.

"To art!" cried Hallaj, raising his glass.

Mona's mother looked surprised, then she got up and came over to be introduced to Bob and Jim. They were polite but then drifted off, Bob to talk to Amr, the younger son, who worked at the bank, and to Hassan, who had finished his Ph.D. at Columbia and was scheduled to go into the diplomatic service of Lebanon, "if there is any Lebanon left," I heard him say wryly. Tall, gentle, he reminded me of his father; Amr in the banker's suit had his mother's sparkle and laugh. He was eyeing the singer in the lilac silk with the pretty pointed face, but Jim had already gone over, I noticed, to refill her wineglass and that of her sister Sonia.

"B.J.," hissed Mona's mother to me in Arabic. "He is handsome still, your husband. You are lucky." She patted my hand. "Poor Abdul Latif. He might as well be dead." She looked strangely calm about the situation.

"It's hard for Mona," I offered.

"Yes, but she has her *work,* you know," emphasizing the word in a somewhat sarcastic way. Then she whispered, with a sidelong glance at Hallaj, "And who is he, do you know him, I never saw him before."

"Just a friend, madame," I assured her. "He came with Sonia. He is an artist."

Old Mme. Aida tossed her head; it was clear what she thought of artists.

Bob had gone with Hassan to see Abdul Latif.

Mona was laying out the rest of the lunch, with her younger son's help.

"We must eat," she announced. *"Tfaddalluu. Le dîner est servi.* Please!"

We filed in and circled the table with its tempting, aromatic dishes, picking up the heavy silverware, the thick damask napkins. Suddenly Abdul Latif appeared, walking very slowly, supported by Bob and Hassan. He wore a dressing gown of old dark green brocade, a color that diminished the ashy quality of his skin. He accepted a glass of tomato juice and sat down near the dining room table, watching the company: the lean bearded Palestinian sculptor in his cowboy boots, the older woman poet, the two pretty young women in the latest Paris fashions, his sons in their business suits, his ancient mother-in-law from Damascus in her tasseled brocade carpet slippers, and us: Americans who had bobbed up unexpectedly out of the past.

Mona came up and put her hand on his arm, then went back to her guests. His eyes followed her. In the black-and-red gown, the red silk ribbon holding back her lustrous hair, she was explaining to Bob and Jim the sources of the Sufi poetic vocabulary, its meanings for Arab readers with knowledge of this rich literary tradition.

But at center of one of her better-known poems is a simple, frightening line: "Despair began to spread like darkness, bullets began to make shadows, pointed shadows."

Not even the half-grown boys who guarded the checkpoints along the scarred line that split the city needed to know their Sufi symbolic heritage to understand that. They heard it all around them, every night, as they crouched, machine guns at the ready, in their lean-tos of old oil barrels and sandbags, four blocks from this house where we were dining elegantly on all the fruits of the Lebanese countryside and the refined wines of the West.

"I am tired, Mona," said Abdul Latif. He rose with difficulty, and Amr and Mona escorted him down the hallway and back to the mahogany bed.

Mme. Aida watched them go, then settled herself in one of the rose velvet chairs, lit still another forbidden cigarette, and waited for someone to bring her coffee.

The taxi driver's derisive titling of the American University as PLO University was not a joke people laughed at. The PLO was real, it was controversial, and it was relatively new on the Middle Eastern scene. In 1956, there was no PLO. Instead, we heard about Palestinian refugees living in camps and supported by the United Nations Relief and Rehabilitation Administration, with contributions from the United States and other well-intentioned countries. We heard about how victimized the refugees felt themselves to be but then the major step on the road to reconciliation was thought to be some form of compensation from Israel for the land it had seized from the Palestinians. The idea of an independent Palestinian homeland was not often discussed among Westerners in the Middle East; for many Palestinians it was a question not so much of a homeland as of returning to their own lands in Israel, a state which was still regarded as an unpleasant aberration which would soon pass.

In 1958 and 1959, while we were living in the United States and occasionally lectured or were interviewed about the 1956 Arab-Israeli war, we also were inclined to express optimism in saying that the passage of time might help, might heal. Young Arabs and Jews would grow up together in the Middle East and come to share similar outlooks and a desire for peace. Common economic interests would prevail; political differences would diminish in intensity. Such optimism was not uncommon among Western "specialists" far more sophisticated than we were at that time; indeed, before the 1967 war, even sophisticated Arabs could be heard expressing much the same sentiment—privately, of course.

What had happened in the past quarter century had completely belied our naïvely optimistic predictions. The "cause," the "desire to return to the homeland," had not disappeared but after the '67 war had taken the form of an ideological commitment superseding the political differences which had preoccupied the educated Palestinians of the fifties and early sixties, and transcending the class differences between the camp refugees and the prosperous Palestinians in other Arab countries. The new generation of Palestinians, whether the children of those driven from their homes or of Arabs still in Israel, became more organized, more determined, and more conscious of their past and their common cultural heritage than were their parents. The Palestine Liberation Organization was born. In 1981, people in Beirut talked about revolution.

Revolution? The word was not mentioned a generation ago except in reference to the still-recent struggle against direct colonial rule, or the current fight against colonial puppets, such as Nuri Sa'id's government in Iraq. Now, among the Palestinians, the *jeel al-nakba* (generation of the disaster) had been replaced by the *jeel al-thawra* (generation of the revolution). But revolution against what? No one could satisfactorily explain to us what this meant.

The issue seemed an interesting one to pursue, for my grant to make an educational film about social change in the Arab world from the women's perspective was to include political change. Since women's participation in the Palestinian movement or revolution was a new development, I thought it might be a good way of documenting both the political activity and the changing roles of women in the Arab world. But when we tried to talk to friends in Beirut about the whole subject, people's attitudes toward the "generation of the revolution" surprised us.

"Why do you want to make a film about the Palestinians?" people would ask. "Why not about us? We have suffered just as much." I replied that I saw the struggle as an example of a people's own desire for self-determination, and perhaps worth recording for the universal human qualities involved, similar to such struggles in other parts of the world and at other times in history.

"But what about us, the Lebanese?" people would insist. Suspicion, amusement, cynicism, disbelief, greeted us. We replied that indeed the Lebanese had suffered a great deal. But they were the victims of—whom? The Palestinians, the Israelis, the Americans? Individuals of various sects and political opinions blamed different groups. To speak of "Lebanese" in terms of a single viewpoint was impossible—except for a universal feeling of being victimized by outside forces. How then could we make a film if the subjects themselves could not agree on the cause of the trouble? I admitted that the lack of agreement might be the basis for an interesting film. Would Lebanese friends be willing to discuss the situation, their doubts and fears, on film? People said no. They said it was becoming too dangerous to speak. "The Palestinians will probably be willing," they said. "They *want* to speak."

But it appeared we could not simply take a taxi to PLO headquarters and ask for permission to film or to visit the refugee camps. We had to be introduced. Thus Dick Scott, longtime professor of philosophy at AUB, took me to visit Anny Kanafani, Danish-born widow of Ghassan Kanafani. Kanafani had tragically died in 1975 when his car was firebombed. A talented painter and writer, he had been a highly visible and articulate interpreter of the Palestinian cause while alive; dead, he became an immediate martyr. His widow, over tea, talked about her homes and kindergartens for the children who had been orphaned by the disaster, the *hijra* (exodus) from Palestine. She talked about the refugee camps. I told her what I hoped to do.

"I want to do a film about women and the family," I said, "not the politics, but the people, and how they are dealing with constant crises."

Mme. Kanafani nodded and promised to make some phone calls.

Ghanem Bibi, a Palestinian publisher of left-wing books and periodicals, invited us to dinner. He suggested we should visit the camps for ourselves and see what the word "revolution" meant to the inhabitants. We said we wanted to do just that. Could he help? He said he had not been to the camps for some time and suggested we meet Rosemary Sayigh. She had written about the Palestinians for many years and had done research in the camps. He would introduce us to Rosemary. She said she would do what she could.

But in the end, it was two anonymous students at AUB who had heard Bob lecture, who called and offered to set up a meeting with Majid Abu Sharrar, a member of the PLO Central Committee. We knew the students only as Hassan and Ali; they never gave us their second names because they said they did not want their parents to know they were involved.

The morning of the meeting, Ali and Hassan picked us up in a red VW bug, and as we maneuvered through the hair-raising daytime traffic—no police, no stoplights, no rules—Ali lectured us.

"The PLO are the only true revolutionaries in the Arab world."

"But what are they rebelling against?"

"It is a revolution against injustice, against the past, a revolution for a better future," said Hassan.

"A revolution for a return," said Ali.

Bob explained that we thought of revolution as a struggle against a particular government, a particular set of circumstances.

"Yes," said Ali. "You are right. That is what we are talking about. That set of circumstances is PALESTINE." His voice capitalized the word.

From the sea, we had turned in and headed toward the airport, where market stalls, more makeshift than the ones along the beach, lined the road.

"These merchants are the ones most recently bombed out," explained Ali. "They don't need a permit here."

Shaded by a striped beach umbrella was a shoe emporium, the wares displayed on shoe boxes; a lean-to bore a hand-lettered sign and contained rows of crockery, arranged into dinner place settings. Oranges were stacked in brilliant careful mounds under the blue sky. Men stood beside these shops, quietly waiting, but few customers seemed to be about.

Ahead, where a large overpass arched over the main road, a heterogeneous collection of vehicles had gathered: old American trucks, Mercedeses, Jeeps, Peugeots. "It's the taxi station for the South," said Ali, "where you would go, monsieur and madame, if you got permission to visit the refugee camps." People with children and chickens and bundles and bags waited on curbs.

I turned around in my seat as we passed the area.

"Saida, Saida," shouted a bald man beside the half-open door of his cab, the motor revving. "One seat left."

"Did we come this way before?" asked Bob.

"Probably not," said Ali. "They just reopened the road yesterday."

Past the taxi station we wound up the hill to the Arab University and turned left into a small street. Beside a store advertising Italian men's shirts at incredible reductions, Ali maneuvered his red VW into an unpaved parking lot and we got out.

Ahead of us on the sidewalk, next to the display of Italian shirts, stood a symmetrical arrangement of sandbags and empty gasoline barrels, like those at the checkpoint stations along the airport road. But this checkpoint was set up next to a building, an apartment building. Two young men in those ubiquitous camouflage uniforms and baseball caps lounged beside the building, which was unmarked except for posters bearing names and slogans and photographs of the young men and women who had, said Ali, died for the revolution. The posters of the martyrs. Some were peeling from age and weather, the poster paper torn and shredded so that only an eye or a bit of mustache of the martyr was left affixed to the cement wall, a wall pocked with bullet scars and pitted by the hits of long-range shells. A few of the martyr posters were new, recently slapped on with paste; the ridges where the paste had not smoothed out showed like ripples of the sea across the young faces—startled, smiling, purposeful, scared faces of dead men and women.

"PLO. The Unified Command Headquarters," Ali said to us in low and somewhat reverent tones.

Bob and I looked at each other, then at the pair of young men in camouflage battle dress by the sandbags, who stood up straighter as we approached. They wore their machine guns over their shoulders as casually as backpacks or golf bags, but as we came nearer, their hands moved across their chests toward the weapons, slowly, purposefully.

Ali said hastily, "We have an appointment with Majid Abu Sharrar."

We were signaled in, to the elevator, and rose upward three flights to a bare hallway where other soldiers stood, guarding the door. "We have an appointment with Majid Abu Sharrar," repeated Ali.

"Not here," said the soldier, barring our passage with a rifle. We stood in the elevator uncertainly, the door opening and shutting.

Ali looked surprised and uncomfortable. "But we called," he said. "We were told to come *now*."

A young girl emerged from a half-opened door that gave onto the hall we faced. She was thin; she wore very tight jeans and a gray sweatshirt. Her hair was cut in a fashionable afro and she wore long gold earrings and Texas cowboy boots.

"Majid will be here soon," she said, tossing us a quick smile. "Let them wait in there. Come on, Youssef, let them in!"

The soldier reluctantly let us by and led us into a small office. We sat down on an overstuffed sofa before a single desk. The girl came in, checked the desk, pushed a button on a telephone, swung her earrings with another quick smile, and left. We waited.

Tea was brought on a tin tray, tea in those tiny fluted glasses with gold rims, not by the girl but by a boy in T-shirt and camouflage pants, wearing combat boots too large for him. He could not have been more than fourteen. He smiled engagingly at us.

"Welcome," he said.

Finally Majid Abu Sharrar appeared, a dark-haired middle-aged man, handsome in dark suit and striped tie. Only the bulge of a weapon on his hip distinguished him from the businessmen lunching in restaurants on Rue Hamra. We shook hands. He looked at us carefully but did not smile. He read through the proposal for a film on Palestinian women, talked briefly with us about how we would do it, agreed it was a good idea, and gave us his personal phone numbers (two). While we sat there, he telephoned the PLO's public relations office to formally announce his agreement to our filming and give his permission for us to visit the refugee camps in the South. Could he help us in any other way? Would we like to see the Plastic Arts Museum?

"Yes," I said. "Hind al-Sayed told me about it."

"Hind has done a good job," he said. "You should see the Palestinian posters. They will perhaps be interesting to you. We will send you over in my car."

We stood up. We shook hands again. The audience was at an end. At the bottom of the elevator, beside the sandbagged barrels and the walls covered with the peeling posters of the martyrs of the revolution, a young man came forward and identified himself as Majid Abu Sharrar's driver. He would take us to the museum in Brother Majid's blue Peugeot 504. Hassan and Ali came with us; they had never been there either, they said.

The museum was small, scrupulously clean, and totally empty of people except for the two young curators and ourselves. Also, it was very cold.

The paintings were a mixed collection: nostalgic Grandma Moses reconstructions of life in Palestine before the exodus; political posters by French, German, Latin-American artists; searing "committed" social commentary, à la Orozco. Mona al-Shafei's friend the sculptor Hallaj was represented in poster and sculpture. Images of violence. The ravaged faces of men and women stared at us from the walls of the silent, cold rooms. Downstairs we could hear the Peugeot 504 running quietly as the driver enjoyed its stereo. Um Kulthum again: "Oh my love," she sang. "My love."

Majid Abu Sharrar was as good as his word. When we returned to Lebanon in the spring, official permission was waiting for us, and we were able to head South to the refugee camps, to begin making final arrangements for filming.

Six months later, after I had taught my morning class at the University of Texas in Austin, a student came up with a recent French newspaper. "Another PLO leader has been assassinated," he said, pointing to a short article on the firebombing of a car in Beirut. A Peugeot 504. The dead man was Majid Abu Sharrar.

Comment

LEBANON AS IDEAL COMPROMISE

AMERICAN SOCIAL scientists with Middle Eastern interests in the 1950s were entranced by Lebanon's apparent success in generating a free, capitalist, and pluralist society in which Muslim and Christian could live and work side by side in prosperity and harmony. The success of this constitutional state in which Muslims and Christians were given equal representation was frequently cited as an example of how religious differences could be mediated through institutionalized relationships, rather than becoming a basis for communal strife. Indeed, compromise and mediation were discovered as a basic form of interpersonal and intergroup relations at all levels of Lebanese society, and studies were devoted to the exploration of this as a model of both rural and urban social processes.

Implicitly it was recognized that Lebanon was well on its way to becoming a class-organized society, but certainly a "healthy" one in which upward mobility, unhampered by ethnic or religious discrimination, would continue to provide opportunity for self-betterment. The Beirut elite included families from all the major religious groups in the country. The American University in Beirut, most prestigious among the several local institutions of higher education, had a student body with representatives from all the minorities, even though the core of its enrollment was the children of the elite and the near-elite of Beirut itself, as well as of the entire Arab world. So, as in America, education provided possibilities for upward mobility available to anyone who could qualify for admission and pay the bills. The need for a college-educated labor force seemed inexhaustible as the banks and businesses multiplied. There was no suppressed minority in Lebanon, it was argued, no underclass of people who did all the dirty work.

Except the Palestinians. Of course, the refugee problem was unfortunate. The poorest and least well-educated Palestinians had ended up in the camps around Beirut while the middle class moved to better districts of the city or went to other Arab countries. This was hardly Lebanon's fault. It was up to the United Nations to take care of training and relocating the refugees. Admirers of Lebanon's model constitution certainly didn't feel the need to take the Palestinians into account in contemplating the country's rosy future.

If political scientists waxed enthusiastic over the constitutional mediation of intergroup relations in Lebanon, social anthropologists were no less excited over the way in which kinship ties seemed to bridge class differences and offer a leg up in the world even for country cousins without benefit of formal education. Ties of blood took precedence over all else, obligating the rich to help their poor relatives. It was a question of honor. A wealthy relative in Beirut could be called upon to provide jobs for village kinfolk or help them deal with government officials or educational expenses. Politicians distributed their favors among kin in return for their support (in elections, of course) and kinship extended outward to include hundreds of relatives over great distances. It was ward politics writ large, tying together town and country, rich and poor, and guaranteeing admirable stability while the rest of the Middle East experienced the traumas of revolution and military coups.

The notion that ties of kinship could mesh with constitutional government and result in a modern, progressive nation was very pleasing to liberal American political scientists and anthropologists alike, for it suggested that modern legal institutions and traditional patterns of human relationship could coexist rather than replacing each other. As long as Shi'a and Sunni, Maronite and Orthodox leadership all had a hand in the Lebanese government, and thus had a portion of patronage and influence to share among the less fortunate members of their respective clienteles, how could differences between the haves and the have-nots become a matter of general importance? The only problem was that each group must continue to get its fair share. But since Lebanon was the principal center of East-West trade in the Middle East, there seemed no reason why local prosperity should falter. Self-interest would continue to make the status quo more attractive than any attempt at radical change.

Thus, class differences and kinship networks were seen to be in complementary distribution in Lebanon. The lines of possible conflict were balanced by ties of common interest. Peaceful coexistence between class and ethnic groups seemed assured.

How does one explain the total inadequacy of this 1950s "expert" opinion about Lebanon? How could the seeds of civil conflict, already taking root in the late fifties and early sixties, have been so completely overlooked or underestimated by American specialists? In part to blame, of course, was the nature of research on which such opinion was based. Anthropologists studied villages; political scientists studied "political institutions." In both cases the forest was overlooked and the trees were a focus of myopic attention, though of course everyone was behaving according to the best tradition of his or her discipline. In fact, even all of Lebanon would not have been sufficient as the unit of study if scholars were to have predicted that this country, a defenseless outpost of Western and Middle Eastern capitalism, was soon to be seized by contesting foreign powers and torn apart. Furthermore, Western social science of the fifties was possessed by a quest for social order; even conflict was seen as producing in-group solidarity, never as the basis for further and greater disorder.

Nor was sufficient attention paid by foreign observers to the fact that Beirut, the center of Lebanon, is a commercial, not an industrial city. Factories, large-scale manufacturers, might have offered opportunities for "free" labor, detached from established sects and kin groups, a chance for a working class to develop which could have included Palestinians along with Lebanese. But a commercial city is full of business people who hire only their own kind. White-collar jobs predominated; a broad-scale working class never developed. Thus the refugees of 1948 were still refugees when they were joined by thousands more Palestinians in the aftermath of the 1967 war, and it was the children of refugees, facing the same future, who provided the rank and file of the PLO.

So it was the Palestinians, their thirst for their lost homeland unrelieved by their position in Lebanon, who were overlooked and underestimated in the 1950s and 1960s by American social scientists—and American politicians. To have reckoned with this unhappy population full of hatred for the Israelis, and equally resentful toward the Lebanese well-to-do and the Americans with their unfulfilled promises, would have been to admit to ourselves a level of blame and responsibility we still refuse to accept.

CHAPTER III
Amman, Jordan
1981

Waves
bow
before
the shore
courtiers
to their king
and then
withdraw

Unknown, ninth century

Men cannot save those
Who cannot learn from Time.

Abid ibn al-Abras
Lament for an Arab Encampment

THE BUS CARRYING us to King Hussain's palace for tea suddenly stopped dead. Ahead, through the rapid crisscross strokes of the windshield wipers, we could see the palace gates through streaking rain—formidable wrought-iron structures, guarding the entrance in the high spiked protective fence that encircled the turreted residence of the Hashemite ruler of Jordan. From this stony hill upon which the palace had been built we had been told there was a fine view of the seven hills of Amman, a view of the countryside and of all approaching persons and vehicles. A hilltop bastion for a much-beleaguered King—one who had survived. Once, twenty years before, we had glimpsed the palace hill from a distance. Today, at the gates, we could see nothing but the rain pouring down out of a heavy dark sky on this late winter afternoon in Amman.

"What's going on?" We craned our necks to see.

The bus driver was shouting out of his side window. The uniformed palace guards were shouting back. The driver revved his motor, but the bus remained immobile.

"I think the bus is too high to get through," volunteered the man in the seat behind, a retired diplomat, one of the Americans, like us, invited here to a post-Christmas conference on Arab resources and foreign policy by the World Affairs Council of Amman and the Center for Arabic Studies at Georgetown University.

"Oh no," sighed one anxious wife. "So we have to run out in the rain?" She had emerged from the hotel hairdresser's only an hour before, her new coiffure created in honor of the meeting with royalty.

The arguing went on, but nothing happened. Two eras of technology, it turned out, were colliding. The protective gates had been set around the palace long before the advent of the Jordanian tourist trade and the development of luxurious air-conditioned buses. The neatly streamlined box on top of our bus, which held the coils and condensers for the air-conditioning system, kept tourists cool on the long hot drives through the desert in summer, through the Jordan River valley to the Dead Sea; to the hidden rose-red city of Nabataean Petra; to Aqaba, Lawrence of Arabia's country. But the box was strung up on the palace gates. The bus was too high. And that was that.

The rain continued to pour down. A gray wet vista at least two hundred yards long stretched ahead of us, and there seemed to be stone stairs beyond, many stone stairs blurring into the distant rain. In a rush to the door, we would all soak our modest finery, donned in some excitement at this invitation to have tea with royalty. For how many kings and queens were left these days to have tea with? Bob and I had said to each other, pleased at the idea. We had written postcards to his mother, to our children; they would get a kick out of it, we told each other. "And," I added, "pageantry has its place, and it's fun for everyone." "True," answered Bob. "And this King really reigns." Now, however, with the rain streaming down the windows of the tourist bus and the light slowly fading, the prospect of much pageantry seemed a bit dim.

But the King's minions came to the rescue—a procession of dark-suited young men bearing helpful large black umbrellas. They shepherded us up the steep, curving slippery palace walk, rushed us up flight after flight of wet stone stairs, and through a heavy oaken door. Here our coats were taken politely.

We stood in a long wide hall, hung with portraits. I recognized Emir Abdulla, founder of the Hashemite dynasty, the strong face and short beard framed by the agal and kaffiya, traditional headdress of the tribes of the area. Abdulla was Hussain's grandfather. Another, darker-toned portrait was of Talal, Hussain's father, deposed for reasons of health in 1952, when Hussain was sixteen years old.

The invitation had read: "You are invited to have tea with His Majesty King Hussain and Her Highness Queen Noor, on Sunday at 4:30 P.M. promptly." Well, we had been prompt, because the bus ordered to take us had been prompt. The conference had started promptly, after the prompt arrival of all the delegates on Royal Jordanian Airlines, courtesy of Ali Ghandour, the energetic and charismatic president. His airline was one of the success stories of the modern

Arab business world. Ali Ghandour had come to Amman from Lebanon ten years ago, and had made Alia (Royal Jordanian Airlines) the most efficiently run and popular Arab-owned airline in the area.

Like many conferences, this one had been a mild success, allowing for an exchange of views and papers by American and Arab participants. And the King and Queen's tea party was to top it off, so to speak. Where were they, though?

The polite, dark-suited young men suggested we might roam about the apartments until the entrance of the royal couple. To warm us, presumably, against the cold dankness of the rainstorm we had just run through, we were served tea, very sweet, in tiny glasses banded with silver, not the gilt-painted glasses of Arab coffee shops and homes, but real silver as befitted a real monarch. Hussain of Jordan had survived numerous attacks on his life, several threats to his crown, and the demise of almost every other leader in the area over the past generation. Even Hassan of Morocco, the only leader to rival him in staying power, had come to the throne in 1961. By 1981, Hussain was the only leader who had been in power when we first went to the area in 1956.

How had he survived? Not by barricading himself in the palace tower, obviously. A combination of astute political moves and assistance from the West, yes. But also a recognition on the part of his subjects of his legitimate claim to the throne. Hussain, after all, could trace descent directly from the Prophet Muhammad. He also represented Arab nationalism—as the son and heir of a dynasty that had led the Arab revolt against the Ottoman Empire at the beginning of the twentieth century. Lawrence of Arabia may have gotten the publicity during the revolt, but it was Hussain's ancestors who assumed leadership. In an area of conflicting powers and interests, Hussain's kingdom looked more secure and prosperous than others; he seemed genuinely interested in social and economic development, and his personal courage and honesty had earned him respect.

"The new Queen has redecorated these rooms," said a voice at my elbow. A gray-haired Jordanian woman in a dark-wine suit, lacy blouse, and gorgeous pearls, she was one of the local participants who had accompanied the American group to the palace. "What do you think?"

"They're very pleasant, certainly," I answered politely. We sat down on a beige-and-white textured sofa, comfortable, under a glittering French chandelier, its polished crystal drops reflecting and refracting the subtle reds, saffrons, and blues of the old Persian carpets that covered the floor. "Is it all new, I mean, since the marriage?" amending my question at the amused yet kindly look in the lady's eyes.

"These rooms, yes," she said. "Upstairs, the bedrooms, who knows?" She smiled again. "Different wives, of course, have different tastes."

Hmm. The King's first wife had been an Egyptian princess, Dina Abd al-Hamid al-Aun. The second, an English girl, Antoinette Gardiner. The third, Alia, a Palestinian. The fourth, an American, of Arab and Swiss descent. Where were they now? Alia was dead in a plane crash, the Egyptian divorced and remarried in Cairo, the English woman reported still living in comfort in Amman with her children. Certainly no traces of that past were evident in the room where we sat. Long, full, heavy biscuit-colored drapes, drawn against the rain, looked new, as did the pleasantly silk-lined walls. Decorative objects of many different cultures and periods had been placed carefully on polished tables of dark wood: miniatures; inlaid boxes; silver cigarette lighters. Against the main wall stood a shelf of signed photographs—photographs of the King smiling beside distinguished world leaders who had visited the palace in recent times: Giscard d'Estaing of France looked out of a silver frame; as did Sultan Qabbous of Oman; Fidel Castro of Cuba; Queen Beatrix and Prince Claus of the Netherlands; Pope John Paul II; President Saddam Hussain of Iraq, the country once ruled by Hussain's own second cousin, Faisal; Helmut Schmidt of West Germany. A strange company, those leaders, their visits testimony to the precarious yet central position the tiny kingdom of Jordan held in the Arab world of the early 1980s.

The palace where we now sipped our tea was a fortress within a fortress. The agricultural and nomadic peoples of ancient Jordan first came into contact with European culture when the armies of Alexander the Great passed through in the fourth century before Christ. Afterward, the Romans came, and the Arabs bringing Islam from Arabia, and the Ottomans from the north, until the West took over again, carving up the Arab world into new countries and distributing them to France, Britain, Italy. The new "country" of Transjordan became a British-mandate territory after World War I, a fully independent nation by the 1950s. In recent years, Jordan seemed to be an armed oasis in a vast desert of sand, wind, barren hills, and sectarian struggles, a fortress barricaded (with the help of the West) against hostile neighbors: Syria, Iraq, Israel. Dismissed as a British invention, a pseudo-nation when Hussain was a seventeen-year-old king, Jordan had emerged as far more than that as it had held on to its sovereignty and independence during a half century of violent political conflict and change.

"Well, Rhonda . . ." Another Jordanian lady's voice brought me back to the drawing room, where we awaited Their Majesties. "What do you expect? Isn't she a decorator, the American Queen? Didn't she get some kind of degree?" The woman sniffed audibly, causing her diamond earrings to swing above her subtly striped silk blouse and beautifully cut black suit. "If she's a professional decorator, the rooms *should* look pleasant if she's doing her job properly."

The first lady, older, smiled, kindly. "Of course. But remember the Queen is young. And also nice, very intelligent."

Although I had not asked, she went on to answer the unspoken question that hung in the air with the words "professional decorator." Queens, the implication was, were not ordinarily, in royal Jordan at least, professional decorators. "Yes, I would say people like the new Queen. But we would all be dishonest if we did not admit that any of us"—her gesture embraced the half-dozen well-dressed Jordanian matriarchs present—"would have been delighted had one of our own daughters become Queen."

The lady in the black suit nodded. "Yes, you are right. And we must remember that the King has had a difficult time. Very sad, his last wife, the Palestinian, dying in an air crash. Politically, that was very important for the King, that she was a Palestinian, I mean."

I nodded quickly.

"Poor thing, if she had lived . . ." Her hands, rose-tipped and flashing with rings, finished the sentence with an eloquent gesture.

The first lady rose. "I fear we are boring our American guest. Enough of politics," she said. "Let us give you a tour of the other rooms. I am sure they will be here soon. . . ."

A group of us followed her friendly direction toward the back.

The topic of the Palestinians was one bound to raise hackles of one sort or another, for the development of a Palestinian guerrilla movement had nearly led to civil war in Jordan; Hussain's own strong support for the Palestinian cause was challenged by the growing strength of the PLO. During 1970, the radical popular front for the liberation of Palestine within the PLO called for the overthrow of the King and radical revolution. The day of Black September, marking the defeat of the Palestinian uprising by Hussain's army, had not been spoken of at the conference. Everyone stressed the need for unity these days, but the old scars obviously remained.

"Here the room is slightly more personal, I think," the kindly lady in the wine suit said. "A sort of vision of what a royal Bedouin leader should have in the way of what you call a recreation room. The idea is American, is it not?"

The royal rec room was the last of the three public rooms, past the entrance hall with its family portraits; the large reception room where the chandelier glittered and the sounds of all footfalls became whispers in the thick pile of the Persian rugs; and past a smaller, salmon-pink reception room, paneled in the French style, where, we were told, the audience would be held. The informal room was fairly small and comfortable, with low couches along two walls, covered with cushions embroidered in the traditional Arab cross-stitch. Here presumably the royal couple relaxed a bit. Bedouin saddlebags decorated the walls; there were a new stereo and a cabinet of records, a shelf of books: volumes on military maneuvers, on planning, a few contemporary English novels; and Jane's huge and classic concordance of military arms and equipment.

A rustle, a movement in the general direction of the hall, was a signal, communicated along the length of the apartments, that the royal couple was arriving. We moved forward to see them descend the stairs, as monarchs should, preceded by the leader of the polite dark-suited umbrella brigade which had escorted us through the rain.

Queen Noor, née Lisa Halaby of the United States, M.A. Princeton (urban planning), the fourth wife, was slightly taller than her husband, King Hussain ibn Talal ibn Abdulla. It was Hussain's grandfather Abdulla and his great-uncle Faisal with whom the Allied Powers had dealt after World War I. In the chaos of promises given and promises fulfilled and unfulfilled, Faisal and Abdulla had negotiated and bargained hard. Britain doled out territory: Iraq as a mandate under Faisal as King; Jordan as a mandate under Abdulla as King.

The present King smiled graciously and bid us welcome. The Queen did likewise. Two circles formed for the audience in the formal salmon-pink drawing room. I found myself in the Queen's group; Bob had gravitated to the King's.

Hussain's hair was gray. His neat mustache was also gray, but he was fit and slim, walking quickly, almost eagerly, to greet his guests. In a dark pinstripe suit and white shirt with dark tie, he looked older than his forty-five years. He had been only fifteen, after all, when he had seen his grandfather, Emir Abdulla, cut down before his eyes by a follower of the then reigning mufti of Jerusalem, Haj Amin al-Hussaini. That was 1951. One year later, when King Talal was deposed because of illness, Hussain became King. He had reigned for nearly thirty years.

"You are most welcome," the Queen was saying. She smiled, a quick smile that vanished as quickly as it had come. She seemed a serious young woman. "We cannot offer you the sophistication or the sights of Paris and London," she said evenly. "We can only offer you ourselves and our hospitality."

"Oh, look at her belt!" whispered a woman behind me.

What a belt it was! The principal piece of jewelry the Queen was wearing, the belt was perhaps six inches wide and fashioned entirely of broad scalloped links of massive gold. I stared at it, as every woman in the little circle must have stared at it, in pure astonishment and envy. My eye kept going back to it throughout the brief audience, not only because of its opulent golden gleam but because the Queen kept unconsciously fingering it, pushing the great buckle down, gently, from her waist, over and over again. The scallops, curving inward, must be pinching, I thought. Oh well, that was obviously the trouble with solid-gold belts: they were simply too uncomfortable! Yet it *was* lovely, that belt, especially over her mid-calf-length afternoon dress, brown chiffon with a gold stripe woven into the fabric. Ruffles at sleeves and neck, a bracelet or two, rings, dark stockings and shoes.

"Yes," answered the Queen. Yes, she said, she had strong feelings about her own Arab identity, through her father, Najeeb Halaby, former chairman of Pan American World Airways.

"When I first came to Jordan," she continued, "I was fascinated by the differences between Arab and American society."

American society was "finished," she said, too clean, too ordered; the "homogeneity" of American society left her feeling discontented and she found she welcomed the "complexity" of Arab society when she first came to Amman to work as a designer (score one for the black-suited lady in the reception room).

"What are the differences you feel most strongly, Your Majesty?"

"Well, I can tell you better when I explain how I argue with my father," she answered. The quick smile came and went. "He believes that rational approaches to problems, as exemplified by the West, are the only way. I disagree with him." She smiled again, lightening the intensity of the expression on her young face, framed by shoulder-length blond hair; she had worn her hair pulled back in a neat ponytail at the formal opening of the conference two days before.

"I am interested in other approaches to problems," she went on earnestly, "alternate approaches." She did not specify what they might be and none of us asked.

The circles began to shift. Waiters in white coats were handing around tiny sandwiches on silver trays: egg salad, cucumber, tomato. Someone asked about the Queen's interest in indigenous art and artists, her newly established National Gallery.

"We are all pleased," she said and pushed down that massive golden belt again. "It is a beginning." She sighed slightly. "We cannot compete with the national galleries of the great powers, of course, but it is a beginning."

Others asked questions. Should I ask about Princess Wajdan Ali's role in the establishment of the gallery? I wondered. For the princess, whom I had met earlier at the conference, was a well-known painter herself, a strong and handsome woman, obviously someone with whom anyone in the Hashemite Kingdom of Jordan who cared about art would have to reckon.

Queen Noor talked about the contributions of Jordanian painters and did indeed pay tribute to Princess Wajdan's assistance and cooperation. Wajdan was Hussain's first cousin; her mother had been Talal's sister.

The Queen was enthusiastic, she was serious, she was obviously making a real effort to be part of, to contribute in some way to, the society whose King had chosen her to be his wife. By local standards, of course, she had already done her duty: she had produced a son. Her first child, Hamza, was nearly one. The rumor in the city was that she was expecting another baby; perhaps that was why she kept pushing down that wide, irritatingly sharp, yet extremely beautiful golden belt!

"Your Majesty!" I heard Bob's voice rising above the series of questions being posed in the audience circle. Was his voice louder than the others', so that the Queen's circle also paused to listen, or was I just conscious of it since it was my husband's?

"I am a cultural anthropologist," began Bob, "and I would like to ask whether tribal loyalties and alliances are still important in the political life of the kingdom of Jordan."

I looked at the King. He had furrowed his brow slightly. I deduced that this was not the usual question he received from American visitors. But then, how could he know that Bob had lived for two years with a tribe of southern Iraq, that we had been guests of the sheikh of one of the largest settled groups there, a sheikh who traced his ancestry, as Hussain did, to the desert, to the seat of the holy places of Islam.

"If you are asking me about Arab character, I am certain," said the King smilingly, "that it is surviving and surviving well."

The audience laughed lightly in acknowledgment and appreciation of the King's parry, but Bob was not going to stop there.

"Your Majesty," he persisted. "I am certain that Arab character will survive. Your own reign is evidence of its strength and this pleasant afternoon is evidence of its warm hospitality." The King inclined his head. He thought Bob was finished. But he did not know Bob. "What I am asking is whether territorial ties and loyalties, tribal ties and loyalties, still have any importance in modern Jordan."

The King paused. He looked directly at Bob for the first time. "Yes," he said finally. "Certainly. They have some importance. Even today."

He looked over us to where the polite dark-suited young man was gesturing. "Ah yes," he said, "please." And his gesture indicated that the audience was over.

We moved through the salmon-pink drawing room into the reception room, where silver urns of boiling tea and a magnificent tea cake awaited us: a confection of strawberries and cream in the middle of January. Truly a royal fantasy. We shook the hands of the Queen and the King and thanked them profusely. The Hashemite ruler and his American bride walked ceremoniously down the hall, away from us, past the portraits of the Emir Abdulla and mad-eyed Talal, and headed up the stairs, presumably both to kick off their shoes and she to unclasp that pesky, if magnificent, golden belt.

The umbrella brigade was stationed by the palace doors. We were shepherded once more through the rain and dark to the formidable palace gates where our air-conditioned transport, product of the latest technology, had been forced to wait outside. In the warmth and light of the enclosed bus, the group burst into sudden conversation.

"I couldn't resist asking the King that question," said Bob. "Do you think it was rude?"

"No, no," I replied. "But he seemed a bit surprised."

"Well, yes. But he owes his life to the Bedouin tribesmen of Jordan and they say the tribesmen are his most loyal supporters today. However, I would guess 'tribe' is not part of the vocabulary of modern kings, at least not in the presence of foreign businessmen and diplomats."

"What did you think of that *belt?*" said one of the wives, turning round in her seat ahead of us.

"Worth a bundle, I'd say," chuckled her husband. "Solid Hashemite gold."

We drove on through the dark rain, and the turrets of the walled, protected bastion of the King's palace receded into the night behind us.

The ruins of the ancient Roman city of Philadelphia lie under present-day Amman. Once Rabbath Ammon, biblical capital of the Ammonites, the city was conquered by King David in the eleventh century before Christ but regained its independence from the Israelites under King Solomon. Ammon was renamed Philadelphia by Ptolemy II, son of Alexander the Great's general who had become Ptolemy I. And as the Philadelphia of the Fertile Crescent, it prospered and grew until the fall of Rome signaled decline for all the Mediterranean and

Near Eastern outposts of the empire. By the seventh century it had been captured by the Arabs and converted to Islam, but it was only a village in 1921, when Emir Abdulla chose it as his new capital.

"So it is really a new city we are living in," explained Amer Salti, a Jordanian banker of Palestinian descent who had invited us to his home for lunch. He had earned a Ph.D. in Arabic literature from the Sorbonne and had also studied in America but had found banking more profitable in the bustling economy of modern Jordan. We were enjoying now one of the results of his labor, a fine new modern house with floors of local marble and wide windows open to the surrounding hills.

In 1960, when Bob and I passed through on our way back to Cairo, Amman had been a city of 100,000, but now, a generation later, in 1981, the ruins of Philadelphia were covered by houses and office buildings, makeshift shelters, markets, tents, and grand villas. The King's palace, where we had been guests the day before, stood high above the plain, and the city itself was spreading across its seven hills and beyond, down into the valley.

"They say a million people are clustered nearby," said Amer.

"A marvelous view," I said.

"Oh," joked Rebecca, Amer's American wife. "Every house in Amman has a marvelous view. It's one of those cities, like San Francisco, with built-in views." Rebecca was working with a British planning team, under contract to the kingdom of Jordan to build model cities to house the rush of migrants, from rural areas within Jordan and from countries outside Jordan's borders, that were pouring into the city every day.

"But Amman's is new, in the best and worst sense," added Amer. "It has few remnants of tradition to live up to, no wonderful medieval architecture like Cairo and Baghdad, where you have lived, Bob. But that can be good as well as bad, you know. New people, new ideas, to meet new needs."

"So many people, though," said Rebecca earnestly, "coming and coming." Her husband wore a banker's gray three-piece suit, but she had chosen jeans, a white silk shirt, a denim vest, boots. An attractive, lively person who obviously felt strongly about her work and its consequences. "And the migrants need so much. There are lots of problems. The government is, I think, sincerely trying to provide what it can, but everything is happening so fast around us."

Rebecca's mother, visiting from Salt Lake City, said, "I find it amazing. Every time I come, the city seems to have added another ten thousand people."

We lunched on excellent kebab and kufta prepared by Amer's mother, who lived with the Saltis and helped with the two young daughters while Rebecca worked full time. I looked around the table. Mother. Mother-in-law. A traditional extended household. Not quite. Most extended families focused on one set of grandparents, though not always. I glanced at Rebecca's handsome mother, younger-looking than she probably was; at Amer's mother, square, dark hair graying, fine aquiline features. The way she moved back and forth from kitchen to living room, the way she helped the younger daughter cut her meat, exuded a sense of authority. Here she was, indeed, in charge.

"Mother has just come from Damascus," said Amer. "In time to meet you."

"You're Syrian?" I asked.

The older woman shrugged. "I am an Arab," she said shortly. "Before, we never needed all these permits and passports to get from here to Beirut or Damascus. It's ridiculous. People are getting crazier every day."

"Well, you know why, Mama," said Amer evenly. "It's the whole business of the Palestinians, and where they are supposed to live."

"Aren't they Arabs, too?" shot back his mother. "What is happening to you, Amer? I thought we were all supposed to be one nation in this life. But people say, are you Syrian, and are you Palestinian, and are you I don't know what."

"We are all Jordanians now, Mother," her son replied. "We are lucky."

The older woman began to clear the plates with a great amount of clatter. I stood up to help, but Amer motioned me to sit down. "You're a guest," he said gently.

Over fruit—wonderful oranges—and coffee, Amer's mother looked at Bob, at me. "Have you been to Jerusalem?" she asked.

"When it was still partly under Jordanian control," Bob replied.

"We can't even go now," said Amer's mother, "without suitcases full of papers."

"Yes, it's hard," agreed Amer, "but as Americans you shouldn't have too much trouble."

We had considered going across the river to the Israeli-occupied West Bank, once a part of Jordan and still a bitterly contested area, for it had constituted one third of the small country's fertile land. But we had decided against it.

"I don't think we'll be going this time," Bob finally said.

No one answered or commented. The subject was too painful. We took our coffee into the living room and sat down on the modern Scandinavian chairs, their spare lines softened by many beautifully embroidered pillows in reds and oranges, tribal work and Palestinian embroidery. A large landscape by Wajdan Ali, the princess painter, covered a whole side of the wall. The other walls were windows onto the slopes where the sheep continued to amble, grazing; the builders added stones to the walls of new villas, and people and carts and cars moved up and down the hills, winding around on narrow roads between olive trees and tussocks of dry grass.

What could one say politely about the issue of Jerusalem, the city whose fate was a major stumbling block to a permanent peace in the area? Revered by all three monotheistic religions, Christianity, Judaism, Islam, the name of the city itself evoked wonder, awe, pride, and fierce factionalism. Internationalization of the city had been suggested as the only solution honoring all factions. But at the word "internationalization," Israeli leaders left the bargaining table. The idea that Israeli authorities were controlling the Muslim holy places, second only to Mecca in importance, was a constant goad to Arab emotions.

"We *are* lucky," repeated Rebecca, "to have a decent place left to live, ourselves, with our families. That should be enough."

"But it's not, is it?" burst out Amer's old mother. "Respect and pride are also necessary." She then rose and, with a fierce look at her handsome banker son, took her younger granddaughter by the hand, excused herself briefly, and left the room.

The sunset was premiering for us, a brilliant winter sunset, the clouds flaring from blood red to orange to palest dim rose. Against this Technicolor backdrop, the single boy herding sheep toward a tent on the darkening slope opposite us looked very small and lonely.

"Do the children of the migrants, like that young boy, I mean, go to school?" I asked.

"Oh yes," said Rebecca. "The government is building new schools, new clinics. But the migration to the city has happened so fast they can hardly keep up with the new arrivals."

"They move to Amman, Bob," said Amer, "partly so their children can go to the free government schools. There still aren't enough schools in the countryside and today you just can't get anywhere without an education."

"But that's not the only reason, Amer," rejoined Rebecca. "They come to make money, this is a real boom town." She paused. "And it's safer here than a lot of other places nearby. Be honest. It *is* safer."

Bob's question earlier to King Hussain about the importance of tribal loyalties seemed not to be such a dumb or rude question after all. In the final two days of the conference, we were entertained twice—once at the new Yarmouk University and once at the American Embassy. In both places, tribal affiliations and traditions seemed to be a factor, but in different ways. At Yarmouk, we were given a splendid *mensif,* the traditional feast of the desert. Whole sheep had been roasted in our honor, but the lamb was served in a manner that deferred to Western sensibilities. No one was expected to pluck chunks of meat from the bones with his or her bare hands, as was customary out on the desert; no, the huge trays that required two men to bring them onto the linen-covered banquet tables were piled with carefully cut morsels of lamb, distributed over great mounds of saffron rice dotted with pine nuts. Spoons were provided for Western guests, and pitchers of delicious sauce: meat broth thickened slightly with yogurt and seasoned with salt and lemon. Another meal fit for a king—or a tribal chief —and certainly for guests of any nationality.

At the American ambassador's residence a varied group had been assembled to meet the conference participants from abroad: members of the diplomatic corps from many nations, Jordanians, other Americans living in Amman for business purposes. But the most striking were the tribal sheikhs in their voluminous robes, fine black wool abas bound with gold; black-and-white kaffiyas, or head scarves, crowned with the traditional agal, or circular rope of black-and-gold thread.

I caught Bob's eye in the throng and moved over to him. "Do you remember ever seeing sheikhs in their robes at diplomatic functions in the past?"

He shook his head. "Well, some of the Iraqi sheikhs were members of Parliament before the revolution but they often changed into English suits for affairs like these. Apparently attitudes have changed."

The sheikhs were numerous. They sat on overstuffed sofas plying amber worry beads between their fingers, eyeing the moving throng. They lounged by the Western-style buffet, looking at the finger food laid out for guests: carrot sticks, deviled eggs, tiny rolls, meatballs to be speared with colored toothpicks. Men drifted past the buffet table in dark suits, women in silken dresses of peacock colors. Here and there one glimpsed a Moroccan caftan fastened with silver, a printed shimmering sari from India, a Sikh turban.

A tall young Jordanian woman in a long-sleeved, high-necked dress tried out her English on me.

"My name is Maha," she said. "And what is your name?"

"Elizabeth." She bent forward, not understanding.

"Beeja," I said quickly, tossing in my old nickname from Iraqi days.

"Ah. The little name from Bahija," she said, flashing a smile. "I am, you see, studying to become a candidate."

"A candidate?"

"Yes. A candidate. Is that not the word? A B.A. candidate. At the university."

"Of course. Of course."

"It is not the proper way, I see." She bent over. "What is the proper word, please?"

I explained about candidates and students and she repeated what I had said.

"That is why we are in Amman. So I can be a can—a *student*—for teaching in the end," she finished triumphantly.

"Your father agreed to that?"

"He chose. We did not choose. My father loves his children, each daughter, each son. He does not have business in Amman, he is from sheep country, goats, he is a sheikh, but he makes the sacrif—the sacrif—the sacri*fice*"—I nodded and was rewarded with another radiant smile—"the sacrifice for us, for his children."

There was a pause. I smiled.

"You have children?" she asked.

"Three."

She wrinkled her brows. "They are with you?"

"No. They are in America, in universities."

She took that in. "They are in America—and you are—here. Why are you not in America with them?"

"I am here with my husband." (I pointed Bob out, talking in a corner to a stout gentleman I did not recognize.)

"Ah." She nodded. "Your husband. He agrees to leave them there? And he wants you to come here with him?"

I nodded.

She peered at Bob again. "I see," she said, and laughed heartily. "Of course. He is young. My father is old. But he is good. And of course powerful."

"I would like to meet him."

She took me by the hand, this beautiful stately maiden, and led me to a Louis Quinze love seat where two robed gentlemen sat stiffly, eyeing, somewhat warily, I thought, the colorful company around them. One stood up when we approached. He was slight and shorter than his daughter, with a dark face, much seamed by age and weather, but when he looked up at Maha his eyes shone with pride.

"Sheikh Abdulla, my father," she said and smiled. Her pride in him was also obvious.

I shook hands with the sheikh and said in Arabic that I was honored to meet him and that my husband also would be honored to meet him. We had friends in Iraq, I went on and felt that I was babbling as I stared into that dark face; I realized I was trying to explain that our friends in Iraq were tribal leaders and therefore—therefore what?

Sheikh Abdulla turned to Bob, who had joined us. They shook hands. Bob tried out his twenty-five-year-old Iraqi Arabic dialect.

"Ah, yes," said the older man. He smiled slightly. His false teeth shone. "I am from the north, the leader of many tribes, but we in Jordan are far from Iraq, and not only in geography these days, my friend. It is sad." He shook his head.

The beautiful Maha tugged gently at my elbow.

"Let us have a cake," she suggested. "I am not on my diet tonight. I wish to talk, if you will, about women in universities in America. My brother is a candid —a *student*—in Oklahoma. I want to go, but not yet has my father agreed."

When I turned to look back, the regally robed sheikh was deep in conversation with my husband.

"Well?" I asked later.

"Well," replied Bob. "Tribes are important here, obviously, but it's not a topic anyone wants to expound upon. The sources of power are secrets in any society, of course; it's hardly a thing you take up lightly at a party like this. He's a tough old man, Sheikh Abdulla. I would guess that King Hussain is lucky to have his allegiance in these troubled days. A palace guard is never enough to meet serious challenges."

Bob was articulating what we both felt, but had not stated, during our visit to Amman. For despite the signs of growth, of building and expansion, in the city and its outlying suburbs, despite the warmth of hospitality extended to us and the King's obvious determination to hold on to his nation, there was uneasiness in Amman, fear of the future. The thousands of people flocking across the borders, often illegally, from Syria, Lebanon, Israel, Iraq, were gathering around the King, the palace gates. Yes, they were coming for education, for economic betterment. But they were obviously also coming for protection. The King had been tested and tried for thirty years, as Jordan developed from a dependent mandate to a complex and quickly growing nation in the vulnerable center of the Arab world. He was perceived as a stable, honest leader with ancestral roots deep in the desert, in Islam. He was trying to hold out.

The Prophet Jeremiah (49:2) cried, "I will cause an alarm of war to be heard in Rabbah of the Ammonites; and it shall be a desolate heap, and her daughters shall be burned with fire: then shall Israel be heir unto them that were his heirs, saith the Lord."

King Hussain was a presence that defied the prophecy and suggested that Amman, though beleaguered, would not be destroyed, but would live as a peaceful, prosperous city in the shadow of the towers and turrets of the Hashemite palace. Like ancient Philadelphia under Ptolemy II.

Comment

COLONIALISM EAST AND WEST

WE AMERICANS, unlike the Arabs, tend to regard our colonial period with pride and nostalgia. Colonial Williamsburg, for example, is a pleasant symbol of the American past. For the thousands of tourists who visit its restored workshops, houses, and gardens each year, it represents the admirable qualities of the early American colony. Americans see demonstrated there the ability to make a living on a new land and to adapt old technologies to fit the needs of a new country—all the virtues of pioneer invention, strength, perseverance, and innovation.

Given our pride in our own colonial past, it is often difficult to relate to the Arab world's reactions to *their* colonial past: rage, shame, anger, the kind of anger that erupted into protest marches, peasant revolts, strikes, terrorism, and guerrilla warfare, that culminated in conflicts far more violent than the struggles of colonial America in its revolution against the British. The American Revolution was fought fiercely, but the residue of bitterness dissipated rather quickly, and by 1785 Great Britain and the new United States of America had established diplomatic and trade relations. The two countries share a long history, a common language, a common religion, and bonds of kinship. We tend to forget that our ancestors, the colonial Yankees of whom we are so proud, were in their time also colonial invaders—of a continent peopled by American Indians. These native Americans may better be able to understand the Arab attitude.

Historically, however, the Arab world has had a far more complex colonial experience. Before the Europeans, the colonial rulers were the Muslim Turks of the Ottoman Empire, who dominated most of the area from the fourteenth through the eighteenth century. Then came the French, the English, the Italians, the Spanish—all of whom were far more foreign than the Turks, however disliked Turkish rule may have been. European colonials in the cities and villages of Iraq, Egypt, Algeria, Morocco, and the Levant spoke a language very different from Arabic and practiced a different religion. Unlike many of the English in America or the Turks in the Arab world, the new European colonists in the Arab world did not settle down, intermarry, and become part of the local population; these Westerners stood apart and looked down upon their Arab subjects or at best considered them as "other." They were strangers as well as foreigners.

There was no shared culture, but rather a long history of conflict going back to the seventh century and the fall of the Christian Byzantine Empire before the victorious Islamic armies. Thus, every reason for misunderstanding existed between the Arab and the European, who had centuries before struggled against each other in the bitter wars of the Crusades.

European imperialism in the Middle East is seen by some historians as in part a reaction to America's success in revolting against the British and buying out the French through the Louisiana Purchase. The declaration of American independence changed the balance of power. Britain and France were deprived not only of taxes but also of a source of cheap labor and raw materials as well as a market for European goods. The Arab lands, so much more accessible than North America, took on new attraction. When Napoleon landed in Egypt in 1798, nearly twenty years after the American Revolution ended, some trade agreements had already been established in the Arab world by foreign powers. By 1853, Sir Richard Burton could write, "Egypt is the most tempting prize which the East holds out to the ambition of Europe." The Suez Canal Company was formed by Ferdinand de Lesseps with a majority of European stockholders in 1858. France conquered Algeria in 1830, Tunisia in 1863, most of Morocco in 1912, and proceeded to bring in French settlers to displace local farmers. Italy invaded Libya in 1913 and also expropriated local farms for the use of Italian settlers. In contrast, virtually no English farmers came to Iraq and Egypt; Britain aimed at political control and economic exploitation, rather than settling its people in the Arab world. Exclusive trade relationships and a guaranteed source of raw materials, such as cotton to supply the textile mills of Manchester, were of greater interest to Britain than agricultural settlements. All the colonial powers, however, were interested in education to different degrees; the United States was no exception. The French Jesuits established a missionary school in the Levant as early as 1734, another in Damascus in 1755. French and British schools were opened in Egypt in the early nineteenth century, and by 1860 the American missionaries alone were operating thirty-three small schools in the Levant. Robert College was opened in Turkey in 1863, the French University of St. Joseph in Beirut in 1874, the American University in Beirut in 1866. It was not enough to merely seek economic gains in the Middle East. Souls were to be saved and the curse of "Mohammedanism" lifted from the ignorant. The missionary effort, seen as part of the "white man's burden" in Africa and Asia, reflected an unshakable belief in the superiority of Christian Europe and in the general need to "uplift" the Islamic world to the level of the West.

The curious mixture of political ambition, idealism, economic greed, and Eurocentric religiosity which constituted colonialism in the Arab world bears little resemblance to our perception of colonialism in American history and is far more complicated. There were some benefits. The new missionary schools and hospitals in the Arab communities provided help and encouragement; indeed, some say the American missionary schools' tradition of freedom of thought encouraged the development of anti-imperialism and Arab nationalism. But overall, the foreign presence had a more corrosive effect on Arab society than was apparent to either side at the time, or than is even recognized today by many former colonials, more than a generation later.

Why was it corrosive? Certainly a limited amount of basic infrastructure was developed, in the form of roads, dams, communication systems, and modern government institutions. What then was wrong with this introduction to the conveniences and conventions of the West? As many colonial administrators said at the time, "We are really helping these people. Why aren't they more grateful? Why don't they appreciate all that we are doing for them?"

To comprehend something of the feelings of the Arab people who were colonized, we need to recognize that the rule of powerful foreigners meant a devaluation of indigenous political institutions, language, laws, religious practices, arts, methods of trade, agriculture, and irrigation. Traditional technologies were disdained as backward and primitive; new Western methods were introduced, forcibly if necessary.

In many cases changes under European rule fundamentally upset local patterns of social and economic relations. In southern Iraq, for example, the British surveyed the countryside and registered all land in the names of the sheikhs of the tribes. But the sheikhs had not owned the land as individuals; they managed it and arbitrated disputes over its use, together with the senior members of their tribe, for whom they spoke. Much of the land was for grazing and used by all the members of the tribe. By registering the land in the names of the sheikhs, the British created a class of large landowners in southern Iraq; as a result, individual tribespeople and their families were impoverished. The old system of tribal ownership was destroyed and traditional patterns of tribal authority were undermined.

In Algeria much of the land held and cultivated by local communities of farm families was simply taken away from its users and allotted to individual French farmers with the justification that the French would cultivate the land more efficiently and scientifically, thus contributing to the overall good of the country. Even though some compensation occurred, many Algerians ended up working as laborers on what they considered their own land. So while European technological know-how was often respected and aspects of European life were emulated by the small elite of foreign-educated Arabs, colonial expropriation of land, devaluation of local ways, and interference with local practices and beliefs were deeply resented and ultimately harmful.

There were other problems. Arabic, the major language of the area, admired by Arabs for its beauty and revered as the language of divine revelation in the Koran, became almost a liability for Arabs with political and economic ambitions. To obtain employment or to conduct major business with the colonial administrators, an Arab needed French, English, or Italian; the occupiers did not learn the language of the occupied. Thus ambitious parents sent their children to the missionary schools to learn the foreign languages so that they might better compete for a high place in the new social order. From these schools emerged many of the leaders of the new nationalist states a generation later. Yet the missionary education was offered to only a few, and was expensive; only the wealthy could afford to send their children to such schools. Thus the colonial schools educated an elite, a tiny percentage of the population, which because of its privileged knowledge could enjoy many opportunities inaccessible to most of the people. In 1956, when Morocco gained its independence after forty-four years of French and Spanish rule, there were exactly forty Moroccan university graduates in the entire country.

Religious belief was also devalued by the colonizers. Islam was seen as stagnant, fatalistic, a religion in decline. "The dead hand of Islam" was something to be cast off, in the view of many colonial administrators, so that the Arabs could enjoy the new advantages offered by Western civilization. There were few converts to Christianity from Islam, however. Instead, proselytizing Protestant sects from Europe and America had to be content with converting local Christians, members of Orthodox and Coptic congregations. Such Christian minorities found special favor with the colonialists and often filled white-collar positions in embassies and trade missions. Islam was so generally depreciated that many members of the elites educated in Western schools turned to a kind of general secularism which discounted all religion as useful in the struggle toward modernization and eventual independence. The result was a serious breach between the religious practices of these elites and those of the majority of the faithful which has only begun to be bridged in the last decade.

Reactions to the colonial presence took different forms. Many large landowners, traders, and wealthy merchants who comprised the local elites in North Africa and the Near East welcomed the French, British, and Italians, seeing in colonial interests a way to improve their own positions. But small businessmen and artisans, the backbone of local mercantile capitalism, were often shut out of the colonial economy, owing to lack of capital and inability to speak foreign languages. Moreover, their children did not attend foreign schools, for they were needed to work in the family enterprises, and so there was little chance that a second generation would break into the closed colonial circle. As for the poor, who constituted the great majority of people in all Arab countries, they simply retreated, closing their doors literally and figuratively against the foreign presence. While the poor could not avoid the economic consequences of colonialism—or the political consequences—they took care to keep foreigners away from their families and out of their homes. It was only after 1912, for example, when the French took over the governing of Morocco and were present in daily affairs, that Moroccan women began to wear the all-enveloping jellaba and the face veil, to hide themselves from the gaze of these strangers.

Not all resistance and resentment were so passive. The Mahdist 1885 defeat of General Gordon at Khartoum and the following thirteen years of Sudanese independence until Kitchener recaptured the country in 1898 showed that the British were not invincible. In Libya, the Sanusi religious brotherhoods established a powerful network of Islamic education and trade centers across the southern desert, centers which became bastions of resistance against the Italian colonialists. Demands for independence were voiced not only by Islamic figures such as Muhammad Abdu in Egypt but even by the Westernized sons and daughters of the rich old elites who were less enchanted with the foreign presence than their parents had been. The British were forced to resort to bombing unruly tribal settlements in southern Iraq as late as 1932, in a decade which also marked uprisings in Palestine and Morocco. Such revolts required larger and larger numbers of European troops to "pacify" the countryside and made foreign occupation increasingly costly.

It was the Versailles peace talks of 1919 that marked the real beginning of Arab nationalism. During the First World War, the Western Allies had vied with the Germans and Italians for the support of the Arabs, each side promising the Arabs in exchange greater independence after the war. As a result, the growing rebelliousness of the area was temporarily restrained. But the peace bargaining table did not produce the promised independence.

Instead, mandates and protectorates over Arab lands were handed out among the victorious Allies as spoils. The Europeans claimed that the Arab people were still not ready to assume the direct governance of their countries. But in the view of the Arabs this was largely an excuse to permit the European powers to secure their own future interests. Egypt and Iraq were to be governed by the British; the Levant was carved up into the countries of Transjordan, Palestine, Syria, and Lebanon under British and French supervision. North Africa was divided between France (Morocco, Algeria, Tunisia), Spain (Morocco), and Italy (Libya). Thus independence, so enthusiastically promised before World War I, turned out to be politically inexpedient when the battles were over.

The division of the Arab world among the European powers did not pass without protest. In 1919, demonstrations took place across the Arab world. Peasant men and women tore up the railway tracks in Lower Egypt to prevent the British troop trains from running. Cairo was the scene of massive demonstrations and of a boycott of British goods. In Iraq, a Shi'a revolt against the British took place in 1920. In Morocco, Abdul Krim's Rif tribesmen rose against the Spanish colonialists in 1921 and marched on to disrupt French markets and attack French outposts. In Turkey, Atatürk defeated the Sultan and the Turkish republic was born—an inspiration for many through the region.

For the next forty years, people throughout the Arab world rose up again and again against the European presence from Fez to Cairo. By the 1950s, a group of young intellectuals had emerged, advocating local independence, following the example of earlier nationalists such as Jamal al-Din al-Afghani and Saad Zaghlul. As Frantz Fanon said, "What is given is not the same as what is taken." The people of Algeria took him seriously; they would retrieve from the French, they said, the land that had been taken from them. Every Arab country, with the exception of Saudi Arabia (which had never been occupied by Europeans) struggled with varying degrees of violence throughout the fifties for self-determination. Some replaced mandate-appointed leaders with more popularly backed candidates, while others rose to push the colonial powers out of the seats of government by force. By 1962, most countries of the Arab world had declared themselves independent. France, Britain, and Italy withdrew from all direct rule in the Arab world, yielding to superior force, changing priorities, or, in some cases, international pressure. It was the end of an era. But eras do not end tidily. Arabs felt they had scores to settle and that they must secure their economies against foreign domination. In Egypt, Gamal Abdul Nasser began to tax foreign companies, insisted that official business be carried out in Arabic, and abolished special courts to try foreign offenders. Nasser's supreme act of independence, however, was his nationalization of the Suez Canal in 1956, twelve years before the French concession would have run out. The British and the French, together with the Israelis, protested Nasser's audacity with troops and bombers, but the United States refused to support the attack and called for an end to the aggression.

The wave of strong anti-Western feeling throughout the Arab world was accompanied by a period of nationalistic concerns. National image became more important; every new country instituted its own airline service; foreign products were "out" and local products "in." New health services and widespread free public education in Arabic became matters of primary importance. Pride in the Arab past was reflected in the arts and literature, which in the fifties and sixties appeared to be entering a new renaissance based on a combination of indigenous and Western models.

Today foreign rule is absent, but the colonial presence remains, albeit in different forms. The West is present through the thousands of tourists who are essential to the economies of many Arab countries, through the Western television programs which fill the screens in many Arab homes, and through the Western consumer goods which flood the markets. The rich Arab countries must reach economic agreements with foreign powers in order to sell their oil; the oil revenues themselves are then invested in those same foreign countries. Poorer nations, to attract the capital necessary for industrialization, must mortgage crops and products for years in advance to foreign countries. The Western presence is also felt in the American support of Israel, which in the eyes of many Arabs is seen as a new imperialist power, one which has already seized Arab lands by force and which has stated aspirations to extend its rule as far as the borders of biblical Judah.

Thus, what seems to be emerging in the 1980s is a new stage in the colonial encounter. Many citizens of the Arab world feel their nations have traded the status of colonies for that of Third World countries, still tied to their colonialist rulers by a world economy over which they have little control. Egyptians, under Anwar Sadat, felt that only the end of financially ruinous conflict with Israel could bring any hope for independent national development. Other Arabs privately agree that peace in the Middle East is essential but remain far from convinced that either Israel or the United States really wants peace. People of the Arab world are now affirming areawide commonalities such as religious identity as a statement of pride in historical tradition. Such a statement is also a defense against what they recognize as a remaining vulnerability to Western interests. Some countries, such as Saudi Arabia and Libya, are even forbidding tourism and restricting the use of Western television programs, in an effort to reduce foreign influence.

Colonialism, then, is both an idea and an experience. In both respects, American and Arab colonialism have differed markedly. No gracious monument like Williamsburg, Virginia, is likely to be built to honor the colonial past in the Arab world today. For the bitterness is too deep and the process of independence still unfinished.

CHAPTER IV

Tripoli, Libya

1979

Religion embraces tradition, which is an
expression of the natural life of the
peoples. Thus, religion, embracing tradition,
is an affirmation of natural law.

Muammar al-Qadhafi
The Green Book, Vol. I, Democracy

WE WERE INVITED to Libya in 1979 by the Arab Development Institute,
with the thought that we might write a book about the new socialist state. By
that time Colonel Muammar Qadhafi had been the leader of the Socialist People's Libyan Arab Jamahiriya for ten years. We went, knowing little more than
what the generally critical press in the United States and the even more critical
one in Egypt had told us about the newly oil-rich country. Actually, the press
had told us about Libya's leader, Colonel Qadhafi, rather than about his country;
he was a much more interesting source of news, an *enfant terrible* whose continued and apparently successful rule contradicted his Western image as an immature demagogue. Thus, in fact, we had little idea of what to expect.

The airport was brand-new and vast, with shining immaculate black marble
floors and smoothly running escalators that siphoned us in single file down
toward immigration facilities, and down another floor to customs formalities.
We had been told that we would be met by a representative from the Arab
Development Institute. But no one was there. So then we looked for a porter to
help with the luggage. No porters were to be seen anywhere, not in the waiting
room or against the rows of spacious glass doors leading to the exits, nor against
the walls broken up with rosette windows and skylights that filtered the sunshine
onto the black marble floors.

In the new socialist republic, perhaps people did not have to work as porters
anymore, Bob suggested. That was all to the good, we thought. We had seen
enough in past years, in Iraq and in Egypt and in Syria and Lebanon, of men and
boys who carried heavy loads for pennies, loads that bent them double and aged

them prematurely, loads like refrigerators and pianos. No one should have to do
that to survive. In the old cruel past of feudal kingdoms, those things happened.
Not now. Good citizens carried their own luggage.

Very well. We would carry our own luggage here, as we usually did in America, and so we did, out to the marble porch, gleaming in the sun, offering us a
platform from which we could see the empty avenue leading away from the
airport straight as a die, its median strip boasting pink and red and white olean-
der bushes, clustered about standards that bore ceremonial banners, like flags, as
far ahead as we could see. The slogans were in Arabic, and we were not close
enough to read them; but the picture fluttering on the nearest banner looked
like Colonel Qadhafi.

We looked for a taxi. There were no taxis outside the airport. Bob noticed
that at the far end, to our right, at the corner, there seemed to be some activity.
In fact, a whole fleet of brown-and-yellow-painted taxis seemed to be parked
there. He gestured wildly. They did not respond.

"You stay here with the luggage, B.J.," said Bob. "I'll go over and see what
gives."

I stayed. There was nothing else to do. The only people who passed by were a
group of Libyans, including two women with babies: one in a white wraparound
garment reminiscent of the Iraqi abbaya, the other in a brown wool dress, a
turban, and smart leather boots. I could have sworn I had seen that same dress
on the rack at Marks and Spencer's in London a few days before. But maybe I
was wrong. The women and the three men, who were carrying several pieces of
heavy luggage, did not look at me, nor did the small girl in pigtails, wearing a
ski sweater and a pleated plaid kilt.

The air was clear, the sky was blue, the avenue ahead was riotous with the
blooming oleanders, and I was totally ignored. No one offered to sell me chewing gum or shoelaces, to take me to a good hotel or an excellent but cheap
restaurant, to pilot me through the native bazaar. No one asked for alms. I was
alone. In the more than twenty years of living in and visiting Arab countries, I
had never felt alone or neglected. Stared at, maybe, importuned, helped, smiled
at, cursed, but never left so alone. Well, I told myself, Libya has a very small
population, fewer than 3 million people on 680,000 square miles of desert,
oasis, and Mediterranean vegetation. Yet—it was getting curiouser and curiouser. The minutes ticked by. Where was Bob?

Eventually he reappeared. "Well, I guess we'll get into Tripoli," he said. "Or
at least I hope so. No one was much interested in my business. After four tries in
Arabic, an old man finally referred me to a kind of kiosk where men were
standing around, some drinking tea. The chief of the kiosk took my name, my
intended destination, wrote out an order form, took my money in advance, and
assigned me to this guy."

"What guy?" The road before us was still empty.

"He's over there, turning his cab around, and will be here in a minute. While
I was waiting the clerk of the kiosk told me all about the taxi drivers' people's

committee. No one is boss, he said, wages are fixed. All very interesting. We certainly don't read about anything like this in the press." Bob paused. "I hope he takes us where we're going, but then, why shouldn't he?"

"Where *are* we going?" I asked, beginning to feel like Alice with the Red Queen.

Bob smiled. "I told him the Libya Palace Hotel, the only place that came to mind. I'm sure I heard someone mention it once, and fortunately it seems to exist. I just hope they'll let us in. Remember what we were told, you have to be sponsored. And here we are, obviously *not* sponsored." He looked around at the broad beautiful marble porch on which we stood, pristine, vast, and devoid of all human beings except ourselves. "Awfully empty, isn't it? I kind of thought we'd be met."

The taxi drove up and we loaded our own luggage while the driver held open the trunk. A ritual motion if ever I saw one, I thought. The driver did favor us with a few curious glances, and I thought I caught him smiling into his splendid black mustache before he adjusted his white skullcap, tugged perfunctorily at his tweed sport jacket, climbed into the driver's seat, and took off at a speed I did not dare to estimate.

Bob put his hand over mine. "It *is* a Mercedes," he said lightly. "They have tough bodies."

We sped along the empty avenue of oleanders and palm trees decorated with the Arabic-sloganed banners, the banners bearing the bust of Muammar Qadhafi in military uniform. The flags of painted images and slogans undulated in the brisk Mediterranean breeze, a breeze made brisker for us, at least, by the rate at which the good strong Mercedes taxi was roaring forward. Miles of semi-empty countryside. Nothing at all to see by the roadsides until wham! we were on the outskirts of a city in the making, and the traffic became suddenly thick around us, cars, trucks, carts. Everything seemed to be happening at once, unlike the building sites in America where a house may be going up in an already populated neighborhood, or an apartment house may be coming down because of rotting timbers. Here were half-finished high-rise apartments, fields measured out with sticks and string into lots of various sizes: house lots? car lots? parking lots? shopping mall lots? A small fruit stand offered oranges for sale next to a newly poured cement slab, several cement mixers turning, great, gallant, bulbous mixers with a German name inscribed on their bellies. Nearby a new mosque was taking shape, its unfinished minaret a jagged tower. Between the half-finished buildings, workers could be seen raking the empty land—in preparation for future slabs that would be the bases for future buildings. Gravel was piled to one side of the workers who were raking. And everywhere were the signs, the slogans in Arabic, signaling again and again that we were in the Socialist People's Libyan Arab Jamahiriya. Signs on standards, signs on billboards, paper signs slapped onto newly built walls.

The older city emerged around a series of traffic circles, whose central pylon held the picture of Muammar Qadhafi in different military poses: hatless, with

his army hat, full-length, torso, profile, head. And with the image of Muammar
Qadhafi were the slogans in Arabic, which we were finally beginning to be able
to piece together out of the blur as the Mercedes taxi roared past.

"Partners! Not wage workers!"

"The nation that feeds itself is an independent nation."

"People governing themselves!"

The taxi driver was a speed demon, but his driving also demonstrated a kind
of inspiration. He wove swiftly and gracefully in and out of an incredible moving mesh of cars: Fiat sedans, Fiat pickup trucks, English Fords, BMWs, Volks-
wagens, and an occasional old, large American Chevrolet. It was always amazing
how large American cars looked outside their natural habitat. All the cars were
going as fast as or faster than we were, and the drivers did not seem to even be
glancing over their shoulders or into their rearview mirrors as they zoomed
around the grassy central circles and headed off into one or another of the
streets radiating out from the circles, each with its pylon, its standard carrying a
picture of Muammar Qadhafi, carrying the nationalist slogans.

"Partners! Not wage workers!"

"God is great!"

From time to time as we moved through town, a small glimpse of blue was
visible between the sand-colored buildings, lower and more modest than the
new constructions rising on the edge of the city. The sea was not far away. But
we were scarcely on a scenic highway. It appeared that the main road had not
been laid out with any thought of charming new arrivals to Libya with a felici-
tous roadside view of the glorious Mediterranean. And the downtown streets of
the city itself, through which we were now passing at an alarming rate, were
those of an older, smaller place. No avenues, no tree-lined boulevards. No
monuments except the banners, the pictures of Qadhafi in the traffic circles.
Two-lane streets, lined with narrow stalls and stores offering a variety of everyday services, rather than postcards, bathing suits, beach balls, and souvenirs of
the seaside. Lots of car repair shops (advertised by a picture of the bulbous
Michelin tire man), gasoline stations (yellow pump), appliance stores (a single
gleaming white refrigerator on the sidewalk), and sensible-clothing boutiques
(sweaters, long scarves, bright blue children's pants, jeans, and pleated skirts
swayed on hangers hooked along the edge of a half-opened door).

As suddenly as we had started, we came to a stop on a narrow incline, a side
street. We looked around, but there was no sign of the Libya Palace Hotel. In
fact, no signs at all. Now what? The taxi driver sat calmly in the driver's seat,
after taking off his skullcap and scratching his head, his only reaction to that
harrowing drive. We sat in the riders' seat. No one moved.

"Uh . . . er . . . where is the hotel?" asked Bob, in extremely polite
Arabic.

"There!" The driver gestured out his window. To the left, it was true, a fairly
tall building could be seen: a bit of shallow border jutted out from a brick wall,

without windows, that hid the building's purpose from public view. Perhaps there was a sign, obscured by the protecting wall?

Bob moved. "Stay here," he said, "and pray they have a room. I don't know the name of any more Libyan hotels. I don't think the good citizens would allow us to sleep on the street. Wonder why no one met us."

I watched Bob move across the street and disappear behind the wall. The driver had laid his arm casually across the seat. He was waiting, too. I racked my brain for facts about Libya that might have stuck in my mind from reading done in advance of our visit. I could remember the population of Libya, the name of its most famous Roman ruin, the city of Sabratha (miles of temples and theaters along a magnificent stretch of Mediterranean coast). I could even, for some reason, remember the number of its new schools (more than a thousand, the book had said, mostly elementary), but I could not remember the names of any hotels in all of the capital city of Tripoli.

"Humph!" The driver made an ambiguous noise as Bob ran out from the wall and crossed the street, smiling. I saw the smile as a good omen, a sign that we might have a bed. On the other hand, I thought wildly, he could simply be smiling at the ludicrousness of our situation. Why were we so worried? Surely we could find a hotel room in the capital of one of the wealthiest independent Arab states in the world. (What was it the book had said? Libya was among the top ten oil producers in the entire world and thus rich, rich, up from nothing in 1951, when it was one of the poorest nations and seen by international planning commissions as a hopeless prospect for development.) However, we had also been told by Libyan friends that their country did not need or want tourists. All visas were authorized and so were hotel rooms. Only our authorizers were missing!

"Well, we have a room," announced Bob. "Thank God for that. I'll tell you the story later, let's just get the bags out and check in."

The taxi driver, to our surprise, insisted on helping us carry our bags into the hotel. Bob fumbled in his pocket.

But the taxi driver held up his hand and refused the tip.

"Welcome to Libya," he said, "the Socialist People's Libyan Arab Jamahiriya!"

He came into the hotel with us, watched while Bob signed in, shook hands with Bob, and left.

"I believe he wanted to be sure we really were going to be let in here," I said, as we crowded ourselves and our suitcases into the tiny (three-person-limit) self-service elevator. Above the bank of floor buttons was a green paper sign, "Partners! Not wage workers!" Citizens did not have to work as elevator operators or bellboys either, it seemed.

"Maybe the driver was just being nice," suggested Bob more charitably. But neither of us felt charitable as the elevator went up and down, stopping at two, four, six, but never at three, the floor where our room was. After several minutes of punching buttons and muttering furiously, we finally gave up. We got off at four and walked down (we later found that the elevator, for some unknown reason, stopped only at even-numbered floors).

The room was small but adequate, with a desk and two chairs, twin beds covered with red slubbed-cotton spreads, a clean bathroom, and a double window obscured by heavy dark green wooden shutters. I threw open the shutters; the view of the sea was splendid, and the sunlight streamed into the small room, but with the sunlight came a draft of winter Mediterranean wind that chilled us to the bone. I quickly closed the shutters and we lay down in the darkened room for a nap before dinner. We had left London at eight that morning; it was now four-thirty. Heathrow, with its bookstalls, its tea shops and pubs, its buzzing, milling groups of English people and tourists passing up and down the escalators of the underground, might have been light-years away. We felt we were in a different world. We *were* in a different world. A nap, we felt, might fortify us for whatever might happen next.

Before he dropped off to sleep, Bob suddenly said, "You know, we are really lucky!"

"Lucky?" I echoed in amazement.

"Yes, lucky. At first they weren't going to let us stay here at all. Back to the airport we should go, and so on. No other hotels would be possible, etc. Just like we were told in Austin. You have to be recommended. The driver was waiting to take us back to the airport, I guess. Five European businessmen were behind me at the desk, pleading and cajoling the desk clerk for this room, any room."

"So how did you happen to be successful?"

"I said the Arab Development Institute had made a reservation for us. The clerk was very doubtful. Where were our hosts? But the reservation was there. I could see it, and I said so. So they must be expecting us. Maybe they never got our telex."

His guess turned out to have been only partly right. The institute was indeed expecting us, and they had gotten our telex, but someone had typed the date wrong, and the institute's driver had spent the entire previous day at the airport waiting for us. If we hadn't been able to speak Arabic, we might still have been sitting in the airport!

Well, we were in Libya, next door to Egypt, but it seemed thousands of miles away, here in the new Socialist People's Libyan Arab Jamahiriya. Libya, until this point at least, was unlike any Arab country we had ever visited or lived in before. Something different was going on. Something new was happening. "Partners! Not wage workers!" What did those signs, those banners, those slogans, really mean in terms of people's everyday lives?

We went down after our nap, looking for dinner. What faced us was a sea of tables—small tables occupied by men, only men, who filled the lobby—a large rectangular room pillared on left and right, paneled in dark wood, and painted crimson between the panels. Small white notices, lettered in green, bearing those same slogans, "The revolution has begun," and "Partners! Not wage workers," and "God is great!" were pasted on all the pillars. From afar they looked like giant Band-Aids. A thick cloud of cigarette smoke hung like a false ceiling over the room, giving a strange surreal effect to the round tables covered with tiny coffee cups and tall orange pop bottles, where all those men in heavy suits seemed to sit in silence, staring—at us, at the front desk, at what? Not one woman was visible. Alice, Alice, I thought in panic, where is your rabbit hole for me to scuttle into? Then I stood up straighter and dismissed such ridiculous thoughts.

"That must be the restaurant in the back, where the doors are," said Bob. He took my elbow firmly and guided me down the long room, between the tables where men of every age and nationality sat, upright Anglo-Saxon types, groups of Arabs clicking worry beads softly, an African face or two. As we passed, a few eyes turned toward us, and I realized that no one at all had been staring at us when we stood tentatively at the entrance to the room. My panic had been quite self-centered. Everyone was staring at the giant color television console that stood in one corner. What was on the TV? I turned back to look. A "Sinbad the Sailor" cartoon went off and the government newscast came on.

At the glass doors, a red-coated waiter gestured us to a table in a corner, by a curtained window. White napery, a rose in a glass vase. Water glasses. Wineglasses. *Wine*glasses?

"Drinks?" said a waiter in an unmistakable Egyptian dialect.

"Drinks?" echoed Bob. "I thought there was no alcohol in Libya," he said to the waiter in Arabic.

The Egyptian smiled at us in a worldly way. He had obviously dealt with foreigners before. "Try the bitter," he suggested, pronouncing it with the soft Arabic *tah*.

We did. "Not bad," said Bob. "Campari minus alcohol. Adapting colonial habits to local needs—an interesting case of cultural diffusion, wouldn't you say?"

The first course came, a good thick lentil soup with excellent local bread. We began to feel better. I looked around. The restaurant was half full, of men, men in Arab robes, African dashikis, European suits. In a distant corner a family—man, wife, and child in a high chair—was visible. Bob struck up a conversation with the waiter.

"I'm from Beni Suef, originally," said the waiter. "All the waiters are Egyptians. We make good money here and send it home."

He brought a plate of meat and vegetables, a kind of stew.

"That's how the service jobs get done here, I suppose," said Bob. "By outsiders. Libyans are rich enough so they don't need to wait on tables."

He was right. The maids in the hotel were Tunisian, one of the "floor managers" was Algerian, and the woman who turned down our beds was Egyptian; she told me she was divorced and had migrated to Libya to work so she could support her three children, who were living with her mother in Cairo.

"Their father doesn't support them?"

She scowled. "He said, you want them, you feed them, and that's the way it is. I'm lucky to make good money like this, but I miss the children."

We had seen the labor migration statistics, but "women" was not a category that appeared in any of the studies we had read. How many women migrant workers were there, I wondered, single, uncounted, living alone or with other workers, working to support themselves and their families? So much for the conventional wisdom of our texts which say women don't go out to work or travel abroad without male relatives. Practices were changing faster than the laws and customs described in books. We were to meet many migrant workers in Libya, male and female, teachers and doctors and nurses and engineers, as well as chambermaids and cooks and waiters. The 1979 estimate of Egyptians working in Libya was close to 400,000—a sizable number in a total population of only 3 million Libyans!

"Partners! Not wage workers!" Were the migrant workers allowed to participate in the committee-directed enterprises under way in Libya? This was a question that would be answered ambiguously during our stay: the obvious answer was no, the fruits of the land should be shared by the citizens of the land. Migrant workers were not citizens. Still, it seemed in practice to be a gray area where things were not clearly defined.

"Partners! Not wage workers!" The voice enunciating the slogan we saw everywhere caught our attention as we ambled up the stairs the next day on our way from lunch. (After several tries with the quirky elevator, we had chosen the stairs for routine transport.)

It was a woman's voice. We came out on the landing to discover two maids and one of the floor managers clustered in the hall discussing the most recent event: Qadhafi had announced nationalization of all private businesses; any company with more than five employees was to become a cooperative, the profits shared between employees and former owners.

"Well, why not?" the second woman answered. "God says that all Muslims should share equally in the fruits of the *umma* [the community of believers] . . ." and she quoted the Koran in support.

"But," replied the man, "that doesn't mean all Muslims should take part in *running* the umma."

"Why not?" returned the first woman. "Partners means sharing the running, too."

"Besides, the people's committees already exist—" interrupted the second woman.

"No, no," argued the man. "It doesn't mean that. . . ." They were still discussing the issue as we shut the door of the room behind us.

That night, the Egyptian waiter confirmed that people's committees of all employees existed in the hotel, and the committees were supposed to run the hotel. Mark up one for the chambermaid and her good Koranic education, I thought to myself. Next day, in our conferences at the institute, the process was explained to us by the sociologists and planners, mostly college graduates from the United States and England.

People's committees were operating everywhere, in the schools and universities as well as in the shops and markets that we visited with our colleagues from the Arab Development Institute. The dean of one of the colleges, a recent Ph.D. from the University of Michigan, welcomed us to his office but remarked wryly that he might not be dean next week.

"The committee is meeting tomorrow to give me a vote of support or select a new dean."

"But that's how deans are chosen at Michigan, too," Bob pointed out. "A search committee makes recommendations and those go to the president, and so on."

"Yes," answered the dean, "but does the search committee at Michigan or Texas include representatives not only of the students but also of the secretaries and the custodial staff?"

We had to admit that it didn't.

"In principle, I agree with the policy," the dean said earnestly, leaning forward, his arms in the sleeves of his Harris tweed jacket flat on the desk. "But practically, there are difficulties, difficulties!"

"Ideals are often hard to implement," offered Bob, a bit sententiously, I thought.

"Yes, yes, and the economic ideal is the hardest. Partners, not wage workers! What does that mean? Why is the market half closed? Some people are protesting, I think, since the nationalization of all the business enterprises."

Bob nodded. "We heard about it in the hotel. But can that really be done?"

"Well, he's doing it, Muammar, our brother. The foreign press says all the market is closed, that everyone is against the nationalization. Go see for yourself. It is only half closed."

The dean paused. "Oh dear, I am remiss. Would you like tea?"

We thanked him.

He rang for tea. No one came. He rang again. No reply. This was something new, unlike the hundreds of offices in the Arab world where we had sat in the past, with a servant rushing in with tea as the bell bonged.

The dean rang again. Still no answer. He went to the door and looked out, but the corridor was empty. He came back, looking embarrassed, and then burst out laughing.

"You see what I mean?" he said. "In principle I *like* Muammar's ideals. But in practice, I want somebody to make us tea."

"Really it doesn't matter," I protested.

"Don't worry about it," Bob added.

"We have money," burst out the dean. "To buy anything we want, meat, tea, butter, but half the time we can't find meat in the market and nobody is available or willing to make tea. I'm a sociologist, you are an anthropologist. Is what we are experiencing the pain of social change?"

"Does anyone make our tea in America?" Bob returned. "And," he added, "social change is often much more painful than it looks here."

The dean nodded vigorously. "Okay. Yes," he said. "You are right. And I remember the slums of Detroit, too. Yes, compared to America, we are on a luxury picnic with a few inconveniences."

"Well . . ." Bob was not about to let that pass without discussion, but he was interrupted by the opening of the door. An elderly man in a white skullcap and a kind of uniform looked in.

"If you would like some tea"—he smiled at us all—"I would be happy to make it for you and your guests."

And so we eventually had tea.

Ibrahim Abdulla came to the Libya Palace Hotel to take us to his home for lunch. We had brought letters and gifts from mutual friends, for he had gone to the University of Texas, but not in Austin, so we had not met him before. Now he taught at the university in Tripoli. He had been home from America about three years.

"You ask about poverty here?"

Bob nodded.

We had cut down to the seawall from the Libya Palace Hotel and were walking along the Corniche, the walkway along the beach, toward his car. Ibrahim had apologized for the inconvenience, but the narrow street in front of the hotel was jammed; the streets nearby were jammed. Parking was obviously one of the new modern inconveniences of Tripoli, where, we were told, the number of cars which had existed in the city twenty years ago might have been listed in one slim registry book.

"Look out toward the ocean, there, that is your best answer to the question about poverty."

He gestured across the seawall. The bright blue Mediterranean glittered under a cloudless winter sky, but between the wall and the sea itself, something new obtruded. Whatever beach had existed for the ancient pleasures of Romans and the more modern pleasures of Libyans was completely obscured, covered with hundreds of regulation-size lift vans—huge metal boxes that convert from truck sections to freighter containers. Orange, blue, green, yellow, arranged in orderly rows as far as we could see.

Those huge rectangular boxes laid down so carefully, in patterns of different colors, looked like so many toy blocks for giant children to play with. And beyond the rows of building blocks which seemingly stretched on for miles, ships were visible; a few flags fluttered in the cool breeze, we could see the smokestacks of freighters clotting the bay of Tripoli, waiting to unload still more colored boxes onto the sand.

"The government is bringing in everything needed by the Libyan people," said Ibrahim quietly but proudly. "There is the evidence. Qadhafi may be making some mistakes, particularly in his relations with other nations, but he is spending money on his people, not like some of the leaders in the other oil states."

"What's *in* all those boxes?" asked Bob curiously.

"Washing machines, television sets, machinery for gas stations, lumber, cement, lots of clothes, even cars. . . . It moves a little every day," went on Ibrahim.

The boxes seemed to lie immobile, and no activity was evident at all; our silence might have indicated our incredulity, for Ibrahim quickly added, "Today is Friday, no one is working. But tomorrow you will be able to see from your hotel that they are moving. First priority is food, second clothes, then machinery."

Ibrahim's car was a white Mercedes sedan, and he unlocked its doors for us. We set out along the seafront road where the scene of the van-glutted beach went on and on. We passed rows of new cars, parked on both sides of the narrow street, Mazdas, gray, white, blue.

"They were unloaded last week," explained Ibrahim, "and are ready for people to pick them up. This model costs about four thousand dollars."

I counted a hundred and thirty-two cars before tiring of the game. We were passing the old port area, and on our left houses were under construction, a mosque, a gas station. But on the right the colored blocks still filled the beach between us and the sea.

"Muammar has promised," said Ibrahim suddenly, "that when every citizen has received what he needs, these boxes will be gone, the port will be cleaned up and the area made into a fine beach for all the people to enjoy."

Bob and I were silent while we careened off the paved road and bumped over stones and through blowing dust to a row of new mud-brick houses, sand-colored, with doors and wooden shutters painted blue.

"Our house is one of the new villas," Ibrahim explained.

Villa. An interesting word, the Italian word. We might have described the houses we were passing as bungalows, since they seemed much more modest than "villas," with their implications of fountains, baths, and mosaics in the Roman tradition.

The children standing in the dusty streets and playing near the unfinished houses looked cheerful and healthy. They did not bother us but spoke politely to Ibrahim. (In fact, the only person who reacted unpleasantly to our presence in the entire time we were in Libya was a small girl who spat at us on the stairs of the Libya Palace Hotel!) This seemed remarkable, given the anti-Western flavor of the newspapers and television programs. But in practice, Libyans were polite to us as strangers, friendly when we met. Many Americans were still working in the oilfields, though at a distance from the larger cities. The country did not need foreign tourists and did not want them. But visits for business, including education, were quite common, and several English and American young people were teaching English in the universities.

Ibrahim was speaking, regretfully, about the refuse that was blowing about in the new, half-finished streets: the bits of paper, wood, the plastic bags and cigarette butts, refuse that in most other Middle Eastern countries we had lived in or visited would have been collected by private initiative, salvaged, recycled, and resold. But there was no market for such garbage here: Libya was no longer a poor country.

"The garbage workers' union still is not inspired to become a proper revolutionary activity group, you see," said Ibrahim wryly, pushing some broken glass carefully out of our way. "But it's not good, letting the garbage lie around like that. If young people see that kind of neglect, they think they can get by without doing *their* duties." He paused. "Now in the old days—"

"Was it different then?" Bob interposed.

Ibrahim paused at the blue door of his parents' house.

"Different? Yes, it was different. You never saw much trash lying around. But of course Libya was a poor country then. There was terrible poverty, poverty everywhere. Sickness. Hunger. These children haven't known it, they don't care, but I was a child then, I remember. We were lucky; my father had a small place in the market; he sold vegetables. We were never hungry. But many others were. Many others."

"And you feel Qadhafi is responsible for the improvement?"

Ibrahim turned. He looked directly at Bob. "Yes. He is responsible. That is why he stays in power. He has made life better for people here."

The blue door opened into a long hall, which led ahead into a courtyard lit by sunshine. At the entrance to the court an old woman wrapped in blue sat on the courtyard floor, her face to the warmth of the sun, her back to the wall. She laughed and waved at us. I started toward her friendly greeting, but Ibrahim ushered us into a room on the right. We took off our shoes, following Ibrahim's example, before we stepped on the thick carpet, and were motioned to cretonne-covered cushions on the floor. We sat down. Ibrahim put more cushions behind our backs, "for comfort," he said, smiling.

After a moment, a pretty young woman came in, in a black pleated skirt, black tights, a heavy white wool sweater over a black turtleneck; she shed her clogs at the door and came forward to shake hands.

"My wife Asma."

"Welcome to Libya," said Asma. "How is Texas?" She smiled.

"Texas is cold right now," I answered. "About like Tripoli."

She sat down on a cushion beside us and smiled again. I smiled. She smiled back. I made a slight adjustment in my back cushion. Bob and Ibrahim sat opposite us, across the thick red-and-yellow carpet, against the whitewashed wall. Cigarettes were offered. We said no, thank you.

There was a pause.

Asma said, into the silence, "Would you like music? We have some cassettes." She got up, and then as suddenly sat down again.

"Oh, I am sorry, I forgot. The machine is out of batteries and the batteries aren't back on the market yet."

"Maybe they're out there in one of the big blue boxes on the beach," joked Bob. This seemed a bit daring, even rude, but Ibrahim seemed to accept it as an ordinary remark.

He nodded. "Yes. Probably," he said, "along with the meat. We always have a shortage of meat. Last year a whole load of lamb from Yugoslavia spoiled while waiting to unload. That is sad. And all this is said, Bob, to apologize, because I'm afraid we could not find any meat for your lunch today."

"Please," said Bob. "We are honored to be in your house. Thank you for inviting us."

"You are welcome here," answered Ibrahim. "But I do remember the wonderful barbecue in Texas."

Asma rose and went out, shutting the door of the room behind her. Ibrahim was smoking. Bob sat silently. I leaned back against the pillow and looked around me. The salon, or room for entertaining guests, where we sat was long and rectangular. Cushions lined three sides of the carpeted floor, and across the fourth stood a big oak wardrobe, an armoire in the old style, Italian-inspired in its swirls of carving around the tall doors. Suitcases were piled on top of the armoire, and on each side bedding had been piled, neatly folded blankets, quilts, mattresses, pillows, some covered in the same pattern of red and beige roses as the cushion I sat upon. The whitewashed walls were decorated with hangings, a black-and-white representation of the sacred Kaaba, at Mecca; a scene of men sitting in a mosque; a group of white-robed men on horseback. The kerosene heater hissed intermittently in the center of the room.

A comfortable, pleasant room, and familiar, from days in the villages and cities of Iraq, from Egypt and Nubia, and yes, from Morocco. The pattern of living was found all over the Arab world, and indeed had parallels in our own society: the parlor was for guests; cooking and cleaning and childcare and sleeping took place elsewhere in the private quarters of people's houses. Only in recent years in America had those boundaries between public and private quarters become blurred, the parlor–kitchen–dining room dissolving into the family room or the recreation room, where everything went on simultaneously. Was it more comfortable?

Lunch was served by Asma, on a large brass tray, bearing several flowered china dishes and plates with large spoons. The four of us gathered around the hot thick soup of vegetables and lentils, the plates of different salads, the bowl of grape leaves, the two bowls of stuffed vegetables, stuffed potatoes. The potato stuffing was flavored with cinnamon and hot red pepper. Ibrahim apologized again for the absence of meat, though Asma pointed out that there was a little in the soup, and also a little in the potato stuffing. Her aunt had found it, after several hours of looking.

"And after all, it's like the old days," said Asma. "What are our Libyan specialties? Mostly bones and beans. Meat has always been hard to find."

"Or to afford," corrected Ibrahim. "Now we can afford it, but we can't find it."

I said how good the potato stuffing was. Bob agreed. We had large, sweet oranges. Ibrahim removed the tray and brought a basin and towel for us to wash with. Then the old people came in with Ibrahim and Asma's son, a toddler who rushed excitedly in ahead of Ibrahim's father, his stepmother, and her two sisters; they had come to get a look at the American visitors. The women half covered their faces but stared at us with great interest.

"Baba!" cried the child and ran to his father for a kiss, then to his grandfather, and he finally settled down next to his mother and also stared at us.

"Welcome!" said the stepmother. We stood up to shake her hand and the hand of Ibrahim's father, who wore a jellaba and skullcap and had made himself comfortable against a very large gold-fringed red velvet cushion at the head of the room. We sat down again. The three elderly ladies settled on the rug in front of the armoire, behind a small tea tray covered with a lace cloth and containing the pots and cups and bowls necessary for the tea ritual.

The three ladies were a sharp contrast to Asma in her skirt and sweater, her dark hair falling free from ornamental side combs. Their heads were bound up in printed head scarves. They wore long shapeless flowered dresses under lengths of material that were wrapped around their bodies, that covered their knees as they adjusted to sitting, that even covered their heads as they sat making the tea. What they were wearing, we were told, was the *hoki,* a local variation of the *haik,* that long piece of cloth traditional rural women wrap around themselves in Morocco, in Algeria. But where in Algeria it might be white, and in fact on the streets of Tripoli was also white, here in Ibrahim's father's house the women wore hokis of different colors, navy blue, striped white on blue, or gold and blue.

In response to my question, Asma went and got another hoki, folded carefully into a neat rectangle, to show me. It was gold on gold.

"Beautiful," I said, fingering the material. "Where does it come from?"

"Here, in Tripoli. It's woven of silk and cotton, like this, or silk itself. Very expensive. A piece like this, five meters, maybe over a hundred dollars."

The old ladies were muttering among themselves and gesturing toward me.

"My stepmother is saying that you don't wear such things in America," offered Ibrahim.

"No, it's true, but I've lived in Iraq and the women wear something very much like this, the abbaya."

The stepmother paused in her preparation of the tea, pouring the liquid back and forth from one blue enamel teapot to another, from a great height, until it reached the desired strength and created, we were told, the proper amount of foam.

"What does she say about Iraq, Asma?" the stepmother said, and I understood and replied in Arabic.

But of course the dialect was different, and the mix of Iraqi and Egyptian usage in my speech caused the old ladies to giggle. Even Ibrahim smiled. Asma translated for me.

"Please don't feel bad," she cautioned, in English, "but what they are saying is that you should be able to tell the difference between a hoki and an abbaya. They are made differently and worn differently. And," she added in a tone that indicated they could not be more dissimilar, "the abbaya is *black.*"

I nodded. "True." I had been too eager to make the connection, and the old ladies had seen through me instantly. I decided to keep my mouth shut and drink the tea, which was hot, very strong, and very sweet.

"It reminds me of the tea I used to drink in the sheikh's guesthouse in Iraq," said Bob.

Ibrahim smiled again. "We are all Arabs," he said. "Many of our customs are similar, though we have our political differences."

I warmed my cold hands on the tiny tea glass decorated with painted flowers. The talk was turning to marriage. What about marriage customs in America? Ibrahim's father was asking. How was the issue of the *mahr,* or dowry, handled there? "I know they call it bride price in America," said Ibrahim, "but you know it isn't really that." His father asked if in America the mahr had increased with inflation.

Bob was not answering directly. I saw he was trying to avoid saying that there was no mahr in America at all, no traditional payment by the groom's family to the bride's family and to the bride to cement the marriage and provide money for setting up the new household. He said instead, rather ambiguously, that parents and relatives and friends are expected to give the young couple generous presents to help them start their new household.

That didn't wash with the old ladies at all. They were indignant and turned to me.

"You married him without a mahr?"

I nodded.

They shook their heads. I was obviously an unfortunate case. "No girl in Libya would ever give herself in marriage without a very generous mahr," said the stepmother; one of the old aunts nodded sagely and the other burst out, "That's why our good Arab boys want to marry foreign girls, they get them free! It's shameful, that's what it is."

"But, Auntie, it is very different in America," said Asma in my defense. "Life is different. You don't understand."

"What's to understand?" returned the old lady. "Don't women everywhere have to look out for themselves, to be sure they're taken care of in old age? A man who has paid a good mahr thinks twice about divorcing his wife."

"Yes, yes," broke in Ibrahim. "That's true. I agree that the mahr is a good custom, but here it is getting all out of bounds. Why, ten thousand, fifteen thousand dollars, that's ridiculous."

"Not for the consent of a fine girl who will bear good children and keep a good household. Not at all." The ladies were speaking rapidly in Arabic and Ibrahim and Asma were getting involved and trying to remember to communicate in both English and Arabic, and the conversation was getting faster, more heated, and harder to follow.

"Ten thousand dollars!" Bob was astounded. "That is the average mahr in Libya today?"

"Oh yes," said Ibrahim's father, "and it keeps going up. Inflation."

"Thank God I'm already married," said Ibrahim, with a side glance at Asma.

"I never would have been able to marry," said Bob.

The men laughed.

"Come on, Bob," joked Ibrahim. "America is supposed to be the richest country in the world."

"It wouldn't fit with our buy-now-pay-later economy," said Bob. I tried to interrupt at that point, but Ibrahim was off again.

"You know Abdulla, Father. He got married last month and the mahr was twelve thousand dollars, plus a flat, plus a car, plus a refrigerator, plus a car *for the bride's mother!*"

The elderly ladies were delighted. "Who was the matchmaker?" they asked mischievously.

"And that doesn't count the gold," went on Ibrahim. "The man must give at least one big piece, a necklace like a collar that reaches to here"—he demonstrated by indicating the bottom of his chest, just above his belt line—"a very long collar, very expensive."

The elderly ladies' eyes sparkled as they switched to the fascinating subject of gold. Gold in America. How much was it per ounce? Although they did not specifically ask how much gold jewelry I owned—I was wearing none except my wedding ring—I felt sufficiently self-conscious to start babbling about giving gold to our daughters on graduation from high school, and at feasts like Christmas, or birthdays, so that just like Libya we really did wear gold chains and rings. . . .

"But you do not get large gifts from husbands when you marry?"

"Well, sometimes we do, but," I finished bravely, "it is not required."

"Not required." One old lady raised her teacup to the other, who repeated, "not required."

The three ladies looked at each other and then at me.

"A woman's life in America must be hard," said the stepmother sympathetically.

Asma, who had been quiet during the animated conversation of the past moments, now spoke up. She looked pained. "Auntie," she said, "some things are better here, some things are better there." She was speaking very slowly, in careful Arabic, so I could understand and recognize her effort to be both truthful and diplomatic.

"In America women work outside the home," she added. "They work as teachers and doctors."

"But they do here, too, now," said Ibrahim quickly, too quickly.

I looked at Asma. "Didn't I hear that you trained to be a teacher in Texas?" I asked her in English.

"Yes, but I did not finish my degree. If I had the degree, I could get a job. But I have to go back to school here to finish and it is difficult—the credits are different—the child—I am expected to help in the house."

"They need teachers desperately, though," I said, "at least that's what we've been told at the institute, and at the university. Lots of teachers are from Egypt because there aren't enough Libyans to fill the places."

"That's true," allowed Ibrahim. But he did not pursue the matter.

The room had quieted. The elderly ladies had sat back on their heels to sip their tea. Their hokis had slipped down around their shoulders, like colorful striped shawls. Ibrahim's father held his empty glass. Everyone seemed to be watching Ibrahim and Asma, except the child, the little boy who ran back and forth between them, pausing en route to snuggle for a few seconds at his grandfather's knee before taking off again across the red-and-yellow carpet to get a kiss from Auntie.

Obviously Ibrahim was in an uncomfortable middle position. The elderly ladies expected Asma's help and company; they felt it was their right after working hard all their lives, and according to tradition they were correct. And Ibrahim also was expected to assume the traditional role. Housing was short in Tripoli. Many of his friends at the university, Ibrahim had said, were obliged to leave their families in smaller towns and villages because there was no place in Tripoli for them to live. They were lucky to have a room in his father's house. It was true that Asma had anticipated a professional career when she studied in Texas, along with her husband. In Texas it may also have seemed a good idea to Ibrahim. But now back in his father's house, faced with both family opposition and bureaucratic obstacles, and with no real financial need, having Asma go out to work may have seemed less attractive.

"Why does Asma need to work?" I could almost hear the older people talking. "Her husband is rich. She should stay home and have more beautiful children."

To make an enormous, probably costly effort to meet the bureaucratic regulations surrounding teacher accreditation and get Asma either enrolled in the university or appointed to some minor teaching post: this was a major effort outside the home which might create other battles inside the home. Ibrahim seemingly was not ready to fight on both fronts; perhaps Asma was not, either.

"I will probably forget my English before anything happens," said Asma sadly, and she rose to take the child to the bathroom.

Ibrahim did not comment.

We left soon after. It was time for siesta. Even in winter, Ibrahim said, his father rested before returning to work.

"He still works in the market?"

"He doesn't need to, Bob. I can easily take care of him, of all of them. But he says he wants to. He says he feels better when he's doing something. He has his same old place in the market. He sells potatoes and peppers and talks to his cronies, just like he did before the oil boom."

"Well, it gets him out," replied Bob. "I can see why he wants to be busy."

Ibrahim smiled. "At least he lets me drive him to work in the morning and pick him up in the afternoon and evening. That saves him some time and trouble." He shook his head. "Can you imagine a country like ours, Bob, where an old man who sells potatoes in a little stall in the market is picked up and delivered by his son in a Mercedes-Benz?"

"Your country is changing fast. But everybody has his own pace."

"Yes, and we have to remember who we are and where we came from. My father hasn't forgotten. Neither have I. But some people—maybe they don't realize their luck, or can't take it in, it's hard, it's happened so fast, with the oil."

We drove back past the rows of new Mazdas, past the shabby old port, onto the paved roads beside the sea where, as far as the eye could see, the colored boxes full of consumer merchandise, treasure chests from the industrial world, lay in rows, waiting to be unloaded. And the ships lay at anchor beyond. Uneven rates of economic development, the experts called it. And perhaps uneven rates of human acceptance and ability to deal with it all.

"Tomorrow we would be happy to take you round the markets," said Ibrahim, as he dropped us off at the Libya Palace Hotel. He smiled at me. "The gold market, however, is still closed, madame, I'm afraid." Had he winked at Bob?

"What a pity!" returned Bob.

Wadi al-Haay. A demonstration agricultural project slightly south and east of Tripoli. We visited the project with a high-level official of the Ministry of Agriculture: an attractive middle-aged woman who held a degree from an English university.

"The nation that feeds itself is an independent nation." This was the slogan behind the large budget allotted for agriculture, Dr. Salma explained to us. Agriculture was the top priority in the first long-range plan proposed by the government, with 21.2 percent of the $2.1 billion budget. Housing came next, followed by industry, electricity, transport and communications, and education.

Model houses for farmers had been spread about the area, plots were staked out, a center for agricultural and nutritional education had been built around a small garden. A pylon with the torso picture of Qadhafi held the place of honor in the center of the garden. We went around the center, talking to an Egyptian woman agronomist who was promoting beekeeping and kitchen gardens, to a Libyan agricultural specialist who worked increasing the cultivation of grains and the expansion of the olive groves that had always formed a major part of Libya's cash crop. Classes in nutrition, in sewing, in weaving of the traditional flat baskets, were held regularly for women. Agricultural programs and literacy classes were held for both sexes.

We visited a model house and had tea with the owners, an older couple who offered us Coca-Cola as well as the traditional tea.

"We can always drink Coca-Cola when we run out of water," said the man with an eye to Dr. Salma, the Ministry of Agriculture official who accompanied us. She responded to that with spirit.

"Everyone knows water is a big problem," she said seriously. "The government is working on it. A solution will be found."

"Yes, yes, and we are glad to have this nice house, aren't we, Ahmed?" said the wife with a sharp look at her husband. "Come," she said, and ushered me to the back of the house where a fine modern tiled bathroom had been installed, sink, shower, and a porcelain Turkish-style lavatory with a flushing mechanism.

"Isn't it great?" The old woman was genuinely pleased.

"Does everybody in Wadi al-Haay have a bath like this?" I asked.

The old woman stared at me. "Of course everybody does. Who told you they didn't?"

"Nobody," I replied lamely. It seemed unused, in fact, waiting for a better water supply.

"In the past, nobody had baths except the Italians," the old woman temporized. "That's true. But that's the *past*. Today *everyone* has them. Muammar promised, and he keeps his promises."

Another high priority in Libya was education (nearly 10 percent of the budget). Everyone we met talked about schools, took us to schools, discussed the quality of education that was provided in the schools and the necessity for increasing the number of schools. The statistics were impressive: in 1950, while still under colonial rule, Libyans in school throughout the country totaled 32,741. In 1962, under King Idris, the enrollment had increased five times, to 167,000. But in 1973–74, the latest statistical abstract from which figures were available, this number had skyrocketed to 610,000. A twentyfold increase in a single generation.

"That doesn't count university students, either," pointed out a statistician. "Do you realize there were only thirty-two Libyan students in universities in 1950, and all abroad? In 1973 we had eight thousand students abroad, and the new universities are adding even more to the total." Such a great leap forward, for that indeed was what it was, obviously presented some difficulties.

"My students can't do simple algebra," complained one college instructor, "but they all think they should graduate anyway." A Libyan oil company administrator told us that the low level of performance on language and mathematical tests was a serious drag on the improvement of the system. "The instruction has *got* to be upgraded from the beginning levels upward," he said.

"We are trying to do that very thing," asserted one of the educational specialists in the ministry to whom we were taken by colleagues at the institute. "It's not easy to leap forward. One sometimes breaks a leg in trying," he added, somewhat ironically, "and then the leg has to be mended. It takes time."

Bob said that it seemed all Arab officials believed the key to progress or improvement in people's lives lay in education. This was also true in America, I pointed out, remembering my own mother and father, both high school teachers in small Midwestern towns, who used to say that schools were the right arm of progress.

"Yes," said the ministry official, "but we can't just copy the West. We are *not* the West. We have different backgrounds, expectations, we have to put together our own kind of education. Go and see for yourselves."

We visited high schools, elementary schools, the university, and the teacher-training colleges. The schools were following the standard Western curriculum: science, language, literature, history, mathematics, art, music, physical education. In one basketball class, two girls were wearing T-shirts with that familiar three-quarter profile of Muammar Qadhafi imprinted upon them. But some things were different. All students had required classes in religion, the Libyan history books I saw had obviously been written from the revolutionary viewpoint expressed by Colonel Qadhafi. And literacy classes for adults were held in each school in the afternoons, when the regular school day was finished.

In one kindergarten, the children stood up when we entered and sang us a raucous, enthusiastic song of welcome. And then they started the song we had heard on the car radio when we visited Sabratha, the ancient splendid Roman ruin.

"Axii—al-thawra! (My brother! The revolution has arrived!)
Uxtii—al-thawra! (My sister! The revolution has arrived!)
Ummii—al-thawra! (Mother! The revolution has arrived!)"

When we had applauded, suitably impressed, the children sat down and folded their small hands on their desks in front of them, bright eyes peering up at the strange visitors while the teacher, a very pregnant young woman, explained to them that although we were from the imperialistic West, in fact were *Americans,* we were still the guests of the Libyan Arab Republic and that was like being guests of the family, and they all knew what that meant, didn't they?

"Yes!" chorused the children. "Welcome to Libya!" they shouted in English.

The teacher smiled broadly, and after the children had been set to work with paper and colored crayons, I asked her about the charts and posters that covered the kindergarten walls. The usual slogans were pasted on the outside doors of the school but here in the classroom were large photographs of animals, of trees, with identifying tags in large, carefully executed Arabic letters. But there were other charts totally unlike those seen in American classrooms. The one that caught my eye especially looked like an enormous Easter egg—a green paper oval that covered almost an entire wall of the room. Within the oval, pictures had been pasted, like fruits or flowers on the branches of a strangely shaped family tree. At the bottom were pictures of a mother, father, children, each bearing an appropriate caption in Arabic, the caption on strips of paper that

could be pinned on or taken off, like the tail of the donkey in the old children's
birthday party game. To the right and left of the mother and father were pictures of the other members of the family, grandmother, grandfather, aunts,
uncles, and cousins. I drew closer to look at the illustrations: grandmothers and
grandfathers wore more traditional clothing: skullcaps, jellabas, head scarves,
hokis; mothers and fathers wore Western dress. Above the "related" family
were pictures of other people, some in military uniforms, some in baggy farmer's clothing, some in suits and ties; yes, these were the "peoples" within the
nation *(watn)*, which the oval represented. And at the top of the green egg a
large umbrella shape had been drawn, its parasol embracing the family *(usra)* as
well as the nation *(watn)*; the umbrella was captioned *umma*, the classical Arabic
word for the family of believers, the larger Muslim community.

"What a good idea!" I said spontaneously, and meant it. "The children pin
the appropriate words to the appropriate pictures and learn civics and Arabic at
the same time."

"And ideology as well," said Bob.

The teacher nodded enthusiastically. "You know, I studied in America," she
said. "And I so admired the practice teachers I met, how hard they worked to
make learning aids for their classes. I always felt something was missing, but I
never could figure it out. Then when I came home, I thought, how can a child
learn to relate to others and to his society if he learns only about *himself*, or
herself. Maybe it's okay for you in America, but not here. In Libya, the child
needs to learn very early that he is part of something, and has to contribute to
something. In the old days it was just the family, and still is, to some extent, but
today children must know more. They belong to the family, yes, but also the
nation and to the umma."

"How does it work?"

At the teacher's beckoning, a small boy came up, twisting a button on his light
blue uniform coverall (in some schools, they were white, and I had even seen
dark blue and orange coveralls). He took a tab from a duplicate pile at the
bottom of the chart (it happened to be "grandmother") and pinned it in the
proper place.

"Now bring your own chart, Muhammad."

He went back to his desk and brought a small replica of the large oval that he
had cut and pasted himself. He showed me that one of the "spaces" on his tree
was blank.

"My grandfather died last year," he explained.

"Thank you, Muhammad," said the teacher.

I looked at the young woman. "Will you leave when your baby is born?"

She shook her head firmly. "Oh no, I have three months' maternity leave, but
I probably won't take it all. I'm needed here."

"What about the baby, though? People tell us that Muammar Qadhafi doesn't
allow people to have servants."

The young teacher nodded her head vigorously. "Yes, you are right. But I'll bring the baby here."

"Here?"

"Of course. To the childcare center in the school." The teacher nodded and smiled. "Yes, I forgot. You don't have such things in America. But how could we work well unless we had proper childcare? Our brother Muammar understands that. Not all schools have such centers, but many do, and more are promised. Would you like to see ours?"

Downstairs, at the end of the hall, we were ushered into a large, sunny room, with cots and cradles in one corner. Several small toddlers played with blocks, a few babies snored in the cots, and a teacher sat on a cushion, nursing her baby between classes.

My hostess, the kindergarten teacher, giggled. "She is on her—what do you call it in America?—coffee break, that's it." She introduced me to the childcare supervisor, an eager young woman who demanded, "Do you have more modern baby and childcare in America? I have been to Sweden to see facilities, but not to America."

"We have very modern childcare if you can afford it," I heard myself saying, "But it is usually not in the workplace, near the mothers."

"Why not?"

I could not think of a reply. Could I tell her that in modern America, the common assumption was still that mothers should not leave their preschool children and go out to work, and that if they had to work, childcare was then their problem? The eager young woman would probably not have believed me. For despite the antipathy toward the "imperialistic West" and the anti–Uncle Sam cartoons in the papers, America was, selectively at least, admired and imitated here in Libya. The pregnant teacher would probably believe me, for she had lived in America. She had picked up some pedagogical ideas in America, but had adapted them to local needs.

Children were a high priority in Libya, loved, indulged, carefully dressed and cared for, the future members of the usra (the family); the future citizens of the watn (the nation); the future believers of the umma (the wider Islamic community). Children were what held the society together and ensured its continuance, and the charts so carefully devised by the smiling young woman before me were designed to stress that sense of importance, that priority, given to children. I did not think I could explain to my kindhearted guide the complicated set of circumstances that had lowered the status of children in the United States, as American women became wage earners.

On our way back to the hotel from the school visit, we passed a long line of camels jouncing up and down merrily between the choked lanes of lunchbound traffic. They did not seem at all concerned, their chins held high, their arrogant necks arched proudly.

"Off to the market," remarked the driver, over the blare of Um Kulthum's old hit song, *"Inta umrii."*

"I need to call and tell my wife to get in line," he added. "We haven't had meat for a week."

Later in the day, after walking through the old Castle at the port and viewing the magnificent Roman mosaics in the ice-cold empty national museum, we strolled back through the inner city, away from those treasure-chest boxes on the beach still waiting to be unloaded. Then we stopped, at the shouting and confusion spilling out from the entrance to a street ahead.

"What is it?" Bob asked a passerby.

"Lining up for meat," he replied laconically and tried to push forward into the crowd.

Colonel Qadhafi's foreign policies, his ill-fated support of Idi Amin, his financing of troops for the Polisario movement in the Spanish Sahara, his dabbling in the politics of Chad and the Sudan, these were scarcely mentioned in Libya. They had filled the press in America and Europe and we asked the people we met about these incidents. Mostly our questions were dismissed.

"Everyone can make mistakes."

"Not everything Muammar does is perfect, but he is helping his own people."

Most people were more concerned with the problems of everyday life: they talked about finding meat, getting in line for new housing, negotiating the mahr in preparation for marriage, caring for their children and following their progress in school, and signing up for the modern free health care (if a health problem cannot be solved in Libya, we will send any citizen abroad for the best treatment, the Colonel had promised). We had listened to that story somewhat dubiously but had been introduced to several people who had received such treatment.

After our forays around the city, to the museum, the markets, the farm cooperative, to the meetings at people's homes and in their offices, we would return to the Libya Palace Hotel. And we found that our interest and our guarded enthusiasm for the new Libyan society were not shared by the other foreigners whom we had discovered there: a French journalist, a Polish gynecologist training midwives, an East German pediatrician, a West German businessman, a Lebanese magazine editor, a British oil worker. They spoke ominously about the future of the Socialist People's Libyan Arab Jamahiriya, even as we sat together drinking coffee in that daunting smoke-filled lobby, in corners away from the afternoon Sinbad cartoons, the government news broadcast, the religious lessons on the television.

"The Cabinet is saying that the Colonel has at last gone too far. Nationalizing business just won't wash."

"It all comes to money in the end."

"But everybody seems to have enough," argued Bob, "so why shouldn't it have a chance, the nationalization, I mean?"

"Can't last. Situation will collapse."

"How?" demanded Bob.

"Oil will dry up, then where'll they be?"

"Leader's losing support, some say."

"How can they live without water?"

"Islamic laws in the modern world? They must be mad. Just won't work."

"I predict the market will remain closed till he changes his mind."

"But the market isn't closed," said Bob in exasperation. "We were there yesterday. The place was full of people buying British tweed, Chinese table-cloths, cooking pots from France. Only thing that's closed is the gold market."

"Well," said the British oil worker triumphantly, "gold's the key to everything, isn't it?"

We were not so sure. The foreigners in the hotel lobby seldom left their coffee tables and mostly talked to each other; the gynecologist and the pediatrician had limited contacts in the hospital. We felt we had been more fortunate, speaking Arabic as we did, and given the freedom to visit what we wished, the hospitality traditional to Arab society.

Maybe the Libyan experiment wouldn't work in the long run. It was too soon to say. Obviously, Libya had many problems. Serious problems. Water was at the top of the list. The educational system was not yet up to its self-assigned task. The acres of multicolored treasure chests clogging the bay were mute evidence of moving too fast, too soon, without what the economic planners called "sufficient infrastructure and support services." The refuse still blew about on the streets. Oil was a nonrenewable resource. It would not last forever.

But the standard of living was obviously a comfortable one, at least for the people we met. And what was missing in Libya was also significant, particularly in comparison to other oil-rich Arab states (and some, such as Morocco, which had no oil). Here in Libya, no conspicuously rich elites paraded about in limousines and lived in palaces. The only conspicuous evidence of the regime was the slogans everywhere. No rumors circulated about President Qadhafi's life-style, suggesting he enjoyed forbidden fruits, or even overly expensive ones. Qadhafi avoided the trappings of office whenever possible. In fact, he was said to be something of an ascetic, who frequently retreated to the desert for contemplation; from these sessions, it was said, had come the Green Books, a series of three pamphlets outlining Qadhafi's ideas about economics, politics, social structure, the family: his plan for a Libyan utopia.

Among Libyans, Qadhafi was called by his first name, Muammar, or called brother, rather than President or some other more glorious title, and he referred to his position as temporary, awaiting replacement by a people's assembly. He regularly convened these people's assemblies, but so far no one had taken his place.

Of course, Muammar Qadhafi did spend money, a great deal of it, not only in

Young PLO soldiers visiting a cemetery, Beirut.

Devastation in Beirut, 1982.

A camel caravan, south Jordan

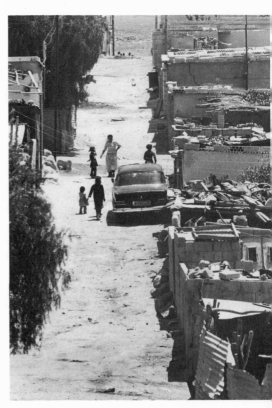

A Palestinian refugee camp in Bekaa, Jordan.

ear the Saudi Arabian border.

Child with a toy gun, Beirut.

Gathering for Friday prayers in a mosque
in Amman, Jordan.

A Bedouin man preparing coffee in his tent, south Jordan.

his native land but in other countries, in support of the Arab cause as he defined it and in unity with Muslims struggling with unfriendly forces. In those respects, his objectives were not far from those of Gamal Abdul Nasser, Egypt's late President, a man whom Qadhafi greatly admired and whose ideals he felt had been betrayed by Anwar Sadat.

Although the matter of Qadhafi's foreign policy, so heatedly discussed in the West, was not much mentioned during our visit, we did not sense any great enthusiasm for these foreign adventures. Domestic matters were of more importance to most of the Libyans we met: individual prosperity, a voice in local affairs, the preservation of personal dignity. And in Libya in 1979 these demands were well on their way to being satisfied, an achievement which had helped make Qadhafi popular and relatively secure for ten years.

Like Qadhafi himself, who became head of his nation in his late twenties, the men and women in Qadhafi's bureaucracy were very young. We met many in their twenties and thirties who occupied positions of far greater responsibility than might have been the case in an older country with a more established bureaucracy. They said that yes, they had a lot of opportunities to exercise personal judgment in their positions, within prescribed limits, of course, and in terms of the specific objectives of the people's republic. Libyan government workers at the higher levels are well paid, often they can travel abroad easily, and they feel involved in the development of a new nation with unexpected wealth—that light crude oil so much in demand in the West. In 1979 these young men and women seemed to be content to wait patiently for the day when the highest level of decision making (foreign policy, for example) might be more influenced by their opinion than it was at that moment.

As for the name-calling, insults, and ridicule that the Western press has leveled at Qadhafi and that he has returned, perhaps this is a reflection of opportunism on both sides. Evoking the presence of a common enemy is a time-honored way for a leader, in the Arab world as in our own, to maintain a high level of internal support and cohesion. However, Qadhafi does have real enemies, and his vituperative attacks upon them perhaps provide a degree of satisfaction to many other Arabs, even leaders, who these days are obliged to express their dissatisfaction in much more muted terms. On the other hand, Qadhafi's personal style and his rhetorical extravagance lend themselves to Western caricature and misrepresentation. But his leadership has brought years of peaceful development to his country, and his 1971 defiance of the West, when he challenged the oil companies and won, gave the entire Arab world a larger share of oil revenues than the colonial pittance it had long received. Thus, according to many people in the Third World, Muammar Qadhafi, with all his eccentricities, has behaved far more responsibly than some of the Western leaders who criticize him. We did not have time to learn much in Libya, but we found it a far different place from what our own media had led us to expect.

Comment

UNITY AND DIVERSITY IN ISLAM

ISLAM IS THE newest of the great monotheistic religions. Judaism, Christianity, and Islam all emerged in the Middle East and share a common basis of belief about the nature of God and humans. Yet the differences among them have fueled strife which remains lively—and dangerous—to this day. What are the differences between our myths about Islam and the realities of living in modern Muslim communities?

The first Muslims, of course, were the Arabs, followers of Muhammad, the prophet who lived in Mecca in the seventh century after Christ. Muhammad received revelations which Muslims believe came directly from God through the angel Gabriel; these revelations were set down in the Koran. Jesus is not God, states the Koran. This verse alone was sufficient for the Christian world to view the new monotheistic religion as a heresy, far worse in many ways than "pagan" beliefs which make no reference to Christian doctrine. Eventually every weapon in the armory of the Christian world was marshaled against the "heresy," including theologians, soldiers, and the thousands of children who marched—and perished—during the Children's Crusade to redeem the Holy Land from the infidel Saracens.

Islam did not originate as an attack on Christianity, however. The Prophet Muhammad is said to have viewed Islam (the word in Arabic literally means "submission") as redressing what he regarded as laxities and depravities which had developed within the religions he knew. Thus, Islam was a reformation of both the practices common to the idol-worshiping peoples of the Arabian Peninsula and those of Byzantine Christianity, with its elaborate ceremonialism and revered statuary. But Islam was not a reform of Judaism, either.

Muhammad saw the Old Testament and much of the New Testament as the heritage of Islam, but he rejected many ideas within the scriptures. The idea of the Holy Trinity, for example, ran directly contrary to the Islamic emphasis on one God. Abraham, Moses, and Isaac were revered as great prophets, as was Jesus. But Muhammad did not see them as divine; in fact, he claimed no divine status for himself and insisted that no human being could make such an assertion.

Islam shares with Christianity and Judaism the same fundamental concerns:

human salvation, good and evil, heaven and hell. As a total way of life, in which law and politics are no more divorced from religion than are commerce and family relationships, it is closer in spirit to Judaism than to Christianity. And it formed the basis of a new society on earth in the most literal sense of the term.

Conditions for the development of Islam in A.D. 622 were very different from the conditions which existed at the birth of Christianity. Unlike Jesus, who faced hostile, foreign authorities and whose early followers faced charges of insurrection or worse, Muhammad and the people of Mecca and the surrounding desert and oases of Arabia had little to fear externally in the beginning. The social and political problems were internal. Raids and warfare among the nomadic Bedouin disrupted peaceful commerce.

In the past, tribal descent had shaped economic and social status, but by the seventh century, such a system did not match the complex changing roles of wealth and status in the urban life of Mecca. Under the new creed, anyone of any race or social origin who submitted to God's will and became a Muslim had claim to equal footing in the community. The door to personal achievement and success was no longer barred by differences in tribal status. The new religious doctrine was well suited to the capitalist economy of merchants and markets, which had developed by Muhammad's time.

In the beginning, then, Islam was truly revolutionary. The Koran provided a totally new charter for social and political life. It emphasized the equality of all persons within the Muslim community. City merchants and desert nomads were united under the same leadership.

Women as well as men were recognized as Muslim persons, with equality before God and legal status on earth. Women were entitled to veto powers over their marriage arrangements, and to inherit a portion of their husbands' and fathers' estates. Merit was gained in freeing a converted slave.

Less than a hundred years after the birth of Islam, Arab soldiers and traders were moving into North Africa, into Turkey, across the Mediterranean to Sicily, Spain, Italy, France. By the early eighth century Islamic armies were halfway across the European world and had they not been stopped in France at Tours in A.D. 732 Western history might have taken quite a different course. As it was, the original Islamic community in Arabia had by this time engendered a new empire which reached into three continents. Intellectual life flourished in the tranquillity of Córdoba and Granada as well as in Damascus and Baghdad. Christian and Jewish philosophers made their way to these centers of learning. Indeed, sizable minorities of Christians and Jews lived throughout the Islamic Empire, for the Koran makes special mention of "people of the book," Jews and Christians, as respected and protected minorities within the Muslim community. However, the actual existence of a Muslim state in southern Spain was seen as an intolerable affront by the growing European powers. In 1492 Granada fell to Christian armies under King Ferdinand and Queen Isabella. Muslims and Jews alike were given an ultimatum: conversion, expulsion from Spain, or death. Members of both religious groups fled to Morocco and beyond.

Though 1492 marked the end of the Islamic reign in Western Europe (as well as the discovery of America), the spread of Islam through conversion by no means ceased. During the following centuries it steadily gained strength in Africa, the Indian subcontinent, Southeast Asia, and China. A Muslim community in the Philippines struggles today with the government for some degree of self-governance. American Muslims are said to number more than 2 million. Nearly 800 million people in the modern world consider themselves Muslims. Only one third live in the Middle East. (The great majority of Middle Easterners are Muslims, though small groups of Christian Arabs and Jews constitute perhaps 5 percent of the total population.)

What is the power of this creed? Why is it the fastest-growing religion in the world today? Islam has a flexibility, a simplicity, an egalitarianism that is seldom mentioned in the Western texts. As Islamicist John Alden Williams has pointed out, " 'Orthoprax' is a far better term than 'orthodox' to characterize Islam; for right practice rather than right theology is primary." Indeed, no generally recognized religious authority declares what is orthodox and what is not; Islam does not have a central ecclesiastic hierarchy. There are no ordained priests or ministers. Rather, communities of Muslims direct their own affairs, through local specialists in Islamic law and theology. Such men (and women) acquire knowledge in the religious schools and universities of their own regions. They are given various titles with some differences in significance depending on local practice: ulema (the group of learned men, including scholars); sheikhs (specialists in aspects of religious as well as secular affairs); qadis (religious judges); mullas (learned leaders of Friday prayers); muftis and ayatollas (religious legal specialists). This lack of a central authority, this freedom for the development of practice, is crucial to understanding not only the Arabs but the whole Islamic world.

Outsiders are often puzzled by the variety of seemingly inconsistent behavior. How is it that the Saudi Arabian authorities can stone a princess and her lover to death for adultery while Muslims elsewhere express their horror at such an act? Aren't they all Muslims? Yes; but times have changed since the seventh century.

The consensus on all issues which existed within the small Muslim community during the Prophet's lifetime is no longer universal. Practice differs, from Morocco to the Philippines. For example: the elaboration of mystical Sufi orders found in North Africa, in which pious Muslims take part in weekly *hadras*—meetings of prayer, trance, and meditation—has no equivalent in Saudi Arabia, which forbids such activities. Polygyny, marrying more than one wife, is illegal in Tunisia but not in Egypt. Also, there are seven distinct schools of religious law, each with its own legal specialists and code of precedents; every Muslim is part of one school but respects the other six. How is this latter example possible, since, we are told, all law is based on the Koran and the Koran is believed to be the literal word of God, and hence considered unchangeable?

The earliest consensus among Muslims was shattered soon after Muhammad's death by the issue of leadership succession. Who was to take the place of the

Prophet? Shiat Ali (the party of Ali, the Prophet's son-in-law and cousin) argued for succession based on descent through blood ties, a variant of the argument for the divine right of kings. The Sunnis (so called because of their following of the Sunna, or proper path of conduct) argued for leadership based on ability and proven merit. Disagreement over this issue continues into the twentieth century: for the Shi'a sect in Iran, the idea of leadership carries with it the idea of divinity. The Sunnis find this view blasphemous.

What, then, are the central doctrines and beliefs that can be seen as unique to Islam, that distinguish it from other great religions, and that form the core of beliefs on which all Muslims, of whatever sect or practice, agree? All Muslims believe in one God, *Allah* (the Arabic word for God); all Muslims must assume the five duties (or pillars): profession of faith, prayer, fasting, the giving of alms, and the pilgrimage to Mecca (if the believer can afford it). All Muslims believe in the centrality and divinity of the Koran as a guide to everyday life and a basis for law.

In addition, they rely on the *hadith,* a collection of the traditions and sayings of the Prophet during his lifetime. Here there is room for theological differences. Local groups interpret the hadith differently and see some hadith as more valid than others. Individual communities often interpret the hadith to fit changing times and local situations, so that in 1972, for example, the grand mufti of Jordan could issue a *fatwa* (an opinion or judgment *for his congregation only)* which states that the use of contraceptives is in no way against the teachings of the Koran, and that Islam allows abortion if the health of the mother or the good of the family demands it.

The issue of *jihad,* or holy war, is another point of concern and Western misunderstanding. Some Muslims would argue that a sixth duty, or pillar, exists, and that is the jihad, the duty of the holy war. While the protection of the Islamic community is cited as the religious reason for a jihad, social and political reasons are varied, just as in European wars. Far more holy wars have been declared by leaders and would-be leaders than have actually been fought; and far more Muslims have ignored the call to such holy wars than have answered it. But certainly Islam, like Judaism and Christianity, may be used to justify war. Islam probably has about as much to do with conflicts between Sunnis and Shi'as in Iraq and Iran today, or among religious groups in Lebanon, as Christianity has to do with the tragic conflict in Ireland. In all cases, religion may be used as justification and encouragement for struggles which stem from other circumstances, ranging from economic distress and political oppression to the personal ambitions of secular leaders.

Much orientalist scholarship emphasizes the fixed, static kind of society which Islam supposedly produces. Yet nothing could be further from either the original statements of the Prophet and the Koran or historical practice throughout the ages. The tenets of Islam provide no divine sanction for the development of any form of social hierarchy; Islam encourages rather than restricts social mobility. This is not to say that many forms of social stratification have not existed in the Middle East in different times and places, however.

Today new class societies are in fact developing in many Muslim countries. In this regard, it is important to remember that Islam in the seventh century posited two bases for Muslim everyday life that appear to have some relationship to our American views of equality and democracy: *tawhid* (oneness) and *ijma* (consensus). Though these two concepts have not always been honored in Islamic historical practice, they are now receiving increasing attention. The great Islamic thinker and reformer Muhammad Abdu published his celebrated essay on tawhid in 1897 and suggested then that modern political and scientific ideas were not antithetical to but rather at one with Islamic principles. "Tawhid" means literally "declaring the oneness of God"; to some modern Muslims, declaring the oneness of God implies the equality of all those who so declare that oneness and, by inference, the responsibility of all human beings for each other —a sense of universal brotherhood. Ijma, or the sense that one is in accord with the needs and ambitions of one's followers, is the ideal to be sought by a political leader. As new middle classes begin to emerge in countries such as Egypt, Tunisia, Algeria, and Saudi Arabia, these concepts are taking on new meanings. Both ideas are being called on by leaders, supporters, and opposition groups who, in different countries with varying social, economic, and political conditions, are attempting to evoke Islamic ideology to construct new societies in the modern Arab world. Colonel Muammar Qadhafi, for example, cites tawhid as the basis for what he terms Islamic democracy: President Anwar Sadat, on the other hand, some say, was brought down because he failed to take seriously the need for many new groups in Egypt to be considered in the construction of a national consensus.

Islam, then, is a monotheistic religion, with a fixed center of belief, but with enough flexibility to allow it to adapt to changing times and the needs of its believers. More than thirteen hundred years ago Islam began by legitimizing a new association of people of diverse social and racial origins. Today it continues to legitimize new and developing forms of community life.

CHAPTER V

Sanaa, Yemen

1981

> The rains came like a merchant from Yemen
> Unfolding his goods on the desert of Ghabit;
> And in the morning we saw, scattered on the sand,
> Like the bulbs of wild onions,
> The drowned lions.
>
> Imru al-Qays,
> *The Muallaqa* (A.D. 600)

WE WANTED to visit Yemen, fabled stronghold of the Queen of Sheba, site of the egalitarian Karmathian sect of Islam, home of traders since recorded time. But it was not as easy as it sounded. Yemen was no longer just one country, but two, the two new countries made out of old kingdoms. The Yemen Arab Republic lay in the north (6 million people, 76,000 square miles), the People's Democratic Republic of Yemen in the south (2 million people, 112,000 square miles). South Yemen, a Marxist regime, had no diplomatic representation in Cairo, so we applied for visas to the North Yemeni consulate. Days passed. No visas. No reason given, despite Bob's frequent trips to their offices.

Our problem, we were told, was not unique. Yemen had never encouraged visitors of any kind but had stayed strictly to itself. This was understandable, given its complex history of uninvited visitors who had always brought trouble rather than peace and prosperity.

After the Queen of Sheba died in the tenth century B.C., Yemen was divided into four kingdoms and prospered until the arrival of the Romans. Jews, Ethiopians, and Persians ruled at different times before the Arabs came, bringing Islam, in the seventh century. The Ottoman Turks were in and out of the region from the sixteenth century. In the 1800s, Britain raised the Union Jack in Aden. Yemen formally became independent in 1918. But then Saudi Arabia entered the picture in the 1930s and began changing boundaries in the Gulf States, at approximately the time the old theocratic ruler of Yemen, the Imam Yahya, is reported to have kept two huge panthers in cages in his palace in Sanaa.

The panthers kept no one out, however. By 1981 Yemen's borders had been changed several times by bloody civil war. In 1962 Egypt sent troops; we remembered a friend's fiancé who had been a captain in the "Yemeni expeditionary force" that left Cairo station in a roar of cheers and goodbyes. The Egyptians, President Nasser said, were there to support "republican elements" against "royalist elements," which were supported by Saudi Arabia.

In 1967 the royalists and the republicans agreed to arbitrate. Egypt and Saudi Arabia withdrew, and a so-called neutral commission was convened in Khartoum, to assume control. But no one consulted the Yemenis about this, and when the commission members arrived in Sanaa, expecting acclaim and gratitude, they were met instead by fierce public demonstrations which quickly turned into riots. The commission retired hastily. Yemen clearly wanted to decide its own destiny, without assistance, and it was finally left to do so, splitting into two countries that now form the southwestern edge of the Islamic world. South Yemen. North Yemen.

And both Yemens, understandably, exercised their right to be selective about who was allowed to cross the new borders.

Bob, as a trustee of the American Institute for Yemeni Studies in North Yemen, felt he should visit the country and the institute while he was nearby and had the time to go.

Once more he trekked down to the Yemen consulate in Cairo and this time came back looking more hopeful. "Today the official finally explained to me why he wouldn't give us visas. The American consulate has refused to grant visas to Yemenis. Tit for tat. So I asked to use the phone and called our embassy myself, right from the Yemeni officer's desk. The American consul said he knew nothing about refusing visas to Yemenis, but promised to look into it."

"North Yemenis are considered subversive or something?" Tom asked. A friend from Austin, Tom lived in Cairo and worked as a free-lance photographer for several news services. He had decided to travel with us to Yemen.

"Who knows why any visa applications are turned down?" returned Bob. "Maybe they don't want any more Arab migrant laborers in California. Complaints from Mexico or something. That's what I thought at first. But it turns out the visas are for Yemeni Fulbright scholars."

Two days later our visas to Yemen were granted, in exchange for America's granting visas to the Yemenis. Tit for tat. We never did discover why the Yemenis had had trouble, for the American consul diplomatically would say only that he had never seen the applications, and that they had perhaps been held up at the lower consular levels, where Egyptian staff did the processing.

Jubilant, Bob, Tom, and I boarded the plane, the only foreigners bound for Sanaa on a damp night in March 1981. We expected to be met by Leigh Douglas, the resident director of the American Institute for Yemeni Studies. The last thing I had done, in fact, before leaving Cairo, was to buy a tempting collection of Hilton Hotel pastries as a house present for Mr. Douglas. But again no one was at the airport, so we took the last cab through a rainstorm to what the taxi driver, after long consultation with Bob and a tiny sketch map, had insisted was the institute. An anonymous blank wall. The driver got out of the car and began to unload our baggage into the mud.

For it was still raining. Someone was shouting from a window in answer to Bob's steady pounding on the wall. From the clearly enunciated if strident English, it did seem as though we had arrived at the American Institute for Yemeni Studies. At last. Now for a comfortable bed, and a cup of tea with a Hilton Hotel pastry. I got out of the cab clutching the pastry box and Tom collected his cameras.

The heavy door in the high wall opened, and a shaft of light streamed through.

"Well," said a tall young Englishman in a bathrobe. "Good evening. I'm Leigh Douglas. Sorry not to meet you. Didn't know when you were coming. No, your telex never arrived. But then," he added, "they seldom do."

I extended the box of pastries, its paper bows now somewhat bedraggled by the rain.

"Oh. Thank you very much," he said formally. "I'll just put this inside. No, you're not staying here, but in the annex. We'll trot round. Just a moment."

"I told you we should have eaten them ourselves," grumbled Tom.

"Is the rain unusual?" Bob asked conversationally as we maneuvered down muddy lanes with our bags.

"Not really," said Leigh, banging on another wall, waking up another person, a man in a nightcap who appeared at a window, shouting in annoyance but finally promising to come down and let us in.

"Afternoon rains," went on Leigh while we stood mutely in the squishy mud, the rain dripping on our faces, our luggage. "Usually stop by sunset. But not tonight. Yemen is an unpredictable country, you'll find. Part of its charm. Ha ha."

By the time we had been ushered into our reserved accommodations I was willing to agree with Tom. A Hilton Hotel cream puff would have helped cushion the impact of our spartan quarters. We set to, with proffered sheets, to make our beds around foam rubber pads on the cement floors of two cell-like rooms.

"Not the Ritz, I'm afraid," laughed Leigh, "but it's the best we can do. Institute subsidies low, you know, and Sanaa real estate skyrocketing."

"Of course," said Bob matter-of-factly. "We'll be quite comfortable, I'm sure. Does the bathroom—er—work?"

"Yes," said Leigh. "From time to time. Just jiggle the chain, like this. The hot water comes and goes, have to watch the spout. Yes. That's it. Ha ha!"

"Ha ha," repeated Tom, but his tone was not amused.

We nodded good night.

"Ten bucks per night per person for this?" Tom gestured around our narrow rooms, the tiny kitchen, the shared rickety bath, and the muddy courtyard with its two sets of doors, now firmly closed and multiple-locked behind us.

"Well, at least no one will steal your cameras, Tom," said Bob. "A burglar would have a hard time getting in here."

"And who, my friend, would want to?" returned Tom testily.

"Adventure!" I cried out in a false gay voice. "We are in the mountains of the High Yemen, lost and forbidden to outsiders for centuries. What do we expect, the Hilton?"

My stomach and watch told me it was morning, but the room was so dark it was difficult to tell what the world might look like outdoors. Presumably there were no windows to further prevent incursions from burglars and other strangers, but a dim gray light did seem to be coming in through a row of narrow slits, high up in the mud-brick wall. I climbed onto the single chair our accommodations boasted and squinted through the slits. The sun was shining weakly through clouds on a large square patch of garden, where a woman in dark trousers and a red print tunic, her head bound up in a scarf, was bent over, weeding. A peaceful rural scene. But we were in the capital city. I could see, however, that the peaceful rural scene would not be visible from the street, for the garden was enclosed on four sides by high walls, walls of houses exactly like the one through which I was now squinting. A community garden, perhaps, shared equally by the four houses? Mixed rural and urban elements, allowing for growing food, even in cities, and house walls to protect the gardens, just as the courtyards and the sets of double doors protected the houses, as Bob had pointed out the night before.

Breakfast. Bob was still asleep, but I was starving. Hmmm. I had another jealous thought about the pastries, but I had brought a small can of Nescafé. Water must be available in the kitchen. Forward I went, to find two strange blond young women, one with a baby, in the kitchen. They said good morning, but did not introduce themselves, nor did I. One of the women began to set up an ironing board and the other sat at the table with the baby, who cried *"Oooo!"* and pointed a finger at me. I smiled, but no one responded. I put on the kettle.

"Well." I cleared my throat. Maybe, since we were sleeping here and they weren't, I was supposed to be the hostess and therefore hospitable? "Would you like some Nescafé?"

"Oh yes." "Thank you."

"There's powdered milk here, I think," said the young mother, "so we can have café au lait. And don't we have some bread, Stina?"

Stina fished out a loaf from her shopping bag. Bob and Tom drifted out of their cells, looking somewhat damp from dousing faces under the unpredictable streams of the faucets in the single sink. We stood in the tiny space, munching and swallowing. The iron hissed and steamed on the board.

"Thank you for the bread," I said.

"Excellent," agreed Bob and Tom.

"And thank you for the coffee," said Stina. "It is very expensive here, like everything in Sanaa."

There was a slight pause, and then all of us began to speak at once, explaining our presence. Bob, a trustee of AIYS, an anthropologist, was doing research on social change. I was to make a film about women's status. Tom was a photographer. Stina, the ironer, who turned out to be the mother of the baby, was Norwegian; her friend was American. They were a nutritionist and a social worker, respectively, just finishing a stint on the Cornell University Breast-Feeding Promotion Project.

I suppressed a smile. How typical of academia, I thought. I had nursed my own children and assumed that most women in the Arab world did the same. This remote rural country was hardly the place that needed an expensive project to promote what everyone was already doing. But social science must go on, I told myself. New topics for research must be found, however silly they seem.

Stina must have caught my expression, for she said abruptly, "It is a very important project here, you have just arrived, you do not understand. . . ."

I sat up at the table, mentally scolding myself for jumping to conclusions; this was what I was always criticizing others for doing and here I was, falling into the same trap. "Tell me," I said. "I'd like to hear about it."

So they proceeded to tell us, at length, or at least me, for Bob and Tom decided at that point to take a walk and get a sense of the local environs, they said. "Bottle feeding," said Stina, "is considered modern here. Breast feeding is considered backward and primitive."

"Just like it was in our grandmothers' day," said her friend the American. "In the twenties and thirties."

I realized they were speaking of my mother's day, but I kept my mouth shut and listened.

The girls changed places, Stina taking up her cheerful baby while her friend assumed the ironing-board chore.

"It's much worse here than I think it has been in America for a long time," went on Stina, in her slightly stilted English. "Lots of babies die here, four hundred per thousand births, imagine that. So bottle feeding to improve infant nutrition seems at first to make sense."

"More coffee?" I served out the mugs, filling them with powdered milk from a huge two-gallon tin with a baby's face smiling from its blue label. Nestlé.

"But you know," Stina continued, "the idea of extra nourishment is based on the assumption that you have pure water to begin with and that you sterilize the bottles." She looked at me expectantly. "Yes?"

"Yes."

"And of course that whole idea falls down here, because you don't have either, especially in the mountain villages where we've been working."

"But, Stina, why would rural women want to bother?" I asked. "I mean, I can see the point with urban women, maybe, but—"

She looked at me a bit disdainfully. "You are basing what you are saying on your *previous* experience." (It turned out she had read my books about women in Iraq, in Egypt, in Morocco.) "Yemen is *not* like other places."

"Yes," I said, "I am beginning to see that."

"In other places where you have been, women don't help with the farming so much. But here they do," and she emphasized her words by banging her coffee spoon on the table. The baby grabbed the spoon and took it up. "Do, do, do," she chanted happily.

I sipped my coffee. I had not expected to spend my first morning in the fabled High Yemen being lectured on breast feeding, but then, why not?

"Women," Stina's friend was saying, "have a very hard time here."

"Don't they everywhere?" I quipped.

She gave me a look. "Yes, of course, but here the problems are *different*. They not only work in the fields, but they must carry water up the mountains every day. And they have lots of babies. So they like the idea of putting the baby in the crib with a bottle. It's safe for a while, and the mother feels good because supposedly the baby is getting first-rate *modern* nourishment."

"And . . . ?"

"And it doesn't work out so perfectly," said Stina, draining her coffee cup. She stood up, kissed the baby, and settled it, gurgling and kicking, into a blue canvas baby backpack set up on the table. "Babies can choke, or get sick if the formula isn't mixed right. Or they die of diarrhea from bad water, or of malnutrition if the formula is too thin. It's really awful!"

She kissed the baby again almost ritually and swung it round onto her own back. "So you see why the Cornell Breast-Feeding Promotion Project is important."

"Yes, I do," I said humbly. "I didn't mean to suggest otherwise. But it did seem rather strange on the surface."

"Many things do," said the ironer rather sternly, folding the shirts and skirts carefully and packing them into *her* backpack. "You have to look deeper."

She was right, of course; I had assumed too much.

"We have to go now," said Stina, "but I'll take you to the market one day if you like and show you all the powdered formula that's sold here. That's the other side of it. It is—" She stopped, unable to bring out a word strong enough to express her feelings on the subject.

"It is *shameful!*" finished her friend, in ringing tones.

I was startled. Powdered formula *shameful?* My skepticism must have been evident, for they stood in the little court, the American girl with her pack of newly ironed clothes, the Norwegian girl with her child jumping up and down gleefully on her back, and delivered a passionate condemnation of the powdered-formula companies of the affluent West, who, "for profit motives alone," plugged their products on Yemeni television and in shops all over the country.

"They have even brainwashed the doctors and nurses," said the American, "with free gifts, so the doctors will push powdered formula too. The doctors say bottle feeding will improve women's condition in Yemen—"

"But it won't," insisted Stina.

No mountain path, it appeared, was too steep for the cans of powdered formula to be carried up, up into the remote areas of the High Yemen. The companies cared nothing for morality or ethics, but only for profit, said the girls. UNICEF figures indicated, they said, that thousands of babies had died as a result.

They continued talking indignantly as we walked out through the double doors that secured the tiny annex, across the cobbled courtyard to the heavy wooden front door, and onto the muddy road where we had arrived the night before, and where Bob and Tom, back from their turn around the neighborhood, rushed up.

"We've been invited to lunch!" announced Tom.

"By Dick Verdery," cried Bob. "You won't believe this, B.J., but I ran into him on the *street!*" We had known that Dick, an old friend from Cairo days, was in Yemen, but had been told he was up in the mountains, implementing a project to pipe water into the villages.

Stina looked interested. "Where will you have lunch?"

"At the Sheba Hotel."

"Ah," said Stina. "It is a deluxe place. Good for you!"

I looked at her quickly, but she was not being ironic. The morning was teaching me that perhaps middle age had made me superskeptical and far too flip. I decided I must reform.

"Take an umbrella," advised her friend.

"Leigh Douglas says it usually doesn't rain till late afternoon," said Bob.

Stina smiled. "Well, you can never be sure. You are in a tropical climate here in Yemen. Not like what you expected, maybe." She waved a hand and was gone with her friend, the two thin, straight-backed young women maneuvering their way around the puddles, the ruts of mud, while the baby, jouncing up and down happily on its mother's back, called back to us.

"What was that all about?" asked Tom.

I was silent for a moment. "I'm getting educated," I said firmly. "Having my preconceptions challenged. Good for me. Just because I've lived in the Arab world before doesn't mean I know anything about Yemen."

Bob looked at me thoughtfully. "I had the same feeling from Leigh Douglas," he said. "Yemen is different, he says, special."

"Yeah, and he didn't even offer us a pastry," said Tom.

"They were a present after all," I responded. "We shouldn't be such Indian givers."

"And besides that we've been invited to a deluxe hotel for lunch," added Bob. "You heard the young lady. But Leigh says it's a very long walk, so let's fortify ourselves with another cup of Nescafé."

We sat around the narrow table to gulp another mug of stimulating brew, thick with profitable powdered milk from Switzerland. At that time, like many Americans, we were unaware of the worldwide boycott against Nestlé, a boycott that by 1983 had succeeded in making Nestlé agree to drop its hard-sell tactics in Third World countries.

The Sheba Hotel, one of the newest grand hotels in Sanaa, is not the Hilton, but its general air of opulence is indisputable. It stands on a slight rise in the center of the capital city and bears the ancient name of Yemen, Sheba or Saba, the rich land of Southern Arabia that boasted the great dam of Ma'rib, and that is immortalized in the Book of Kings:

> And when the queen of Sheba heard of the fame of Solomon . . . she came to Jerusalem with a very great train, with camels that bare spices, and very much gold, and precious stones. . . . (I Kings, 10:1–2)

The architect must have read his Bible, for the hotel evokes ancient splendors while it incorporates modern conveniences. The Sheba shines and shimmers with the accoutrements of luxury: deep soft carpets, overstuffed sofas and armchairs, tiled splashing fountains, central heating, lush plants in finely wrought brass-and-copper urns. Decorative paintings hang in the softly lit pastel wall panels, paintings executed in the style of old oriental miniatures. In the dining room, for a king's ransom, it seemed, we lunched with Dick on subtle curries, rice with real saffron, imported out-of-season grapes and melons. The service was impeccable, and the rooms, according to Dick, "are more than comfortable, and always full, though they cost an arm and a leg. Reputedly they even have television." He laughed. "What more could one ask?"

The Sheba belongs to an Indian hotel chain, and although it might seem to us to evoke the legend of the High Yemen, a kind of exotic never-never land which outsiders were until very recently not encouraged to visit, it was obviously established to make a profit in the new situation of the eighties. Today, with Yemen's doors partly open, Sanaa thronged with a new breed of traders, coming not to buy frankincense and myrrh and precious stones, but to negotiate business contracts for the purchase of the exotic fruits of industrialism: television sets, refrigerators, calculators, drip-dry fabrics, and machines to make everyday life easier: water pumps, computers, tractors, washing machines.

Yemen today is rich, rich with the indirect revenues of the oil boom in the Persian Gulf. In 1975, of a total population of 6 million, 8 percent, or over 300,000 people, were working abroad, in Saudi Arabia. By 1981, when we arrived in Sanaa, that number was estimated to have doubled. And that figure did not include the Yemenis working in Kuwait, the United Arab Emirates, and the United States. From a minimal subsistence agricultural economy a generation ago, when the entire city of Sanaa, according to Dick Verdery, who had come on a UNICEF mission, boasted perhaps a total of eight automobiles, Yemen was leaping into a new kind of world. Foreign traders were helping.

It is said that all trade in Yemen (and hence all contract signing) is in the hands of thirty-four families, but if so, they were not visible in the public rooms of the Sheba Hotel. Only European and Asian businessmen and international-agency representatives (the UN, the ILO, U.S. AID, Holland Aid) could be seen, walking purposefully across the lobbies, well dressed, as the ambience of the Sheba Hotel demanded, in the custom-designed clothing of their countries of origin. They hovered discreetly by the windows, looking for cars that were to take them to prearranged contract consultations (the Yemenis, understandably, preferred to do business on their own turf, which was usually the multicolored guest room, or *mufresh,* of their homes). The traders from abroad sat in the overstuffed chairs, awaiting important calls from the ivory-colored telephones thoughtfully scattered across the public rooms, on small, exquisitely inlaid tables. Stationery was also provided by the hotel, thick and cream-colored, on which the trader-visitors might write discreet messages to their Yemeni contacts, should the telephones not work or the cars not arrive as promised.

What could be further from the luxury of the Sheba Hotel than the village efforts of the Cornell Breast-Feeding Promotion Project? Stina's earnest lecture on breast feeding and Western powdered-formula profits that first morning had been a realistic introduction to the complexities of Yemen. Yemen seemed unlike other Middle Eastern countries where we had lived, not only because of the different problems the country faced, or because of the tropical rather than desert or riverine oasis climate. Here we had no Yemeni friends to serve as reference points, as sources of interpretation. We wandered about by ourselves, observing without understanding.

According to Marty Kumorek, a Peace Corps volunteer whom we met, a split always exists between the world of everyday life for ordinary Yemeni people and the world of Yemen experienced by foreign visitors. Mythical worlds, insisted Marty, exist in the minds of all people who live and work in cultures other than their own, worlds fabricated from snippets of history, secondhand descriptions of "the natives," moments of experience and bits of illusion. Or self-delusion. He laughed, adding that any similarity between the mythical world developed by the foreign visitor and the real world of the country in question was purely coincidental.

Yemen's high-walled houses, its polite but indifferent people, encouraged such mythmaking. Like others who had tasted the consumer goods of the West, Yemen wanted them. And therefore it would put up with foreigners, for certain purposes. Foreign businessmen were trying to make sales; it was in their interest to be pleasant and accept the Yemenis on their own terms. Yemenis, we were told, kept to themselves.

Meeting and socializing with other foreigners allowed some testing of our own perceptions of Yemen, in the sense that the social maps of other personal landscapes could be compared with our own. But with all the differences in detail based on individual experiences, the strangers' land of Yemen remained a special expatriate land, a land of conundrums and puzzles, but of great charm and seduction, a land which many chose never to leave. For the romantic Westerner, Yemen had elements of Oz, Shangri-La, the heart of darkness. We found ourselves full of contradictory impressions.

For Stina's suggestion that we had expected something else was quite accurate; we had expected to feel more at home in Yemen, because of our experience in other Arab countries. There were some similarities; the religion was the same, but its expression was different. Even the call of the muezzin seemed harsh to us. We would be startled out of sleep on our foam rubber pads by the high electronic cry from the mosque next door, calling the faithful to prayer, calling, calling, calling.

Arabic was spoken, of course, but the dialect was very different from Iraqi, Egyptian, Moroccan, the dialects we had spoken in other years, in other countries. And we noticed great differences in food, dress, public behavior.

North Yemenis are small, wiry people, with finely chiseled features. They are pleasant and polite, but not outgoing. Having never been colonized by the West, they do not view Westerners with quite the emotion found in newly independent nations, such as Algeria or Morocco. They exhibit neither aggression nor affection; they are as indifferent to Westerners as we are to strangers in America.

We wandered alone through the muddled and often muddy streets of Sanaa. Midafternoon almost certainly brought a deluge from the always clouded skies. No one solicited our business. No one offered to guide us through the market. It was March, cold and damp, a tropical spring in the highlands. We marveled at the conglomeration of international consumer goods available. Piled high on shelves in tiny shops, hardly more than cubbyholes, we saw Heinz ketchup, Big Texas canned grapefruit juice, English marmalade, Chiquita bananas, Egyptian oranges. Drugs from all over the world were available without prescription. Larger stores held American freezers which were filled with Stouffer's TV dinners, ice cream, frozen German sausages.

And everywhere, in every shop, large and small, were the ubiquitous cans of powdered formula. Stina was as good as her word, and she had taken me on a guided tour of the powdered-formula offerings. The European Common Market was well represented by Nestlé (Switzerland); France-Lait (France); Nido (Britain); Frisian (the Netherlands); Nono (Austria). America offered Klim (a Borden product). Yellow cans, blue cans, orange cans, each with a smiling, chubby, pink-cheeked European or American baby on the label as mute testimony to the nutritious quality of the contents. Western cows were feeding Yemen's babies, but the only seeming beneficiaries were the milk companies.

"How can people afford these prices?" we asked. Expatriates, with large cost-of-living allowances, shrugged.

"Tremendous inflation," responded one economist.

"What about local products?" we asked.

"Bread is subsidized by the government," we were told, and we did find the local bakery, a quarter of a mile from our annex rooms, where it was possible to get, each day, thick round wheat loaves from the oven (three for twenty-two cents, as opposed to one egg for twenty-two cents).

"Yemenis only eat bread?"

"With *helba*," said Chuck Swagman, a young anthropologist from UCLA, who took us to the local equivalent of Burger King to eat Yemen's national dish. Helba is fenugreek, a plant called Greek hay in ancient times. Could the dish possibly be composed entirely of fenugreek? It did not seem likely. And of course it wasn't. What was put down on the rough wooden table in front of me, and everyone else in the restaurant (all others were men), was a clay bowl of steaming—steaming what? Taken from a great blazing oven at the side of the restaurant, rather like a crude pizza oven, helba looked—unusual.

"That's helba," said Chuck, eyeing me critically as I hesitated with my spoon. Was it burned, or was that blackish-yellow cast just an exotic crust that I was too finicky to try?

It wasn't bad. But it wasn't very good. At first it seemed like a meat pie with a crust, but it wasn't that either. As I dug in and tasted, it seemed more like tapioca or porridge mixed with hot peppers and fenugreek and cooked together to a liquid, stringy mush. And topped with leathery cheese, but no, it wasn't cheese. Haggis in a pot? Baked in a pizza oven rather than boiled in a calf's stomach? Though it was hot and spicy where haggis is bland, helba in conception seemed more like haggis than anything else I had ever eaten.

"Eat up, B.J.," said Bob, smiling a little. "It will stick to your ribs, as your mother used to say."

"She didn't and I can't," I said. I put down my spoon, and Chuck shook his head. I was obviously a failure. "It is filling, though."

The national dish was indeed different from those of other Middle Eastern nations, totally unlike the tajine and couscous of North Africa, the rice and grilled meat of the Fertile Crescent. But we were, I had to remind myself, at the southeastern tip of the Arab world, near the Red Sea, not far from the Indian Ocean. Helba did not appeal to me particularly, but I was lucky, I had grown up in an affluent society where one did not need to utilize the limited resources of a mountainous land. Spices from the Queen of Sheba's time had helped to make a reasonably edible dish out of subsistence ingredients.

Qat was another local product for sale at special markets throughout the city. Qat, a mild mood heightener, supposedly nonaddictive, is the focus of male social life in Yemen. Bundles of the branches of this shrub, *Catha edulis,* their leaves fresh and green, were laid out for inspection each day in every shop, to be carefully selected for price and quality by discerning users. Qat-chewing was a social activity: one invited one's friends to an afternoon chew and was invited by them in return. It was essential to offer the best-quality qat one could afford.

"Not such a big deal, as far as highs go," reported Bob, after chewing qat at the home of a Yemeni teacher. "You chew up the leaves and stuff them into the side of your mouth like a squirrel. Makes the saliva flow and you swallow the green juice. Pretty soon you have a big wad in your mouth."

"After a couple of hours you feel kind of like you've drunk a pot of strong coffee, sort of strung up," said Tom, "but it takes a lot of chewing to get any effect at all. And makes the sides of your cheeks sore. Is it worth it, Bob?"

"Takes practice, I guess," said Bob.

Most of the chews were for men only, but women were beginning to chew as well, Stina said. I decided to pass up the experience, thereby coming down firmly, Dick told me, on the side of most Americans and other foreigners, who opted for alcohol, their own familiar drug, rather than dabbling in the local specialty. Even though a minority of Yemeni men disapprove of qat-chewing, the use of qat does separate most Yemenis from foreigners, including other Arabs, for a lot of serious business and most socializing took place within the setting of a "qat chew."

What seemed more serious than the mildly narcotic quality of qat was its cost, according to the Yemeni teacher who had invited Tom and Bob to chew. A chew might set the average family budget back from eight to twenty-five dollars, depending on how many guests had been invited to the session. Further, the Yemeni teacher explained, qat had become so profitable in modern Yemen that most of the agricultural land was now devoted to its cultivation. More grain and vegetables had to be imported from abroad, along with the powdered formula, the automobiles, and the television sets.

"It is bad for the long-range economy of my country," he had said, "but what to do? Everybody chews qat, and likes it, including me."

Wealth from migratory labor in oil-rich Saudi Arabia had made increased use of qat possible, a mixed blessing, thought many Yemenis, who welcomed other conveniences and improvements brought by economic development: new construction, improved health care, more schools, and more paved roads, from country to city, and within the city itself. Wide avenues now ran along the medieval walls of the old Ottoman part of Sanaa, past the airline offices, the Sheba Hotel, and the new government buildings, and near the long line of trees where we were staying at the American Institute. And with the paved roads had come a burst of joyous, carefree motorized traffic. Gone were the days, twenty years ago, when eight cars lumbered down the streets of the capital. New cars, trucks, motorcycles, and buses roared around the new paved avenues in happy abandon and at high speeds, paying little attention to car lanes, stoplights, policemen's whistles, or pedestrians. But a few blocks outside these main arteries, the city streets still lay, as one might say, in their natural state; the daily afternoon rains turned them into sloppy seas of mud. The tales of the Queen of Sheba never prepare you for mud, I thought as we edged along high ground at the sides of house walls to try to avoid plunging above our shoes in the mucky centers of the streets and to keep out of the way of the spattering raised by a passing car or motorcycle.

"Must be why Yemenis are so thin and agile," joked Tom. "They begin walking by jumping over mud puddles."

The Yemenis of Sanaa were indeed adept at jumping puddles, and in wet weather had to go about with the hems of their garments held up in one hand. The traditional dress style didn't seem well suited to broad jumps.

The garments were diverse—and many were unfamiliar. Some of the men wore floor-length shirts topped by Western-style suit jackets. But instead of a head scarf secured by a rope crown, the Yemenis wore turbans. Black turbans, green turbans, white turbans; each signified a particular status or group, just as did the black Karakul Russian-style hat which the American anthropologist Carleton Coon is reported to have had to wear, as a Christian, when he visited Yemen in the thirties.

And some Yemeni men wore a kind of wraparound skirt, woven in multicolored stripes, belted and centered by a dramatic dagger in a sheath. Just as the Highland Scots wear their sporran center front on their kilts, so did the Yemenis wear their daggers in the middle of their skirts. The Yemeni skirt, however, was more modest than the kilt, covering rather than revealing the knees.

"No, the black dress worn by some women is *not* borrowed from Egypt," Dr. Fathiyya said to me, firmly and politely, in answer to my question. Director of legal services in the Ministry of Development, she had been kind enough to grant me an extensive interview. We sat in her office in the ministry. She looked very small and unassuming behind the big desk, but the battery of secretaries and retainers I had passed through to reach her suggested the importance of her position.

I smiled. "I just thought maybe the new movement for Islamic dress was having repercussions here, too. Return to roots. It *looks* like the same all-enveloping black garment."

Dr. Fathiyya smiled back, briefly. "We have never changed, as did Egypt, in our attitudes toward Islamic dress. So perhaps"—she clasped her hands together —"they borrowed it from us!"

She herself was wearing an ankle-length plaid skirt, a white blouse, a gray flannel blazer, but her head was uncovered. This was normal dress for what she called "the new educated Yemeni woman."

I asked about the new Yemeni woman, about how Yemen's rapid social change was affecting her role.

Dr. Fathiyya looked at me directly. "Her role is still to be a wife and mother, the center of the family."

"Yes," I said, "but you yourself—"

"I also am a wife and mother," she replied. "And I consider that an honorable role. Don't you?"

"Of course." What was happening to me that wherever I went people lectured me—Stina on breast feeding, Marty on mythical worlds, now Dr. Fathiyya on woman's place? Did I look intolerant? Reactionary?

Dr. Fathiyya talked about combining work and family, about education.

I talked about my film project, to look at social change from the woman's perspective. Perhaps Yemen was a good example? Things were changing so fast?

"No," she said. "No filming. There is nothing to film. We cannot demonstrate, on a large scale, that any great change in women's position has taken place. Give us two or three years. We need time. And remember that women lead different lives in Sanaa than they do in the mountain villages."

"I understand that," I answered, "but—"

"I stress that point," interrupted Dr. Fathiyya, leaning forward to emphasize what she was saying, "because all Westerners seem to think of us as one large mass, women are all the same, imprisoned, oppressed, etc. What nonsense. Obviously there is diversity to begin with, and that affects the way change is introduced and takes place."

I switched the subject. "You were educated in America?"

"In England. My father is a qadi, a religious judge, he went to London to do legal research; we all went with him, and he encouraged me to enter the university."

"How did you like England?"

Another small brief smile. "It is also a damp climate," she said. "The university was very good. I was not, however, impressed with what I could gather of women's position in the West."

"Perhaps you did not have enough time to do that, or meet people who could explain it," I started in defensively, realizing as I said this how it might indeed be turned to apply to my own position, at this moment, in Yemen. How many women had I talked to so far? Four, five. "Legal rights . . . right to work . . ." I was getting warmed up, but Dr. Fathiyya just sighed several times and I stopped.

"You still do not get equal pay with men for equal work," she said.

"We are campaigning for that exact purpose," I said, my voice rising in spite of myself.

"Yes, yes, but you have had *generations* to do it, and you still haven't succeeded. So why do you criticize us, when we are just beginning?" She stopped. "Excuse me," she said gently. "Will you have coffee?"

"Thank you."

"I'm sorry," she said. "I tend to get impatient. We are just beginning, and yet the West is so critical, particularly women's groups, where we might have hoped for support. Forgive me. You are a guest."

We drank the tiny cups of thick Turkish coffee, a legacy from the Ottoman occupation.

"Come back," she said, "in three years, and make a film. We will look at how women here combine different roles successfully. We will have made great strides then! Come and see!" She smiled and shook my hand.

Women like Dr. Fathiyya who combined work and family roles were an exception, it seemed. The majority of women still stayed at home and cared for the family; and those we saw on the street were covered from head to toe. The black costume I had described to Dr. Fathiyya was the traditional dress of a conservative urban middle-class woman: a blouse and long pleated skirt of heavy black silky material, covered by a kind of waist-length cape, also black. A black face veil fell from a black satin headband, and some of these women also wore black gloves and black shoes and stockings. Their skirts were a little shorter than those I had seen in Egypt, presumably a practical variation to avoid the mud. Other women were more colorfully if more loosely covered in a rectangular wrap-around that looked like an Indian bedspread but turned out to be a specially designed garment called the *sitara,* made in Indonesia, navy blue or red with designs of variegated flowers and lotus blossoms around the border and in the middle. The women who wore the sitara also wore a black face veil, but many chose a veil that was far more startling to the Western observer, what Tom and I first called the "bull's-eye veil." This, we were told, was the *marmoukh,* a length of black silk or nylon imprinted with a pattern of red and white circles, in pairs, like double bull's-eyes.

I bought a marmoukh and tried it on, in the privacy of the AIYS annex, and discovered that the bull's-eyes were not meant as bull's-eyes at all; they were to distract the stranger's gaze from the possible location of the forbidden attractions of the face underneath. For the eyes of the woman so veiled did not, as I had assumed, look out through the brightly painted bull's-eyes, as if through dramatically outlined spectacles, but through the black expanse between. Like the entrance to an old Islamic house which opens not into the house itself but into a dark, dead-end hall, the Yemeni marmoukh was designed to deflect the stranger's gaze.

The exotic sitaras and the women's black costumes caught our foreign eyes, but there were also the unveiled schoolgirls in their uniforms, carrying brief-cases and rushing down the streets at the end of classes; and there was Dr. Fathiyya. She was an exception, our friends repeated, though there were other women like her in the colleges, the universities, studying abroad in medical school. Would it have been possible, a generation ago, for Dr. Fathiyya to sit at the large desk in the Ministry of Development and order men to make us coffee? It seemed unlikely. Things were changing, and we were not familiar enough with what Yemen had been before to be able to understand exactly what was going on.

"Dr. Fathiyya, after all," Bob's Yemeni teacher friend pointed out, "is from a very old, very highly respected religious family. Even though she is a woman, you cannot even think of her as being in the same class as, say, a peasant woman from Thula."

Class. Yes. Coming from America, we did not think of class differences as a major factor. But of course they were, and especially in a society like Yemen, closed for so many centuries, where people's place in society was determined first by birth, then by wealth. The combination of the two gave one, man or woman, an immediate running start in life, and a great advantage in any period, including one of rapid social change.

"Sanaa is not Yemen, either," added the Yemeni teacher. "You must visit the countryside."

"We are hoping to do that," responded Bob.

"Yes," said the teacher friend. "It is a different world. Many of the villages are still practically independent and self-sufficient communities. The government more or less leaves them alone. They are sort of like what you would call city-states?"

"Village-states," returned Bob, pleased at his own bon mot. "Are they remnants of the old Karmathians, the ones we read about in the West, the Islamic sect that believed in strict social equality?"

Our teacher friend smiled. "You have been reading too much propaganda put out by the People's Democratic Republic in the South." Then he turned serious. "I am not sure," he answered, "but many of the communities interpret the law more equally than do the sharia courts here. As I say, they're independent. They do what they like."

"And we might find some of the traditional cooperative organizations still in existence in the villages?"

The teacher nodded. Bob was speaking of the local development authorities, village councils organized around the Islamic concept of *hashr,* the common good. Some of the foreign aid programs were said to be working with the councils.

"They are Islamic in origin," said the teacher. "A certain percentage of the *zakat*"—the religious tax—"goes into the funds, to purchase things everyone needs."

Dick Verdery was working with the local development authorities in his water project; Diane Pontasik, an economist with U.S. AID, had explained how the LDAs worked.

"They are self-generated," she had said, "and seem to be real grass-roots organizations. For example, up in a village near the eastern border, the council met and voted to establish a medical clinic. The men working in the Gulf contributed funds for the building, the equipment, the medicines. Then they came to us and asked for nurses to help train Yemenis. That's the sort of thing they're doing now."

Utilizing old structures for new purposes. Yemeni social change did seem to be progressing in a special way, though Bob pointed out that what was special was not just the existence of self-generated village organizations but the recognition by Western assistance agencies that local structures were worthy of serious attention.

And of course he was quite right. Twenty-five years ago, when we had first come out to the Arab world, foreign aid personnel tended to accept the attitudes of local urban sophisticates who viewed traditional organizations—tribes or village councils—as hopelessly mired in their unprogressive ways. Tribes must go, new forms of organization such as Western-style cooperatives must come in. What was not recognized at the time was that Western colonialism had already irrevocably changed these tribes and councils. Tribes in the past had ruled by consensus; land had been owned in common; resources had been often shared. These old patterns of government disappeared when Western colonial powers introduced modern forms of central authority, backed by tanks and planes. Communal lands also disappeared as land registration for tax purposes ignored collective ownership or use. This had sometimes resulted in the entire tribal land package being registered in the name of the then-ruling sheikh. His grandsons had taken advantage, had indeed become absentee, feudal-style landlords. This had happened in Iraq with the British, in Algeria, Morocco, and Tunisia with the French. The colonial powers justified their actions as "modernization" when what resulted was a replacement of old communal ownership patterns with the concept of private property. Which was of course easier for the foreign occupier to understand and control—and tax.

Yemen had been bypassed during the Western colonial period, and thus, Bob's teacher friend pointed out, some of the old communal institutions still survived. The Ottoman Turks never pushed their control so far or concerned themselves with most average-size villages.

"What about conflict, fighting between villages, sheikhs?"

"There is some, of course. Even now. But these days people are more interested in improving their lot and those of their families. Now that we have the opportunity," he added with a smile. "With our new income we are becoming big consumers like you in the West."

"So you have no trouble traveling around alone?"

Bob's friend shook his head. "No, as long as you stay away from the borders, where there are still skirmishes between villagers and the soldiers of the Front." He used the term as it was used throughout Sanaa: the Front meant the National Liberation Front of South Yemen.

So Bob, Tom, and I went into the countryside, in an old Land-Rover rented from the American Institute for Yemeni Studies, sharing the costs with a Japanese graduate student who had come to Yemen to study Arabic, and an American author-architect from Michigan, Norman Carver. Norman had produced a beautiful prizewinning book on Italian hill towns, and had come to Yemen looking for new photographic possibilities.

Two miles outside the clutter and sprawl of burgeoning Sanaa, the car was suddenly plunged into a deep fog, the kind of dense swirling mist associated with the magical appearances of genies from bottles in old illustrations of *The Arabian Nights*. We felt enclosed, cut off, transported suddenly into a tunnel, through which only our Land-Rover moved, barreling along in a noisy sputtering deliberate way on the narrow blacktop road unfolding ahead of us.

The minutes passed, and the mist slowly began to rise, like a veil lifting, disclosing a balding hill, a tiny village tucked into a cleft of rocks. Around a sharp turn, a few pocket-handkerchief-size fields emerged in a deep valley to our right. A man was plowing, followed by a woman in a printed dress who scattered seeds, sowing where he turned over the land in the furrows. Again Stina's image of the hardworking Yemeni farm woman came to mind. Was her baby in the crib with a bottle of Nestlé's formula? Was the baby ill or thriving? The mist came down again.

There was a mountain, its top wreathed in fog, rows of narrow cultivated terraces built into the steep sides, green and triumphant evidence of human industry edging to the dun brown of the rocky slopes. As many as three hundred terraces, one above the other, can be counted on the side of a mountain. I remember reading that about Yemen. The terracing technique, it is said, was brought to Europe all the way from Yemen in the days before the Crusades. Islamic conquerors from the Arabian Peninsula established the Western Caliphate in Andalusia and branched north and east. With the teachings of the Prophet they brought scientific knowledge and agricultural methods. The same terracing patterns are found in France today in the hills of the Ardèche, where the grapevines that grow on those narrow ridges produce the wines of the Rhone.

The veils of mist were moving away, and the morning light fell through the fog, picking out, as with a weak spotlight, a flock of sheep beside the road, a deep ravine with a stone castle crowning its adjacent hill, goats leaping in and out of the mists, like bewitched creatures first appearing, then disappearing, before our eyes. Soon an entire settlement could be seen, ribbons of mist circling around the stone houses.

"Now then!" breathed Carver. "Could we stop and get closer to the houses, do you think?"

The two photographers leaped out, equipment around their shoulders, Bob and I lagging behind, in some obscure way not wishing to be closely associated with the picture-taking. The Japanese student elected to stay in the car; he seemed to be suffering still from jet lag or a combination of jet lag and culture shock.

There was a small stone mosque, with a whitewashed dome and a square-towered minaret. The beautiful multistoried stone houses raised walls and turrets around us; their austere gray lines were accented with whitewash—along a doorway, around a narrow slit of window—which added to their noble, elegant air. But at our feet, along the narrow earth paths between the houses, lay a new detail: bits of industrial rubbish, blue-and-pink plastic bags intertwined with mud, and flattened soft-drink cans—a trail of nonbiodegradable trash.

Those garlands of garbage were a kind of leitmotif, a symptom of change in local habits of consumption. Wherever we went in the sputtering old Land-Rover, up broken roads, across washed-out hillsides, into the markets, the garlands were there. The village streets were otherwise clean, the houses' pure lines sullied only by those blotches of modernity on the roads, red and silver for Coca-Cola, blue and pink for sodden plastic.

"And they call this progress," said Norman Carver disdainfully, aiming his camera so as to exclude the garbage from the frame.

"Well," said Bob, "it's easy enough to say that, but you and I both know, Norman, that soft drinks and plastic bags are tempting, easy, and useful. They haven't the means to cope with this kind of mess."

"Look," put in Tom, "if we didn't have garbage dumps, our streets in Austin would look like this, too. Only worse. Beer cans . . . old car junk . . . pieces of tire . . . We're just good at hiding them away."

"That's fine," said Carver. "I don't want to look at it."

The Japanese student said nothing. He was not asleep anymore, but his English was minimal and, after all, what was there left to say? Garlands of garbage. Great colorful tins of powdered formulas. Mixed results of open doors and new trading policies.

In Shibam we met four Egyptians in the weekly rural market. The two women looked startling in their tight jeans and high heels. We nodded and stared at them, they stared back. The Yemenis were too polite or indifferent to stare. The market offered none of the Queen of Sheba's precious stones, no exotic goods as we had half hoped. There were mounds of secondhand hinges and bolts; wooden stirrups for horses; a small pile of navy blue sitaras; tomatoes; bolts of cloth; one traditional sheathed dagger displayed on a length of ragged green cloth; some bits of silver and beads.

But there was lots of qat. Bundles on the ground beside nearly every stall, bundles in baskets being hawked by several old men. Tom was in the middle of bargaining for the dagger when the seller, apparently bored, suddenly stood up, chose a bundle of qat from a passing peddler, rolled up his dagger, and departed, presumably to head home for lunch and a good chew. Other merchants were doing likewise.

We went back to our Land-Rover, where we sat and devoured our hard-boiled eggs, brown bread, and tomatoes and washed them down with water. Foreigners in a foreign land.

Chuck Swagman invited Bob and Tom to visit the village where he had been living for nearly a year, doing anthropological research. They flew to Hodayda, on the Red Sea coast, took a taxi inland, and then headed straight up the mountain, along narrow trails and rock-strewn paths, between the high terraces. It took them eleven hours of hard climbing to reach Chuck's village.

"But what got to me really, B.J.," said Tom, recounting the adventure later, "was the men on the trail, carrying big beams as wide as that"—he measured off a span the size of a foot—"and wooden boxes full of TV sets, and they kept passing us. *Passing* us, and we could hardly make it on our wind."

"Very steep," agreed Bob. "I had a hard time. Getting old."

Tom laughed. "You may be older, but I'm out of shape. We did about the same time." Bob looked pleased.

They climbed into the clouds, they said, from the heat of the foothills to the evening chill when they finally arrived near midnight. The houses in the high villages were of the same stone found in the valleys, the mosques had whitewashed domes. And what was in the markets? Powdered milk, fenugreek, piles of qat, soft drinks. Local development authorities planning local improvements? Yes, said Chuck, there was some of that. A road was on its way. And wound around the houses and spilling down the mountain paths beside the villages, the eternal garlands of garbage, red for Coca-Cola, blue and pink for plastic, to last another thousand years.

Kawkaban is reputedly one of the highest villages in Yemen, and also the site of an active local development authority or village council. It also boasts two fine examples of cisterns, both Yemeni and American friends told us. Cisterns? My memory of cisterns involved my grandparents' Wisconsin farm, where my cousins and my brother and I were allowed as a great treat to look into the cistern, the rain barrel that all prudent farmers in those days kept as a hedge against dry seasons. But they were dangerous and deep, these rain barrels and cisterns, and our cousins told us dark tales about children who had fallen in, never to be seen again.

Yemeni cisterns were not of such plebeian cast, we were told. Rather they were large, spacious masonry tanks, architecturally famous since ancient times, designed to catch and store the water from the summer rains in different basins at different levels so as to flood the fields in dry season as well as provide bath and laundry water.

Kawkaban is visible for several miles, a cluster of stone buildings that seems to perch on the very tip of the mountain. Although it is perhaps only forty miles from Sanaa, the trip took us five hours in the old Land-Rover, on a back-breaking, axle-cracking narrow road. Tom and Bob and Norman Carver took turns driving; the Japanese student sat behind me in the back seat and kept his eyes firmly closed. Broken and washed away in places, boulder-strewn, the road offered a selection of hairpin turns and breathtaking switchbacks to challenge and excite the most daring mountain mule. The only problem was that we were in a sputtering old car.

We passed below and through the wreaths of mist to emerge at the end of the road. The village lay not on a slope or a peak but on a high mesa; sheep and goats were cropping the short green tufts of grass that sprang up between the stones, in what looked like barren earth.

The village was large, but we saw no human beings at all. We parked the car and decided to walk. Norman Carver went off with his cameras; the Japanese student elected again to stay in the car.

"It's midday," said Bob. "People must be inside eating their lunch. . . ."

"And chewing their qat . . ." put in Tom.

The place had a silent eerie quality, and Bob, Tom, and I walked more quickly than necessary through the narrow winding streets, past shuttered shops and anonymous walls, a small mosque. Not even a child came out of the closed doors of the houses; we kept walking and in ten minutes we emerged on the other side. The mesa stretched ahead, and one of the cisterns lay on the left, some distance from the last village house, near the stony lip of the mesa.

The Yemeni cisterns put my grandfather's modest rain barrel to shame. This was a sophisticated structure, the size of a community swimming pool, oval in shape; a very small amount of water lay in the bottom of the cistern, below the stone steps that had been built at the four corners to allow access to the basin. Near the bottom of the stone walls, pipes were visible through which, presumably, the water was let out onto the small terraced plots below the mesa.

Tom was clicking photographs while we stood and admired the careful dressing and matching of the stones, the more recent patching of cement.

"Good afternoon!" The soft voice speaking English in this silent place near the top of the world made us all jump.

Two men stood there, smiling and extending their hands in greeting. Both wore snow-white dish-dashas (floor-length shirts) with suit coats; one man's suit coat was brown, with a brown skullcap, a belt, a dagger. The other, in a navy blue blazer with brass buttons, said in excellent English, "You are admiring our water basin." He was wearing, I noticed, a row of tiny lavender mountain wildflowers in the handkerchief pocket of his blazer.

"Yes," said Bob. "It is most impressive."

"Now we have an electric water pump," he said. "It is more efficient, but this is also useful."

"How did you get the pump?" asked Bob.

"We bought it. The village council bought it. Just like you could, in America. You are American, aren't you? I spent three years in America. In California."

"Oh yes," said Bob. "We used to live north of California. We live in Texas now."

"Texas," said the man. He smiled again. "They have oranges in Texas, too. But not Cesar Chavez, I think."

"You are right," Bob replied. "But maybe in the future."

The man in the navy blue blazer looked at us. "Come and see the view from here," he said.

We walked forward with him to the edge of the mesa and admired the magnificent panorama before us: the ring of mountains, their peaks still wound around with pale strands of mist; the valleys darkened blue; small settlements showing green terraces, tiny squares of fields, stone houses in hollows and overhangs on both sides of the deep valleys. Blue, gray, white, green. The red-and-blue garbage garlands were not visible from this distance.

"Here it is exceedingly clean," said our acquaintance with the pocketful of flowers. He spoke proudly, as though he had read my thoughts. And he was right, we had seen no garbage on the streets of Kawkaban. Maybe our host had imported Hefty garbage bags from America and instituted a dump? "No dust," he went on, "no smells, very nice, not like Sanaa, ugh!" He made a horrid face and translated rapidly into Arabic for his friend, who nodded and smiled in agreement.

"Here all is very good," he continued. "Have a happy time in Yemen! I am happy to be in my home and to welcome you here!"

"Thank you!" said Bob formally. "Your country is very beautiful."

"Yes," assented Tom.

Our friend waved goodbye and set off, walking along the edge of the wide mesa with his companion and gesturing toward distant spots.

Three years in America picking oranges? It sounded like it, three years as a migrant laborer to save up enough to contribute his share to the community electric water pump, to support his own family. Would he be able to stay home now, or would he have to leave, to become a migrant laborer again? There did not appear to be much work available in Kawkaban, though the vistas were indeed magnificent.

Clearly, our earlier image of Yemen as a remote country long isolated from the rest of the world had to be modified. It was true that only in the last ten years had foreigners been able to travel to Yemen relatively freely. But it was not true that Yemenis themselves had been shut off from the outside world. For many generations, Yemeni men have traveled to Saudi Arabia and the other Gulf States to work, experiencing the modernization which was taking place beyond their borders and bringing it home to their families. By 1981 Yemen, even in the villages on distant mountaintops, was full of foreign-made consumer goods—electric generators, television sets, cassette recorders, purchased with the wages of these migrant laborers. Even more important, the men were far more traveled and far more sophisticated about world affairs and about their own interests than the traditional architecture or the colorful national costumes might lead a visiting Westerner to believe.

Yemen, unlike most other Arab countries, has never been colonized in the sense of being controlled by an effective foreign administration. There existed a strong tradition of local governance, of self-rule, which we had not encountered in Egypt or Morocco. Even at the time of our visit, many districts in the mountains were essentially independent of the new republican central authority. And with such independence come pride and indifference to foreigners. Although the traditional code of Arab hospitality prevailed in the case of guests, perhaps Yemenis have enough of foreigners when they work outside Yemen.

The new pattern of migrant labor and the consumerism were not without problems, however. Yemen was becoming dependent on the income from workers abroad. Where labor migration might once have been an occupational alternative for some people, a means of acquiring extra money for limited goals (such as land purchase or marriage), it was now becoming a national necessity to purchase basic foods. Inflation was rampant, and with eggs at two dollars a dozen, a Yemeni householder could no longer make ends meet without outside income. And the local economy was no longer producing much except qat.

For the educated Yemeni, the neglect of so many of the terraced farms and the growing of qat on many of those still cultivated were a matter of grave concern. Qat is not nutritious, nor is it a good cash crop, for it is largely consumed in the country and not exported. Qat is grown instead of badly needed food crops and also weakens the soil. Yet qat commanded a high price on the market, higher than any other crop, so it was difficult to persuade farmers not to grow it.

It occurred to us, as visitors, however, that indulgence in the pleasures of qat, a habit specific to Yemen, was not so much the cause of economic dependence on labor migration as it was a result of that situation. We were Americans, coming from a society which consumes more drugs—recreational and medicinal —than any other country in the world. Thus we could appreciate that Yemenis had developed their own way to relax—or even escape—after working as wage earners, taking orders from foreign bosses and customers.

But the larger problem remained. How was Yemen to escape from its dilemma, its current dependency on migrant labor? How would its people be able to cope with the rising inflation? How could the country maintain its traditional independence when it was part of an international market system in which human labor was its major export?

We regretted not being able to see how the self-proclaimed Marxist state of South Yemen was handling its economic problems. Perhaps another time, travel there might be possible for us.

Comment

LABOR MIGRATION, OLD AND NEW STYLES

TODAY IN THE Arab world millions of people are traveling back and forth across national boundaries each year in search of work. This movement—labor migration on a historically unprecedented scale—is probably of greater long-term importance to the future of the area than the Arab-Israeli conflict, but it has thus far received little attention in the Western press. In the last decade, oil wealth has transformed human labor in the Middle East into a marketable commodity to a degree which was scarcely foreseen a generation ago. At least 3 million Egyptians are working outside their native land; over half the Saudi Arabian labor force is made up of foreigners from many different countries. And the movement is not limited to blue-collar workers. Migrants include electricians, architects, stonemasons, farmers, doctors, teachers, plumbers, librarians, engineers, and administrative and clerical workers, as well as servants.

No planning preceded this new movement. Contemporary Arab labor migration is a grass-roots phenomenon of unexpected scope and far-reaching consequences.

In 1959 it was commonly stated that Egyptian fellaheen, or peasants, would never leave Egypt, though the possibility was raised even then as the population crisis loomed. But in those days labor migrants were defined in roles already recognized in the area: traders, servants, artisans. Migration of the Arab population from the eastern shores of the Mediterranean, for example, was well established before the beginning of the twentieth century. Syrian-Lebanese traders were among the first traveling salesmen in the Third World, the first to transport and sell industrial manufactured goods to customers in Africa and South America. As front-line representatives of the new capitalist mercantilism, they worked shoulder-to-shoulder with the missionaries and the colonial administrators. Some of these traders eventually returned home to retire in Lebanon or Syria. But others settled permanently in colonially administered lands and new nations, where they live to this day; in Spanish settings they are still called *sirio* or *turco* families.

Mercantile migration has also been a long-standing pattern among Yemenis, who shipped goods by dhow to the shores of East Africa and across the Indian Ocean in export-import businesses that were family-owned and -operated. Within Egypt, nineteenth-century records show that Nubians came to Cairo and Alexandria from their homes a thousand miles away in the south. They worked as servants, cooks, doormen. Sa'idis, natives of Upper Egypt, became the fruit salesmen/brokers of Egypt's northern cities. But these highly traditionalized forms of labor migration, preindustrial in origin, created little stir, as the numbers were relatively small, the practice developed gradually, and the resulting social contacts were limited.

Modern Middle East migration bears little resemblance to these earlier forms. To begin with, the number of people involved is enormous, some say up to 4 million or more. Secondly, the migrants' wages are high, often two or three times an average home-country salary. And demand exists for all skills. Rich countries such as Saudi Arabia, Kuwait, and Libya want the advantages of advanced technology and science now, and they want the services that must accompany such technology, so that the material benefits can be enjoyed to the fullest. They are willing to pay well. Thus farmers from the Nile Delta, paid two hundred dollars a month plus expenses, work side by side with Saudi Bedouin who are trying to establish new farms on recent land grants. A skilled construction worker from Egypt can earn forty dollars a day in Iraq, an unskilled worker nineteen dollars. Egypt also is the only Arab country with a surplus of college-educated men and women, thanks to Gamal Abdul Nasser's open-door university policy of the sixties. Thus Egyptian schoolteachers, along with many displaced Palestinians, still staff the thousands of new schools and universities which have opened in the oil-rich states during the last decade.

The new labor movement which has been developing since the mid-seventies is also radically different from the post–World War II pattern of Arab migration to Europe from Algeria, Morocco, and Tunisia. North African migrants, like all workers moving from less developed to more developed countries, have generally filled blue-collar jobs and therefore have had limited relationships with the resident population. Arabs in France live within communities of their own, in low-income districts. In Aix-en-Provence, a rich provincial town in the south, social intercourse between the Arabs and the French is at a minimum. The Algerians and the Moroccans clean the streets and perform much of the town's heavy menial labor but, except for taking orders from their employers, have little opportunity for social exchanges. Even the workers' special needs in terms of food and bread are filled by small Arab-run stores. An Algerian man or sometimes an entire Arab family may occasionally occupy a bench in the public squares and parks of the city, but none are found in the chairs of the chic cafés which line the Cours Mirabeau. While some cross-cultural contact does take place among younger people, French residents and foreign tourists can live in Aix, as in many other cities of France or Belgium, practically unaware of the significant Arab component in the population. A similar pattern is found with regard to Turkish workers in Germany and Scandinavia.

But in Saudi Arabia, the situation is very different. Representatives of many nationalities, who often share the same language or religious faith, encounter each other every day. In a Saudi Arabian city, the barbershop may be staffed by an Indian from Madras while the corner grocery is owned by Pakistanis, as is the nearby catering service. A Yemeni may run a restaurant next door to an Egyptian establishment. Shirts are tailor-made by Delhi Indians. School is taught by Egyptians and Palestinians. All day Pakistanis in bright yellow uniforms patrol the streets, picking up trash, including throwaway plastic and glass bottles which have no more value in Saudi Arabia than in America. Throughout Saudi cities, houses of reinforced concrete and cement blocks are being built, plastered, wired, and painted by Tunisians and Egyptians. A Palestinian doctor, educated in Lebanon, does physical checkups; an Algerian dentist fills teeth. Business in the offices of a government that dispenses money to its citizens through a complicated system of grants and subsidies may be conducted jointly by a Saudi citizen and an Egyptian administrator, though the supervisor will always be a Saudi. In short, Saudis are in constant contact with people of many nations, and Saudi public life is filled with male foreigners, mostly alone, and most of them in the prime of their lives. (Thus it is perhaps not surprising that the present King has recently assumed a more conservative attitude toward the already limited public roles permitted to Saudi women.)

The new pattern of migration of all kinds of workers has had different effects on the migrants' home countries. Egypt is suffering from severe labor shortages, particularly of skilled artisans such as plumbers and electricians. Construction sites remain unfinished. And although the loss is perhaps less obvious, some of the finest intellectual talent has left for better-paying jobs in other parts of the Arab world. The family life of migrants is obviously affected. Wives whose husbands are abroad on two- or three-year contracts find themselves running households, shops, or farms alone for the first time, as well as managing a significant cash flow of remittances. Other male members of the absent husband's family, however, are likely to be more involved in spending those remittances than would be customary in the United States. In Egypt, the consumerist binge has become a part of life at all but the poorest levels of the society. Egyptian television, now accessible to more than two thirds of the population, has primed the consumer demand with its commercials and its soap operas depicting prosperous Egyptians living in comfortable homes filled with modern appliances. Migrant workers' earnings are often used to buy cars, refrigerators, washing machines, television sets. Mud-brick homes in rural villages are being replaced with cement and fired-brick houses. The infusion of foreign salaries has fueled the rise of inflation, and many local incomes have not kept up with the cost of living. Thus talented government workers find themselves tempted to join the ranks of labor migrants or, failing that, must take on two or three jobs in Egypt to make ends meet.

Labor migration in the Middle East today is distinctive in still another way: it exists outside of direct political control. Though some border restrictions are enforced, particularly between Egypt and Saudi Arabia, and migrants are supposed to have official work contracts and visas, thousands of workers slip across borders each month. Even the deteriorating relations between Libya and Egypt did not affect the flow of labor migrants, nor did the diplomatic freeze placed on Egypt by other Arab countries after its recognition of Israel. Diplomatic relations have been severed between Iraq and Egypt, yet scores of workers line up at the Iraqi-interests section of the Spanish Embassy in Cairo each day to apply for work visas. International labor migration has become a necessity for both giver and receiver countries, a reality with which Arab political leaders must live, whether they like it or not.

The result of this massive new movement of human beings will be, in the view of one Egyptian social scientist, "a new social order." The sharing of everyday life by people for whom no language barrier exists and among whom Islam is a common faith is producing a new international Arab community of a far more substantive nature than that conceived by Gamal Abdul Nasser, who popularized the idea of political Pan-Arabism. Public opinions are currently being created which every Arab national politician will have to consider in the years to come. A recognition of common economic interests and a sense of common Muslim identity are becoming evident. In the future, such developments may come to supersede sectarian and national differences.

CHAPTER VI

Rashadiya Refugee Camp, South Lebanon

April 1981

Here I stand and make
Both myth and reality in my own way
And live the violence of my dream and of my reality.

Jabra Ibrahim Jabra
A Poem Sequence

SPRING WAS COMING. The time to begin filming was fast approaching, for the crew was scheduled to arrive May 15 in Cairo, where Bob and I had been living. Marilyn Gaunt, who was to direct the film, and I were to meet in Beirut on April 8 and explore the possibilities of filming in one of the Palestinian refugee camps. Bob had said goodbye to me that April morning and cautioned us not to take any unnecessary risks. If I had read the newspaper before leaving Cairo, I might not have gone at all, for according to those reports the Beirut airport was closed owing to heavy shelling from mixed sources.

Marilyn, en route from London, had been warned by the stewardess that the plane might not be able to land in Beirut. But things changed while we were both in the air and the airport reopened. In the nearly empty waiting room, Marilyn and I fell into each other's arms in relief. We had arrived safely and things seemed calm for the moment.

Yes, I had permission to film in the refugee camp. We could visit Rashadiya first, the camp closest to the Israeli border. "But it's going to be hard," I said, "to keep the focus on women and the family. Everyone will want to speak their piece on the political situation."

"Well, let's go and see," said Marilyn. We had worked together in Marrakech and had planned this new project over many cups of tea and discussions far into many nights. It was important to us—and it was about to begin at last.

"Eye on women, not to worry about politics, right? Effect on the family, on women's roles in prolonged stress."

"Right."

And thus we headed down the road to South Lebanon on an April morning, thinking but not speaking to each other about the warnings of friends in Beirut, including Phyllis Salem, the sensible, cheerful director of the AMIDEAST office with whom we were staying.

"Don't go," she had first said. But when it was obvious that we were determined, she had lectured us about prudence, caution.

"You don't realize," she had said. "The country *looks* beautiful, but there is danger everywhere." Wife of Elie Salem, who was then dean of AUB, Phyllis had lived in Lebanon for thirty years. "This country used to be a paradise, but it's far from that now. If you must go south, don't be misled by appearances; be careful. We really don't know what's happening there!"

Phyllis was right. The country looked beautiful.

Away from Beirut, on the winding road south that followed the sea, one could believe one was still back in happy old Lebanon, oasis for the Arab world, ancient center of trade and commerce for the whole eastern Mediterranean. One could believe it, that is, if one looked at the sea, blue and calm on this magnificent late spring day, and noted with pleasure the beach clubs and the striped umbrellas of families taking their ease on the sand and splashing in the water during the Easter vacation. Easter was a long vacation in Lebanon, including both the Latin and the Eastern Orthodox celebrations. The pastry and confectionery stores in Beirut displayed splendid concoctions of chocolate and colored sugar, fantasy eggs in clear plastic gift boxes tied with gold and silver ribbons.

But on the other side of the sea road another scene unfolded: gutted buildings where refugees had set up housekeeping; makeshift huts and tents of squatters. A woman in a long red dress was hanging out pants and shirts on a clothesline strung from a corrugated tin roof to a collection of old gasoline cans that marked off a bit of territory where chickens scratched. Beyond, across an empty lot studded with rubble, an old man in baggy black trousers and coat, a black-and-white kaffiya on his head, herded sheep. Children raced through these dismal settlements with sticks held high. No one looked up.

"People from the South who are afraid to go home since the Israelis came across the border in 1978," explained our guide, a representative from the PLO office in Beirut who was to accompany us on our visit to the refugee camp.

"But that was three years ago," I protested.

"Why doesn't the government of Lebanon do something about them?" asked Marilyn.

Jamal, our guide, answered. "What Lebanese government?"

The taxi driver spoke up. "If people would leave us alone, everything would be fine," he said in English.

A derisive laugh from Jamal. "Look what happened in 1976 when you were left alone. Christians started killing Muslims, Christians killed Christians, Muslims killed Muslims. You don't know what government is." He spat out the window. "Now the Palestinians—"

"Don't give me that," retorted the driver. "If it weren't for the Palestinians—"

"Okay, okay, don't blame everything on us." Jamal switched quickly into Arabic and the argument continued: young people knew nothing but violence, Palestinians, Shi'ite Muslims, Maronites ruining the farms, the irrigation, the militias. . . . The taxi driver careened faster and faster around corners on the seaside road while we clutched our seats and wished, prayed, that we might arrive at the refugee camp in one piece. Faster, faster. Jamal's voice rose, the driver's voice rose, we passed an oil refinery, and then we pulled up to a dead halt in front of a small store by the side of the road.

"Coca-Cola," said the driver, smiling, "good cakes, and beer. Lebanon has everything to offer."

"After this speed trip can there be anything more dangerous ahead?" asked Marilyn, as we crawled, shaken, from the taxi.

"How much farther is it?" I inquired, and to my intense annoyance, my voice quavered.

Jamal smiled. "Not far," he answered, and added, "Don't worry, madame, we always argue, we Palestinians and we Lebanese."

"Were your parents born in Palestine?" I asked politely, trying not to notice that our seemingly reckless driver was drinking his second Amstel beer in the middle of the morning.

"Yes," said Jamal, "but I am sorry to say that although I love my parents very much, they are capitalist bourgeois types."

Marilyn stared, I suppressed a smile, but Jamal was in deadly earnest.

"Yes," he said. "My father had a large factory in Palestine but it was taken over by the Israelis in 1948. Then he went to Africa and set up another factory, and he was doing very well, but the Africans nationalized their private-sector industries last year, so now he has nothing. He lives in Beirut. He is trying to start up a business again, but with the unsettled conditions here, it is not easy."

"It must be hard for him, your dad," said Marilyn.

"Yes," said Jamal. "But then such capitalist exploitive industries should be abolished in any case."

"What about your father, though?" I asked. "What about you?"

"I have the revolution," said Jamal proudly. "My father is— Let's go, the driver is ready."

Back in the taxi, I persisted. "You were saying your father is . . . ?"

Jamal looked at me, looked away. "My father is passé," said Jamal. "The things he stood for are wrong. Only the revolution provides us with the right approach to economic life. Capitalism is finished. The people must govern themselves . . . must share the profits from the means of production. That is what the revolution teaches us."

Marilyn and I looked at each other and then fell silent. Soor (ancient Tyre) was coming into view; the waves of the sea washed over the edges of a city in ruins. The cement and stone walls along the Mediterranean were in pieces, as though smashed by giant hammers. But we did not go into Tyre; we cut into a side road and stopped beside a blank wall, where Jamal got out and disappeared.

"Where's he off to?" asked Marilyn.

"What's going on?" I asked the driver.

"He's checking in," said the driver. "With Azmi. You have to get permission to go on to the camp. You can't just drive in."

"Who's Azmi?" Marilyn asked Jamal when he returned with the required papers and we had started on the inland road to Rashadiya, the Palestinian refugee camp for which we were headed.

"Azmi is a brave man," said Jamal formally. "He is a hero. Of course, that is not his real name. He is the commander of all South Lebanon."

"He commands the *Palestinians* in South Lebanon," said the driver cuttingly.

"What do you mean by that?" burst out Jamal.

"Are those orange trees?" I asked quickly to avoid another heated discussion. Obviously they were orange trees, couldn't I smell them, didn't they have orange trees in America? These were wonderful oranges, the harvest was finished, but maybe we could find an orange, would we like an orange, we could easily stop . . .

"No, no . . ." we protested, but we stopped anyhow and got some oranges, and Jamal peeled one and offered segments to us, and to the taxi driver with whom he had so recently been arguing furiously. Delicious, sweet, fresh tree-ripened oranges. "The last of the season," he said.

The orange groves came to an end and we wound into a leafy country lane overgrown with fragrant flowering bushes where that now familiar setup stood: a checkpoint. Sandbags and barrels smeared with paint stood beneath the flowering trees, and young men in camouflage battle dress with fingers casually close, too close for my taste, to the shining triggers of the machine guns slung carelessly over their shoulders. The machine guns looked clean, well cared for. Perhaps it was the combination of the leafy flowering country lane and the ominous shining weapons that caused me at that moment to have serious doubts about the forthcoming film project. Was it worth it? Why expose myself and the crew, four young women with longer lives left to live than mine, to the dangers that lay ahead? What was I doing here on a beautiful spring morning? I told myself sternly that I had gone too far to turn back now. But no, one could always turn back.

"What are you thinking about, B.J.?" said Marilyn in a low voice while we sat in the taxi, being given the once-over by the camp guards, young men with dark hair and curious eyes who talked to Jamal but kept looking over and gesturing at us.

I told her.

"Now, luv, no offense but maybe you've been out here too long," said Marilyn lightly. "We've only come to get a look at the place. Maybe it isn't right.

Also, who in the U.K. or America has seen a refugee camp on the tube? What do these folks mean when they talk about revolution? We're here. After that drive, it's a relief. Might as well look. Can always leave, say no, whatever."

She talked on, soothingly, as we wound through the camp, down toward the sea, amid gardens where men and women, weeding, raised their heads to look at us, past a school on a hill, past houses that looked almost permanent, so pleasant did they appear in comparison to the ugly squatters' huts we had seen en route.

We had said we wanted to make a film about women's role in violent political upheaval. Could this possibly be the place to do it? Houses, schools, gardens. Where was the violence?

"Those guards with guns aren't there for their health," said Marilyn.

Would we be able to make the film we wanted? It was all very well to have official permission, but that was only the first step. We wanted to do something that reflected women's own views, not Jamal's revolutionary slogans. But maybe they were the same. "Okay, let's see," said Marilyn.

We were ushered into what we were told was the office of the mayor of Rashadiya, actually the living room of his house. We presented our letter of permission to film from the central PLO office in Beirut. The mayor, who introduced himself as Ali, read the letter. He looked up at us, and began to deliver a speech.

"Mr. Dulles of the U.S.A. thought the Palestine problem would go away," said Ali. He was a slender young man whose gentle manner and pleasant smile of welcome were belied by the pistol on his hip and the intensity of his words.

He wore a freshly pressed khaki shirt and slacks and he offered us coffee.

"Dulles thought we would disappear under the feet of the Western powers. But he was wrong. The revolution is stronger now than it was in 1948. Then we were pitiful refugees. Today we have a purpose, a cause, the revolution!"

"What is the goal of the revolution?" Marilyn asked.

"To regain our homeland," said Ali earnestly. He rose and pointed to an old lithograph on the whitewashed wall—a faded greenish picture of a valley, a house, some trees. "This is our homeland. This is my ancestors' house. This"—pointing to a sprig of olive branch encased in plastic and pinned above the lithograph—"is from my father's olive tree. A man from *Time* magazine brought it to me. He went to our village in Israel and brought it back to me."

"He interviewed you?"

"Yes. Did you read his story in the magazine?"

We had to admit we had not. We did not add that we had not even heard of Rashadiya a month ago. So great was our ignorance, our indifference, that in our minds, all Palestinians were either lumped together in squalor in camps with UNRWA schools attached or were living in other Arab countries where they held well-paid professional positions, as economists, teachers, engineers. Bob and I had known some of them in Baghdad, Cairo, Casablanca, Amman. They had no citizenship, of course, no place, but we had not taken this very seriously twenty-five years ago.

Ali was continuing. "We thought others would see our plight. Arabs, Americans, British, French. We were wrong. No one cared about the injustice that had been done."

Jamal, I noticed, watched him with approval.

"We realized that no one would help us. We had to help ourselves."

My mind began to wander, rejecting the rhetoric, the rehearsed quality of Ali's words. But then in response to Marilyn's specific questions he began to give us specific information.

Rashadiya was a small town, he said. One of the oldest camps. It had a population of 9,000 people, 16,000 before 1978; it had five schools.

"Five schools?"

"Yes, and a clinic, several shops, training camps for revolutionaries. It has a governing people's committee."

"Like a town council?" I asked.

"I suppose," said Ali. He took a breath and began again. "Here all of the people consider themselves revolutionaries. We call it a people's committee, not a town council."

"Are there any women on the people's committee?" from Marilyn.

He nodded.

"We would like to meet them," said I.

"Of course," said Ali. "Women's role is important here."

And that is how we came to know Um Zhivago and her husband, Abu Zhivago—called, as most married couples are in the Arab world, Mother (Um) and Father (Abu) of their oldest son. They had five children, Zhivago, the eldest (as their own names implied), plus Rami, Lara, Shama, and Alia.

"Why did you call your son Zhivago?" I asked that first day. "It is not an Arab name."

Um Zhivago smiled. "Didn't you see that film about Dr. Zhivago, the poet, the fighter, the idealist? That Russian film?"

"Yes," I said. "I saw it."

"And didn't you think the hero was great?"

I nodded. Marilyn nodded.

"Well, I was pregnant at the time," said Um Zhivago. "So when I had a boy, we decided to name him—"

"Zhivago," finished Marilyn, "after the hero."

"Right." Um Zhivago smiled triumphantly. "And he is a good example to all the boys here, Zhivago. He works hard in school and he does guard duty once a week—watching the camp from sunset till dawn."

Marilyn and I looked at Um Zhivago's face, bright, open, proud. She was serious. To her, Zhivago was already a hero.

The beach in Rashadiya is beautiful, fine clear sand sloping down to the sea. But it is totally empty. Children are forbidden to play in the sand unless accompanied by their parents. This seemed incomprehensible to me. What did they think, that Israeli frogmen would come out of the sea from the other side of the border, six miles away, and steal the children?

"No, no," said Abu Zhivago. "That is not it at all." He was a middle-aged man, thickening now and balding, but patient with our rudimentary questions. A pleasant person. He taught Arabic in the elementary school, he ran the boys' athletic club, and his responsibilities went beyond the confines of Rashadiya: he was the general secretary of the Palestinian Football Federation.

"There are still bits of bombs in the sand from 1978," he said. "They are shiny. They are round. The children pick them up because they look like balls. You know how children are. Then the bits explode. The children are blown up, at the same time. . . ."

I stared at Abu Zhivago. What was he talking about?

"I see you do not believe me, madame," he continued. "But it is true. There is a name for it in English, but I cannot say it. . . ."

Something stirred in the back of my mind, a news story somewhere, or a television report . . . cluster bombs; could he be talking about cluster bombs?

He smiled broadly. "Yes," he said, stroking back his thinning hair, a nervous gesture which must have been captivating when he was younger, slimmer, athletic, captain of the soccer team. "That is the word. Cluster bombs."

We found this hard to believe and said so, since cluster bombs had been declared illegal under international law. Abu Zhivago offered to take us to visit the neighbors whose child had been blown up last fall. No, we said hastily, we did not want to meet the bereaved parents. We believed him.

The largest school yard was cut in half by a row of bomb shelters. The corners of the streets, laid out in the grid pattern of the French barracks it had been a half century ago, were marked by bomb shelters. We looked at them curiously and asked to see the inside.

"You will see them soon enough," said Abu Zhivago, smiling his charming smile.

We smiled back, not believing a word. For some reason, they did not want us to visit the bomb shelters. Well, we would see about that tomorrow. But that night, dropping off to sleep, we heard the noise, first a long whining whistle, a sickening thud, finally a crackle as of fireworks exploding.

"B.J.," said Marilyn. "What's that?"

The sounds came again, whistle, thud, crackle, boom. A bomb? Surely not. Someone was banging on our bedroom door.

"Yalla!" cried Abu Zhivago. "To the shelter! Quickly!"

"B.J., hurry, for God's sake!" Marilyn had jumped into her jeans, but I struggled into clothes (how could I appear in the shelter with all those strange people in my worn-out old nightgown?). "Hurry!" cried Marilyn. Another whistle and a thud came, and the following explosion shook Um Zhivago and Abu Zhivago's house. Alia was crying. She was just two years old.

The lights were out in the camp. Someone shouted in Arabic to Abu Zhivago that the generator had been hit. In the shelter, crowded with people, candles had been lit. A row of people shifted closer together to make room for us on their blanket.

"So!" cried an old lady, white-haired, her head covered with a scarf, a sweater hastily buttoned over her dress. She peered at us out of very bright eyes. "These are your Americans, Um Zhivago?"

"I'm English," said Marilyn stiffly, but no one was listening.

"Yes, yes," said Um Zhivago, holding on her lap Alia, who was sniffling, from fright or cold one could not tell. "That's right."

"Aha!" cried the old lady. "Hear that!" as the thud and whistle came down, and the crack and explosion sounded close by.

I nodded. "Yes, I hear it."

"How can ye miss hearing it," breathed Marilyn. "I didn't live through the blitz, but—"

"There come your tax dollars, my dear," hooted the old lady. "You paid for those bombs to come across here. Now why did you do that? Do we look like terrorists? Do we look like we would hurt other people? All we want are our just rights. We want to go home to Palestine."

A child across the room burst into tears and was shushed by an adult. "Mama," the child cried. "She's coming," said the shusher.

A hiss, far distant, signaled another explosion. Wham! It came, and we were all silent. The line of people sharing their blanket on the concrete floor with us looked at me. They were expecting a reply. What could I say?

"Not all Americans agree about spending money that way for bombs to go to Israel," I began. "I don't think it's a good idea. I think it's a terrible idea," I said as the ground rocked with another explosion.

"Then why not speak up for us, dearie?" went on the old woman. "Isn't America a free country where everybody says what they think? Huh? Without going to jail, I mean, huh?" She laughed mirthlessly.

The child across the room continued to sob.

"Yes, yes, it is, I will, yes," I sputtered.

"Right on," murmured Marilyn.

"Here, have a bit more blanket," said the old lady, "give some to Um Zhivago, there, for Alia," and I passed along the extra inches of blanket as we paused, almost breathless, to listen to the chilling sounds above—hiss, thud, boom!

"Where is Daddy?" whispered Alia.

"Checking around," replied Um Zhivago.

"She'd be out there, too," put in another woman, younger, with a small baby in her arms. "Um Zhivago, I mean. But she's here because of you. She sends the kids down to us, and she goes around. Looking for wounded, seeing if the old have made it down here."

I looked at Um Zhivago and she nodded. She was as tall as I was, but younger. Short black hair fell down over her eyes, she pushed it back, a perennial gesture with her, I was to learn.

"That is because I am responsible," she said. She used the word in the sense of a noun, "one of the responsible ones," i.e., a member of the people's committee where leadership presupposed personal risk.

The candles flickered; from the one nearest us, green wax dripped onto the cement floor, and a child scraped the wax up, rasping on the cement with a small fingernail.

"Stop that," said a woman sharply. The child pulled away her finger. The green wax continued to drip onto the cement. The candle was burning down.

The crying child across the shelter had fallen asleep, lying curled up next to an older child—a sister? Alia was asleep in Um Zhivago's arms.

One of the guards in camouflage uniform with a shiny triggered machine gun clattered down the stairs. I realized there had been no sickening hisses, thuds, or explosions for some time.

"It's clear. You can go," he said to us.

And we all filed up the stairs and back to our beds. Above the darkened camp, the stars blazed bright in the night sky. We had no idea what time it was. Um Zhivago was whispering. "No one hurt tonight, thank God," she murmured.

By late morning, Um Zhivago had finished her washing, the children had gone to school. The kindergartens, which she supervised, were in full swing. She had been by to check. Now she said she had to visit an old lady who lived alone two streets over and then deliver a baby present. Would Marilyn and I like to come along? We had barely reached the end of the next street when the shelling began again. She pushed us into the nearest shelter and I steeled myself for another lecture on American responsibility for the attack. But none came. The women in the shelter were worried and confused. They were not interested in us.

"They never shell in the morning; what's going on, is it another invasion?"

"No, no," said Um Zhivago.

"But—"

"It's a fluke, it won't last," insisted Um Zhivago, and as if to prove her point, she stood up. "Let's go."

"Don't take your guests out in this," urged the women, staring at me. I found it reassuring to be seen for the moment as an individual, not to be held responsible for my government's policies. ("We don't hate you, Bob," an Iraqi friend had once said to my husband. "We just hate your government.")

Comforting thought, but not so comforting a prospect ahead. I found I was very reluctant indeed to follow Um Zhivago out of the relative security of the shelter into the clear day outside, with its unknown quota of shells lobbing toward us across the border. And Marilyn obviously felt the same, for she whispered, "What are we doing outside the shelter, B.J.?"

"There must have been a successful commando raid last night," said Um Zhivago conversationally, "so the Israelis are retaliating."

"So you are more or less at war," I said. "All the time. And both sides are responsible."

"Of course," said Um Zhivago. "We fight. They fight. It is the price of revolution."

Revolution, revolution. What did she mean by revolution? By now the sky was clear of the white puffs of smoke left from shells fired and returned. The sea came into view as we climbed the uneven rock path between the houses, avoiding the center drains where the waste water was channeled down the hill. Music blared out of an open window where a blue shutter banged, back and forth. Just like an ordinary morning in an ordinary village. But next to the blue-shuttered house another house lay in ruins. Weeds grew through the cracks in the floor. Had it been bombed? Shelled? My mind jumped again. I didn't want to be standing out here in the open, in such a vulnerable position.

"We have to go back home," Um Zhivago said to Marilyn and me. "Can you believe it? I forgot the baby present. What's the matter with me?" Um Zhivago laughed shortly.

"You have your mind on other things," I suggested, picking my way carefully down over the slippery stones where someone had tossed the wash water not too long ago, past the fallen roofs and the banging blue shutter.

"Do many people go to the shelter?" asked Marilyn.

"Many. But you get tired sitting in there all the time. I can't stand it. I send the children, though. The children are more important than anything."

"More important than the revolution?" I was being provocative and I knew it.

She stopped dead and stared at me. "The revolution is *for* the children," she said vehemently. "If we die, they will carry it on. It's a revolution of generations."

I recognized the slogan. I nodded. But Um Zhivago was not satisfied. "You don't take me seriously," she said.

"Yes, I do, I do," I said fervently. "How can you say that? This, this . . ." and I gestured helplessly at the vista before us, the schools with their smashed windows where children sat and did their arithmetic and spelling, the rows of barrackslike houses made into homes by the addition of courtyards, grapevines, blossoming bougainvillea. Geraniums planted in old tin cans decorated the porches where laundry dried in the sun, and in a distant garden plot someone in a bright blue kerchief was weeding. Yet the ugly snouts of the bomb shelters could not be hidden, and the sea, the beautiful, rippling, grape-blue sea had an empty beach where children could not play, because of the cluster bombs in the sand.

"Of course I take it seriously," I said.

"It's because we don't understand, Um Zhivago," Marilyn put in, "how you can go on and . . ."

"You *have* to go on," said Um Zhivago. "It's like life. You have to."

We stared at her.

"It's—it's—like cooking, really. Can you live without food? But before you start to cook, you see what you have in the cupboard and you try to make the best meal you can out of it, so you and your family survive. That's how you can go on."

"Maybe the Israelis feel the same," I ventured.

We were walking along the main street now, heading back to her house. The street was empty. Everyone must be in the shelters, I thought wildly; what are we doing out here when we could be wiped out at any moment by an American-made shell?

"You must be joking," said Um Zhivago. "The Israelis want to get rid of us. To them we are all terrorists, even little Alia." She laughed bitterly. "Who will speak up for us except ourselves?"

"In the film you can speak for yourself," I said.

"Yes," added Marilyn, "and many people will listen."

"You're not just saying that?"

"No, no." Marilyn and I glanced at each other.

Um Zhivago must have caught our look, for she said, "It's just that many people have come here, television people, film people, they say they will do something, then they go away and we never hear of them again. Are you like that?"

She stared us in the eye, first Marilyn and then me. We said that we were serious, we were going to make a film and show it. I hurried ahead slightly, not avoiding Um Zhivago's eyes, but because I desperately wanted to get under cover before the shells came out of the calm blue sky and hissed, thudded, and boomed down upon us again.

In the house, she found the gift she wanted, a boxed baby bonnet and sweater set—in washable blue acrylic, bordered with white stripes. But there was no wrapping paper, so we had lunch instead. Ground meat, cooked in a sauce of tahina and onions, flat bread, tomatoes. Abu Zhivago said, *"Tayyib."* (It's good.) The ultimate compliment.

When Lara came home from school, she was sent to borrow some paper, blue with a pattern of pink pandas, so the present could be wrapped properly and delivered to the new mother.

"Remember," said Um Zhivago, "the revolution is *for* the children. Each new child that is born will carry on when we are gone."

I nodded. But the slogans made me uncomfortable. As though they were canned, planned, automatically produced. Yet, Marilyn and I decided, there was no doubt in our minds of Um Zhivago's sincerity, her belief in the slogans, whether or not the phrases had a familiar clichéd ring to us.

She giggled. "You were scared this morning, weren't you?"

I nodded. "Yes, I was," I said.

Marilyn nodded too.

"Well, you don't get used to it," she said philosophically. "I'm scared all the time. . . ." She nodded her head, almost as though she were telling herself something. She pulled herself up, the good figure beginning to thicken like Abu Zhivago's, and pushed her black hair out of her eyes again.

"And that business about the Israelis," she said. "Do you really think they want peace? If you lived here for a while, you wouldn't believe that for one minute."

She looked at me and smiled. "But we have to excuse you, I guess," she said. "After all, they really brainwash you in America." She giggled again; it was an infectious giggle.

"And in Britain, too?" asked Marilyn lightly.

"Yes," said Um Zhivago. "In Britain, too."

Um Zhivago put her hand on my shoulder. "Stay here and rest a bit. You had a hard night," she said. "I have to go get Alia. *Then,* if no more shells have fallen, we'll visit the old lady and deliver the baby present. It's hard to keep a schedule on a day like this."

She banged out the door and was gone. We were left alone in her bedroom, with the family portrait on the wall, in a gilt frame, the shelf above the double bed lined with the knickknacks and mementos from family vacations: a Damascus mosaic cigarette box; a trophy from the Palestinian soccer federation, a prizewinning school drawing of Zhivago's. The music box on the dresser played "La Marseillaise." The double bed was wide and smooth, covered with a pastel print spread that harmonized with the light wood of the headboard. We sank down onto it. "Forty winks then," murmured Marilyn, and I was asleep before I realized what had happened to me. What *was* revolution?

I explained to Ali, to his sister Alia, who was secretary of the Women's Union, to Abu Zhivago, and to Um Zhivago that I wanted to make a film for schools and universities in America, about Palestinians as people, and about Palestinian women in particular. It wasn't to be a political film, or a film about the PLO or about the Palestinian revolution. It was to be about women and the family in a revolutionary situation.

"And all the crew will be women, too," I added. "If we come back, they will be with us."

"You mean the technicians?" said Ali.

"Yes," said Marilyn, "the camera, the sound, will be women."

"Good idea," said Abu Zhivago. "Good idea, why not?"

Um Zhivago invited us to stay in their house while we were filming, but Jamal suggested it was perhaps not possible, or maybe not even permitted, for us to come back and stay in Rashadiya for such a long time as two weeks, the time span I had requested in my letter to Majid Abu Sharrar.

"Not permitted?" Um Zhivago was indignant. "Who says it's not permitted? This is my house, I invited them. . . ."

Jamal tried to explain. "Well, you know, in Beirut . . . and because of the shelling . . . and permission . . ." He trailed off at the fire igniting in Um Zhivago's eyes.

"Don't tell us what is permitted," interposed Ali. "We are on the front line. She had permission from the Central Committee. That is enough for me. If Um Zhivago and Abu Zhivago invite them to stay, they stay. As responsible persons, we also have something to say about who comes and who goes; we too have our place, we don't let Beirut dictate our actions. . . ."

I looked at him in surprise. Gone were the rhetoric, the consensus slogans. Jamal must have sensed that urgency, too, for he looked flustered. "Yes, yes, of course, I understand, Ali. I'm sure it will all work out."

"For the good of the revolution," snapped Abu Zhivago.

"For the good of the revolution," repeated Jamal hastily.

"Good! Now let's have some coffee," said Abu Zhivago. "My wife makes the best coffee in Rashadiya."

Um Zhivago smiled and rose. She was very pleased. "We will paint the room for them," she said proudly. "It's needed it for a long time," and she looked pointedly at her husband, who looked away and then offered us all cigarettes.

"You know," she said to me, "I think it's a good idea to make a film about women for a change. Where would they be without us? Where would *anybody* be? They wouldn't be here, that's where they'd be. No people, no kids, no food, no laundry, and . . . no revolution." She laughed.

I told her I liked that slogan, and I thought women everywhere would go along with it.

"Even in brainwashed America?" She laughed.

"Even in America," I repeated firmly. "And in Britain, too, right, Marilyn?"

"Right."

When we got back to Beirut from Rashadiya, we discovered that the shelling we had experienced had not been limited to the South. Long-range shells had done so much damage to the runways that the Beirut airport was closed again.

"The airport's closed?" Marilyn couldn't believe it. "When will it open?"

No one could say.

"We're due in Cairo tomorrow, B.J."

"True."

"Let's go overland somewhere and get a plane there."

"The only way is through Syria and that's impossible. We can't get visas."

"What do you mean, luv? We'll just go to the Syrian Embassy and get them."

"No Syrian Embassy in Beirut."

"So what do we do?"

Nothing to do but wait. People were paying enormous prices to take private boats to Cyprus. We could not afford it. But our friend Jim was going up to his fiancée's family's house in the mountains for the Orthodox Easter vacation; we were welcome to his apartment at AUB, he said. We said thank you, and moved in. Marilyn came down with bronchitis. We waited.

Every day I went to the travel agency, full of hope, and every day I came back again. Middle East Airlines closed their offices. British Airways allowed that the airport might open in about three weeks.

"Three weeks?" Marilyn started up from her sickbed. "The crew's coming out in three weeks. We haven't confirmed the Cairo locations. The budget . . ."

I knew about the budget, too. Marilyn and I had made up the budget together. We stayed indoors, because there were new incidents every day. The telephone rang.

"The airport's open," guessed Marilyn, half asleep.

"B.J.?" The soft voice on the other end of the line was not that of the travel agent.

"Mona!"

"I thought you left a week ago."

"We couldn't. The airport is closed."

"Oh yes . . ." Her voice trailed off. "B.J., Abdul Latif died the day before yesterday, if I had known you were here, I would have told you, but—"

"Mona! Oh, Mona, I am so sorry."

"It was very peaceful. We were with him, Hassan, Amr, and I. Mama had gone back to Damascus. The funeral was yesterday."

"I will come," I promised.

"No, you mustn't. It is dangerous, B.J."

"I will come."

Marilyn and I set off in a taxi on our way once more to the Green Line. The desolate scar across the city that was not at all green.

"The line has moved up," said the taxi driver, almost to himself, and as we drew up to the familiar apartment house I saw that he was right. Two men in short-sleeved khaki shirts rose from the doorway and adjusted their weapons. The line had moved up—right to the entrance of Mona's house.

"Where are you going, please, madame?" the taller armed man asked politely.

"To Dr. al-Shafei's house here, for the condolences," I replied.

The soldier nodded. "The poet? Whose husband died two days ago?" He had not shaved that morning, and though he was very young, his eyes were red with fatigue and rheumy like those of an elderly man.

"Yes. She is my friend."

Marilyn and I stood there, waiting for the soldiers to do or say something (shoot us? order us away?). The taxi driver, a middle-aged man in a thick gray sweater despite the warm April sun, got out of the cab and shut the door of his car.

"Would you like me to wait for you, madame?" he said conversationally, without looking at the soldiers.

I was surprised at his concern, for to persuade him to take us, I had had to argue with him, explain about Abdul Latif's fatal stroke, tell him about my long-standing friendship with Mona. In Muslim society, visiting the bereaved after death is as much of a duty as it is in Christian society, maybe more. The driver had apparently decided I was sincere, for he had shrugged his shoulders and opened the door for us. As we left, he had hollered in Arabic to the driver behind him in the taxi stand beside the British Embassy, "If we don't die today, Youssef, we die tomorrow, hey?" and laughed uproariously.

Did I want the taxi driver to wait for us? The silence grew between the driver, the two young soldiers, and us.

"No, thank you," I said finally to the driver. "I don't know how long we'll be here." It was true.

"But—"

One of the soldiers looked at the driver, shifted his weapon from one shoulder to another. "If they're such good friends," he said, "won't the poet find a way to send them back?"

Strange, I thought, that these completely unknown men were trying to look after us. Why? They had no reason to care about our well-being, one way or the other, two Western ladies, one young, one middle-aged, wandering foolishly near the battle line in the civil war that still existed in supposedly peaceful Beirut. Perhaps they all admired Mona's poetry, I thought. Everyone read the respected newspaper *Nahar* each morning in Beirut, and Mona's poems appeared once a week. Everyone in the Arab world admired poetry, read it, and often wrote it as well. The only person with a publicly accepted right to interrupt a head of state on a ritual occasion was a poet. So perhaps friends of a poet, like us, had allowances made for them. Or perhaps the Christian soldiers and the Muslim taxi driver were outdoing each other in a display of chivalry.

The second soldier, who had been silent all this time, waved his gun in a somewhat flamboyant manner, an indication, apparently, that we could pass by him into the lobby, press the button to the elevator, and go up to the apartment where friends and relatives were extending condolences on the death of the head of the al-Shafei family in Beirut—Abdul Latif, physicist, longtime dean of AUC, but known to these young soldiers as a poet's husband.

I paid the taxi driver and thanked him.

"My God, B.J.," murmured Marilyn as we entered the lobby under the watchful eyes of the two young soldiers, "are you sure this is okay?"

"We're here. Let's go in."

The door to the apartment was open. We heard the Koranic chanting, clear and high, the ancient Koranic verses recited slowly, reassuring the listeners that all was being done that could humanly be done to mark the death of Abdul Latif, the end of his life on earth and the beginning of his life in another, better world.

Marilyn and I hovered on the edge of the room. When the session of chanting ended, a tall robed servant brought in a tray of coffee, bitter and strong, in tiny lusterware demitasse cups. Some men and women in dark suits and black dresses moved in to shake hands with Mona and with Hassan and Amr, who rose from their seats on the crimson velvet sofa. We took places in the salon.

"Al-lah—ah . . ." The chanter was a young man, wearing a dark suit like everyone else in the room, distinguished from the other mourners by the thick Koran he held in one hand.

He cocked his head slightly to one side, covered an ear with his hand, and closed his eyes. "Al-lah-ah . . ." The rich voice dwelt on the phrases, stretching or shortening the syllables of the sacred verses in the style he had been taught by older chanters whose holy art, dedicated to the evocation of the presence of God in the hearts and minds of men, stretched back hundreds of years.

Marilyn and I listened to the prayers that were being recited in many other Lebanese homes that day for men, women, and children struck down in the streets and in their houses by stray bullets, by shrapnel from antiaircraft defense, by unexpected explosions in the anarchy of an unfinished civil war. A kind of dignity; human beings could still think, feel, honor the dead, despite the chaos about them.

Mona had her eyes fixed on the chanter. Amr and Hassan looked down at their dark-suited knees, but the older man sitting next to them (introduced as Abdul Latif's older brother) focused on the ceiling, occasionally pulling on his yellowing white mustache.

"Al—" The rest of that phrase was drowned out by a volley of shots, the boom of a distant shell. Another boom answered. The French windows in the salon and in the dining room rattled and shook, and an unseasonal breeze rushed through the open windows, filling the room with a strange heady scent.

Without a word, Amr, Hassan, and their uncle moved to close the windows, draw the glass curtains, and pull the heavy golden drapes. The sounds of the fighting receded, muffled until another boom sounded very near. Again Hassan stood up. His brother Amr joined him and the two strong young men moved the heavy mahogany table against the windows, the one from which we had dined so lavishly only three months before.

"A—meen." The chanter brought the sura to its predetermined end, and many of the people rose quickly, pressed Mona's hand, and left. The afternoon shelling had begun, and people obviously wanted to get home before the incident became worse.

We stood in line to shake hands and offer our sympathies. When my turn came I put my arms around Mona. "You must stay to lunch, B.J.," she said. "You and Marilyn."

"No, thank you."

"Yes, do. Amr will drive you home."

"No, no, Mona. We will get a taxi."

"I am going toward West Beirut," one of the guests offered. "May I take you?"

"Thank you."

"Don't go," cried Mona.

"We'll be back. I'll call you. I don't want to trouble Amr. The shelling is getting worse. He would only have to drive back again."

"Yes, you are right. I will call you." And we embraced once more. Marilyn and I shook hands with the uncle, with Amr and Hassan. The two young guards by the front door had moved inside, out of the sun. One was asleep, propped against a pillar near the elevator.

Three days later the airport was still closed. At Mona's suggestion we set a new plan in motion, the only possible recourse open to us. We took a taxi to Damascus and were stopped at the border. No Syrian visas. No passage across. We activated the next step in the plan, which involved giving the driver fifty dollars in cash and our visa applications and asking him to please drive into Damascus, pick up our visas, and come back. "What if he just runs off with the fifty dollars?" Marilyn asked. "Then come back to Beirut," Amr had said. "You won't have lost much. And you'll probably get through."

The plan worked. Six hours after we halted at the Syrian border, the driver returned with our visas. We paid another fifty dollars to go on into Damascus, over the barren hills and into a sprawling, thriving, crowded metropolis that did not seem as if it could possibly be the same city we had seen rising from the plain on our way to Baghdad twenty-five years ago. The streets were unfamiliar, jammed with cars, with people. We were speeding to get to the airport, for if we missed the plane to Cairo we would have to stay in Damascus until the next flight was scheduled—at least three days. In my heart of hearts, I half wished we would miss the plane so I could settle in, walk slowly down the ancient street called Straight, where we had bought brocade in 1956, have tea with Mme. Aida, visit the great Omayyad Mosque. But I knew we had to get on: we were way behind schedule already and the film crew was due to arrive in Cairo, with thousands of dollars of rented equipment, in two short weeks.

We made the Cairo plane with five minutes to spare. The aircraft rose high and fast over the city, and I looked down, hoping to see the old outlines of Damascus or at least one familiar landmark. But the edges of the city were blurred, frayed by new houses, new factories. It was obviously not the same Damascus I had visited with Mona, nor with Bob even earlier.

"Ladies and gentlemen," said the stewardess in a clipped British accent, "we shall be in Cairo in one hour and forty minutes. It is our pleasure now to serve you supper."

"I never," said Marilyn. "The stewardess is a Brit. You know, B.J., I never thought I'd think of Cairo as home, but today that's what I feel like. I can hardly wait to get there."

"Me, too." I wondered whether Bob had gotten my telexes. He had not replied. But in the days of closed airports and scrambled communications, one did not expect replies. One only hoped messages arrived.

"We can perhaps just manage the confirmations before the crew comes," went on Marilyn, "but it'll be tight, B.J."

"Yes."

"You're thinking about Mona."

"Well, yes."

"We'll be back in Beirut, you know, luv, in six weeks if we're lucky, to do the Palestinian bit. We can visit her then."

We landed in Cairo and took a taxi home. Bob had received no word from me at all. He said he hadn't been *too* worried.

Marilyn, with a glance at me, said, "You should have been more worried than that, Bob. It wasn't a fair, my friend. And then B.J. here, at the height of the bombing, had to get *dressed* before going to the bomb shelter."

And she launched into a grimly humorous but slightly exaggerated account of my struggle to get my nightgown off and my dress on before the next bomb fell.

Bob said modesty always was one of my weaknesses—and we went off to dinner and the slow unwinding of tensions we had brought back with us from revolutionary Rashadiya and from besieged Beirut.

CHAPTER VII
Rashadíya
JUNE 1981

Teach the night to forget to bring
Dreams showing me my village
And teach the wind to forget to carry to me
The aroma of apricots in my fields!
And teach the sky, too, to forget to rain.
Only then, I may forget my country.

Rashid Hussein
Tent 50 (Song of a Refugee)

THE CAIRO FILMING was finishing up. The crew and I were due to return to Beirut in early June to begin the Palestinian segment of the film. A week was scheduled for preliminary errands and for reconfirmation of permissions with the PLO Central Committee. Two weeks had been set aside for shooting and three or four days in Beirut at the end to organize for the return home, to mark the film cans, the tapes, finish the work sheets, and pack everything for the film editor in London.

But in Cairo the news from Lebanon was worrying. The country, supposedly under a cease-fire, was hardly at peace. A British television crew had been taken captive in the Bekaa Valley. The airport closed, opened, closed again. Scattered "incidents" were reported in Beirut, the American University hospital emergency room was the scene of a bloody confrontation between militias of different factions, and long lists of casualties appeared in the French as well as the Arabic newspapers.

"Perhaps we better not go at all," suggested Marilyn.

"Have you been able to insure the equipment?" Diana Ruston, the sound recorder, asked. I had just discovered that our expensive London insurance did not cover war zones. And Lebanon was defined as a war zone.

I shook my head. Lena Jayyusi, our assistant, looked upset. "But I thought it was all arranged," she said.

"It was. It *is*," Marilyn corrected herself. "But the situation changes every day. Who knows what we'll find now?"

"I think we have to go and at least *try*, B.J.," said the camerawoman, Diane Tammes. "If we can't do it, we can't. We'll come back. But otherwise, Marilyn, you know what people will say in London—"

"That women crews are chicken," said Diana.

"I vote to go," said Lena. And we agreed.

So we set off for Beirut, the five of us, somewhat nervous and uneasy, but determined to make the attempt. I felt that we also owed it to Um Zhivago, who had stood up for us so stoutly when the PLO representative had tried to curtail our plans. Bob had offered to come with us as far as Beirut, in case, he said, there was "trouble." We accepted his offer with alacrity, and none of us tried to define what kind of trouble might await our arrival. We were not sure, for example, whether we would be allowed to bring the film equipment into the chaotic city without previous arrangements with a designated bureaucrat. But we touched down in the airport on a bright, clear summer day. It was June 11. By that time, there was little central governmental machinery of any sort left in Lebanon. In the nearly empty reception room, several eager independent customs brokers came forward to solicit our business.

"Not bad so far," Bob said cryptically as we headed into the city by still another circuitous route.

"Got to change the way practically every day now," said the taxi driver.

The Mayflower Hotel had not gotten our telex requesting reservations, but they made room for us. The city was nearly empty, it appeared. Everyone who could afford it had departed for an early vacation, in order to avoid the troubles that had been predicted. The middle-aged manager of the Mayflower stored our equipment in a downstairs room "at no extra charge, madame," he said with a slightly twisted smile. The equipment was heavy. "But, please, I warn you, ladies, do not go out after dark, it is not *advised*." He laid heavy emphasis on the last word, looking straight at us, Diane with her camera balanced on a thin shoulder, Lena carrying bags of various sizes, Diana with her Nagra tape recorder, Marilyn and I hung about with valises, shoulder bags, briefcases full of papers. "Not advised," he repeated.

The security officer at the American Embassy telephoned and advised me not to go south. "We have no idea what the Israelis or the Syrians are planning, Mrs. Fernea."

"I understand."

"We cannot be responsible for your safety, ma'am."

"I understand that," I repeated.

A number of people in Beirut, including Lebanese, Americans, and Palestinians, advised us not to go south. This was not exactly calming but then, as Marilyn pointed out, our last stay in Rashadiya had not exactly been calming either. We decided to make a preliminary run south to see if we were still welcome in the camp. If the situation there looked relatively stable, we would then take the crew and equipment down and give it our best effort until whatever trouble had been predicted burst out and forced us to depart.

Yes, the taxi driver near the Mayflower would take us to Rashadiya—for a rather high price. But then, why else would he want to take the risk? Marilyn and I made another ritual trip to PLO headquarters to obtain permission to go south, were assigned an escort, and set out once more along the sea.

Um Zhivago welcomed us with open arms. "I knew you'd come back," she cried. "And look! We painted the room blue! You can all stay there together."

Two days later we prepared to go down as a group, five of us in two taxis, with thousands of dollars' worth of film equipment packed into the trunks. Uninsured. What would I do if the equipment was blown up by an American shell?

"Spend the rest of your life paying for it, I guess," said Bob.

"We'll help, B.J.!" promised Diane, Diana, and Lena. "Yes," said Marilyn. "What we need, I think, is a bit of luck. Now let's go!"

"And I shall go back to Cairo," Bob announced. "Obviously, I'd love to go down to Rashadiya with you all, but that's not really fair. It's your show, not mine. And it sounds as though you'll be okay."

"Inshallah." The ritual phrase, "God willing," sprang to my lips unexpectedly. We put our arms around each other and parted, each heading for a different destination.

I told myself sternly that of course we would be all right. But on the way south there was a moment, a moment when we stopped once more near the commandant's military headquarters to get the final papers which would allow the crew to remain in the camp. Jamal—for it was Jamal, our first escort to Rashadiya, who had been assigned to us for the entire period—had gone inside the offices. We eased ourselves out of the taxis after the wearying ride. We stood together in the sun beside a mud-brick wall, which was covered with crimson bougainvillea but guarded by two burly young men armed with machine guns. And a child came running down the street toward us, a small dark child in shorts and a sleeveless T-shirt. He stopped when he saw us, five alien ladies loaded down with bags and bundles and cameras flanked by soldiers. He said, "What are you doing here?"

Jamal must have had his doubts too, must have sensed our anxiety. After we had taken off again in the cab and passed down the leafy lane that looked like the driveway to a country house but was in fact the armed and guarded camp entrance, and emerged on the road leading to Um Zhivago's house, he said, in Arabic, "Don't count on staying the whole time, B.J."

"Why not? We need the two weeks to do what we want to do. I have permission, Jamal. You know that."

"Yes, B.J. But . . ." He paused. "There might be a strike at any moment and then I would have to take you out, for your own safety. I promised them in Beirut I would."

I did not share these possibilities with the crew. They had enough to worry about. For filming in Rashadiya was not easy, despite our permissions, despite Um Zhivago's support. We spent a lot of time waiting—and discussing. Waiting for each proposed sequence to be approved by the authorities. It seemed to take forever.

"But we're in a war zone, B.J.," Jamal kept pointing out. "You don't want to put people in danger by filming things that shouldn't be filmed, do you?"

What things? I wondered, but no one answered my question.

Why were we filming only women and families? I explained. Um Zhivago explained.

Why didn't we interview more men? We explained. Jamal explained. Um Zhivago explained.

Earning trust in the camp was a slow and difficult process.

"People are tired of helping the media," Jamal said. "It doesn't do any good. No one listens."

Yet slowly the shooting proceeded. And Jamal, I felt, began to take us seriously. In the beginning, it seemed, he felt we would not stay long; he had brought only one shirt. But after three days of dawn-to-dark work, he apparently decided we were in earnest and would stay the course, despite the dangers and risks involved, for he went into Soor and bought himself two more shirts.

Um Zhivago insisted on cooking for us—meat with tahina and tomatoes, stuffed grape leaves, rice with noodles and meat. We ate with the family; Abu Zhivago and the children sat closer together so we would all fit around the table. I began to feel we were an undue burden on the budget, but Um Zhivago brushed aside my offers of help. "You are our guests," she said.

"But Arab hospitality is only a duty for three days in the desert," I pointed out.

"This is not the desert," she answered, smiling. "This is the *revolution*. And it's taking a lot longer than three days."

"But—"

"What's the matter, B.J.? You don't like my cooking?"

"Um Zhivago, we *love* your cooking," said Marilyn.

She laughed at me. "*You* may, but B.J. doesn't. We'll have to let her cook and see if she can do better."

So I made spaghetti sauce. The family ate it politely, though not enthusiastically. The next day I insisted on taking everyone to lunch in Soor, since we had to pass near the city to scout out the soccer game we hoped to film. But when I asked for the bill, the waiter announced that Colonel Azmi had paid—Azmi, the commandant of South Lebanon, "the brave man," "the hero." Where had he been? Eating in the back room, out of sight, with his retainers.

"I'd like to meet him," I said, "and thank him for his help."

"Have a party on the last day," said Um Zhivago, "and invite him."

"Good idea. We'll invite everyone who has helped us, and maybe Azmi too."

"And you can cook American food for us all," she suggested.

"Um Zhivago, how can I cook for fifty people when I'm supposed to be filming?"

"You don't want to have a party?"

"Yes, I *want* a party. But let's order roast chickens from Soor. We can afford it. Really."

Um Zhivago smiled. She was delighted. Abu Zhivago was delighted. I was pleased that we could repay in some way the hospitality that had been offered to us.

We filmed by day, we translated tapes by night, we sank onto our narrow beds "like kippers in a tin," as Marilyn said, and snored in Um Zhivago's fresh-painted, if somewhat small, blue room. The days passed, and no bombs fell. The film went into the cans, the tapes into boxes. Um Zhivago suggested a menu for our proposed farewell party. We invited guests. Abu Zhivago suggested the boys' club as a site, "because the table is big enough for everyone to sit down." We would have half a roast chicken per person, bread, salads, and of course fruit. Whipped garlic sauce to go with the chicken. We would make the salad at Um Zhivago's house and carry it down to the boys' club in great basins which she could borrow from neighbors and friends.

"Will that be enough food?" I asked.

"Oh yes," said Um Zhivago. "It will be a real feast."

"Could we have music?" asked Marilyn.

"Of course," said Abu Zhivago, "I will arrange it. And you must invite the doctors, too, B.J."

"Yes," I answered. "Thank you, Abu Zhivago." The clinic, like all the clinics in the refugee camps, was staffed by volunteers from Solidarity, the European labor movement. Rashadiya at the moment was served by a Dutch woman doctor and two Swedish nurses.

"It will be a good party even if Azmi doesn't come," confided Um Zhivago.

"Why won't he?" I asked naïvely.

"B.J." Um Zhivago sounded exasperated. "By this time I thought you might realize. Azmi is a military *officer,* the commander of all South Lebanon. They're saying to expect a strike anytime, so don't you think he might be needed else-where if there's trouble? You know. Revolution. Remember?"

"Yes, of course. How silly of me," I answered. Yet even after all the time we had spent in Rashadiya, the meetings with people who had lost sons and daughters and land, who had had their houses damaged by shelling, we still found it difficult to reconcile these described events with the events of everyday life which we had been filming: cooking, cleaning, school lessons, a mothers' meeting to decide about a summer daycare program, a workshop to teach sewing to the girls, the play-off in a soccer competition.

"But don't you see?" Um Zhivago would say to me patiently. "Revolution is our life, every day it is our life, along with the cooking and the children. Revolution is the thing that moves us, that keeps us going."

"Yes," I answered, and tried to think how I could explain what we were feeling. "It's hard," I began. "It's hard for us to see the connections you do, Um Zhivago. We have nothing like this in America or in Britain."

"You are lucky then," Um Zhivago answered shortly. She was stirring rice on the two-burner kerosene stove and I could not see her face. "Although many things may come from the revolution."

"What?" asked Marilyn.

"Many good things."

"For women?" I asked.

"For everyone," she answered. "Now call the girls. We need some tomatoes before I can finish this dish. . . . And, Marilyn, I hope you and B.J. show us well in this film of yours."

"We will do our best, Um Zhivago."

She shook her cooking spoon at me and laughed. "You'd better. If it is good, maybe it will speak up loud for us in many places. It's about time somebody listened to women." She stirred. "If they did, wouldn't that be a revolution?" She turned to her oldest daughter. "Lara," she said, "I want a kilo of tomatoes and some cumin. Hurry! Your father wants to eat early."

The crew was down near the beach, redoing some final cutaway shots. I had left them beside the sea, the waves pounding in, dark blue in the late afternoon light, onto the ominously empty shore. We had been lucky. No bombs had fallen. Whatever strike was planned had not yet arrived. We were nearly finished. We would leave in the morning. But the people of Rashadiya were not finished. They were staying. They would be there when the bombs came. I walked up toward Um Zhivago's house, to help her peel cucumbers and tomatoes for the salad. The houses that lined both sides of the street looked almost inviting in this light, the harshness of the plastered cement blocks softened, the bomb scars in shadow. This was our farewell party. The meal was to be served just after sunset.

Abu Zhivago had gone to Soor to pick up the chickens and garlic sauce we had ordered two days before. Um Zhivago had produced from somewhere an enormous white cloth and we covered the table in the boys' club and set the places. She and I, with her daughters Shama and Lara helping, and the baby, two-year-old Alia, shouting "Eat! Eat!"

"We'll have Ali here," mused Um Zhivago, seating people, "and his sister and then Hassan, who sings, over there, and Abu Zhivago next to him. Azmi will be at one end and you at the other."

For Azmi was really coming, it seemed. A car drove up outside. Was the commandant of South Lebanon arriving early? No, it was not Azmi yet. It was Abu Zhivago and his two sons Rami and Zhivago, bringing in the big fragrant boxes of spiced chicken roasted on a spit. Paper plates were laid down, the basins of salad placed strategically within reach. The fruit was arranged down the center of the table, pyramids of grapes, melons, peaches. Halves of flat fresh bread marked every place and small bowls of tahina were near enough for dipping; to drink, there was fruit juice, a new mix of pineapple and orange in plastic cartons, one to a person, with straws included. The chickens smelled marvelous, and a whiff of the pungent garlic sauce filled the room.

"Napkins!" shouted Um Zhivago. "Where are the napkins? They can't eat the chicken without napkins."

Zhivago produced them, two boxes of white paper napkins with flowered borders.

"Now we are all ready, Beeja," breathed Um Zhivago.

"Looks good," said Abu Zhivago.

"Is it enough, do you think?" I ventured nervously.

"More than enough, it is fine," returned Abu Zhivago. He pursed his lips briefly and stared at the festal board—chickens, bread, fruit, juice, vegetables, tahina, salad, garlic sauce; was something missing?

Another car roared up.

"It's him," shouted Zhivago, then lowered his voice when he saw his mother's face.

"You must go to the door and meet him," fluttered Um Zhivago. "You probably should have worn your blue dress, Beeja, but I guess that thing is okay." She gave grudging approval to my brown Liberty print.

"You come too," I urged.

"No, no." She shrank back. "I'll talk to him later."

"You will, will you?" from Abu Zhivago, but his perennial worried look had been replaced by a smile.

"Yes, I will. He never gave me the money for the old lady who lost her son last winter in the raid. But I'll get it from him tonight. It is his duty as a revolutionary to support that poor old thing."

"Yes, yes, now go on out," said Abu Zhivago. In his nervousness, he almost but not quite pushed me out of the room to the door, where a procession of men in freshly pressed army uniforms was heading toward us. Let them not have machine guns, please, I said to myself; then I saw that they wore pistols at their hips, like Texas Rangers.

"Azmi!" said a short dark-haired man. I looked past him to a great towering figure, next in line. Was that Azmi?

The short man laughed.

"The short one's Azmi," hissed Um Zhivago. "Him." And poked me in the back.

I shook hands with the short man. "Beeja," I said, and the reception line was shaking hands, Azmi, Marilyn, Diana, Lena, Diane. We all filed into the banquet hall and sat down.

Azmi sat at the head, surrounded by his bodyguards and retainers. We were at the other end, surrounded by the women and the members of their families we had filmed. But not everyone had come and Um Zhivago looked annoyed. The place next to Ali was empty. Where was his sister? "Yes, where?" hissed Um Zhivago, her eyes angry.

Jamal was in the middle. The musicians were on one side, the Solidarity doctors on the other.

After a clatter of chairs and a preliminary rush of conversation, the room fell silent. Everyone was eating. Azmi was the first to finish. He wiped his fingers on the flower-bordered paper napkin and stood up.

He began to speak. In classical Arabic. He made a speech about the revolution, and about us. Jamal signaled to me. "You must reply," he said.

"Get up, Beeja," whispered my good friend and mentor Um Zhivago.

"On your feet," prompted Marilyn. "Come on, luv!"

I stood up. Everyone looked politely in my direction. I swallowed hard, smoothed down my Liberty print, and spoke haltingly in Arabic. I thanked Azmi for his help, I thanked Abu Zhivago and Um Zhivago for their hospitality, I thanked the people of Rashadiya for putting up with us. I knew, I said, that many other filmmakers had come to Rashadiya, but I hoped that our film would help Americans and Britons understand what life was like for the people in Rashadiya.

I paused.

"Don't forget the revolution!" It was a loud whisper from Um Zhivago. But I could not do it, even for her.

"And Um Zhivago reminds me about the revolution," I said, and sat down. I was afraid to look at Um Zhivago, fearing her displeasure at my refusal to go along with the slogan, but she only smiled.

Everyone applauded.

Thank God, I thought.

But now Azmi was on his feet again.

Another speech emerged, words of appreciation, thanks, understanding.

He sat down. There was more applause.

There was a pause. What do I do now? I thought. Jamal caught my eye, gestured for me to stand up again.

"This time in English," I said, "and you translate."

Jamal stood up and looked pleased.

I repeated myself, but in more flowery phrases, and Jamal did a good job of elaborating those phrases, for people smiled with satisfaction, and even Azmi nodded his head.

I sat down. Jamal sat down. But Azmi got up again. What, I thought wildly, is there left to say? I've said it all, all I believe in, I cannot, I will not just reel off slogans, not even to be polite.

But Azmi merely was thanking us for the meal and toasting the crew: Marilyn, Diane, Diana, Lena. "Now music," he ordered, clapping his hands.

A drum was produced, and a pipe. A pitch was struck. In a moment the room was filled with song. People nibbled at the grapes left on the festal board. Azmi sat back and lit a cigarette.

Everyone was singing, and we joined in the clapping. I looked down the table at Azmi, short, stocky, yes, magnetic. A sense of strength and authority emanated from him, all down that long table. A warlord relaxing, surrounded by his guards, his retainers, his musicians, the doctors. Who were we? What were we in this medieval banquet? Artisans, I thought later. Instead of a banquet table or an ode, we have produced a film. The people of Rashadiya were singing about their lost homeland, their lost loves, their lost comrades. People composed new stanzas and the refrain went on. "My country, my homeland." The revolution. We sat there, five foreign ladies being entertained by the warlord and his people who were engaged in a revolution. But a revolution for what and against what?

Jamal had said, "Against capitalism." "Against the enemy," said Um Zhivago, "and for our children." For return. For the future. But realistically what could the future possibly hold for the displaced, disenfranchised, and now regalvanized people of Rashadiya? How could the border battles achieve anything but more violence? A new strike was supposedly on its way. There would then be retaliation. Such actions were scarcely conducive to peace, a peace where little Alia could sleep in her bed without being hauled out to the bomb shelter in the middle of the night. Where Zhivago, Rami, Lara, and Shama could go to school without fearing bombs, and Um Zhivago could cook up new dishes for her family. They were singing, I decided, to enunciate hope amid hopelessness. What was the revolution, then? A purpose? Meaning in an otherwise chaotic and torn world? What else could it be?

Azmi stood up. Chairs clattered backward all down the table as the retainers, the bodyguards, the musicians, the doctors, the citizens, and the film crew did likewise. The warlord was finished. The feast and the speechifying and the entertainment were over. Time to get back to business—the fighting part of revolution.

"Come, come quickly." Um Zhivago jerked me along by the hand to where Azmi's yellow car was waiting outside, its motor racing.

"What's happening?" I cried.

She rushed ahead, dragging me behind her as hostage. Azmi stood by the running board and waited for us.

"You forgot the old lady," cried Um Zhivago. "You never gave the money for that poor old thing, whose son gave his life for you."

Azmi reached in his pocket and pulled out some paper notes. "Not for me, Um Zhivago, for the revolution."

He nodded at me, climbed into the car, and was gone.

"He is a brave man," said Um Zhivago, "but, like all men, he needs to be reminded of his duty once in a while."

We walked back to the boys' club, where the crew and many of our friends were sitting outside on the benches surrounding the tiny fountain. Coffee had been served.

"Good party," said Um Zhivago. "It went well." She laughed with pleasure. "And the boys will clean up. So they can eat the leftover fruit. The only thing that makes me mad—"

"Yes, Um Zhivago. What makes you mad?"

"Ali wouldn't let his sister come. He may say he's a revolutionary, but he's only half a one. What do you say in English, he's a—a sho—sho—"

"A chauvinist, a male chauvinist."

"Yes, that is the word."

"You're right, Um Zhivago, he is," agreed Marilyn.

The filming was over. We would be gone from Rashadiya in the morning.

We had three days in Beirut before flying out, Diana, Diane, and Marilyn for London, Lena for America; I was bound for Cairo to meet Bob. Um Zhivago and Abu Zhivago had come to Beirut with Alia, their youngest child, to say goodbye. The crew shopped for presents to take back for family and friends; the selection was small, but the souvenir shops were opening again. Down by the ruins of the old St. George Hotel along the sea, two new and lavish establishments had recently opened in the midst of the rubble, offering Lebanese textiles, caftans, glass, antiquities, rugs, Damascus tablecloths, brought somehow across the embattled Syrian border.

Jamal appeared at the Mayflower Hotel to announce with a flourish that we had been invited to tea by Abu Amr.

"Abu Amr?"

"Our leader," said Jamal, a bit huffily, I thought. "Yasir Arafat. That is what we call him, the 'father of our struggle.'"

I looked at the crew. "Do we accept?"

"It is a great honor," continued Jamal.

We said thank you, we would be happy to accept. "And Um Zhivago can come, too," I said.

Abu Zhivago agreed that she and Alia could stay the night with us and return to Rashadiya after the historic meeting. We were all delighted! Diana, Diane, Marilyn, Lena, and I were to await a car, said Jamal. It might be a private car and it might be a taxi, he wasn't sure what would be available, but he would be in the car. We were not, he repeated, *not,* to get into any other car that came and said it had been sent to take us to Abu Amr.

We exchanged glances.

"When shall we expect you?" Marilyn asked, excitedly.

"Probably this evening after dinner." Jamal smiled.

But when Jamal returned, his face was glum. The meeting, he said, had been postponed.

"Well, never mind, Jamal," I said. "It would have been interesting to meet Yasir Arafat, but we realize he has other things to worry about."

"No, no," interrupted Jamal. "He wants you to come. It's to be tomorrow night."

"But—" began Diane, and looked quickly at Um Zhivago. "By that time, Um Zhivago will have gone home."

Jamal nodded and looked down. So that's it, I thought. The command doesn't want her to meet Abu Amr, for some reason. Not too much exposure for women perhaps? Well, I thought righteously, then we won't honor him with our presence either. After a hurried conference, the crew agreed unanimously.

"What hypocrisy!" cried Marilyn indignantly. "All that talk about women's liberation through the revolution, and then not wanting a woman who is actually *working* to get any public appreciation."

"Why shouldn't she come?" asked Lena. "What's wrong, Jamal?"

"Are they afraid of her?" asked Diana.

Jamal looked uncomfortable. "No, no, it is just policy. It—" He faltered before the six pairs of eyes focused on him, the beginning of a sob from little Alia. "It is not considered . . . appropriate . . . I guess." He added, "I don't make the policy, B.J."

Um Zhivago wiped away tears and explained that she had expected this all along. "I knew it was too good to be true," she said. "They don't want women to be in on important things."

"Well, we're not going," I said stoutly. "Maybe Abu Amr will get the message."

Um Zhivago looked at me. "Get what message?" she brought out sharply. "That you're afraid to go out in Beirut at night, with all the bombing? That's what they'll tell him. Don't be silly, B.J. Go! Go and tell him about what women are doing in Rashadiya to help the revolution."

Jamal said nothing, but he looked very hard at me.

"Perhaps we should, B.J.," said Diane.

"We could tell him about your work in the camp, Um Zhivago," said Marilyn.

"Splendid idea," said Diana.

"Yes, yes," added Lena.

Um Zhivago blew her nose. "Yes," she said firmly. "Tell Abu Amr that. He needs to hear it. And then tell *me* what he says." She almost managed a smile before she turned away to comfort Alia, who was clutching her mother's knee and whimpering.

Thus on the following evening we found ourselves in Yasir Arafat's office, or at least in the particular office he was using that evening. As a man whose activities were at the very least controversial and generally provoked a range of reaction from adoration to intense hatred, he lived in constant fear for his life and thus moved his headquarters, we were told, every few days, and sometimes every day, to improve the odds for survival.

The taxi, with Jamal in front beside the driver, had picked us up at the Mayflower Hotel at 11 P.M., certainly an odd time to have tea, I thought, but no, said Jamal, this was the usual time at which Abu Amr honored people with his audiences. He stressed the word "honor," as if to remind us of our luck. We had wound through a bewildering string of back streets in the dark, from one end of Beirut to another, until we ended up in the office where we now sat: the top floor of an anonymous unmarked apartment building, a small room with an open door leading to a narrow balcony. Something glinted on the balcony—a rifle? One of those ever-present machine guns? I leaned forward a bit in my chair. Yes, the balcony held two chairs and on the chairs lounged two rather large young men in combat fatigue uniforms, their glinting guns beside them. Obviously. Guards. Why should I have been surprised?

I looked at my watch. It was 11:30 P.M.

The office, in addition to the five chairs we sat in stiffly while awaiting our host, contained a large teak desk, designed with supports of modern stainless steel tubing. An old-fashioned cross-stitched sampler, of the kind our grand-mothers used to make, hung behind the desk. But instead of asking God to bless the house or to remember the birth of a child, this sampler urged revolutionary activity on the viewer. The slogan was stitched in the red, green, and white colors of the Palestinian cause, those colors we had seen on flags, on the photos of martyrs pasted on the walls of houses, on the posters in the boys' club in Rashadiya. A flag was worked into the center of the sampler and a pattern of crossed swords and guns formed the border. To the right hung a sepia print, elaborately framed in gilt, of an onion-domed temple in North Vietnam, and behind us was a large reproduction of Brueghel's "Winter." Here on the steamy wall, in the hot summer night of Beirut, the peasants of the Low Countries looked a bit incongruous trudging across the frozen landscape.

My reverie was interrupted. A banging of doors, the clattering of heavy boots, and a clamor of men's voices brought the two young balcony guards to attention. The glint of the guns disappeared and became a gleam, winking and reflecting weakly on the matte-finish surface of the teak desk.

Abu Amr was coming, it appeared from the way the guards snapped to and nearly leaped over our collective feet. Diana, Diane, Marilyn, Lena, and I sat demurely in the office of the revolutionary chairman who had invited us to tea at —yes, it was nearly midnight.

He came in, hurrying, a bit stooped, his hand outstretched in welcome, a small man in rumpled army fatigues, the black-and-white-checked kaffiya of the traditional Arab tribesman held in place by the black rope of the agal, but folded back carefully along both sides of his faintly bearded face so that it was not hidden but revealed, a bit fleshy, pouched under the eyes, cheeks taut but chin beginning to sag. Abu Amr. Father of the Struggle.

We stood up.

Abu Amr, barely my height, nodded and shook hands.

"Yasir Arafat," he announced simply.

"Sharaftunna!" I stuttered out the classical Arabic phrase. "We are honored!"

He smiled happily, and the smile totally changed his face. The face came to life, seemed less pouchy, less fleshy.

"You speak Arabic, madame," he said in perfect English. "You are most welcome. We have heard of the filming in Rashadiya."

The flashbulbs began to pop. Me and Abu Amr. Marilyn and Abu Amr. Diane and Diana with Abu Amr. Lena and Abu Amr. Arafat paused and looked care-fully at Lena.

"You are Palestinian," he said. "You live in Beirut."

"No, in America."

"Why?"

"I am with my husband," said Lena simply.

Abu Amr raised his eyebrows slightly. "Ah yes," he said noncommittally, and ushered us into what Jamal described as the conference room. Abu Amr took his place at the head of the long oval table, and gestured to us to be seated also. We wore our modest best, skirts and shirts; I had decided at the last minute to wear my pearls, despite the slightly amused looks of the younger, less traditional crew. Three British citizens, one American, one Palestinian. At the other end of the conference table sat a handsome dark-haired young man, introduced as Abu Amr's adviser. His wife was next to him, a blond young woman who told us she was Belgian, a correspondent for several European newspapers. She was, she said, primarily interested in the phenomenon of the new revolutionary woman, who was emerging as a vital force in the political life of the modern age in which we lived. I smiled at her politely. The other crew members, I noticed, glanced at her clothes, which were impressive. Like her husband, she wore beautifully cut khaki trousers and a campaign shirt, but her costume was embellished by several gold chains and bracelets.

I tried not to stare rudely at Abu Amr as he offered sugar for the tea and plates of English tinned biscuits from a tartan can, following the traditional code of Arab hospitality. How could this diffident, ungainly man with undistinguished features and what appeared to be a permanent five-o'clock shadow have molded a group of refugees into a fighting force and wielded enough power to be either violently denounced or fervently blessed every day by hundreds of thousands of people all over the world? Sitting next to him, I felt none of the vitality and controlled energy that had vibrated across the room from Azmi at our farewell feast in Rashadiya. But when Arafat turned and looked at me, something did happen. He did not exactly stare, but I felt the same way I had felt as a child when faced by our fire-and-brimstone priest of St. Anne's Church (retired early by his diocesan supervisors for what was termed health reasons). When Father Du Blois stared at me I felt guilty and squirmed in my seat, as if he were asking silently, "Are you having holy or unholy thoughts? Are you thinking good or evil?" Abu Amr seemed to be asking me silently about my true feelings about the revolution.

But what I heard myself saying, without prompting (yes, Father Du Blois), was how impressed we had been by the strength and spirit of the people in Rashadiya.

Diana, the sound recorder, who sat across the table, spoke of the strength of the women in the face of great adversity.

Marilyn spoke of Um Zhivago's work in the kindergartens.

Abu Amr directed a question in Arabic to his adviser: "Who is Um Zhivago?"

Taking that as my cue, I launched into a description of Um Zhivago's political activity, the Women's Union, the sewing workshop, the weapons training.

Lena elaborated.

Diane, our camera operator, spoke again about the strength of the women, their persistence and determination.

There was a slight pause while we sipped our tea and nibbled our biscuits.

Abu Amr spoke of the achievements of the Palestinian people and of the revolutionary movement. "We have," he said, in his good if stilted English, "transformed pathetic, even pitiful refugees into freedom fighters."

Jamal, I noticed, was nodding vigorously, and the aide's Belgian wife was taking notes with a gold pencil.

"We have given Palestinians a sense of dignity," continued Abu Amr, "and people cannot live without dignity. But you know, er . . . uh . . . ladies," he said, with a glance around at us (perhaps to see if that word applied in modern times), "you see, ladies, there are two revolutions."

"Two revolutions?" echoed Lena.

"Two revolutions. . . . One is political, but the other, more important one is an educational revolution." He sipped his tea and cleared his throat. "Of all the ethnic groups in Lebanon, we Palestinians have the highest percentage of children in school, and the highest scores on the government baccalaureate exams. I am prouder of that than of anything else," he said, "because that means the people are no longer ignorant. We will work next on the medical aspect. Now—" He was interrupted by a phone call and excused himself.

"It is your duty to speak about women's liberation in the camps," the Belgian woman was admonishing us firmly. "How the revolution has freed all women from the shackles of family, of tradition—"

"Well . . ." I paused and looked around me. I was sure at that moment that Lena, Diane, Marilyn, and Diana were thinking as I was thinking, that the Belgian lady was perhaps overimpressed by the rhetoric of the revolution. We knew that the sewing workshops couldn't start until 11 A.M. because the girls had chores at home, we knew that some families would not even let their daughters leave the house to attend a Women's Union meeting, much less participate in a sewing workshop or a revolutionary group. "I gave my foot to the revolution, my son is paralyzed from a bullet in his back," one man had said to Um Zhivago when I had gone with her on a routine visit to the wounded. "So I am *not* going to give my daughter too."

"You must say it," insisted the Belgian woman. "The great awakening of women to their true identity that is happening there—the freeing force of the movement."

Abu Amr came back into the room and sat down. The tea was removed by a teenage boy in combat fatigues. Coffee was served.

I cleared my throat and resisted that stare of the Belgian woman in her khaki pants suit and gold chains. I was not going to go along with her rhetoric and slogans. I would have betrayed my own beliefs, and also Um Zhivago, who felt so strongly about the need to improve the status of women. After all, when the mayor of the camp would not even allow his own sister to attend a public dinner, what kind of liberation were we discussing?

I spoke instead of the purpose of our film—to try to show the effects of conflict on women and the family, so that Palestinians, like all groups, could be seen as human beings. In the West, I said, the Palestinians were viewed as terrorists, not as women with children who were hungry, husbands who were sometimes brave and sometimes forgetful, girls who wished to get an education and improve themselves.

The adviser burst out, "And just why do you have that image in the West, madame? Why, that is the Zionist conspiracy! And America cannot admit to it—but that is what it is. . . ."

I demurred. "I don't think that is the whole story," I began.

"America does not want to admit that the Zionist racist conspiracy and the Zionist aggression exists," he charged on, "because then they would have to admit to their *own* conspiracies and aggressions—against *blacks,* against the just claims of the American *Indians,* against the—"

"Nonsense!" Abu Amr's voice was so loud I jumped. "What you are talking about, my friend, is history!" Then he lowered his voice and began to lecture, father to son. "When you look at history, you see that every people, every nation, has done terrible things. . . . Why, we did it to the Spanish ourselves back in the early days of Islamic conquest. . . ." His eyes blazed at the young adviser sitting opposite him. He was not quoting revolutionary slogans now, repeating phrases prepared for the visiting media that we had heard many times before. "The Spanish did it to us in Andalusia. . . . We cannot dwell on that, that is past, my son, we have to go *forward* to try to *improve,* as best we can with what we have."

For a moment I considered quoting Um Zhivago on revolution and cooking —the analogy seemed so apt to his discussion—but before I could speak, he had turned and asked me a question.

"Do you think that your film, madame, will ever be permitted to be shown in America?"

"Of course," I said. "I already have two distributors. I wouldn't have made the film unless I had some way of distributing it so people could see it. Otherwise, why bother?"

Abu Amr looked surprised. "That is wonderful," he said. "But are you sure?"

While I nodded, he said in Arabic, to his adviser, "I thought you told me that no films on the Palestinian people would be allowed to be seen in America. Is she lying or are you?"

Jamal said, quietly, "Madame understands Arabic."

The adviser looked down at the table. His wife suddenly became very busy writing in her notebook.

"Well," said Abu Amr, "thank you for coming. We look forward to seeing your film."

Jamal rose. We rose. The audience was over. It was 11:45 P.M.

At that very moment, while we stood smiling politely at each other around the table below a painting of a girl with a great bloody hole in her heart, gunfire rang out—rat-tat-tat-tat! Machine guns—rat-tat-tat-tat—seemed all around us, spattering bullets at the windows like fiery hail.

We continued to stand, the smiles somewhat fixed on our faces, while Abu Amr turned and saw his phone blinking red in the other office. He signaled to the adviser. "Get me the Democratiya!" he shouted in Arabic. He turned to us and said gently, "Please sit down, ladies, this will be over in a moment."

We sat down.

The windows, one, two, three, four, five, six, seven windows, across the front of the audience room were unprotected. Two stood partly open. I resisted an impulse to leap up and close those open windows, realizing how ridiculous a risk that was. Obviously machine-gun blasts come right through ordinary window glass and this certainly looked like window glass. One, two, three, four, five, six, seven windows. Rat-tat-tat-tat—the firing continued, the raucous deadly voices of the weapons speaking and answering each other, increasing in volume and intensity.

Lena, across from me, had closed her eyes. Then there was a pause, one, two, three seconds, followed by the horrifying sound we had heard on our first trip to Rashadiya, hiss, thud, the crash, and the booming explosion of a long-range shell. I looked down the table at Jamal, who smiled reassuringly.

Father Du Blois. I had not thought of my childhood catechism teacher for forty years, and this was the second time tonight. Why now? Was he signaling me from the other world that I was about to meet my Maker and had better begin saying my prayers, articulating contrition for my evil thoughts, my thoughtless deeds, my blasphemies and worldly actions? The machine-gun fire started up again. Rat-tat-tat-tat—the spattering went on and on, deafening us, rattling the glass in the windows.

I looked once more at Jamal. He had begun to sweat and this upset me considerably. After all, it was he who had more experience and—

"Stop it! Stop firing!" cried Abu Amr into the telephone. He was speaking in Arabic. "All right, someone fired, but you should not have fired back. Stop! No, just stop. Stop! That is how great catastrophes begin. By firing back when there is no need. *Stop firing!*"

I wondered if any of the hundreds of journalists who had interviewed Arafat had ever described him as a peacemaker, a mediator.

The adviser rushed out again, came back, and said, in Arabic, "The ladies must come into the hall away from the windows."

So it was indeed ordinary window glass. I was in the hall, with Lena, before Jamal had even translated the order for Marilyn, Diane, and Diana.

Swish! The hiss seemed closer. The sickening thud came and the explosion rocked us even in the hall.

"Stop it!" Abu Amr was still talking on the phone. "Yes, this is Arafat; who the hell do you think it is, Begin? Stop firing, I tell you."

People rushed back and forth. The Belgian wife had disappeared. We stood in the hall, five waxen pieces of immobility and fear, but what else could we do? The firing went on unabated. Would I see my children again? Had this attack been planned because someone had tipped off the enemy that famous (or notorious) Yasir Arafat, revolutionary chief, was having five Western media ladies to tea in the middle of the night?

Arafat was shouting to us, to Jamal, his hand over the mouthpiece of the phone.

"You must leave, B.J.," said Jamal. "It is not safe. Abu Amr is afraid for you."

"I think I'll just lie down on the floor here," sighed Marilyn.

"Me too," said Diana.

"No, you must go, *go!*"

A vision of our taxi driver passed through my head. Where was he now? Caught in cross fire? Presumably he had the sense to get under the seat of his car? How would we get home?

"Abu Amr is sending you in his car," said Jamal, pushing us (presumably before we lay prone and were harder to budge) out the hall and down the stairs, clattering to the ground-floor garage. The garage was protected by a fluted screen of corrugated iron, but not for long. Even as we stood there, *whang!,* shots hit the screen. Jamal was ushering us into a white Mercedes, its motor already racing. But I found I did not want to get into the car with the burly armed guard and the burly armed driver. I just wanted to lie down on the ground until it was finished, the spatter, the hail of machine-gun fire, the dreadful thuds and crashes of shells, which seemed to be coming closer. Father Du Blois, bless me for I have sinned. Grievously. Well, maybe not too grievously. I did not want to die, and I wanted to see Bob, Laura Ann, Laila, and David again. Father Du Blois . . .

But there we were in the car, Diana between the two burly men in the front bucket seats.

"It's okay, B.J., his car is bulletproof," shouted Jamal, and then I did not see Jamal anymore for the car shot out into the night and the firing and the boom of shells combined into total violent sound that enfolded us, enveloped us in a deadly fog of sound, a blanket of fearful, deafening noise that surrounded the speeding Mercedes, seemed to be slowing it. . . .

Father Du Blois . . . Diana's head hit the front windshield as we careened around a corner, faster than our disdainful beer-drinking cabdriver had traveled on the sea road south, how many days, months, years ago.

"Diana! Lean back!" I shouted, and she did, her head on my knees as we raced, squirreled, and screeched through the dark, reverberating shell-struck violent night of Beirut, onetime oasis paradise of the Arab world, jewel of the Mediterranean, Switzerland of the Middle East. And then we were in a different world, the empty, dark, quiet streets of West Beirut. The apartment building where Abu Amr was calling on the troops to stop firing and the bullets were falling like hail was only a few miles away but might have been on another planet. In what seemed like ages, but actually turned out to be sixteen minutes, we found ourselves in front of the Mayflower Hotel. The driver and the guard got out of the white bulletproof Mercedes. They shook our hands, we thanked them, they thanked us, and with a great screech of tires they were gone, back to Abu Amr in the besieged apartment block, presumably to await the next assignment.

While we stood there, a bit stunned, looking at the lighted door of the Mayflower, the middle-aged night clerk came out to look at the cause of the disturbance. He smiled and waved tentatively at us. Another car drove up, in a screech of tires, emitting Jamal. He had been told to stay away until the incident was over.

"Come and have a drink," I suggested. The bar was closed, so we sat in the lobby with our tax-free bottle of brandy. Father Du Blois. Bless me, Father Du Blois. But he had receded once more into the past of my childhood.

"I wasn't frightened, really," said Diane.

"Well, I was," said Marilyn. "I was scared to death."

"Me, too," I added.

"Do you know any Western songs about struggle?" asked Jamal. He was not drinking, but he wiped his sweating face with a clean white handkerchief, over and over again.

Marilyn launched us. " 'The Minstrel Boy to the war is gone,' " she sang. " 'In the ranks of death you'll find him!' "

Her voice broke on the last note.

Lena began to cry.

It was not quite one-thirty in the morning.

Next day a message was delivered from Arafat's office. The pictures of us all would be somewhat delayed owing to circumstances beyond the chairman's control. Arafat sent his regrets.

Three people had been wounded in the incident, but the streets were quiet at the moment.

The film shooting had come to a dramatic end, but the revolution for the future and against the past, however it was defined, did not yet seem to be finished. And the PLO, which had not existed when Bob and I first came to the Middle East twenty-five years ago, did not seem as if it were going to disappear. Resolve seemed to be hardening, rather than weakening, in the face of unbelievably impossible odds. This determination had impressed us all in our days in Rashadiya, and we had come to sympathize with the plight of the people who lived there. But we would never be true believers. Of course, as Um Zhivago had pointed out, rather sharply, none of us had had our land taken away from us and none of us had lived for years, as the people of Rashadiya had lived, in constant fear for our lives. "I've been here fourteen years, and I am proud to be here," Um Zhivago had said. I had once tried to suggest to her that revolution and conflict wouldn't solve everything, that revolution did not necessarily improve people's lives, particularly women's lives. She had looked at me as though I had struck her, and in some way I had—struck at the very core of what gave meaning and purpose to her life.

The problems of Um Zhivago and the other women in the camp—raising and educating children, supporting husbands and sons and brothers, maintaining some personal identity while keeping life going—these were problems of women everywhere; they were our own problems, in England, in America. These common dilemmas cut through the specific political ideology of Rashadiya and in some sense brought us together. But in the end we were not revolutionaries, the crew and I. We could not accept violence as the solution to violence. We felt that somehow peaceful negotiations had to begin if the problems of the people of Rashadiya were ever to be solved.

The one person I wanted to see again in Beirut was my friend Mona al-Shafei the poet. I had tried calling several times and finally reached her at seven-fifteen the morning before we were to leave the city. The connection went through with a strange plonking sound, and there was Mona on the line.

"Will you have lunch with me today, Mona?"

"If it is somewhere near where Amr works," she answered. "Then he can give me a ride home."

"I thought there had been a new cease-fire."

Over the phone Mona's voice was unclear. The line crackled. Could she be laughing? No, I did not think so.

"Well, more or a little less," she allowed.

We met at Ajami's, the splendid new establishment that had replaced the old restaurant, destroyed in the civil war with the rest of the city center. Ajami's was by the flower market, where Bob and I had eaten dinner more than twenty-five years ago. Mona and Abdul Latif had been vacationing in Damascus then, she said, and the tangled affairs of the Arab world had looked as though they might untangle constructively, given time and planning.

What had happened to the plans and the planners? What had started the slow deterioration of the ideal, the downhill slide that had led to the collapse of social and economic institutions in Lebanon? The presence of the Palestinians, restless and impoverished, without a home, without a place? The indifference of the Lebanese merchants, rich and getting richer as Arab trade shifted from Haifa to Beirut in 1948? The increase in the number of Muslim citizens, upsetting the balance between Christian and Muslim that was supposedly the basis of the political compromise that made Lebanon possible? The ideas of free enterprise carried to their logical extreme, where each person felt responsible finally only for him- or herself and no one accepted responsibility for others, even to cooperate in order to pick up the community garbage? Or was it the smugness of the West that tried for its own reasons to paper over ancient rivalries and hatreds, old gaps between rich and poor, with slogans and development money, tried to solve Middle Eastern problems with Western solutions?

"We don't know anymore, B.J.," said Mona. We sat at a quiet corner table in the new Ajami's, a table covered with heavy pale pink linen, centered with a slender crystal vase of pink rosebuds and white baby's breath. The *mezze,* countless tiny dishes of delicacies, was spread out before us. We nibbled on miniature fried fish, chick-peas with tahina and olive oil, black olives, wrinkled like the cheeks of very old people, bite-size spiced meatballs, tiny egg rolls stuffed with feta cheese and herbs, marinated eggplant.

"It's hard to get used to Abdul Latif's absence," Mona said in answer to my question. "He was the center of my life for thirty years and in many ways the best friend I ever had."

"Will you keep on writing? You should have more time now!"

Mona glanced up at me and down. "Yes, there is *time,* time to fill up in some strange way, I never realized it would be like this. Here, try the *zattar.*"

The waiter, tall, with a trim dark mustache, stood before us in immaculate white coat, black trousers.

"Yes, madame?"

"Have the *sayyadia,* B.J.," urged Mona. "You will never get it so well prepared as here."

"But I'm already full!" I protested, belying my own words by dipping a last bit of bread into the zattar, that pungent mixture of wild thyme and olive oil.

She smiled. A bit of the old ebullient Mona was coming back. "Shall I begin to recite you poems about food to encourage you?" she asked. "There's a nice old quatrain—"

"All right, all right," and I ordered sayyadia, surrendering my waistline to the delight of the dish, a mélange of fresh fish, spices, pine nuts, and rice. The dish was decorated with sprigs of fresh parsley and other pale green and gray leaves I could not identify, and served with a flourish by the handsome waiter.

"They want me to do a regular column for *Nahar,*" said Mona. "It means probably eventually working for them full time. Maybe as an editor. Should I do it?"

"Do you want to?"

"Do I want to? What a curious question. You Americans always ask those kinds of questions. Do I want to? What do I want? What do you want? I suppose I want peace. Of course I want peace, and I want to continue writing. What do you want, Beeja? Isn't that what they called you in Iraq, when you were just married and on your honeymoon in a mud house?" Her face softened as she looked at me and she shook her head, whether at my foolishness or at my advancing age, I could not tell.

I didn't answer her question. "Come to America," I burst out. "Maybe we could arrange lectures."

She laughed out loud. In the softly lighted and elegantly upholstered room of

Ajami's new restaurant, protected, I was told, by bulletproof glass, people at other tables turned from their plates and looked around at us. I realized I had heard very little laughter during my time in the Beirut of the eighties.

"Westerners," she said in explanation, "Westerners, and especially Americans, always think you can solve everything by moving. In the end, it doesn't work. The problems are still there in your head."

The handsome waiter was there beside us again, wheeling up the pastry cart, loaded with irresistible confections: fruit tarts sprinkled lightly with powdered sugar, candied nuts, baklava, chocolate mousse, napoleons, *kunafa*. . . .

"You remember that kunafa store in Cairo, where we used to get pastry for big parties? They had good *Um Ali*—"

"Yes, I remember."

The pastry cart was still beside us, the tall waiter standing expectantly, a finger beside his nose.

"Madame?"

"No, no sweets." Mona dismissed the waiter. "We're getting too old for that," she added slyly. "But we might have one last coffee and talk of the past. I don't want to think about the future anymore today."

"Let's have Turkish coffee."

She ordered it. Strong. Bitter. No sugar. But a bit of cardamom for old times' sake.

"Let's talk of poetry," she said. "Art. Okay? No more personal discussions."

"Okay."

"What about American poetry these days? Quote me a few good lines like you used to when we were both young in Cairo."

I racked my brain. The old sonnets wouldn't do, the new poetry, or the little of it with which I was familiar, did not seem to meet our needs that day. Yeats was too close, too terrifying. The center obviously did not hold here. The past stretched behind us, looking in retrospect like golden days, for the crises of childbearing and childrearing had faded. Abdul Latif was dead, AUB and AUC were no longer the Western witnesses we had thought they were. Damascus was bursting out of its confines, and Beirut was falling into ruins around us. Bob waited anxiously in Cairo for me to finish filming the role of women in revolution. What could I possibly quote to my old and dear friend, the famous Sufi modern poet who sat beside me in her black mourning clothes, that would have meaning for both of us? For I felt unreasonably that this was some kind of crisis; surely we in the West had *something* to contribute.

"Come, B.J., you've never been speechless before," teased Mona, and then, as though she had read my mind, "Has the West nothing to offer us in the way of poetry? Then maybe the West is dead, and the Arabs have been right all along."

"I . . ." And then they came to me, the last lines of Wallace Stevens's poem "Sunday Morning."

A scribe helps a woman with a legal problem in Yemen.

Traditional Yemeni architecture blends with t▶

As Yemen's economy expands to include pickup trucks and taxis, gas stations are built everywhere, like this one high in the mountains.

ugged mountain environment. This village is near Sanaa.

Three young women entertainers from a village troupe near Sanaa, North Yemen.

Social occasions in Yemen, in this case a homecoming, are often centered around the chewing of qat. Qat is a leafy plant with a mild stimulating effect.

We live in an old chaos of the sun,
Or old dependency of day and night,
Or island solitude, unsponsored, free,
Of that wide water, inescapable.
Deer walk upon our mountains, and the quail
Whistle about us their spontaneous cries;
Sweet berries ripen in the wilderness;
And, in the isolation of the sky,
At evening, casual flocks of pigeons make
Ambiguous undulations as they sink,
Downward to darkness, on extended wings.

"Yes," said Mona. "Yes. That is poetry, even if it has a particularly American context. True poetry speaks across and to us. Poetry, my dear, survives."

Comment

THE IDEA OF THE FAMILY
IN THE MIDDLE EAST

IN AMERICA, "family" has come to be thought of simply as "parents and their children" or even a single parent and child. In the Middle East, the Arabic word for family, *ahl* or *ahila,* is a more inclusive term and can be used to mean, according to the dictionary, "family, relatives, kinfolk, clan, inhabitants, companions, partisans; people, especially persons of a special group or place; members, followers; possessors." At its ultimate level, it is the umma, the family of believers in Islam. But however and wherever defined, the family is a human invention dealing with human needs, and its basic functions include the survival and reproduction of the group. In the Middle East, the larger family unit also has until very recently been the major political and economic institution of the area. Only since the birth of nationalism has the state, rather than the family, begun to be a major factor affecting individual well-being. Thus the condition of the family in the Middle East is not seen as a merely personal issue, divorced from economic and political matters, as it now tends to be in American society. For it is the family, not the individual, that is considerd not only the basic unit of social organization but also the focus of social change currently in progress throughout the area, from the Persian Gulf to the Mediterranean.

In America, where "family" problems are peripheral political issues (except in election years, perhaps), where family violence, child abuse, the care of the elderly, and teenage pregnancies are relegated to the bottom of the list of political priorities, below highways and transportation, redistricting, and interest rates, the view that the family is of basic political importance seems, somehow, unbelievable to us.

How reasonable is this difference in political rhetoric between America and the Middle East? Does it indicate real differences in the functions and powers of the family group? In traditional Middle Eastern society, the family has undertaken many of the social tasks now expected of business and the state in the West. For thousands of years, the family group, in the words of Arab sociologist Halim Barakat, "has constituted the basic socio-economic unit of production and [has been] at the center of social organization in all three Arab patterns of living (bedouin, rural and urban) and particularly among tribesmen, peasants and urban poor. As such the family also constituted the dominant social institution through which persons and groups inherit their religious, social class and cultural identities."

In the past, and to a great extent today, the family has been expected to provide economic and emotional support for its members, which might consist of groups as large as two hundred or more persons, for not only mother, father, and children were included in the definition of the group, but also grandparents, uncles, aunts, cousins, to several degrees on both sides of the marital connection. In exchange for the allegiance of its members, the group served as an employment bureau, insurance agency, child and family counseling service, old people's home, bank, teacher, home for the handicapped (including the insane), and hostel for others in time of economic need. Men and women both remained active members of their natal families all of their lives, even after marriage. A divorced woman returned to her natal family, which was responsible for her support until remarriage or death. A divorced man returned to his natal family, and his parents cared for his children. In exchange for these services, the individual members were expected to place the group's survival above their personal desires, especially at the time of marriage, and to uphold the reputation of the family, by behaving properly, "maintaining the family honor."

This, of course, was the ideal. In everyday life, such expectations do not always work out so perfectly. Still, the institution persisted because it filled real needs for people, people for whom no other institution existed. The shift that took place in the West, the assuming of economic and social responsibilities once belonging to the family, first by the religious hierarchy and then by the secular state, has not yet taken place in the Middle East. Though programs of pensions and social security are now in place in many Middle Eastern states, only a small minority of the population, in most cases, is fully involved in such plans. Therefore, the current debate on the place and function of the family is a crucial debate, for it not only involves the suggestion that more responsibilities should be passed from the family unit to the state but also raises questions of the definition of basic individual rights: those of women, men, and children. The status of women is at the core of the whole debate, for the woman has always been seen as the center of the family unit, the hub around which all its economic and personal and political activities revolved.

Today life is changing radically in the Middle East. War and revolution have taken their toll, as has the effect of nearly two centuries of Western colonialism. A redefinition of men's and women's roles has become necessary as the old largely self-sufficient agricultural society disappears and the area becomes more industrialized, more dependent on other nations and other nations' goods.

Industrialization and urbanization have benefited some people in the Middle East and disenfranchised others. In oil-rich countries such as Kuwait and Saudi Arabia, for example, per capita income is high enough that only one member of the family, the traditional member, the father, needs to work so that the family may survive. Women in Kuwait have gone to work at what they define not as jobs of economic necessity but as "personally fulfilling" jobs, much as some wealthy Americans have done. In Saudi Arabia, this same wealth supports an ideology according to which women are not allowed to work in public, in the presence of strange men, for this is seen as violating a woman's proper roles as wife and mother. Foreign migrant workers help fill the labor gap in this expanding economy. However, the luxury of hiring foreign workers also poses problems. Recently a joint council of ministers from the Arab Gulf States (including Saudi Arabia), who all share OPEC oil wealth, issued a warning about the dangers of employing foreign nursemaids to raise the area's children. So whether women must work too much, in factory and home, or work much less, because of the presence of servants, the position of women and hence the nature of family life are changing.

In Egypt, women whose husbands travel abroad as migrant laborers are left to raise their children and manage their households alone. And although Egyptian women have entered professions such as law, engineering, and medicine, as well as teaching, business, and government, the great majority of these women, like American women, work at lower-paying jobs: in factories, shops, and offices, and in service positions, including street cleaners, janitors, hotel and household servants, hospital aides. These jobs are performed to put food on the table.

How then can the Middle Eastern family unit remain the important institution it has been? Some of the same anxieties that prompted *Newsweek* magazine in the United States to focus an entire issue on "Who's Minding the Kids?" are also propelling the Middle Eastern media and Middle Eastern leaders to reassess ideals and goals in view of current events and upheavals. Economic affluence, as in Saudi Arabia, and economic poverty, as in Egypt, both prompt concern about the proper raising of children and the conduct of men and women. Hence the debate in the Middle East today: some thinkers argue, in the press, on television, and in learned academic journals, that women must not be allowed to work outside the home, and that men must reassert their role as supporters and protectors of the family. Others, equally fervent, argue that Islam allows for equal participation by both men and women in the formation of a better future for all, and that today, women are needed to work so that the family can stay together, whether this is seen as the smaller family, the extended family, or the Muslim community.

There is much evidence that the Middle Eastern family, far from disintegrating, is rather regrouping and reorganizing in answer to modern needs. In places where the kin unit itself is deteriorating, owing to war and natural disasters, the values and the functions of the family are resurfacing in different forms.

Suad Joseph, in her study of a working-class district outside Beirut that had once been a refugee camp, found that women without family ties tended to form the same kinds of ties with neighbors. Migrant workers abroad group together in foreign cities around old family ties; men entering new industrial jobs find jobs in the same plants for their sisters, cousins, or uncles. For men of elite political groups, family ties continue to be important as political party bases shift. Newcomers to the city make "connections" through family members. Men who are newcomers in the city, without family, may turn to religious "brotherhoods," groups where, as they themselves say, "they feel like one family."

These adaptations of the family should not seem foreign to Americans, who have witnessed similar adaptations in times of traumatic change. The settling of the Western frontier, for example, was done not by individuals, for no single person could have survived alone, but only in groups: groups of people with family, economic, or military and national ties who banded together for common survival. Yet in America, in an industrial society, we tend to romanticize or idealize the lone individual and forget the support groups we still need.

Today Middle Easterners, organizing themselves, as all human beings have done in times of crisis, for survival, are still resisting the lonely individualism of an industrial economy. And in their struggle, they have some assets: one is an interdependent and flexible social institution that seems still, despite transformations throughout history, the best way to provide for individual needs as well as group survival. If Islam is viewed as the soul of the Islamic Middle East, then the wider extended family might be seen as its body. And, says a Moroccan merchant, "The governments may come and go, Spanish, French, Moroccan, but my family has been here for four hundred years and it is still all I can rely upon."

Middle Eastern leaders may argue and debate about the purposes of the institution, and how women and men should assume roles within its framework, but they have not as yet found an institution to replace it, either in daily life or in ideology. One might question as well whether the state or the corporation has really adequately replaced the family in America.

CHAPTER VIII
Marrakech, Morocco
1971, 1976

> A magic castle,
> A gate of light
> Opening on a time of legend,
> The palm of a hand stained with henna,
> A peacock ascending through the heavens,
> Its rainbow tail spread out.
>
> Ahmad Abd al-Mu'ti Hijazi
> *Caption to a Landscape*

THE JACARANDA TREES were blooming when we first saw Marrakech in late spring 1971. The purple blossoms flared before the red walls of the houses and against the red medieval gates of the city. Heat hung in the air, the heat of an inexorable approaching summer, but it had not yet settled on the wide tree-lined streets of Gueliz, the newer, French-built section of the city; on the narrow winding streets of the medina, or old city; or on the great square of Djemaa al-Fna that bridges the divided provincial capital. Standing in the square, in the warm clear twilight, against those fabled red walls, we watched acrobats and snake charmers, fortune-tellers and dancers, and a man who walked barefoot over the sharp bright-green shards of smashed Coca-Cola bottles.

We were hooked on Marrakech from the very first moment of our first visit. Bob had a Fulbright research fellowship to expand his Middle East anthropology experience from east (Egypt, the Fertile Crescent) to west (North Africa). We could have settled in Fez or Rabat or Casablanca, but we came to Marrakech instead. It was all very well to say that it was an important bridge city between the Sahara and the Mediterranean, that Marrakech had been a stop on the cara-van route between Timbuktu and the Barbary Coast. It was true.

It was important to remember, as Bob pointed out, that as an oasis city Mar-rakech lay between the agricultural plains and the tribes of the mountains, a good place to observe rural-urban relations. He was right. But we were as soft on fantasy and exotica as all the other Westerners who had ever visited Marrakech. We'd read those books, those poems, those tales about the Dionysian city of the south. So we moved to Marrakech with our three children and settled down in a traditional house on Rue Trésor, in the old city.

A few weeks of marketing, doing the laundry, and looking for schools for the children dispelled somewhat our first impression of fantasy and exotica. The tinsel in our heads went up in smoke as we tried to deal with the problems of everyday life. Marrakech may have had red walls and purple jacarandas in the spring and jugglers in the square, but it was also a city adapting to the difficult realities of life in a newly independent nation, a nation only fifteen years old after a long period of French, Spanish, and Portuguese rule. Slowly we made acquaintances and friends, we listened and began to learn about the Marrakech that lay behind those legendary red walls. As we learned more, our view of the city changed, but we never lost the sense that Marrakech, mysterious and romantic, would never reveal all of its secrets to us, the strangers.

Hajja Kenza, a rich widow, was our landlady. She lived next door with her only daughter Naima and gave us plenty of advice, whether we wanted it or not. And she came in unannounced until Bob finally asked for—and got—*her* key to *our* house.

Aisha Bint Muhammad worked for us. She and her husband Khaddour and their four children, Saleh, Abdul Krim, Youssef, and Najiya lived across the street. Aisha was a sharifa, a descendant of the Prophet, a fact she disclosed quite early in our acquaintanceship. Hajja Kenza, though rich, was not a sharifa, Aisha said. With Aisha's help, I began to find my way in the often bewildering byways of the old city; I learned to market; she took me to religious festivals and introduced me to many of my neighbors.

Bob was aided greatly in his discovery of the city by Omar, son of a jellaba merchant, and came to know, through Omar, many of the merchants and traders in the great central Semmarine market. Omar's father, Si Abdulla, explained that the family had lived in Marrakech since the Moors had been expelled from Spain—around 1500, he said carelessly. He was not a descendant of the Prophet, he said, but his wife, Lalla Nezha, was, yes, indeed, so therefore his children were fortunate enough to be so endowed.

And there was Abdul Aziz, the first Moroccan to be allowed to teach French at the local Mission Culturelle Française, where we went with the children each evening to improve our language skills. For the first thing we had learned was that French was the language foreigners were expected to speak; Arabicization was under way, but much business was still conducted in French. Bob found he needed French to do his interviewing throughout the city.

All of these people, in different ways, tried to explain to us what it meant to them to live in an independent Morocco.

"Our government is a Muslim government now at last," said Aisha.

"The officials we pay our taxes to are just as mean, but at least they speak Arabic, even if the papers are still in French," said Hajja Kenza.

"The schools are full," said Abdul Aziz. "People are thirsty for education.

Did you realize that in 1956, when we got independence, there were only forty Moroccans in the whole country who had graduated from universities? The French did *nothing* but try to keep control."

And Omar had said, "We are in a new age, the age of a free Morocco."

Yet by 1971 the early euphoria had passed and signs of discontent were visible. Marrakech particularly was bitter about its students and teachers who were still in jail as a result of the 1965 riots against the central government. Students and teachers from Fez, Meknès, Casablanca, and Rabat had been tried and most of them released. Marrakech was different, an old imperial city, luke-warm in its allegiance to the central government, thus a potential scene for trouble, Omar thought.

"He won't come to Marrakech, the King," said Aisha. "He won't dare."

Aisha's feelings notwithstanding, King Hassan II did come to Marrakech during the year we lived there. He was a sharif too, a descendant of the Prophet, an heir of the three-hundred-year-old Alawite dynasty, son of Muhammad V, the beloved sultan who in the fifties had rallied the recalcitrant tribes as well as the urban nationalist intellectuals against the French. He had been exiled for his actions, a fatal error on the part of the French, for exile bestowed the mantle of martyrdom upon him. He returned in triumph in 1955, to become the first King of modern Morocco.

Muhammad V found a country temporarily united against a common enemy but historically divided. In the first flush of freedom, he promised everything: a constitutional monarchy complete with Parliament; political parties; free public education; free health care; and quick economic development.

Promises are easy to make, as all politicians (including kings) know, but harder to keep. Muhammad V died in 1961 and his thirty-one-year-old son inherited the promises. They had not, could not, all have been kept during Hassan's brief reign, but it was hard to explain that to the new politically con-scious citizens.

In 1971 we could see the school problem on our own doorstep. We had taken Laura Ann, David, and Laila to the local public school, thinking that it would be an important experience for them to attend class with children from Rue Trésor, to learn Arabic in the process. After we had spent ten minutes in the crowded hallways, talking to the polite but harassed administrators, it became obvious that our children's presence would only aggravate the press of people demand-ing their right to education: over forty in a classroom, often two children shar-ing a single seat. And, despite the expressed aim of returning Arabic to its rightful place as the national language, the classes were not held in Arabic. Why?

"Well," said the young principal, drumming his fingers nervously on his desk, "not enough teachers have yet been *educated* in Arabic. We have to have teach-ers, so we use those that are available."

"So?"

"So," he said, "some classes are in French, some are in Arabic, and some"—he paused and smiled engagingly—"some are taught in a mixture of the two!"

Abdul Aziz, when Bob told him this story, explained that of course many details had to be sorted out. "It will take time, you mustn't be so critical."

"I'm not being critical, Abdul Aziz," Bob insisted. "I'm just asking. Why do you presume all Westerners are critical?"

Abdul Aziz had drawn himself up a little. We had not known him very long then. "Because the French always were critical. We were considered inferior beings."

"Oh, Abdul Aziz!"

"We are trying, Bob. Give us a chance."

Abdul Aziz was right. The government was trying very hard, training teachers, building schools, planning curricula. And despite all the problems, it was doing a good job. Perhaps too good a job. The number of children in school at all levels had quadrupled in nine years (from 320,000 in 1956 to 1,283,000 in 1965). A fantastic achievement! But thousands of young people who had studied and taken exams successfully were now beginning to find that there were no jobs for them in the white-collar positions and professions to which they aspired. They did not want to go back to the farm. They wanted to stay in the cities and lead a better life.

"That's what the 1965 riots were about in the beginning," Abdul Aziz explained. "Too many degrees and not enough jobs. But that is not the fault of the Ministry of Education. That is the fault of the Ministry of Economics and the Ministry of Labor."

"But things are calm now. Are there more job opportunities?"

"Well, yes and no." Abdul Aziz was patriotic, but he was always honest. "A lot of people work part time, you see, but things are better; of course, we had excellent harvests in 1968 and 1969."

King Hassan II must have breathed a sigh of relief, we thought, as those bumper crops were stored in silos. He had dissolved Parliament in 1965 after the riots, and was counting on the army as his principal support. It therefore came as a nasty shock when the army organized the palace coup of July 1971 and tried to assassinate the King on his own birthday.

Bob and the children and I were in Casablanca at the time, living in an *internat,* or dormitory, while Bob directed a summer educational exchange program in Middle Eastern studies for fifty-six American students. The students, except for three who were ill, had taken off around the country that weekend.

"The King is dead, monsieur," announced one of the guards at the dormitory gates.

"What?" returned Bob in amazement.

Then the phone rang. The American consul advised Bob to keep "all your student charges inside the compound for the duration, until things are calmer."

"Is the King really dead?" asked Bob.

The consul did not know. "We think so, we're not sure."

"Well, the students are scattered all over, they're away this weekend," explained Bob.

"Oh, I see."

"Nothing I can do," explained Bob.

"Right," said the consul, then paused. "Would you call me if you hear anything important?"

Bob promised he would.

At dusk the elderly French manager of the internat, a burly *colon* named M. Bonne, told Bob he was leaving. By this time the rebellious officers were broadcasting messages over the captured government radio station, asking people to keep calm and accept the new regime.

"You're leaving? Why?"

"I must," announced M. Bonne tersely. "Lock the gate after me. The guards will remain at their posts."

Off he went into the colonial sunset, so to speak, roaring out through the high iron gates in his enormous vintage Oldsmobile, his blond Spanish wife beside him clutching a small locked leather briefcase on her lap (gold, valuables?). M. Bonne was making a quick getaway.

We felt we had been left behind to play bit parts in a grade-B thriller, and we were scarcely jumping for joy. The ill students rose from their beds and wandered mournfully about the compound talking about an early death. What would their parents think? Their friends? Our children, undismayed, jumped into the swimming pool.

Bob tried to reassure the students, but I could sense his uneasiness. We were literally locked in, at the guards' mercy, in a French-owned compound whose director was not known for the milk of his human kindness. And the radio station had stopped broadcasting. In fact, the radio station was dead. Would the guards open the gates if who knew what kind of crowd were to storm them?

The night passed, and we were wakened in the early dawn by a banging on the gates.

"Is the war coming, Baba?" asked David. "Will they put us against the wall and mow us down, like in the movies?"

"David, don't be silly." But Bob rushed out to see what it was, and there was M. Bonne, skulking back to his apartment, beside him his blond wife still clutching the briefcase. "What happened?" he said.

"It's over. The King is not dead. He is back on the throne. Rule of law. He was taught by the French," explained M. Bonne tersely. "It tells, in the end."

Rule of law. Yes, Hassan II, strengthened by his near-escape from death, was back on the throne when we settled in Marrakech. But, we discovered, the word "rule" was defined differently in Morocco and the process of governing could not be compared to, say, Egypt's, any more than Egypt could be compared to the United States. Like many new nations in the second half of the twentieth century, the Moroccan nationalist independent government consisted of old elements, in new combinations. The old elements, according to the political science books we had read, were the *bled al-makhzen,* or territory controlled by the central government, represented, above all, by the Sultan or King; and the *bled al-siba,* literally dissident territory. In the latter areas, the rural tribes had existed for centuries more or less independently of the makhzen. In the sixties and seventies, however, some fresh yeast was evident in the old brew, the ideas and ideals of the young people trained in the West or educated under the new national system. The young idealists came from both the makhzen and siba areas; they tended to put loyalty to the nation ahead of loyalties to the old units.

"One has to be realistic," said Abdul Aziz, "but here I truly believe that realism can be joined to idealism. The old *can* be joined to the new. But some things must change. Land system, for example. Taxes on property must be raised."

He invited us to the local cinema to see *The Earth,* Youssef Shahine's powerful film about injustice in the Egyptian land-tenure system, based on the novel by Abdul Rahman Sharkawi.

"Our problem is not as great as Egypt's," Abdul Aziz said after the film, over coffee in the Renaissance Café. "We have good land and water, but there is inequity in the rural areas. You know my wife Zaynab is from the tribes. She is Berber. Her village is a good example. But the government is doing something about land reform."

"Really?"

"Yes," said Abdul Aziz, "but things don't change overnight."

"Uh . . ." Bob started to speak. "You realize I'm not being critical, Abdul Aziz, but . . ." and they both laughed. They were beginning to trust each other.

The new combinations of old elements seemed evident in Abdul Aziz. He was an Arab city boy (from the bled al-makhzen) who had married a Berber tribal girl (from the bled al-siba).

At first Abdul Aziz had explained that it was necessary for Berber and Arab to unite, to marry, so that the old divisions between groups, so evident in the ethnographies and studies we had read about North Africa, could be erased. But then it turned out that Zaynab was actually distantly related to Abdul Aziz. Ties between city and country, between Arab and Berber, had always existed, on some levels anyway, despite what the books said.

"Of course the city and the country work together," said Aisha. "How can Marrakech live without the farmers? If the crop is bad, the city has no bread. And the villages can't buy the other things they need."

Thus, in addition to the traditional *bay'a,* or pledge of recognition by which the tribes would on ritual occasions publicly express their allegiance to the Sultan, there was another, older, more subtle tie between country and city: the economic one. A complex web of relationships had developed over the centuries between country people who brought their sheep and goats and cows into Marrakech and the artisans who made the hides into beautiful soft Morocco leather, who wove the wool into fine rugs; between the traders who brought in knives and tea and bolts of cloth from Japan, India, and more recently Europe, and the farmers in the villages and the mountains who hauled sacks of barley and wheat into the cities to make into flour.

The makhzen and the siba territories could not survive for long without each other, clearly; political acts of swearing fealty, such as the bay'a, simply reinforced the economic connection. And it was these economic ties Bob had decided to study. In his year in the markets of Marrakech, talking to and interviewing merchants, farmers, middlemen, auctioneers, he developed new respect for the way the traditional methods of personal negotiation still persisted even as the tourist trade continued to reorient many of the goods and services.

"What's really interesting to me is that the old ways still work," Bob said to Omar. "The merchants adapt to new practices; they adjust, change a bit here, a bit there, use calculators instead of abacuses, speculate on the money market rather than on the crop productions, but still rely on the old contacts, the old routes."

"The old ways work better today," Omar pointed out, "because there isn't so much trouble. When the Pasha Glaoui ruled Marrakech for the French, there was always trouble."

"Which was bad for business," said his father, Si Abdulla. "Trouble is always bad for business."

In 1971 and 1972, the bloody days of Pasha Glaoui, darling of the Paris salons, were long over. No more decapitated heads of executed rivals were displayed in Djemaa al-Fna as warnings to political dissidents. Glaoui was pardoned by Muhammad V; one of his sons is in the diplomatic corps of Morocco; another is one of the nation's finest painters; still another runs a marvelous and expensive restaurant in Marrakech. The entertainments in the square were pleasanter, more amusing, though Aisha suggested that many of the storytellers were there with political messages, thinly veiled in metaphor, to deliver.

And in August 1972 the King survived another coup.

"He has *baraka* [God's grace]," Aisha said, the same Aisha who had insisted in 1971 that the King would not dare to come to Marrakech. "Something has saved him *twice*. Of course, he is an Alawite, a descendant of the Prophet, like me. I should remember that."

In 1976 I went back to Marrakech alone, for the first time since we had closed our door on the Rue Trésor behind us. I went back with Melissa Llewelyn-Davies, a director with Granada Television of London, to help make an ethnographic, educational film about Muslim women.

The acrobats and the fortune-tellers were still there in Djemaa al-Fna. But many of the musical groups, Aisha said, were from religious organizations, or *zawiya*s, bearing witness to their beliefs and hence recruiting for the lodges. There was an upsurge of interest in religion among young people, she said, and Omar confirmed it.

"It's the Green March that's done it," he said when we went to lunch at his house. "The King is very clever, he has put religion and politics together so everyone likes it!"

We had read about the Green March to the Sahara in the American newspapers, watched the television coverage of the unarmed volunteers walking south, green flags waving high. The King himself led them, their religious as well as their political ruler. "We are only asserting our just rights," Hassan II had declared on television when he asked for volunteers to occupy the phosphate-rich territory of the Spanish Sahara.

It was the fall of 1975. The International Court of Justice in The Hague had issued a long-awaited advisory opinion on the legal status of the Western Sahara, a Spanish colony. The court stated that legal ties of allegiance existed historically between the Sultan of Morocco and some tribes living in the Western Sahara, but that these ties were not equivalent to Moroccan territorial sovereignty over the entire area. The King took the position that the historical legal ties constituted a legitimate claim, and that it was therefore only right that Moroccan citizens, volunteers from all the nation's provinces, should march peacefully to the South and further that claim.

Abdul Aziz had written Bob about the event and had sent us a book that the King had written, Le Défi. "A good book," his letter said. "You will understand the situation in the Sahara better after reading it, Bob, and," he had added slyly, "it will be very good for your French, which I am sure you are losing in America!"

This from Abdul Aziz was high praise for the government, since, in 1971 and 1972, Abdul Aziz, though supportive in principle, had often been extremely critical of the King's policies.

When Melissa and I arrived in the spring of 1976, the popular song about the Green March, "Al Ayun," still echoed back and forth across Djemaa al-Fna from the tape recorders and transistor radios carried by the young men of Marrakech. The cloth merchants continued to do a brisk business with their Green March designs for caftans (gold and green for the sun and the grain). But the Green March was not working out as planned. The tribal people of the Sahara had not all bowed down to the King and sworn fealty. Many had pulled back, regrouped, and announced that they did not want to be part of Morocco; they wanted their own independent country. Algeria and Libya offered aid to these peoples, through the Polisario Front for Saharan self-determination. Thus, a war was actually in progress in the South.

"But it is nothing serious," Omar insisted. "Merely skirmishes. It will be finished in a few days, a few weeks, but you should not try to film in the South, B.J., it is too dangerous, you must think of your children."

"We are focusing on the women's point of view," explained Melissa, "so it won't be necessary to head South."

"Ah," said Omar, smiling charmingly. "You must speak to Mme. Aisha, B.J.'s good friend."

"We have," I said. "And she is going to work with us. We're going to her village tomorrow. Did you know she was a landowner, Omar?"

"I am glad to hear it," said Omar.

In the years we had known Aisha and her family, we had never visited the village of her birth, though she had many times invited us. Her husband Khaddour went back and forth, and cousins came and stayed while shopping in the big city. Once several sacks of grain had been delivered to the entrance of the passage where Aisha and her family lived in three tiny rooms off a central courtyard. The grain, Aisha explained proudly, was her annual share of the crop from her own land. We had said she was most welcome to spread the grain out on our roof (Hajja Kenza's roof, of course) and she did so, picking out and discarding the stones and bits of dirt, turning the precious wheat over carefully to let it dry properly before taking it around to the flour mill in Bab Agnaou. City and country. Each was indeed tied to the other, through people.

Aisha's village is small and not on the map. It lies near Sidi bou Othman, a town twenty-four miles north of Marrakech on the Casablanca road, where the rural market is held each week on Mondays. The town is named for the holy man to whom the two shrines are dedicated. The guidebook states that Sidi bou Othman is famous for other reasons: first, Moroccan tribal soldiers made a last stand against the French here, in 1912; they lost and the French broke through to Marrakech. Sidi bou Othman is also the site of a twelfth-century dam, which held the mighty waters of the nearby river in check and stored it into cisterns against the years of drought, cisterns which still exist and which, archaeologists say, must have held nearly half a million gallons of water.

Today the river is only a narrow cut of shallow water beside clumps of old, wild jujube trees, but it marks the way to Aisha's home, the village of Sidi bin Slimane. Our rented taxi took off from the road and followed the river, as she directed (leaving the jujube trees behind and heading across what seemed a barren plain). There were tufts of grass and some prickly bushes, a solitary donkey. Aisha rolled down the taxi window to look carefully at the donkey but announced that she did not know the rider.

"If Aisha's land is out here, it won't do much for her," Melissa remarked crisply. I agreed inwardly. It was pretty desolate.

We bounced over a slight rise, and a whitewashed dome was visible, set into a little grove of trees. "There it is!" cried Aisha. "The shrine. The *moussem* festival is in August, after the harvest. You should stay and make the film then. It is a wonderful moussem!"

The excitement in her voice did not seem justified by the landscape. Except for the shrine and the surrounding trees, there was only a row of mud-brick houses, laid out along a low hill, the same color as the ground upon which they stood.

"There! There! There's my sister's house!" And she jerked the taxi driver's sleeve to indicate where he was to turn, beside a metal door. The door swung open as we approached; a tall woman stood just inside.

"Hajiba!" Aisha cried, jumping out of the taxi and embracing her sister. She was home.

Aisha beckoned to us peremptorily to come in. Here she felt clearly in charge. She settled herself on the carpet in a long room in her sister's house, indicated that we were to sit beside her, called for more pillows, ordered tea.

"It's nice to be home," she said, pulling down the hood of her jellaba and removing her veil.

"Nobody veils here," she said. "Tell your friend Melissa that. Here no one needs to veil. We are all related to each other, so we are one big family—except for four strangers."

When this was translated, Melissa smiled. "How would *you* like to be one of the strangers?" she asked.

Our interchange had been watched carefully by the older sister, who now looked somewhat quizzically at me, patted my knee, and said to Aisha, "This is your friend, the American?"

Aisha nodded. She looked me over carefully.

"I like her skirt," she announced. "But where are her children?"

I produced pictures, wondering what Aisha had said about us during that year she had worked in our house, walked me around the medina, showed me the ways of the shops, introduced me to my neighbors, and taken me to the women's religious organizations in the zawiyas, and on pilgrimage to the shrine of Moulay Ibrahim. "And what about her?" A jerk of her head in the direction of Melissa, tall, fairer than me.

"That's B.J.'s cousin," explained Aisha. "They're going to make a film about women in Morocco."

Aisha had made Melissa my cousin just to keep things simple, perhaps, and, I thought, to forestall any objections that her sisters might voice about strangers and cameras. She was already our advance agent.

"A film? Like on television?"

"Like on the television!"

The sister smiled delightedly. "And will she turn the camera?" pointing to Melissa. "No," said Aisha. "Other women will be coming to do that."

"Oh," said Hajiba. She looked from me to Melissa and back to Aisha.

"They will come on the airplane when we are ready for them," said Aisha airily.

The sister nodded. She was a bit taller and plumper than Aisha, her face more wrinkled with sun and age, but she had the same upright bearing, the same high cheekbones.

Others had entered, another sister, two older women identified merely as "relatives," and a younger woman, very beautiful with black hair and red cheeks and a flowered caftan tucked up partially around her waist, her hands behind her back to support a baby in the traditional sling. Aisha introduced her as Rabia, her brother's son's wife. They kissed each other warmly.

"I am very close to her," said Aisha to me, touching the younger woman's rosy cheek lovingly. "She's like my second daughter, B.J. It's her husband that works my land for me, and I give him part of the crop."

"Film," "cinema"—the words went around the group, were discussed, taken up, put down, discussed again.

"You mean a film about real people and not a story?" asked the beautiful Rabia.

"Yes," I answered. "Why do you ask?"

She laughed. "Because if you want a story, you came to the wrong place. We don't have any good stories here, just work in the fields, and children, and sometimes a wedding or a feast."

When I translated that for Melissa, she looked pleased and said to tell Rabia that was exactly the kind of thing we were interested in. "So the West doesn't think there are only belly dancers and camels here in Morocco," I added. I thought I was being diplomatic. I was wrong.

"We used to have some camels!" cried the older sister. "And we could use them now. Donkeys are so slow and small. But camels are too expensive."

"Where are those women from again?" one of the older relatives asked, giggling behind her hand. "France? Was that it?"

"No," I answered. "I'm from America and Melissa's from London."

"Isn't it all the same? France and America and that—that other place?" She covered her face in mock confusion but was obviously laughing, teasing us.

Aisha looked slightly annoyed, but she took it up. "Maybe people who live in backwoods places like *this* think those places are all the same, but they're not. Why, they don't even speak the same language!"

The older woman uncovered her face. She pointed to me and to Melissa. "They don't speak the same language? Of course they do. I hear it. It sounds funny."

"No, no, I meant in France," Aisha explained hurriedly.

"We're not so dumb as you think, cousin," retorted the old lady.

Rabia spoke into the muffled laughter: city cousin was not always going to get away with murder where country cousins were concerned, but the bantering was good-hearted enough, I thought.

"Do you have rooms as nice as this one in America?" she asked.

I looked around for a moment. It was a very pleasant room, long, low-ceilinged. Whitewashed walls below the log-and-thatch roof, red rug on top of carefully swept reed mats where we sat against the multicolored pillows and drank tea. A sitting room like many others in Morocco except that here someone with a good deal of natural talent had covered the whitewashed walls with murals in bright colors. Red flowers and green trees, white-domed shrines, a man hoeing in a green field, a donkey being unloaded for market.

"Look, B.J., that's the shrine of Sidi bel Abbas, in Marrakech." Aisha pointed it out. "See the green roofs, and there is Moulay al-Ksour, where we went to the hadra, remember, and then you know the Koutoubia by Djemaa al-Fna."

I had seen wall paintings in many parts of the Middle East—in Nubia, particularly, and in Upper Egypt. Berber houses often had finely painted geometric designs on the wooden ceilings, but I had seldom seen scenes as finely executed as these.

"Does everyone in Sidi bin Slimane paint their walls?" Melissa asked.

The older sister shrugged when the question was translated. "If they feel like it," she said. "You don't have to. Some do. Some don't."

"Who's the artist?"

The older sister looked up, "Why, Khaddour, of course. Aisha's husband. When he came to fix my roof, he would paint when it was raining and he couldn't work."

Aisha looked proud and pleased. Khaddour. I could hardly believe it. That big, lumbering man of few words whom Aisha referred to only as "he." Who had no steady job and picked up money from time to time by loading and unloading crates of vegetables and tinned goods in the market. Who had a vacant look in his eye and seemed, though pleasant, to be a born loser, unable to deal with the world of the new, changing Morocco. Khaddour was an artist of no mean achievement; the lively colorful scenes showed that.

"Well," said Aisha. "That can be one part in your film, B.J. Khaddour painting. I'll hold the paints." She laughed and the ladies in the room laughed with her. "And then we take pictures of my sister with the chickens." The sister giggled, pleased.

Aisha went on planning the film while we went out into the courtyard and she explained that the three clay structures, like monolithic modern sculptures, were actually silos, one for each sister, "to keep their grain dry. I can show you how to get the grain out, that would be good in the film, too."

We walked through the village. Aisha's relatives' houses were identified, as well as an innocuous pile of stones that was, according to Aisha, "the beginning of a new shrine." We toured Aisha's garden of fig and almond trees where Rabia's older children climbed up and shook down some green almonds for us. "Rabia, that mint patch needs to be weeded," Aisha announced. "Get your daughter to do it. See," she said to me in a different tone, "we have mint and parsley and coriander. We don't have to buy these things in the market. They are ours."

The surrounding fields were pointed out, long sloping stretches of land where grain and vegetables were coming up. They looked quite undifferentiated to me, but Aisha indicated the single tree, the hedges of prickly pear, the line of stones that marked off the plots, hers, her sisters', her brothers'.

"And don't the brothers sometimes take their sisters' land?" Melissa asked.

I translated and Aisha bristled indignantly. "Of course they try," she said. "You have to fight for your rights. Everybody does. Brothers as well as sisters. Some brothers are mean and selfish. Some sisters won't stick together against a

brother who acts like that. But I've always cooperated with my sisters, even"—
she put a hand on my arm and smiled—"the one who teased us. And my husband backs me up. Even though we're in the city, he comes and helps, fixing the roof, helping with the harvest—"

"And decorates the walls with beautiful paintings," I added.

She nodded.

"You still think of it as your land?" Melissa persisted.

"It *is* my land," Aisha said doggedly. "It is my right. That is what the Koran says. That is what my father taught me. And I'll give it to my daughter Najiya when I die."

"Not to the boys?"

"No. She needs it more," and to me, very low, "because of her health." She and I both knew she meant Najiya's tragic deformity, the hunchback that had frozen her height at an early age and deprived her of the beauty her face promised.

"Thank you, Melissa," Aisha said carefully in English as we settled into the taxi for the return trip to Marrakech. "Tell her"—she poked me—"that I enjoyed the visit. It's good to see my sisters and to see that things are going right."

Melissa smiled. We sat quietly, looking out at the sparse landscape, the tufts of grass, the prickly pear, the low outlines of Sidi bou Othman far in the distance.

"Ah, B.J., we will make a very lovely film together," said Aisha. And she pounded my knee affectionately as her sister had done.

Hajja Kenza. I had been putting off the call to Hajja Kenza, because I still found it difficult to face the fact that the house on Rue Trésor, where we had lived in 1971 and 1972, was no longer our home, nor anyone's home. It was a hotel! The Hôtel d'Ouriké. When I first saw that sign above our old door, I found myself perilously close to tears. Get a grip on yourself, I admonished myself firmly, stop behaving like a sloppy old lady returning to the sentimental scenes of her youth. It's Hajja Kenza's house, not yours. If she wants to dynamite it, she has every right. But I still would have found it easier to accept the dynamiting than the fact that she had turned that beautiful house into a hotel. What fuss, what fury, had exploded on Rue Trésor while we still lived there, when another neighbor had reputedly dickered with a hotel company that wanted his house. Hotels were bad for the reputation of the neighborhood, stated the petition that went around. Hotels attract bad people, such as strangers and tourists. The good housewife who brought the petition to my door allowed that yes, we were strangers, but we weren't tourists, and since we'd lived there so long we were not *as* strange as some might be. We had signed the petition. Hotels would have nefarious influences on the children. Yes, we agreed. But that hotel had opened despite neighborhood efforts to stop it; and now here was Hajja Kenza, the loudest complainer of all in those days, running a hotel herself, a *public place,* as the good petitioning housewife had defined it, speaking as though the words might corrupt her mouth and rot her teeth.

"It's just because Hajja Kenza got so mad," Aisha had explained during my first visit to her after my return. "The people who took the house after you got a lawyer and sued her."

"Sued her? Why?"

"About the water heater. They said it was included in the contract. But when they got in the house, it was gone. Hajja Kenza took it out after you left and sold it."

I suppressed a smile. Why was I smiling? It had not been a laughing matter at the time; the issue of the ownership of the water heater had caused harsh words between Bob and Hajja Kenza, between me and Hajja Kenza. Aisha had gotten caught in the middle, and I had always regretted the stormy scenes because, in the end, it was Aisha who had been hurt, whose relationship with Hajja Kenza had suffered.

"It was awful, B.J. They took her to court and in the end she had to pay for the lawyer and for the judge and for the water heater, too! She was so mad for so long we thought she might just have a fit and die. I kept trying to calm her down, but it never worked."

"Still—a hotel?"

"One day she just said she was finished with renters. She was going to open a hotel and make real money."

"Does she?"

Aisha had nodded, somewhat reluctantly, I thought. "She seems to be doing well."

"So you and she are on good terms again?"

Aisha sighed. "Oh yes. It wasn't just you, B.J. She's always been a hard woman. I see her from time to time. No bad feelings. But I refused to work for her in the hotel. I'm not *that* poor."

I told myself that what had happened five years before lay long in the past. Aisha and she were more or less reconciled, why was I fussing? I was here this time to do a job, to help make a film about the women of Marrakech. And I had thought of Hajja Kenza. If one wanted a character in the film that belied the Western public's stereotype of the passive hidden Muslim woman, what better could one find than Hajja Kenza, the widow, the independent entrepreneur, amassing wealth by her own hand, albeit with a little initial capital from her father, her right under Islamic law, like Aisha's plot of land in Sidi bin Slimane.

Thus I was on my way to pay a call to Hajja Kenza. I even had an appointment, and I knocked on the door of her house on the dot of four-thirty. The door had a new coat of paint, but no one answered. Above the door, the window was closed, the window where she used to lean out on the sill and harangue the passersby, including me. I knocked again. A little boy pulled on my skirt and pointed to the hotel door. Of course, she was in business, she was in her place of business, not at home. I thanked the little boy, moved the few steps along Rue Trésor, and banged on what had once been our own door. Stop it, I told myself, stop being silly, it's not your house anymore. Even the silver knocker in the shape of the hand of Fatima was gone, replaced by a more serviceable, cheaper one of flat copper.

"Lebas." A very thin, very small old woman answered the door, looking at me sideways. So Hajja Kenza was doing well enough to have hired help.

"Who's there?" That raucous voice I would recognize anywhere.

"It's me, B.J., Hajja Kenza."

"Let her in," ordered that voice.

The old woman stepped aside, looking not at me but at the ground in an annoyingly servile fashion and I had a pang of fury; how much, I wondered, did Hajja Kenza pay this poor old lady?

"Come in, come in." I scarcely had a second to glance into the courtyard and register that the fountain was still there when a door opened directly on my right, where no door had been before. The double window of different-colored panes of glass—blue, red, green, amber—the window of our living room—had given way to this door to Hajja Kenza's office.

"Ahlan wusahlan!" Hajja Kenza stood up, in a neat beige caftan, an elegant brown scarf, and behind her in the small office were, no, it couldn't be, yes, it was—two strange men!

"Lebas, how are you, B.J.?" We shook hands. Hajja Kenza and I had never been much into kissing even in the early halcyon days of our friendship.

"Sit down. Sit down."

I sat down in a chair against the wall. Hajja Kenza sat down by the door, flashing a very golden smile and almost but not quite chortling. The two men, one in uniform, one in a dark suit, also sat down.

Well, what had I expected? I was not sure, but it was certainly not this. Our former landlady, who had complained of bloat and cramps and pains, who had looked drawn and ashen only five years ago, looked rejuvenated. She was slimmer, straighter, her complexion faintly pink, her eyes—was Hajja Kenza wearing eye makeup? No, it couldn't be, she would not let her daughter wear lipstick, go swimming, ride a bicycle without covering her head, her body to the ankles. But it did look as though Hajja Kenza was wearing very discreet eye makeup. If anyone had wanted an advertisement for the tonic effects of work, here it was, and I would bear witness. She would be wonderful, I thought fleetingly, on film.

Hajja Kenza was speaking. She had stood up, I was being helped up, Hajja Kenza's strong hand under my elbow, pushing me along toward the two strange gentlemen like a child that is being taught to say hello.

I shook hands, as instructed.

M. Sefraoui, tourist administration.

Captain Hamid, police.

They were tall, dark gentlemen, not young. They seemed to know Hajja Kenza, at least from the looks that went back and forth between them, the golden smile that flashed from Hajja Kenza's obviously newly capped teeth.

Hotels were indeed good money, it seemed. But what were the men doing here, I wondered, inspecting the premises?

Hajja Kenza, without getting up, opened the door and hollered "Tea!" in the general area of the courtyard.

"How do you like my office, B.J.?" She gestured around the small room, its newly whitewashed walls without windows. "You see what I did. I cut the salon into three parts, two rooms and this. No waste space. And I took the colored-glass windows out and sold them to a French person." She laughed at her own cleverness in spotting foreigners' weaknesses for such silliness as colored glass!

The thin old servant knocked and brought in a tray, bearing a teapot, a kettle of hot water, four glasses, and a bunch of mint. Hajja Kenza waited until the old servant had shut the door behind her and then reached down to a ring of keys attached to her belt, a pleasantly braided concoction of beige and brown, matching the beige-and-brown trim that bordered the sleeves and neckline of her caftan. Middle-aged chic. Ah, Hajja Kenza, you *are* doing well, I thought.

With a large key she unlocked a wooden box on the office desk. It looked as though it might have held papers. It did hold papers, but she burrowed under the first pile and came up with a black lacquer canister of tea and a box of sugar lumps.

"You have to watch everything these days," she said happily, as though she enjoyed the process. "Otherwise people steal you blind."

The man in the dark suit cleared his throat. "You are a tourist, madame?" he asked me. "You have stayed in Hajja Kenza's hotel?"

"Tell him what a good housekeeper I am," Hajja Kenza rushed in before I had a chance to answer. "And how I abide by all the rules—"

"The ministry is of course very concerned about hotels," the dark-suited gentleman went on, ignoring Hajja Kenza's interruption. "It is for your protection, of course. Tourists are considered important to Morocco by our nationalist government and by His Majesty King Hassan II, may God keep him safe."

"I understand," I answered, "and I—"

"Tell him. Tell him!" prompted Hajja Kenza, smiling that gold smile again as she spooned the tea into the pot. The keys at her waist rattled and clinked.

"We rented from Hajja Kenza when we were here some years ago," I began carefully, "when I was here with my husband and children."

"Ah yes," Hajja Kenza interrupted again, as though she had forgotten something. "And how is the family, Mister, and Lorrie Ann and that Laila, and David —does he still play soccer?"

"They are well," I replied formally. "And Naima?"

"She keeps the books for me, so the school was some good, even though she didn't finish her baccalaureate. Isn't that what children should do, help their parents, hey?"

"Yes, they should," I agreed.

The dark-suited man took hold of the conversation again. "And your husband? Is he in Marrakech with you?"

"No, he is in America, but he will be joining me soon, and my oldest daughter also."

"Ah." The dark-suited man said something under his breath to the man in the uniform.

This did not seem the moment to raise the issue of filming with Hajja Kenza. In fact, it did not seem the moment to raise the issue of filming at all. I wondered whether the officials' visit was unexpected. Or whether Hajja Kenza had planned it this way, using me for some obscure purpose. To testify to her honesty, her good character, her long and successful experience of dealing with foreigners? After five years of absence, one half hour with Hajja Kenza had roused all kinds of uneasy and ambiguous feelings in me again. I shook myself. I felt I was being ridiculous.

"Ha! See how generous I am with the sugar." Hajja Kenza spoke, drawing attention to herself as she loaded lumps into the teapot with the mint and black tea and poured the boiling water over it. She laughed again, but it seemed a pointless, false laugh. Generosity was accepted in Marrakech as a virtue, not a joke. And one didn't ordinarily draw attention to its exercise in this way. No, something was up. Permits not filled out properly, books cooked by Naima, taxes not paid according to the proper scale? I did not know, nor did I want to know. I resolved to drink my tea quickly and leave as soon as I could politely do so, without getting involved in whatever Hajja Kenza might have in her head.

"Do you speak French, madame?" Up to now the conversation had been held in Arabic.

"Yes."

"Most Americans do not," he answered conversationally in French. "I understand that in America people speak nothing but English, what a tragedy for them." He smiled. I stole a glance at Hajja Kenza and saw her expression change, her mouth harden at the sound of these words that she could not understand. I was tempted to goad her further, to go on speaking French, but remembered that I was a guest. It is rude to speak when other people cannot understand what you are saying, my mother would have said. I switched back into Arabic, stealing another glance at Hajja Kenza as I did so.

"Yes, it is a shame. We need to know more languages."

I was right. Hajja Kenza had relaxed. She was pouring out the tea.

So I finished my glass, excused myself to M. Sefraoui, Captain Hamid, Hajja Kenza. And left.

In the end, we did not film Hajja Kenza at all. When I went back, first by myself to discuss the film possibility and the second time with Melissa to see what might work, she welcomed us into her office and ordered tea. She was superpolite, even effusive, as she explained that she had inquired about the process of cinema from "people who knew." She had been told that movies cost a lot of money. Budgets, she had been told, were very large, into the millions of dollars, she said, her eyes actually rolling in anticipation.

"So," she said. Her eyes glittered. So what? I thought.

"I would be happy to appear in your film, B.J., five minutes for only ten thousand dollars. This is a special price for you" (hand on my arm, mouth stretched out in that fake smile). "Tell your friend, the director."

I translated Hajja Kenza's offer to Melissa, whose reaction was immediate and expected. She laughed.

"But, B.J., tell her you can also film in the hotel, not just me." She flung open her office door and pointed out into the court where no water splashed in the fountain now; the balcony whose painted doors and windows of multicolored glass through which the children had played games with the sun, the moon, had disappeared, sold to "French persons." They had been replaced by plain wooden doors, one, two, three of them, each for a tiny room within the spacious ones we had once enjoyed.

"I have eight lovely rooms," said Hajja Kenza, the frantic saleswoman now. "Would your friend like to see them?" She pulled at my arm and jerked her head in Melissa's direction. Her caftan and pale green scarf were as neat and chic today as they had been when the gentlemen were visiting; it was her eyes that were wrong—glittering, anxious.

"No, I don't think so, thank you," replied Melissa crisply.

I turned back to Hajja Kenza and tried to explain that Melissa was not from Hollywood, that our film was to be used in schools, on family television, not in big theaters where people spent a lot of money on admission. And therefore we could not possibly pay what she asked, our budget was small and—

"Films for schools?" Hajja Kenza echoed incredulously. "Come on, B.J., you don't expect me to believe that. You are joking. I can see you are joking." And to reinforce her point and emphasize the ludicrousness of my statement, she gave me a rather sharp, if playful, slap on the arm. Accompanied by a giggle, just to show she meant no harm. It was all in good fun. But, her eyes said, it wasn't all in fun. Hajja Kenza obviously thought I was trying to cheat her out of hard cash.

Melissa was moving toward the door. Hajja Kenza gave it one last try. She held on to my arm firmly and gestured upward to the balcony where we had sat on summer evenings, where the children had raced around the second floor, playing tag.

"Isn't it beautiful? Tell her!" she hissed. "I could come down to five thousand dollars; you don't realize, B.J., you are new to this game. Movies have lots of money, even in Morocco—"

"No, no," said Melissa.

And I repeated, "No, no, the boss says no."

Hajja Kenza let go of my arm.

Melissa was already out the door, standing under the sign, Hôtel d'Ouriké.

"Sorry," I said, and extended my hand. Hajja Kenza shook it absently, her eye on Melissa's retreating back.

"Beeja," she whispered conspiratorially. "I *might* come down to three thousand."

I had had enough. It was not only seeing our house cut up and destroyed, it was Hajja Kenza's unabashed greed.

"Hajja Kenza," I said, "we were going to do *you* a favor. It is only because I suggested it that Melissa was even *interested* in the hotel. You would have gotten a lot of free publicity. Many people would have come here. So you should be paying *us* for the privilege of filming *you!*"

She stared at me. Her mouth actually fell open.

"Me pay *you?*" Hajja Kenza just couldn't believe it. She laughed disdainfully. I was obviously mad. "I never heard of such an idea. And I never heard of any films in schools either," she added in a final shot.

Melissa was calling from the street.

"Goodbye, Hajja Kenza. Give my best to Naima."

When I turned back to close the door behind me, Hajja Kenza still stood there, staring after me and muttering. I fancied I could just make out that she was saying "Films for *schools.*"

In August the filming was finished. We had taken part in a wedding and made a pilgrimage to a distant mountain shrine. Omar's family had invited us to film a hadra, or religious ceremony, held in their house. Aisha had taken us back to her village, and the camera had recorded Khaddour's paintings on the whitewashed room and Aisha's description of women's land rights guaranteed by the Koran. Bob had come to Marrakech to spend a few days with me before we all left for home. Abdul Aziz, our old teacher of French, had come to call. He had been away while we were filming, in France on "a special project," he said. "Education. Lectures.

"It was an experience, Bob," said Abdul Aziz.

"How do you mean?" Bob himself had just come from six weeks as an academic guest in France, an exchange scholar.

"Well, for me, you know, a Moroccan, it is strange. All my life I have been taught that France is the fountain of civilization; in school, in literature, in the audiovisual course that you and your wife took."

Yes, I thought. I remembered the stories and pictures of the Thibault family, their boring children Paul and Sylvie and their holidays in the country with the grandparents where they played in the attic—a concept that poor Abdul Aziz had had difficulty explaining to his Moroccan students, born and raised under flat roofs. But Abdul Aziz was talking again.

"Now. . . . I cannot explain. This feeling of attraction for the beautiful city of Paris, and at the same time I felt—upset, I disliked it."

"Why?"

"Well, Paris is full of migrant workers, you know. Moroccan, Algerian. Sixty percent of the men in the Moroccan Rif area work in France. They are everywhere. Is that independence? They come to parks and wander around silently. They walk by cafés and don't sit down. They are poor. No one speaks to them."

"Paris is like that," said Bob. "Even French people don't speak to other French people they don't know."

"But at least they are the same color. They don't call them *monkeys*."

"Someone called you that?"

"Oh no," said Abdul Aziz earnestly. "Everyone was polite to me and applauded my lectures. Education in Morocco. Social Change. That sort of thing. And I quickly learned to wear jeans like you, Bob." Abdul Aziz laughed heartily. When he laughed, his earnest manner dissipated and his face looked younger. "It is only the poor workers who wear the dark suit and tie, as I did when I taught your class."

I served coffee. Abdul Aziz apologized for not bringing Zaynab, who was up in the mountains visiting her family. He picked up the coffee cup, set it down again, and shook his head, as though ridding himself of bad thoughts.

"It's silly to talk about France," he went on, "when we are Moroccan. But then, we are still tied to France. We have to face it."

Bob looked surprised. "Most of the French have left Morocco. How are you tied?"

"Economically, of course. French cheese in the market, French clothes in the stores in Marrakech, haven't you noticed? Who else will we deal with? The King was educated in France, you know. Oh, I support the King, I am proud of what he did in the Green March, but sometimes I wonder where Morocco is going."

"It's hard to do everything at once." Bob was trying to be considerate, as Abdul Aziz's pain was evident.

"About France . . ." He returned to the subject, unable to stay away from it. "It is racism I am talking about—"

"We have racism in America, too," Bob pointed out.

"It's different, it's . . . I mean, even *I* had nothing in common with those Moroccan workers in Paris. . . . I feel ashamed of that feeling. . . . I have not said that to anyone. . . . In America, how do you get away from that—"

"We haven't, we haven't."

We drank our coffee and discussed children, music.

Abdul Aziz said that his work was going well, that he was writing a new book of instruction for preschool children, to combine Koranic education with some of the "more advanced childhood education precepts of the West. Have you heard of Piaget?"

"Yes," said Bob admiringly. "If you can combine Piaget and the Koran, Abdul Aziz, you will have solved the problems of social change all by yourself."

"You are kidding me, Bob." Abdul Aziz laughed.

"Only partly," said Bob.

Bob and I went around together and said goodbye again to old friends: Aisha, Abdul Krim, Najiya, Youssef, Saleh.

Hajja Kenza wrung Bob's hand and told him that I still did not understand the world. "They cheated her, Bob, she is too good-hearted, those movie people have *lots* of money, they just told her they didn't."

Bob smiled. "Yes, Hajja Kenza." She showed him the hotel and he nodded absently. "A good enterprise," he observed. "You are doing well."

"Yes, I'm doing well, thanks be to God."

"And to your hard work."

She smiled appreciatively. "Your husband knows what life is about," she told me and flashed a final golden smile.

Bob insisted on taking Omar to dinner in downtown Marrakech. We ate by the swimming pool of the Hôtel le Marrakech and discussed the future of Morocco.

"It is just beginning to work itself out," said Omar. "Come back again and see for yourself."

We said that we would.

CHAPTER IX

Marrakech, Morocco

1982

Don't throw out the old fire until
you have found the fire maker.

Moroccan proverb
from the High Atlas

THE DROUGHT HAD ended. It was raining in Marrakech, a gentle steady rain that had been falling since our arrival the night before. The members of the 1982 Smithsonian study tour which I was leading looked crestfallen as we checked into our first-class hotel. *Rain* in Marrakech, and the climax of the trip.

"Oh, but it's wonderful!" The hotel desk clerk was almost rhapsodic. "Three years of drought, ladies and gentlemen. It has been terrible. Thank God it is broken. Thank God for the rain!"

In the years since 1976, the letters from our friends in Marrakech had spoken of the drought but not the Green March. The Green March had lost its glory. The skirmishes in the Sahara dragged on, a war neither won nor lost that was draining the nation's resources. Morocco's population had doubled in a genera-tion, and the country that had once exported wheat was now importing 70 percent of its grain.

"People are becoming desperate because of the drought," Omar had written. "I have been to see your friend Mme. Aisha and she is in good health but her family in Sidi bin Slimane is not doing well." Omar's message meant that no sacks of grain had been coming from the village to Aisha's house on the Rue Trésor for the past three years; rather, Aisha and her family were contributing to the rural family budgets.

But now it was raining. Winter wheat gleamed green in the fields as the tour bus crossed the plains. Rain had come earlier, and again now, a crucial moment in the growing season. It began to look as though there would be a good harvest.

"The rain," said the bellboy who took up our bags, "is a gift from God."

Even without an umbrella, the gentle rain felt good as I walked toward the medina to visit Aisha. Her daughter Najiya had died three months before; I was leaving the tour group briefly to make the customary call of condolence. Rue Bab Agnaou seemed more crowded than I remembered: what looked like a population explosion was pouring out of the cinema, and another seemed to be pushing to get in. Horns honked, donkeys brayed, and people shouted as the traffic snarled, screeched, stopped. I was glad to turn off into the narrow Rue Trésor, our old street, where the wet, uneven stones gleamed and the rose-red walls of the houses were blotched with blessed patches of damp. I looked up and stopped dead. The street was literally festooned with signs. For a festival? Hardly. These were hotels, new hotels, *six,* I counted them. Hôtel d'Ouriké; Hôtel des Îles; Hôtel Essaouira; Hôtel Ramzi; Taroudant Hôtel; Aziza Hôtel.

Six hotels. Our old street was obviously no longer residential. The bakery was still there, that wonderful aroma of fresh bread cutting through the damp, the smell of the drains. There, too, was the bath, horse and cart drawn up as usual beside the door, men unloading logs of wood for the fire that heated both the bakery oven and the water for the public bath. Years ago, to entertain our children, Bob had made a lesson in conservation out of the fire that served two purposes at the same time. And men were going into the bath. Business was probably booming, given the spate of new hotels. It seemed doubtful that any of them had private baths. Knowing Hajja Kenza, she had probably sold our bathtub to some "French person" at a good profit.

The rain poured down in a sudden burst, and a bicyclist whizzed toward me, under the multicolored hotel signs, splashing my legs as he passed. Why was I standing in the middle of the street getting drenched and indulging in reveries about the past? There was Aisha's passage where it had always been, opposite our house, now Hajja Kenza's splendid new enterprise, the Hôtel d'Ouriké. Go in, go in, I told myself. This is why you've come, to offer your sympathies to your old friend Aisha.

Quickly I ducked out of the rain into the low passage, dark and wet underfoot. I put my hand on the rough stone wall and groped my way ahead. Eleven years since I had first met Aisha; six years since I had last seen her. How would she have taken this blow? A terrible blow. Her only daughter. Dead at twenty-eight.

When I had come with Melissa to make the film six years ago, Najiya had helped us, as had Aisha. It had been a difficult project, trying to create for a Western audience a documentary about traditional Muslim women's lives in Marrakech that would be accurate, honest, personal. At one point Aisha and Najiya had even taken me to our old fortune-teller friend Saadiya, "to make you feel better," Aisha had explained. "My treat." And Saadiya had droned, in her deep rich voice, "Ah, your path is strewn with great rocks, iron rocks, but if you work hard and persist, all will be well in the end." A judicious fortune, the kind for which Saadiya was famous, a prediction applicable to everything from a difficult pregnancy to a documentary film!

But Saadiya had proved right. The film had turned out quite well. Aisha had helped. And Najiya. Six years before. And now Najiya was dead.

The door at the end of the passageway was closed. Strange. Aisha's door had always been open, except late at night. I knocked, but there was no answer. Had she moved? Where would she go? How would I find her? I knocked again. I could hear somebody inside rattling pots and pans. I pounded a third time. The door was decrepit, light filtering through cracks in the worn wood.

"Aisha?" My voice rose. I hadn't meant it to.

"Who's there?"

"Me. B.J. From America."

The door creaked open. A familiar small figure stood there in the courtyard in the gentle rain. I had forgotten how small she was, Aisha my friend. She wiped her hands on a towel, her caftan tucked up neatly around her waist as always when she was working around the house, revealing the striped bloomers below. A greenish head scarf, much faded, was tied carefully around her head.

"Welcome! Welcome!"

I stepped down into the court and she reached up and put both arms around my neck. We embraced in the rain, and then Aisha recovered herself. "Come, come, what are we doing, it's pouring, come in, come in," pulling me across the court toward her little sitting room and shutting the door behind us.

"There!" She smiled at me, an exercise that eased the new deep lines in her forehead, down both cheeks. Aisha looked much older.

"Oh, Aisha!" I blurted out. "I'm sorry, so sorry about Najiya," and embarrassed myself by bursting into noisy tears.

Aisha began to cry, too, but in a more dignified and quiet way. While I rummaged for a tissue to blow my dripping nose, she arranged herself cross-legged on a flowered cushion on the floor and began to tell me, as though we had met only last week, about Najiya's last days.

"It was winter, she had just come home from work," began Aisha. "Not yet dark. She liked the work . . . it was good. . . ."

"What was she doing exactly?" Najiya had done well in her exams and had been offered teaching jobs in Agadir, in Errachidia, but she had never wanted to leave home. I dried my eyes and tried to listen calmly to Aisha, but I did not feel calm at all. Najiya had been dead three months, yet the details of her last day were so vivid in Aisha's mind they could have happened yesterday.

"She was working in the municipality, in the office," Aisha answered proudly. "A good salary. And people were polite, she said they were very polite, they never . . . never—" Her voice broke.

"They never bothered her about her health problem, you mean—"

"Yes, yes." In the eleven years I had known her, Aisha had never once mentioned specifically Najiya's "health problem," her hunchback. The closest we had come to discussing it was once, years ago, when she had invited me to go to the fortune-tellers with her and Najiya. "We are going for a special reason," she had explained, "and I'm taking two chickens."

"Chickens?"

"Chickens," and she opened her market basket to show me two live, fine feathered hens, their feet tied together, their eyes still slightly open.

We had waited in the courtyard of Saadiya's beautiful house in the Kasba, a courtyard far larger than ours, with a pleasant garden. Fortune-telling was a lucrative business in Marrakech, it seemed; times of change and uncertainty created anxiety, wasn't that what the social psychologists told us? And what better way to dispel anxiety than with a nice comfortable prediction about the future? "Your way is strewn with iron rocks . . . success in the end," etc.

"What are we waiting for?" I had asked Aisha.

She had frowned. "Shh," was all she said. One of the chickens in the basket clucked feebly.

Saadiya herself, large and dark and imposing in white caftan and scarf, opened the door of a room on the courtyard and beckoned us in.

"Sheikh Ahmed," she introduced us to a man standing in the room beside her.

Aisha proffered the chickens. Sheikh Ahmed nodded and the chickens went back out the door, presumably to a waiting assistant. We sat down.

Saadiya whipped out a filmy bright green scarf and laid it over Najiya's head and shoulders. The sheikh, a tall thin man in white like Saadiya, with a green turban and a walleye, launched into a chant, a litany, with Saadiya as his respondent.

A single fly buzzed in the small room. Aisha and I were slightly to one side of the ritual trio, but I could still see Sheikh Ahmed's head clearly, his walleye, with a pupil that wandered across his eyeball, then jerked quickly back like a tic. He put his hand on Najiya's covered head and spoke, he put his hand on her shoulders and spoke. He put his hand finally on that rounded hump on her back, the heavy unmentionable lump of bone and flesh that had telescoped her poor back. The language was heavy with rhetoric and words I could not understand, but he seemed to be asking God to release the "tightness," to ease the pain, to mend what had been broken.

"*Ameen,*" intoned Saadiya.

"*Ameen,*" whispered Aisha next to me. She was clutching her knees tightly with both hands.

A laying on of hands. At the time, I had wondered what the treatment was expected to produce. Did Aisha believe that the hump would melt away under the green scarf and that Najiya would emerge, like the princess in the fairy tale, transformed into the beautiful woman she was meant to be, her back straight as a young tree?

"It's her headaches," Aisha had said to me suddenly.

The séance ended. The sheikh departed. We were to wait a bit till Najiya woke. After a time, Saadiya removed the green scarf and Najiya sat up, rubbed her eyes, and smiled. The hunchback was once more revealed.

"You feel better, my daughter?" Aisha asked quickly.

"Of course she feels better," Saadiya said shortly. "Sheikh Ahmed's gifts are great."

"Yes, I feel better," Najiya had said.

Headaches. Had that been a sign of something? She had always had bad, blinding headaches, even eleven years ago. We had assumed the headaches to be a result of stress. For Najiya, though she had always been self-conscious about what Aisha called "her health," had nevertheless determinedly pushed herself out into the world to get an education. Eleven years ago she had been in secondary school, and from our bedroom window I would see her emerge from the dark passage on rainy mornings, walking her bicycle. Her face set and anxious above the neat jellaba, under the stylish scarf tied beneath her chin, she would look carefully up and down the Rue Trésor before mounting the bicycle awkwardly and pedaling off slowly to class. Perhaps the students mocked her? The headaches had always seemed to come on after school.

Aisha touched my knee, bringing me back from my ruminations about the past. ". . . She had just come from work and I asked her if she wanted tea, but she said no, she was cold, she'd just lie down and cover up and watch the television and have tea later.

"So I left her and came out to reheat the meal. I'd made *harira* soup that day. It's good in the winter."

(I remembered Aisha's harira. I sometimes made it in Austin on winter evenings; take a quarter kilo of meat, brown it, add chick-peas and lentils, and beans, an onion, lots of turmeric and pepper and coriander and salt, some water. Cook slowly. Put tomato sauce in later, to thicken it. Delicious!)

"And I turned the gas down on the harira so it would warm slowly and not burn. Saleh was coming soon from teaching, and Abdul Krim. Youssef was working late, her father too. I came back to this room where the television was on. Najiya looked at me, and she shrieked once, and then—" She stopped and could not go on.

"And then?"

"I couldn't wake her." Aisha broke down. I put my arms around her.

"Aisha."

"She didn't speak to us again. Ever. Just that one shriek."

A massive stroke? It sounded like it.

"When the boys came, we got a taxi and took her to the hospital and they said a crisis of the heart, but there was no hope, take her home and keep her warm, they said, and we did, but . . . four days later"—a slight sniffle—"she died, B.J., she just died. She died right here."

Aisha was crying.

"I still can't believe it, I just can't believe it, Najiya, my daughter. And she had just gotten the job and she liked it and it seemed everything was coming out well for her and—" She put a finger to her eyes, and wiped the tears away, one by one, gently, turning her face from side to side as she did so.

"And the boys?"

"They're all right." Aisha, with effort, stopped crying. "Saleh got his teaching job back. I work two or three days a week cleaning. Najiya wrote you that, didn't she? We make it, but it's hard. Specially because of the drought. No grain last year from Sidi bin Slimane."

"Najiya's letter said that Abdul Krim didn't go on the Green March because he was sick?"

"Yes. He's sick."

"He can't work?"

"No. He can't work." She paused. "But there is no work anyway. So even if he weren't sick he couldn't work."

"And Youssef? He was doing so well in school."

Aisha stood up. "Let's have tea."

She left me abruptly and closed the door against the rain, which no longer beat on the uneven pavement of the courtyard but was dripping slowly and gently, like Aisha's tears. I looked around me at the little room where Najiya had died, where Youssef and Abdul Krim and Saleh had studied their lessons, at the neatly tucked piles of bedding, the mirror, the pictures on the wall: Muhammad V, Morocco's first "independent" monarch; Aisha's father, a mustached man in a skullcap; Aisha and Khaddour at marriage; Youssef as a little boy; Abdul Krim in his warm-up suit at a high school gymnastics tournament; and the pictures of my own children, pictures that Laila, Laura Ann, and David had given Aisha before we left Rue Trésor ten years ago. The pictures, discoloring from age, were curling at the corners, Laila at ten with two blond ponytails; eleven-year-old David, laughing at the camera; Laura Ann, serious, nearly thirteen. How long ago it seemed. The door banged open.

Aisha busied herself with the tea tray. She handed me a glass, one so full of fresh mint that the glass shimmered green in my hand. Then she settled back with her own glass, one knee up to support her elbow.

"Youssef," I repeated. But Aisha did not answer immediately.

"Is it sweet enough?" she asked.

"Oh yes." I sipped the tea.

Then Aisha sighed. "Youssef. Poor Youssef."

"What's happened?"

"Well, they opened another bakery two streets over, and the baker wanted an apprentice. Steady work. Youssef wanted to do it. I begged him not to quit school but he did."

"And is he doing well?"

She shook her head and looked at the ground, holding the steaming tea in one hand.

"The bakery went broke in less than a year. Youssef's out of work, and now he can't go back to school, either. Once you've gone, you can't go back."

"Oh, Aisha, that's bad."

She turned the palm of her free hand up in a gesture of hopelessness.

"Where is he now?"

"He goes out every day to look for work. Some days he comes home with a few coins; I think he works in the market or finds a tourist to take round Djemaa al-Fna. And Abdul Krim just sits in the room. He is so sick. His hair is falling out."

"His hair is falling out? Oh, Aisha, you must take him to a doctor. Let's go tomorrow. I'll get the names of some good doctors tonight."

This was something to do, something I could do, to break through the sense of hopelessness, death, inertia, that seemed to fill the tiny room.

Aisha said, "Thank you, B.J. But we've already been to the doctor."

"Oh, but maybe not the right *kind* of doctor," I insisted. "It sounds to me as though Abdul Krim needs a specialist," and I used the French word, to emphasize the importance of my point.

Aisha sighed again. "Well, all right, we can try again."

A knock on the door preceded the arrival of Abdul Krim himself. He shook hands and smiled at me, a ghost of the old lighthearted Abdul Krim.

He did look ill. His face was puffy and pale, not the cheerful healthy face I remembered. I told myself that perhaps he was just balding early and needed some vitamins and some hope. If he sat about, idle, all day, how could he not be ill—Abdul Krim who had been so full of life, working out at the gymnasium by the hour, winning ribbons in the gymnastic meets?

Najiya's death. Abdul Krim's ill health. Youssef's failure. At least Saleh was still teaching French in secondary school. The situation had seemed desperate for a while, when Saleh had been fired along with hundreds of other teachers who had demonstrated against the King in the troubled years after 1972.

"No, they will not get their jobs back," Abdul Aziz had written to Bob, in response to our inquiry. "It is too sensitive an issue and many hundreds of graduates are waiting to take those posts."

Saleh was lucky. He was taken back. He earned about four hundred dollars per month, Aisha said. This sum, with minor assistance from his mother and his father, was supposed not only to feed, clothe, and house his own family of six people but to contribute to the support of the extended family in Sidi bin Slimane. In 1982, an economist friend told Bob, the average salaried worker in Morocco supported eleven people. Saleh was supporting more than that. The benefits of economic development were distributed unevenly, social scientists had concluded. Yes, indeed. Certainly in Morocco the war in the Sahara, the three-year drought, the rising inflation, did not help.

"Have you seen Hajja Kenza?" inquired Abdul Krim, settling himself on the banquette beside me and accepting a glass of tea from his mother.

"Not yet. I'm hoping to stop by tomorrow."

"The hotel isn't doing too well."

"Really? I thought she was getting richer." I smiled. "At least when we were here to do the film, things looked good."

"Yes, but—" began Aisha.

"Mama . . ." Abdul Krim cautioned her, then turned to me. "There have been complaints against her. The government is investigating."

"Money, money," burst out Aisha. "She has so much, why does she want *more?*"

"Is Naima still doing the books for the hotel?"

Mother and son glanced at each other across me. Aisha looked down. I remembered then an evening during the 1976 filming, when I had come to see Aisha, in despair because it seemed that none of Melissa's and my plans for filming were working out. It was summer, and we sat in the courtyard, Najiya, Aisha, and me, Abdul Krim slightly out of the circle, reading. Naima, the daughter of Hajja Kenza, who lived across the street, had suddenly appeared. After a barely perfunctory general greeting, she had plopped herself down beside Abdul Krim, putting her arm quickly around his neck and leaning her head on his shoulder in fatigue.

Abdul Krim had set his book aside and put his arm around her bent shoulders.

The two young people had sat there, in the shifting light of the summer dusk, like lovers, like brother and sister, dark, good-looking, comforting each other. Naima had grown prettier in five years, shapely, tall, with fine eyes. She had worn a sleeveless short shift that night, and had obviously just come from home; for no one, no woman who cared about her reputation, walked about on the streets of Marrakech in a miniskirted sleeveless dress. But I told myself she *was* at home here, and always had been, slipping across the street to Aisha's house for warmth and tea and acceptance, as I had done that day, as she had done ever since she was a small child.

And Abdul Krim had patted her shoulder and said, "Now, Naima, you work too hard."

She had laughed shortly, without enjoyment. Aisha offered tea, but she refused. Lovers. Brother and sister. Brother consoling sister. An old pattern, for some say that the tie between brother and sister is the most important emotional tie in the Middle Eastern family structure, rivaling in importance the tie between mother and son.

Still, it looked strange to me, the outsider. A public embrace. Abdul Krim and Naima were not actually brother and sister, but the society considered them so. No Moroccan observing that embrace would have found it strange, if they knew that Aisha had nursed Naima with Abdul Krim when they were both babies, for Hajja Kenza had had no milk. It was that gift, that milk tie, that responsibility, that was still a bond between the two women, Aisha and Hajja Kenza, a bond that my presence had threatened years ago. The milk tie prevented Abdul Krim and Naima from ever considering each other as potential mates, even though that evening they had looked like lovers.

Naima. Abdul Krim was talking about her again, but it was not summer now. It was 1982, a rainy winter night. And Najiya was dead.

"Naima nearly got married last year. A good man. But at the last minute it was called off."

"Why?"

"Hajja Kenza was against it."

"But that was what Hajja Kenza always said she wanted, that Naima marry a good, rich man. She even asked Bob to approach Omar, our friend in the jellaba market."

Abdul Krim opened his eyes. He laughed outright, a pleasant sound in the room. "She didn't!"

"Oh yes she did. Bob asked Omar, but he wasn't interested. So what happened to call off this new marriage?"

"Everything was going on well with the negotiations, but Hajja Kenza wouldn't shut up, you know how she is, talk, talk, talk. She had her finger in everything, back and forth. Well, when the contract was drawn up, and the qadi read it to her (she can't read, you know), she found the groom had said that she, the mother-in-law, would never be allowed to live with the couple."

"Really?"

"Really. And she was so furious she tore up the contract on the spot and that was that."

"And now?"

Mother and son looked at each other again, across me.

"Naima doesn't do much of anything now," said Aisha slowly. There was something in her glance, in the way she spoke, that said more, but she did not enunciate whatever was in her mind. If she had stronger opinions, perhaps they had been mitigated by the realization that Abdul Krim wasn't doing much of anything now, either. Although his reputation, his honor, would not suffer as Naima's would, quickly and sharply, when she was seen walking the streets, eventually Abdul Krim's reputation, his honor, would be diminished also. A man is self-supporting; he is a provider; he marries and has children. A real man does not lie about on the bed in his mother's house all day and watch television —unless, of course, he is sick.

"I'm amazed at all the new hotels on Rue Trésor," I said. "What's happened?"

"The street is becoming commercial," said Abdul Krim. "It's valuable property, so near Djemaa al-Fna. They're raising our rent and trying to sell the house and make a lot of money from the developers that want to come in."

"That's why the courtyard looks so bad," said Aisha. "And you saw how the door's cracked. The landlord won't fix anything."

"We need to get out of here," said Abdul Krim. "They're going to sell the roof over our heads. It's only a matter of time."

"Yes," I said, "I can see that. Aisha wrote me." I gulped and pushed on. (It had to be said.) "I *wish* I could help you buy a house, but we just don't have that kind of money. Our children are in college, and my mother, and . . ." My voice trailed off as I met those two pairs of eyes, one young, one old. What could I say?

The dilemma was not new. They had written for help several times during the drought, when Saleh lost his job, before Najiya found hers. I had sent some money, what I could afford. Now how could I expect them to believe that I did not have enough money for anything, when here I was again, coming to Marrakech on a long expensive airplane trip with no apparent hardship to myself. Six years ago, I had come with a crew of young, eager film technicians from England, bringing thousands of dollars' worth of expensive equipment to make a film for schools, for television. No wonder they looked at me that way when I said I did not have ten thousand dollars to help Aisha buy a house, away from the commercialized growing center of Marrakech, to give her some security in an uncertain world. "What I pray to God is to give me a place of my own," she had said in an interview in the film. I had not forgotten that interview, that message. I could not respond adequately to that plea. I did not have ten thousand dollars, or even a thousand, to give her. And she could not quite understand why I didn't.

All people, of course, form reciprocal kinds of relationships, every year of their lives, whether in Morocco or America. But people who live in the same culture, even if their positions are unequal, can usually find a mutual understanding, for some shared understanding of the ramifications of each other's economic position exists. But cross-culturally, it is harder. To Aisha, I seemed incredibly rich, and in comparison, and by Moroccan standards, I *was* incredibly rich.

During 1971 and 1972, when we lived on the Rue Trésor and Aisha worked for us, we paid her a regular salary. When we left, the salary ceased. When we came back to film in the spring and summer of 1976, I suggested, and Melissa agreed wholeheartedly, that Aisha be put on regular salary, as a member of the crew. When the filming ended, the salary ended. But the relationship had not ended with the end of the jobs. There was more between us—concern for each other, friendship. But probably there had been different expectations from the beginning. Or had there? Was the issue here simply money? What I felt as a responsibility, almost a duty, toward Aisha and her family was not duplicated with Omar and his family, nor with Abdul Aziz or Hajja Kenza. Omar's family had offered us their house as a location for one sequence in the film. They had invited the crew to lunch. Omar and his sister Malika and his brother Ibrahim and even his mother Lalla Nezha had told us more than once how they had enjoyed the experience. "Why don't you make a film about the jellaba business now?" Omar had suggested half jokingly. "Maybe we can get Omar Sharif to act the part of my father. He's old enough now." But Omar's family was well off. Aisha's family was not.

"How is Lorrie Ann, and Laila and David and Mister?" Aisha was consciously, politely changing the subject. "And Melissa, how is she?"

I described my children's activities, produced new pictures, which were passed to Abdul Krim. "And Melissa has a little girl," I added.

"Didn't Saadiya say so when you were here and had your fortune told?" cried Aisha triumphantly. "She is very good, Saadiya, she knows spirits, if only . . . Najiya—" and she broke down again.

"Now, Mama." Abdul Krim looked embarrassed. He tried to comfort her, but Aisha would not be comforted. The tears came again, slowly, and she wiped each tear away again, delicately, with a single finger.

"It's . . . that I miss her so much," she said, seeing me out across the wet courtyard, through the low passage to the Rue Trésor. Night had come and the rain had stopped while I had sat with Aisha and Abdul Krim. A cloudy sky lay above us, illuminated by a single light bulb above the sign that Hajja Kenza had installed to advertise her unsuccessful hotel. The door was shut tight. The door of Hajja Kenza's own house was also shut, as was the window where her pot of white geraniums had sat on the sill long ago. What was it a Moroccan friend had said? "Some people are like good bread. Some people are like stones." Aisha. Hajja Kenza. Their relationship was unequal, too. Where did I stand in that friendship, which had started when the two women were children, had continued when Aisha nursed Hajja Kenza's only daughter, Naima, who now did nothing much at all? What responsibility did I bear? Had I helped to sour the relationship? I could not face the myriad of possibilities at the moment. I repeated the ritual words of condolence once more and said goodbye. We were to meet next day to take Abdul Krim to the doctor.

Unfortunately, the doctor whom we visited the next morning proved to be too busy to see us. But Aisha and her family were still very much on my mind when I set off to lunch with Omar's family that day, although I was unsure whether I should say so.

I had received the invitation early in the morning. "Come to the shop at one," it said and was signed by Omar. The rather superior desk clerk at the elegant hotel where the Smithsonian group was staying had handed me the note in a very deferential fashion.

"Is everything all right, madame?"

I looked at him, surprised. "Yes, thank you."

He shook his well-groomed dark head. "It is only that—Is M. Omar a friend of yours?"

"Oh yes, we've known his family for a long time." I smiled pleasantly, I hoped.

"Ah, I see." He smiled back. "Well, madame, he came himself, you see, to look for you. . . ."

"Yes . . ."

What was all this about? The clerk was going on and on. "So, if there is some problem, please let us know, and we will try to rectify it."

I nodded, a bit puzzled. When I repeated this conversation later to Omar he had laughed.

"Ah!" he said importantly. "You have forgotten my duties, B.J. Remember, I am in charge of the office which takes care of tourist complaints about hotels. *That's* why he looked so worried. I handle complaints against Hajja Kenza's hotel; why shouldn't I also slap the hands of the people who own the most elegant hotel in Marrakech? We are a free country now, Morocco; every complaint can be investigated and offenses punished!"

Omar had suggested I meet him at the family jellaba shop, and he would take me from there to his house for lunch. I had followed his instructions, and gone to the market at the appointed time. It was raining again, a fine drizzle, as I crossed the square of Djemaa al-Fna and passed into the covered market, down the wide street of the Semmarine, the street that never failed to dazzle me, no matter how many times I walked through its displays of silks and velvets, its caftans laced and bordered with gold and silver. At the herbalists' corner I turned off, not having time today to peruse the jars of powdered verbena and chamomile, the bottles of orange water, the secret dark jars of stronger cures, dosages: belladonna, deadly nightshade, crocodile tails, and other specialties. Si Abdulla's narrow jellaba shop was just beyond. But Omar was not there as he had promised.

Ibrahim, his brother, came forward. "Omar had an important case to finish in the office," he said. "He'll be late. I'll take you home, and he'll be there in time for lunch. We're living at our uncle's place because we're redoing the house."

"Your uncle and aunt are with you?"

"No, my uncle has another house, a rent house that is empty at the moment."

Ibrahim pulled down the wooden shutter door and locked the shop. The rain had ceased, and the clouds were moving fast across the sky, pulling apart from time to time and letting the sun through. We set off, deeper into the labyrinth of the market, past the woodworkers' corner, fragrant with the odor of argan wood. One of the luggage merchants had decided to nap in his shop and snoozed against the stock: painted tin trunks of blue, pink, red, piled up on each side of him, like multicolored walls. The rows of leather shops gave way to the specialty belt and ribbon and scarf shops. Here hung the braided ropes of imitation amber beads mixed with colored wool and glittery sequins, the fringed scarves waiting for Berber women customers who wore the ropes around their heads, their waists.

"You are completely renovating your house?" I asked politely.

"Yes, the wiring had to be redone. We have two television sets now and my mother wants a washing machine. So we decided to do the whole thing—new bath and so on."

"I see."

"But Omar thinks we should build a villa outside the city."

"Omar?" I was surprised. He had always defended the medina for its convenient location, its comfort and quiet, its easy access to shops and mosques.

"That's what he says." Ibrahim paused. We had reached the fork which leads to the shrine of Sidi bel Abbas, the patron saint of Marrakech. The green-tiled roofs were just visible down a narrow alley.

We turned left, away from the shrine, toward the family house. The streets were beginning to feel familiar.

"We all want to stay in the medina, madame, except Omar. Maybe he wants to marry and has not yet told my father." I thought he smiled to himself. Ibrahim of the brooding eyes, as we had named him, did not often smile. He was not happy with his assignment in the family business while his brothers branched out to tourism, customs, away from their father.

We were walking now in a quiet residential area. There were no more shops, only long stretches of blank walls plastered with the red clay that is distinctive to Marrakech. Massive wooden doors were set into the red walls, doors with brass knockers, silver knockers, all in the shape of a hand. Since Roman times the classic symbol to ward off evil, the hand is called in Islamic countries the hand of Fatima, the Prophet's daughter.

It did not seem that ten years had passed since Bob and I and the children had walked these streets.

Ibrahim, after his outburst, was silent. I did not feel it appropriate to comment on the possibility of Omar's secret marriage plans or the suggestion that father and sons were divided about where the family house should be established—or reestablished: in the old city or the new burgeoning upper-middle-class suburbs —not Gueliz, with its French memories, but the newer areas near the palm groves and the Agdal Gardens. I wondered why he was confiding in me. We were friends of the family, it was true. But of course my presence was temporary; I would be leaving again in a day or two; I could be confided in, therefore, since I had no permanent place here, to help or to hinder whatever might develop.

"My father sold some of his land in Bab Doukkala," said Ibrahim, adding more to the picture. "That's maybe why he might agree to a villa, but keep the medina house, too. We could rent the medina house. Marrakech is growing so fast."

So that was it. The family was getting into real estate development. But even in the past Si Abdulla had always had many strings to his economic bow. The jellaba shop was only one of several enterprises. Ten years ago Omar had explained to Bob that his father believed in diversifying his financial interests. "It's better for business. And for taxes. Also, if the jellaba market is bad one year the leather market may be good."

Bob had said, "Ah yes, diversifying investments, otherwise known as 'not putting all your eggs in one basket.' " (How much sillier that sounded in French, Bob added.)

A similar Moroccan proverb existed, Omar had declared happily. "But not everyone is smart like my father," he had pointed out. "Look at our friend

Muhammad, the rug merchant. He's made a big mistake. He's expanded his shop so it looks like a French store."

We had noticed that in 1976.

"He'll be sorry," Omar had predicted to Bob on that earlier visit. "The foreign tourists may like it, but they come and go. Only once has he had a famous movie star like Burt Lancaster in his shop. Tax collectors are always around and his rate has already gone up. Everyone can *see* he's getting richer."

"That attracts the evil eye?"

Omar smiled. "Yes, the evil eye. You foreigners are fascinated by the evil eye. But what *is* the evil eye? A symbol of bad luck, is it not?"

Bob agreed that it was.

"For Muhammad, the evil eye is the eye of the tax collector," he finished triumphantly, and laughed at his witticism. Then he became serious. "But you see, Bob, the point is, it is not magic, it is real life. I have told Muhammad, but he does not pay any attention."

"I'm surprised," said Bob. "I always thought Muhammad was eminently practical."

"Maybe," allowed Omar. "But he's from the country; he doesn't yet understand the big city."

"How many generations does it take to become a Marrakshi?" asked Bob, smiling a bit. "Muhammad was born here, you know."

"He's learning," Omar had admitted, "but he still has a long way to go."

Afterward Bob had repeated this conversation to me. "Interesting, isn't it?" he said. "The process of succeeding in business is seen so differently in different cultures. What does an up-and-coming young businessman do in America? He buys a house with a twenty-year mortgage, a new car he can't afford, a three-hundred-dollar suit, all to advertise to the world that he is doing well, with the idea that this will attract more business. Here it's just the opposite. The old ways militate against public display. Why? To protect what you have against less successful relatives, greedy tax collectors, thieves, and other unpredictable forces. Here people have been capitalists for centuries without the encouragement and protection that capitalist governments provide."

"I thought things were changing in the new Morocco," I had offered.

"Omar says some things are changing, but not the tax collectors!" Bob had replied.

I was brought back to the present by Ibrahim, who had stopped at one of the tall doors. For a moment I felt as though I still *was* in the past, entering Omar's old house. The general plan of this house was the same: the short dark dead-end foyer, the spacious tiled central courtyard open to the sky, rooms opening around it on all sides.

But the kitchen was to our left, rather than the right; the courtyard was not strictly symmetrical, narrowing at one end, perhaps to accommodate an older house next door. And the doorframes around the courtyard were plain dark wood, not carved and painted, as at the other house we had known.

"Please." Ibrahim held open a door. Two young women stood up to greet us from their places on the banquettes against the wall.

"Malika!" I said.

Omar's older sister smiled.

"Welcome," she said. "This is my friend Tahiya from the college."

"How do you do?" The friend, dark-eyed, dark-haired, eyed me curiously and extended her hand. *"Comment allez-vous?"*

So this part of the conversation would be in French.

"Tahiya is from Fez. She is in my class at college; she lives with us during the school year," explained Malika. Both girls were fashionably and carefully dressed, Malika in a gray crepe de chine mandarin-style blouse, a gray flannel skirt, a gold Koran on a chain around her neck; her friend Tahiya in a black sweater and skirt with a silky crimson print overblouse.

"In the medical school?"

Omar had written of Malika's acceptance to medical school, where places were reserved for those who placed highest on the competitive government examinations.

"It is wonderful!" Omar had written. "The whole family is honored."

"The family succeeds, not the individual," Bob had commented. "Omar, a minor clerk in the ministry, his older brother in the customs house, another brother in the shop selling jellabas, and their *sister* gets into medical school. In America, I'll bet the brothers would have been piqued."

If Malika was in medical school, why was she in college here in Marrakech? The medical school was in Rabat.

But Malika, it turned out, had not chosen to attend medical school. She had decided to go into research medicine and was working on her Ph.D.

"What did your father think about that?"

Malika smiled, fingering the tiny gold Koran on the chain around her neck. She looked across at her friend.

"Our fathers both were a bit surprised," she acknowledged. "But they have opened up a science faculty here in Marrakech and I can go on for my doctorate right here."

"And at the end we are guaranteed good jobs," said Tahiya. "The country needs scientists, in all fields, especially medical science."

"So our fathers agreed," said Malika.

"What's the program like?"

"It's good, but it's hard. And some of the books are in English, which makes it *especially* hard. English is not my best language."

Her friend assented vigorously. "It's the computer book that's the worst. Would you like to see it?"

"Computers?"

"Research methods with computers," explained Malika. "Everyone has to take it. They are a great new tool, computers."

I obediently thumbed through the textbook on research techniques with computers, reading an occasional passage aloud that the girls pointed out to me.

"Isn't that *hard?*"

"Yes," I said fervently, adding that most of the material was completely incomprehensible to me, though I was supposed to understand English!

The door opened, and a tall young man came in, smiling.

"*Bonjour, Mme. B.J.*" We shook hands.

Malika looked from him to me. "You don't recognize Ahmed, my younger brother, B.J."

I had to agree that I didn't. He had been in elementary school in 1972, when we had come to dinner. I had a hazy memory of a small dark-haired boy who had played with his baby sister.

"He is into computers, too."

The young man stopped smiling and became earnest and eager. "It is the way to the future," he said, in the tone of the true believer. For five minutes he lectured me about the benefits which computers could bring to his country.

"Now, now, enough of this school talk!" It was Lalla Nezha, Omar's mother, a bit older, a bit plumper, but smiling and bustling in the same no-nonsense way.

We embraced and she inquired after my family. I produced the pictures of Laura Ann, Laila, and David and Bob. Lalla Nezha passed the pictures to her computer-enthusiast son.

"Why don't you study computers in America, Ahmed, instead of France? See how nice B.J.'s girls look, how pretty they have become."

Ahmed's expression changed; strain was evident in the way he was holding his hands, directing his words. "Yes, Mama, they are very nice indeed, but you know it is already arranged for me to go to France."

"France! France!" Lalla Nezha looked annoyed. "France used to be our enemy, the enemy of Morocco. Now suddenly France is our friend. What has happened to change everything? Your mother hasn't been to school, my dear, she doesn't understand."

"Mama," said Ahmed, once again in that careful voice, "we have to be realistic about our relationship to France, we have to think of the future, of trade—"

He was interrupted by the arrival of Omar, who burst into the room, shaking hands, kissing his mother and apologizing.

"I am so sorry, B.J., how is Bob? I had this difficult case that had to be written out and submitted, because it goes to court next Wednesday, some doctors conspiring with the biggest pharmacy in the city to overcharge for some medicines. . . . You won't believe it, Malika. . . . The typist had to do it over *three times. Bonjour,* Tahiya. Ahmed, can you get me some matches, please?"

He sat down. Ahmed, as younger brother, was sent to serve his older brother. The lecture about the future of Franco-Moroccan relations was suspended in favor of lunch. For it turned out that the father of the family, Si Abdulla, had also arrived. He came in, leaving his slippers at the door. Ahmed was dispatched a second time, to bring his father a glass of water.

Lunch. Ah, lunch. Once more Lalla Nezha had outdone herself. There was couscous. Dishes of salads. Cabbage with fennel. Chopped beets with vinegar and pepper. Tomatoes with cumin. Lalla Nezha excused herself, she would not sit with us, she said, she had something that must be finished, but she would join us for tea later. But everyone else gathered round the big table in Uncle's house: Malika, her friend Tahiya from Fez, Ahmed, Ibrahim, Omar, and eleven-year-old Faneeda, the baby with whom David and Laila had played so happily ten years before. I felt warmed, cheered in this prosperous Marrakshi household, only regretting that the rest of *my* family was not at the table as well. Si Abdulla sat beside me, offering choice pieces of the day's main dish, a delicious chicken tajine with olives and pickled lemons.

"Your children are grown, madame?" Si Abdulla inquired between bites.

"Yes, thanks be to God."

"Thanks be to God," he repeated. "Children are the heart of life. That is what we work for, do we not?"

"You are right, Si Abdulla."

I looked around the table and thought that Si Abdulla had a right to be proud of his family, all of them, in various ways, adapting beautifully to Morocco's independent new society. The problems of alienation, of stress, which was so much discussed in the texts and monographs on social and cultural change, were distributed unevenly, just like the benefits of economic development, it seemed. They were not apparent here. Perhaps with enough property, enough resources, it was possible to adapt to any new situation and turn it to one's advantage. But it was as a family that these new adjustments were being made.

The same relationships existed between Aisha and her family in Sidi bin Slimane. The difference, of course, was that Aisha's family did not have as much to share. They had survived, but barely, during the recent drought, on reciprocal relationships. The simple truth was that the effects of rapid social change were more immediate and devastating if one was poor. And if one had less to lose, like Saleh, one demonstrated against the status quo. No one in Omar's family had felt the need to march in protest against the King.

I made a quick decision. I broke the comfortable silence and told them about Aisha's son and the unheeding doctor, about Najiya's death, about Saleh who had lost his job for political reasons and how he had regained it, about Youssef and the disastrous bakery apprenticeship. And I asked for Omar's help, to ensure that Abdul Krim would get to a good doctor. I would be leaving Marrakech the next day, and would not be able to go back to the doctor with Aisha.

There was a silence at the bountiful family table.

"Wasn't Mme. Aisha here when you filmed in the house?" It was Malika.

"Yes," I said.

"She's a sharifa, too, like Mama," said Omar.

"Well, of course you must help," said Malika in French.

"I will, I will, I promise." Omar looked at me keenly. His hair was thinning, too, I noticed, but the pallor of despair did not hang about him as it did around Abdul Krim.

"It is our duty, as good Muslims, to help others," said Si Abdulla, rather pompously, I thought. Though his manner tended to run to the rhetorical phrase, the ritual gesture, his actions often belied his style; and I was relieved.

"Yes, Father," said Omar. To me, in French, "You have always been a good friend to Mme. Aisha."

"And she to me," I responded.

"That is true," he replied.

"Please be sure to give our regards to your husband, and his family, and also to your family," said Si Abdulla, rising.

"Thank you," I answered. "And now you must think of coming to America and visiting us. It is our turn to entertain *you*. You would be most welcome in our house."

He inclined his head and went to the courtyard, where he sat down with Lalla Nezha to drink mint tea before siesta, the traditional way to settle the stomach after couscous and tajine.

With the departure of Si Abdulla, the conversation around the table became more relaxed. Ahmed started in on computers again, Malika asked about biochemistry in America, and Omar could not resist telling me that he had received more complaints about Hajja Kenza. As for her daughter, he shook his head.

"La pauvre," he said. "With a mother like that . . . I would walk the streets too."

"Come and watch television," said little Faneeda, taking my hand. "I will come and see you in America, shall I?"

"Faneeda!" Malika scolded. "Don't be rude."

"No, I would love to have her," I answered sincerely. "My own children are grown now, remember."

"You can see television in America," said Omar. "I want to show you how we are renovating the house."

Omar, Ibrahim, and I walked down the narrow street to their old house. From the outside, it had not changed. But once past the door, it was unrecognizable except for the courtyard floor. The slate-blue and white tiles were still there. But the rooms were gone, the tiles ripped from the walls, exposing the wooden struts laid in as support against the mud bricks plastered outside with Marrakech red clay. Pieces of wire, parts of pipes, hung from different levels, as though some giant beast had been nibbling at the walls. Two workmen were sitting in one corner of a wall, eating lunch in the sunshine. I was not certain why Omar had brought me here, with Ibrahim.

"It is good to do a big cleaning like this to change things, to get rid of the past," said Omar. "But it costs money."

"Yes." The sun had come out and a bright haze rose from the courtyard floor. The tiles were steaming as the rain evaporated.

"At least you'll keep this floor," I said, relieved.

"Oh no, that will go when the rewiring is finished and the new water pipes are in."

"You will keep *nothing* of the old house? It was such a nice house, Omar."

"B.J., we're keeping the basic structure. See." He drew out a rough plan, and it was true, the basic structure would be the same when the renovation was finished. "We are rebuilding from the inside. And we'll have new tiles, from Moroccan factories, not from Spain like before. I would be interested in your selections. What do you think of these?"

I looked at the samples. They were certainly not Spanish. One pale gray with a pattern of roses, rather French in feeling. Another flower motif in blue. Some geometric patterns, white and green; and the last sample was an adaptation of old Berber wooden ceiling designs: brown etched diamond shapes and whorls on white. I had noticed similar designs on the new mosques throughout the countryside, high in the mountains. White plastered minarets with these same patterns of diamonds and ovals in brown, or in green, the Prophet Muhammad's color.

"They are very nice. I like the brown and white, the Berber one," I said.

Omar smiled. "So does Malika. She and Ibrahim want this tile in one of the salons. My father and I prefer the green. My mother says she doesn't care but she wants the rose tiles in the kitchen and maybe in the bath. Why not one of each? Brown Berber design in one salon, the green and white in the other. They are all Moroccan designs."

"Even the roses? They look rather French."

Omar looked pained. "We have beautiful roses right here in Marrakech. You see them in the market every day."

Omar went to speak to the workmen before we left. "What do you think, B.J.?" Ibrahim asked, in Omar's absence.

"I liked your old house very much," I said truthfully.

"She liked the old house," Ibrahim repeated to Omar as we headed out the door.

"Well, but it was worn out, it had to be replaced. One has to change with the times, and thank God we have the money to do that."

"What about building a villa in the palm groves?"

Omar's eyes flickered. "In the future, maybe. First we have to restore what we already have. Whether we live here or not, it's a good investment for the future—fixing up the old house for the new times."

We shut the door of the old house behind us and stood in the street where the beggar had sat, years ago. He was not there now.

"I must go. Thank you for everything. Come visit us in America."

"God willing. Regards to Bob. Be sure and tell him we miss him."

"I promise."

We shook hands, Ibrahim, Omar, me. "Thank you, again," I said. "And please don't forget Aisha."

"It is my duty," said Omar. "I won't forget. I promise."

And we parted, Omar cutting through to the modern city and his office in the ministry, Ibrahim back to the jellaba shop in the traditional market of the Semmarine, where merchants had traded in Marrakech for nearly a thousand years.

"It's not our affair, you know," Bob said later. "I mean, I'm sure Omar and his family feel they have enough responsibilities without taking on Aisha and her family—just like we do."

"Yes, but I felt I had to try to do *something,* Bob."

"Just so you aren't kidding yourself."

"Kidding myself?"

"Yes—into believing that charity and good works and all that will solve all social inequities. It won't, you know. If it did, the Salvation Army would have taken care of things long ago."

"Bob—"

"It's true."

"I know. But it helps some."

"And *you* feel better."

"Yes," I admitted.

Bob smiled, a bit wearily, I thought. He reminded me that our Muslim friends had a far more realistic attitude toward charity than we did. The Bible says very clearly that an act of charity benefits both giver and receiver. But in Muslim tradition, it is still true that the giver, not the receiver, benefits the most from giving, for he has fulfilled his duty, both to God and to his fellow man.

Comment

THE BUSINESS OF MARKETS

THE STATEMENT is frequently made that Arab-world economies are becoming increasingly Westernized. Presumably this is a good sign, a statement of approval. Western economies, after all, are based on industrial capitalism and this means the things with which we are familiar: factories, corporations, supermarkets, banks, stocks and bonds, international cartels—the institutions that have made the West what it is today. The assumption is that Westernization is improvement, but we do not consider what kind of economy is being replaced in the process of Westernization. We can imagine what Arab society is getting, but what is it losing? More important, what consequences may this loss, this replacement of one economic formation by another, have on the patterns of life in the Arab world?

This is too wide-ranging and complex a question to answer in a few pages of discussion; it is central to the whole structure of Middle Eastern society and the relationship of these societies to the world economy. However, one aspect of the process of Westernization affects the most commonplace activities of daily life in Arab communities and can be appreciated without benefit of economic theories or complex statistics. We refer to the part played by traditional markets in Arab communities and the consequences of the Westernization and transformation of those markets which is in progress today.

In fact, the changes which are taking place in this everyday activity affect the whole rhythm of community life and the legitimacy of its political processes. Much more is changing than merely the way in which groceries and clothing are bought and sold. If we understand change in the market, we can begin to see why the Westernization of Middle Eastern economic life has far-reaching consequences, many of which have not yet been fully integrated into Arab communal life.

From Saudi Arabia to Morocco, a great many Arab cities and towns today have two distinctly different shopping districts in their centers. One is much like that to be found downtown in a European or an American city: straight, wide streets along which are ranged, in orderly rows, large glass-fronted stores, office buildings, and specialty shops of various kinds. Signs indicate the contents of each building. In these districts an American visitor finds little that is particularly "foreign" except the language of the advertising—Arabic—and often English or French is added to help the visitor along.

But nearby perhaps, or in an older section of town, will be found another market center. Here, to the visitor, confusion seems to reign. Rows of small shops, side by side, open-fronted, are filled with what seem to be the same goods; there are few if any signs; narrow lanes twist and turn in a bewildering way in all directions; and above all, there are noise, confusion, and milling crowds. To visit the Muski in Cairo or the great medina markets in Marrakech or Fez for the first time is a formidable experience for the Western tourist, but the same kind of market is to be found in smaller cities or villages, with fewer shops and probably less commotion. Such markets are still a ubiquitous feature of the Arab world, even though in big cities such as Cairo or Baghdad they are no longer the centerpiece of urban life. Indeed, such "Arab" markets are to be found with local variations throughout most of Asia and Africa and in parts of Latin America. They are a feature of the so-called Third World, but they should not necessarily be considered a sign of poverty or "underdevelopment." Such market forms are rather a historical development of considerable antiquity and resemble in many ways European markets as they were before the Industrial Revolution. Some scholars see in them what remains of the central manifestation of mercantile (as opposed to industrial) capitalism. Adam Smith found them inspiration for his views of free enterprise. For these markets are not just different in terms of scale (small versus large stores); they are part of a whole way of life which is intensely personal, competitive, and open to public knowledge and participation. They are also the arena for much of the political and religious life of the city.

The traditional or preindustrial type of market was highly personal in the sense of providing its patrons with the opportunity, indeed, the necessity, of developing face-to-face relationships with a cadre of merchants and artisans whose goods and services provided the necessities of daily life. A cloth merchant in Marrakech described his regular customers as "fish." "You need to attract them but you must also provide them with something if you expect them to come back," he said. This includes not only the product itself but also the conviction that the product they have purchased is a good one at a good price. The merchant's personal responsibility is to provide such a conviction so that the customer will at least start at the same store the next time he or she has similar needs. For the traditional market provides the convenience of many shops together; it is always easy for the customer to walk a few feet farther and look at the same, or nearly the same, goods offered by a different merchant. Competition exists on the spot and the merchant must be alert to deal with that phenomenon. The traditional market is actually a collection of markets, each one devoted to a different category of goods: cloth, spices, baskets, copperware, radios, pottery. The Marrakech market has over thirty separate markets for different goods and several smaller markets located at different points in the city where the same goods are sold.

At the Feshawi coffee shop in old Cairo, near Al-Azhar University, one of the oldest universities in the world, founded in the tenth century.

Seza Nabarawi, pioneer Egyptian feminist.
In 1923, Mme. Nabarawi and Mme. Hoda Sharawi,
on returning to Egypt from an International
Women's Congress in Rome, dramatically
removed their veils in public. The gesture is
seen by many to mark the beginning of
the Egyptian feminist movement.

Many young professional wome
in Egypt and other Muslim countrie
are adopting what they ca
"Islamic dress," a kind

Hosni Mubarak, President of Egypt.

The Western s

odest dress that is a new style
n the Arab world. These four girls
"Islamic dress" are in Kena,
Upper Egypt.

Sheep on a country road in
the outskirts of Cairo.

t a Cairo disco.

Father and children in a Cairo
amusement park.

Cairo mosque.

"Picturesque, yes, but what an inefficient system," the foreign tourist re-marks, arriving back at the hotel after visiting the traditional market, walking long distances, and purchasing few items. "The bargaining is so difficult, far too personal as a steady diet." Americans express discomfort at what they feel is the hard sell. We are used to being left to ourselves when we make most of our purchases; most clerks would be taken aback if asked to express an opinion about a vegetable or a set of dishes. To the Marrakshi merchant and his custom-ers, however, personal advice is part of the business, something they expect.

Business on a personal scale also has other advantages. The merchant/propri-etor can handle it himself, both literally and figuratively. He knows his custom-ers, his sales, and his inventory, and if he has need he is not far from the source of supplies. For the market is usually within walking distance of his home and/or small storage rooms where additional inventory is laid away.

It is also true that merchants in these markets tend to regard partnerships, which might permit a larger operation, as a source of trouble, and prefer to have members of their own family working with them, their sons if possible. Such family relations in business do not mean that the market is entirely closed outsiders. "The games of the marketplace are open to anyone who can buy t dollars' worth of potatoes and push them around on a cart," said a Marrak friend. "A bit of luck and the next day you may be able to start out in morning with an inventory worth twenty dollars." Many merchants began th careers as peddlers or shop assistants, often at a very early age.

Merchants depend upon, as well as compete with, each other. If the custo wants something he doesn't have, the merchant may go to one of his fe merchants to find the style or size required. The other merchant will e similar favors another day—or may share in the profits. Merchants stan gether in matters of taxation and import duties, in concern for the ph condition of the market, in all matters of common interest. In Marrakech, selling the same kind of goods belong to an organization with a recognize who can speak for the group and who will arbitrate disputes between me of the organization should the need arise.

So the merchants are on personal terms not only with regular custom also with each other. Not surprisingly, standards of behavior exist in setting which are violated only at the risk of ostracism by the fellow m with whom one both competes and cooperates. For instance, trying to lu a customer engaged in looking at a neighboring merchant's goods is co very bad form—though a sly wink may pass without remark. The m collective scorn is reserved for the peddlers with goods over their arm scarves or dresses or baskets, perhaps, at cut-rate prices. Such salesme along with those selling from carts or offering goods on blankets laid ground, are often confined to the outer edges of the market area. T depend on a loud voice and a convincing manner to catch the custo he or she plunges into the main market. But many dignified, establ chants passed from such humble beginnings through several met

before reaching the prestigious splendor of the cloth bazaar with its clean, well-swept stores and often luxurious merchandise.

A traditional market such as that in Marrakech serves not only the people of the city, but also Moroccans from the plains and mountains of southern Morocco and tourists from around the world. Agricultural goods arrive daily from within a radius of a hundred or more kilometers around the urban center. Many of the people from both city and country who visit the market come not only to buy but to sell the goods they have produced, for the market is a production outlet for the same region to which it sells. Manufactured goods, both local and foreign, are sold and country products bought—not only vegetables, grains, and animal skins but items like rugs and wood carvings.

All the merchants have a keen sense of their customers' tastes, depending on origin and age. A rug merchant specializing in foreign tourists knows that the Danish prefer the flat kilim rugs, while the French like thick-pile carpets; he also is aware of the rug size limits for foreign air travel. He selects his stock accordingly, when he visits villages looking for hand-made rugs or assesses those brought to him from homes in Marrakech where families are involved in rug-weaving.

On the other side of the Arab world in northern Saudi Arabia, in the city of Hail, a town of approximately seventy thousand people, there is also a traditional market of small shops and stores, though it has recently been rebuilt, its lanes straightened and cemented. Hail is a market town serving dozens of surrounding agricultural oases. Bedouin families drive to market in their pickup trucks, stopping first in the animal market to sell a few sheep, then proceeding on to the food or dry goods markets to buy supplies for the next week or two. The gold jewelry market is always crowded with women, putting their extra money into that safest of investments or selling a bracelet to meet the extra expenses of a wedding or a trip. The old mud-brick market was torn down and rebuilt by the government as one of the development projects which have transformed Hail into a modern city. Here the shops are all taken and there is no indication that the old style of marketing is disappearing even though Western-style shops have opened in other parts of the city. Families, both nomad and settled, say they are more comfortable in the traditional more private setting. On the edge of this market (as in Marrakech) veiled women sell used clothes and in the vegetable market they are also to be found sitting on the ground selling ripe produce from crates. Women play a secondary role as merchants in traditional markets, but they are there. And everyone comes to the traditional-style market, rich and poor, young and old, male and female, a mix of sexes and ages not so apparent in the large stores in the modern downtown area.

The consumer goods of these "traditional" markets, whether in Morocco or Saudi Arabia, are by no means limited to handcrafted or homegrown local products. On the contrary, all these markets offer goods of foreign manufacture, in greater or lesser quantities. In Hail, for instance, it is difficult to find anything which is made by hand these days and Yakima, Washington, apples are as com-

mon as in American Safeway stores. High-tech products, such as video and TV sets, calculators and digital watches, are available in great profusion. Such is the result of the high standards of living made possible by oil wealth. However, in the less affluent Moroccan society of Marrakech, handmade items are still available. The best jellabas (the colorful, full-length garments customarily worn by Moroccans) are hand-tailored and sewn from handwoven cloth and decorated with handmade cording. The division of labor in the market involves both families and hired labor. The work includes people of all ages and both sexes. (Women do a great deal of sewing for the market in their homes.) Perhaps the best-known products are leather ones, which begin as damp skins carried through the market from the slaughterhouse to the tannery, where they are prepared for cutting and sewing by different sets of specialists. Moroccan leather has been famous in the markets of the world for centuries and the craftsmen of Marrakech still turn the skins of the sheep and goats from the Atlas Mountains into everything from fine book bindings to leather hassocks.

The traditional market is more than simply an alternative to the American system of retailing, from malls to convenience stores. In the Arab world, the market was the center of social life before it began to be replaced by its Western counterpart. This is still largely the case today in a market like that of Marrakech. Mosques and religious shrines are part of the market landscape, permitting visitors and merchants alike to stop and pray during the day. The newest mosque in Hail, currently being constructed of marble and tiles, is rising alongside the modernized traditional market. Lawyers and scribes along with barbers and blacksmiths had (and still have) offices and shops in the market. Entertainers perform in Djemaa al-Fna, the open square near the Marrakech market; some are actually witnesses for their religious organizations and are raising funds for their lodges. Blind beggars stand at the market entrances accepting the alms of the faithful. In a market like that in Marrakech, boys are socialized into adult roles, learning how to manage in the world of commerce, taught such skills as tanning, leather design, tailoring, or metalwork. Girls learn to sew for the market working with their mothers at home.

Of perhaps even greater importance was the role of the traditional market in providing an arena for the development of public opinion and an opportunity for men to win their standing in the community in a public manner. A man's reputation was earned on a daily basis doing business before the community at large. It was merchants who constituted the majority of the "respected men," those whose counsel was sought by the Pasha or Sultan in time of trouble. Trust and accountability were highly valued qualities in the traditional market; a man's word sufficed and the system managed without the profusion of written contracts and legal proceedings so necessary in our contemporary Western business world. Indeed, while rulers, often appointed in distant capitals, came and went, the merchants constituted the local elite. For a landed gentry was lacking in much of the preindustrial Middle East, unlike in preindustrial Europe, where merchants often did not enjoy so high a standing.

Thus, in exchanging new forms of markets for the older form more is lost than simply a variety of handmade objects, a style of buying and selling. What is being lost is an important center for the formation of a community: of leadership and of consensus over matters ranging from religious and political concerns to the proper conduct of business. With the disappearance of these markets other means must be developed for these purposes. The problem is becoming easier, perhaps, with the increase in literacy and the spread of radio and television, but these sources of opinion are also more easily subject to authoritarian control than is the word-of-mouth communication of the market setting. The development of newly rich middle classes is of great importance in this regard, but it is also the source of new problems. The two styles of markets, as in Saudi Arabia and Morocco, can only reinforce the growing gap between rich and poor. And in this changing setting, the sources of community consensus remain unclear as the traditional markets give way to the Westernization of the Middle Eastern economy.

CHAPTER X

Egypt and Nubia

1959

> We need an angry generation,
> A generation to plow the horizons,
> To pluck up history from its roots,
> To wrench our thought from its foundations.
> We need a generation of different mien,
> That is not forbearing, and forgives no error,
> That knows no hypocrisy, and falters not.
> We need a generation of leaders and of giants.
>
> Nizar Qabbani
> *What Value Has the People*
> *Whose Tongue Is Tied?*

WE ARRIVED IN Cairo at the end of a revolution. Seven years had passed since the Free Officers' Revolt, which had been, as revolts go, a rather decorous occasion. Little blood was shed, and the King abdicated peacefully. King Farouk, descendant of another soldier, Muhammad Ali, an Albanian who wrested power from the Turkish Ottoman rulers in 1811 and assumed control of Egypt, was allowed to sail away on the royal yacht, carrying as much personal treasure as his vessel could hold.

Egypt was now a republic, under the presidency of Colonel Gamal Abdul Nasser, son of a rural postal clerk. Three years had gone by since President Nasser had nationalized the Suez Canal, causing international outrage and disbelief. He said at the time that he had acted because of the sudden withdrawal of American and British loans promised for the construction of the High Dam at Aswan, symbol of the new Egypt. The Suez war followed, the British-French-Israeli attack on Egypt to regain the Suez Canal. The United States intervened and hostilities had come to an end after eight days. All these events lay well in the past. It seemed to us that the worst uncertainties of the revolution were over and the time of building was under way.

Bob had accepted a three-year contract to teach anthropology at the American University in Cairo; I was seven months pregnant with our first child. After two years of research in southern Iraq and a year at the University of Chicago while Bob wrote his dissertation, we had decided to go back to the Middle East, rather than to Kansas or Wisconsin. We liked the Middle East, we liked the people we had met, and we set off for Egypt with high hopes and great enthusiasm, despite dire warnings from colleagues about the dangers of burying oneself in the lotus-eating atmosphere of foreign climes.

"It's just a good excuse not to do any work," said one anthropologist friend lightly, and "You'll be far from the cutting edge of the field," said another. So our farewell parties in Chicago had been ambiguous in tone. It was obvious, people joked, that we had opted for travel and adventure rather than serious academic endeavor. Bob replied a bit defensively that for an anthropologist interested in the Middle East, three years of employment in the area was a great opportunity to be a participant observer, particularly at a time when the area was changing so rapidly.

"We have a chance to see Egypt in the process of building a new nation," Bob said, a bit sententiously. "A chance to witness revolutionary change firsthand."

"Some revolution," commented a critical colleague. "Nasser is just another two-bit dictator."

Bob shook his head. We did not think of Gamal Abdul Nasser as a dictator. He seemed to us like a new kind of leader in the Arab world, the first indigenous leader in centuries. Even Muhammad Ali had been a foreigner. When we had stopped in Cairo in 1958 on our way home from Iraq, the Egyptians and the expatriate Americans and British we met spoke of Nasser with respect. "The nationalization of the canal was one thing," said Geoffrey Godsell, a correspondent of *The Christian Science Monitor,* "but now Egyptians are running it themselves at new levels of efficiency, thank you very much; that's what's giving people pride in being Egyptian." Godsell had lived in Egypt and knew the country well. "I think it is going to grow," he added, "that pride, that self-respect."

Western commentators at the time who were concerned with East-West relations viewed with alarm President Nasser's new alliance with Russia, who had stepped into the breach and offered aid for the Aswan Dam. But it was withdrawal of American aid that had resulted in the alliance in the first place. What else, we said to ourselves and our doubting friends, was Nasser to do?

Egypt, it seemed to us in 1959, was demonstrating a more positive form of postrevolutionary development than any other Arab country. Morocco, Tunisia, Lebanon, Syria, Iraq, Sudan, had all gained their independence from colonial powers by the mid-fifties. Algeria was still battling the French, but the others were fledgling nations, and Egypt, we thought, was a model for those nations. In 1959 and 1960, Nasser's pro-Arab movement was attracting supporters all over the Middle East. Nasser had taken another revolutionary step when he joined with Tito of Yugoslavia and Nehru of India in declaring that the so-called Third World countries must get out of the cold war. "Why should we be drawn into the quarrels of the superpowers? World peace can be better served by our neutrality," they said.

Omar, a young Egyptologist who befriended us early (he had gotten his Ph.D. from the University of Chicago, too), echoed Geoffrey Godsell's remarks about national pride. Nasser's greatest achievement by 1960, Omar said, was not just schools or clinics or land reform or legal secularism or the Aswan Dam, though these were indeed important. His greatest achievement had been to give Egyptians self-respect. It was no accident, Omar continued, that President Nasser was allocating more funds for improving the Egyptian Museum, for restoring and preserving the Pharaonic and Islamic monuments, that he personally insisted museum admission should be free on some days so that all Egyptians could learn about their own glorious past.

"The new Nile Hilton has picked up the Pharaonic theme, too, I notice," said Bob.

Omar nodded. "And why do you think they hauled that enormous statue of Ramses II all the way from Memphis and put it up by the railroad station?"

"I thought it had always been there," I answered. "It seems to fit, with the fountain and all."

"No, B.J., it was only put there in 1955. And remember, it is of Ramses II, the great builder Pharaoh. And where? Not in the museum or the university but near the train station, in the center of the working city, where everybody passes by and sees it every day."

"Come, come, Omar," said his sister Aziza lightly. "Don't get carried away. A symbol, yes. But it's too much, that statue. Too *big.*"

Omar was from an upper-middle-class landed family, but he supported Nasser in those years. His sister Aziza, who had kindly taken me around Cairo to upholsterers, drapers, and picture framers while I tried to furnish our first home, was not so enthusiastic.

"All of our past belongs to all of us," Omar would say earnestly.

"Yes, I agree," Aziza would say, sipping tea in our new half-furnished study and nibbling on the good raisin pound cake which Abbas, our Nubian cook, had prepared. "But—"

"But *nothing,* Aziza. We must reclaim our past. After all, we have been colonized by foreigners for hundreds of years, and they looted our riches, not only the natural resources like cotton, but our cultural treasures too. First the Ottomans, then the French, the Germans who stole Nefertete's statue, then the British—"

"And now the sons of postal clerks," put in Aziza, rather sharply, "destroying the old Egypt while they say they are building it up. Taking away people's property, nationalizing the land. For whom, Omar?"

"For everyone, Aziza," said her brother, glancing about somewhat uneasily as though someone might be listening on the other side of our apartment walls. "It must be done."

"Radical change is never easy," put in Bob. "In revolutions, they say, the losses always seem greater than the gains—at first, anyway."

"Well, the whole country is losing—"

"Aziza!"

"It's true, Omar. Lots of people who are losing their property are leaving Egypt for good."

"Let them go—the rich . . . the King's family—"

"Not just them. Many other well-educated people who have much to give . . . Nasser is trying to move too fast—"

"But the problems are overwhelming," I said. "Poverty. Health. He feels he has to show results."

"He's not moving fast *enough.*" It was Omar, glaring at his sister. Bob and I might not have been present at all. This was obviously a family argument that could be going on in many upper-class Cairo households in those days. "Would you really like to go back to the days of the thirties, Aziza, when Egypt was owned by foreigners—French, English, Italian, Greek—when there were special *laws* for them, so they didn't have to pay taxes or even go to jail for crimes committed against *us,* the real Egyptians?"

Aziza tried to laugh. "Of course not, Omar, you know that. It's just that you've been away a long time in America, where things are different."

"All right," said Omar, facing his sister. "But you can't have *any* improvement in people's lives here when a few big landlords own most of the country. That's what Nasser is trying to avoid."

The arrival of other guests, less well known to us, put an end to the discussion. Open criticism of the government was a foolish risk in front of strangers. But Aziza and Omar were not alone in their feelings. Not surprisingly, many better-off Egyptians were divided on the issue of nationalization, sequestration of property, and land reform. Landlords who had lived comfortably off their estates for generations, going and coming to Europe and America, did not like the controls being placed on their travel and their capital by the strict financial measures of Nasser, who was keeping a tight rein on the country's economy in an effort to balance the budget. Those Egyptian landlords who had applauded the nationalization of Greek and Italian and British enterprises were not pleased when similar measures were taken against themselves. Yet Nasser was not quite as headstrong as Aziza implied. He had allowed each Egyptian citizen to keep a maximum of two hundred feddans (a little more than two hundred acres); in a large family where each member was allowed those two hundred feddans, many estates were hardly touched. This was not sentimentality on Nasser's part. He knew that he needed the agricultural expertise of the old landlords if the fields of the Delta and Upper Egypt were going to continue to produce food and high-quality cotton.

But many people were leaving, especially foreigners, Europeans who had been in Egypt for generations. With the abolition of their special law courts and their nontaxable status, many merchants and industrialists felt Egypt was no longer a profitable or safe place to do business. The landed aristocracy—pashas and beys, many of Turkish origin—also were leaving. Every week the newspapers advertised auctions of their belongings.

An entire economy was being forcibly transformed from one of peasants, landowners, and foreign merchants to something else, though just what the shape of the new society might be wasn't yet clear. Certainly it was more *Egyptian* than under King Farouk. But a lot of the old bureaucracy was still in place; most of the old elite, even if they had lost some land, still had lovely homes, lots of servants, automobiles.

President Nasser, himself an army officer, gave privileges to the army. Army officers were in. Or were they? What was left of the upper class and the descendants of the pashas took care to keep the less important army officers out of the sacrosanct rooms of the Gezira Sporting Club, the Muhammad Ali Club, the Automobile Club. So the army officers formed their own club, a far more splendid edifice than the aging Gezira Club. The engineers and other groups such as lawyers did the same, and a plethora of new professionally based family clubs sprang up all over the growing city of Cairo.

With General and Mme. Fahmy, the parents of an Egyptian friend in America, we went often to the Police Officers' Club, where excellent food was served and, on holidays, the best entertainment in town was to be found. One feast day we were lucky enough to witness an early performance by a young dancer named Nagwa Fouad, who charmed both sexes of all ages into participatory clapping and singing, with her sensuous combination of beauty, dance, and wit. We discovered early that belly dancing is family entertainment in Egypt.

Our own parents were far away in America, like the Fahmys' children, and thus the surrogate roles we filled for each other were a source of comfort for us both. Also, we were foreigners and Mme. Fahmy was of Greek descent, while General Fahmy was an Egyptian Muslim. Under Nasser's new laws, army officers could no longer marry foreigners; thus the Fahmys, like us, were somewhat anachronistic in the new Egypt.

It was Mme. Fahmy who stood up as godmother for our firstborn daughter Laura Ann, when she was baptized in the Roman Catholic chapel of the German nuns' school in Bab al-Loukh, another remnant of old colonial times.

General and Mme. Fahmy also belonged to the Gezira Club, but, said the general's wife, "the food is really much better at the Police Officers' Club, even if the clientele is a bit arriviste."

"Now, Jenny," cautioned her husband gently. Retired from the army, he supported President Nasser, while at the same time expressing some reservations about his methods.

"Well, I have no one to talk to here," explained Mme. Fahmy reasonably. "So many of my old friends are gone."

"But it is a comfortable place, don't you think?" General Fahmy asked Bob. We looked around the large lounge, heavily carpeted, with easy chairs arranged in family groups so that mothers and children and other relatives could drink tea, play games, and chat as though they were in their own private living rooms. New Egyptian-made materials, printed with lotus and papyrus motifs, in the clear colors found in Pharaonic tomb paintings, had been used for the drapes and the slipcovers.

Mme. Fahmy sniffed. "They are trying, but they have not yet quite developed a modern patriotic style," she said, smiling a little, and I tended to agree with her.

"It all takes time, Jenny," said her husband. "Took France hundreds of years."

"Yes," agreed Bob, and finished his Egyptian beer before rising for lunch. "The beer, I will say, is excellent here."

"It's a German process—" began Mme. Fahmy.

"—but Egyptian workmanship," said the general, leading the way to the dining room, "and it's Egyptian water. You know what they say about the waters of the Nile, Bob?"

"I certainly do," said Bob. "Whoever drinks of the Nile will always return to Egypt."

"But there's something else," persisted General Fahmy as we waited on the sunny patio for a table to be readied. He smiled. "The Nile, my friend, is supposed to have great powers of fertility." He slapped Bob on the back. "But I see you already know that."

It was true. I was pregnant with our second child.

Taste. Decor. Although some things were changing, much seemed the same. The auctions of the goods of departed aristocrats and foreigners always attracted the army officers and their wives. Louis Quinze love seats, old china, Persian rugs, silver plate, English and Italian furniture, European bibelots or paintings of any school—all commanded enormous prices. The taste of a departed elite was still the preferred style. In fact, the standard technique of the auctioneer, when he saw the bidding begin to flag, was to mention the names and titles of the goods' former owners. Names. Titles. The sound of those words stimulated the bidders and the prices would immediately rise again for such items as Prince H.'s desk, or Mme. C.'s dressing table mirror.

One winter morning, I saw twelve Haviland fruit plates and a matching footed epergne, the property of a departed French family, fetch a thousand Egyptian pounds. The Haviland was old, true, and the epergne quite beautiful. But—a thousand pounds? I turned to Aziza and shook my head.

"The family was important," said Aziza, and shrugged. "Mme. Gaudet gave very exclusive dinner parties."

A thousand pounds for a memory? For the thrill of trying to participate vicariously in the social activities of a foreign elite? An elite whose private lives had been closed and forbidden to Egyptians, and who had now disappeared forever? Whatever the reasons for the high prices, a small percentage of each auction's proceeds went into Egypt's republican treasury, where it was needed badly.

Newly prosperous wives could be seen in the flower shops along Kasr al-Nil and Suliman Pasha streets, buying enormous arrangements of roses in the fall, huge sprays of almond and apricot blossoms in the spring, bunches of tuberoses in the winter, whose insistent fragrance perfumed the entire shop. They lingered in front of the show windows where Egyptian shoemakers were displaying good copies of Italian and French designs. They flocked to the boutiques where French embroidered baby clothes and English-style smocked children's dresses were still for sale. Though the new Egyptian Ministry of Industry was pushing locally manufactured goods, those goods often imitated familiar European patterns. Even in the delicatessens and pastry shops, European influences continued. More indigenous pastries like baklava and kunafa were available from the "Syrian" bakeries near the Opera House and the Ezbekiyah Gardens, but Simonds in Zamalek and Heliopolis and Groppi's in central Cairo were crowded with people vying for essentially European delights: meringues, pound cake, napoleons, ladyfingers, chocolates in beribboned boxes, marrons glacés wrapped individually in golden paper—the sweets of a vanished European population. Fresh Italian ravioli and French pâté could still be purchased, together with fanciful sugar Easter eggs, for the Egyptian Coptic, Greek Orthodox, and other Christian groups, as well as the small foreign population (that now included us).

In Groppi's tea rooms, where we drank café viennoise hot in winter and cold in summer, we saw the old class and the new class meeting, but not speaking. Army officers' wives, in new clothes, very high heels, and bouffant coiffures spooned ice cream confections next to elderly men in old-fashioned suits of excellent if shabby tweed, who might nurse a single Turkish coffee throughout an entire morning. The ancient waiters in Groppi's, I noticed, never tried to run these old men off for holding on to their seats too long. They knew well that such men had probably had their apartments sequestered and their furniture auctioned, and were economically useless in the new Egypt. But they still had stature of a kind recognized in Groppi's.

"Let's take Laura Ann to the puppet shows," suggested Aziza.

Aziza was finishing some courses at the university but had a lot of free time "while I think about when I want to get married," she had once explained to me in a burst of confidence. Thus she had taken me around the city and had "adopted" Laura Ann almost from her birth.

So Laura Ann put on her best dress (from one of those Kasr al-Nil shops) and was taken by Mama and "Auntie" Aziza to the puppet show, "Imad al-Din and His Donkey," the dramatization of an old Egyptian folk tale that was drawing full houses, of adults and children, to the theater in downtown Cairo. "It is part of the new Egyptian culture," Aziza said.

Laura Ann, aged two and a half, watched entranced as the puppet donkey plodded along the stage, maneuvered from below, and the puppet peasant plodded along beside him. And she laughed delightedly when the puppet donkey brayed in a most convincing manner, "like ours," she said.

"What?" Aziza cried.

"Ours," responded Laura Ann.

"I think she means the donkey that pulls the garbage wagon," I explained. "It's her donkey as much as the garbage man's, she thinks, since it goes by our house and stops by the *ganeena,* the park where she plays every day."

Aziza looked a little taken aback, but I said quickly, "I guess she's learning about all aspects of Cairo, Aziza."

A new indigenous dance group, the Reda troupe, was formed to choreograph and produce authentic Egyptian folkloric programs; a large tent, the Balloon Theater, was raised in the Dokki district of the city, so many people could watch the Reda troupe perform variations on traditional Egyptian themes. The Reda troupe, begun by an engineer, was distinguished also by the fact that the engineer's own daughter was one of the dancers, a breakthrough in a nation where, until recently, female entertainers were called "artistes," a word often used as a synonym for prostitutes.

The legitimate theaters were refurbished, revitalized, like the cinema industry, "like the poetry, the literature," added Omar. "It is a cultural renaissance for Egypt." So it seemed.

And foreign policy somehow became a part of that renaissance as European powers vied with each other to offer Egyptians the best cultural events of their nations: Russia sent the Bolshoi Ballet for three weeks, with Ulanova or Plisetskaya dancing every night. Germany presented fine string ensembles. Bulgaria and Rumania sent folkloric troupes and invited the Reda troupe to tour their own capitals. Italy provided a season of opera performed in the local replica of La Scala, built in 1869 for the Empress Eugénie's projected visit to Cairo in conjunction with the opening of the Suez Canal; Verdi was asked to write *Aida* for that occasion. France sponsored a season of new films; Britain sent a Shakespeare repertory company. The United States sent choir and jazz groups.

We went to many of these star performances, benefitting from the cultural by-products of the cultural cold war. And afterward we would sit with friends on the Victorian porch of the old Semiramis Hotel, beside President Nasser's new riverside Corniche: drinking Egyptian beer and tea with Omar, Aziza, Nicholas Millet, an archaeologist from Chicago, Susan Spectorsky, an Arabist from Radcliffe, Mona and Abdul Latif al-Shafei, then of the American University in Cairo. And while we contemplated the eternal Nile, we felt that we were truly fortunate to be in Egypt at this time. The river, black and gleaming by night, remained the same, but Egypt was changing: an ancient nation was being reborn, we believed, awakening from years of domination by others to assume responsibility for its own destiny. At the time we recognized that there would be some problems along the path to progress. How could there not be problems?

"Egypt is such a poor country," Abdul Latif, the Syrian dean of the American University, would point out. "The President has very little to work with. Now if it were Syria—"

"Or Lebanon," his wife Mona, beautiful, warmhearted, and Syrian-Lebanese in origin, would always add. "I like living in Egypt, you understand, but really, B.J., the food in Lebanon is so much better."

"That's because they have greater natural resources, my dear," Abdul Latif would reply solemnly.

"Nasser is doing his best. He just needs time." Omar sounded a bit defensive.

"Time to run us further into the ground?" his sister quipped mischievously.

Omar glared and Nick broke in to end the argument with a joke. "Oh, there's a new joke today about Nasser and two army officers."

"Tell us."

" 'What do you think of President Nasser?' one army officer asks the other. 'I can't talk here,' his friend replies, 'let's go where people can't hear us.' And so they go to the coffee shop. 'What do you think of President Nasser?' 'I can't talk here, it's too crowded, let's go somewhere else.' "

"Yes, Nick, get to the point." Bob was impatient in those days.

"Well, they go on a bus, walk farther, farther, and finally, way out on the desert, miles from anywhere, the officer says, 'Come on now, *what* do you think of President Nasser? Out with it!' And his friend looks all around him and then whispers, 'I *like* him!' "

President Nasser went further. The nationalization and sequestration of lands, he said, should not be limited to foreigners and Egyptian large landholders. He struck at another important establishment interest in the old system: he nationalized religious property. By creating a Ministry of Wakfs to handle the management of religious endowments, he hoped to remove the dead weight of real estate, often some of the best property in Cairo, which was frozen in charitable trusts and could not become part of the modern economy. In so doing he also ended any semblance of an independent religious establishment. From then on, mullas and sheikhs were government employees, paid out of the national treasury like the majority of other middle-class Egyptians.

President Nasser's new entente with the religious establishment was demonstrated in a historic 1962 television broadcast on the issue of family planning. By then, the good news from the health-care programs indicated a decline in the death rate. Fewer babies succumbed to dehydration, fewer children and adults were dying of smallpox and cholera. But the bad news was that, partly owing to the declining death rate and an improvement in diet (and, people whispered, new hope for Egypt's future), the population had grown from 21 million in 1956 to 26 million in 1962. Nasser, however, appeared on television, flanked by the rector of Al-Azhar University, the leader of the Islamic community in Egypt, to declare that family planning was necessary for the good of the nation. Nothing in the Koran or in Islam forbade family planning or the use of contraceptives, said the rector, provided that these measures were used not for sinful purposes but "to improve the condition of the family," the most important institution in the Islamic world. President Nasser said that the population increase needed to level off, or Egypt would not be able to keep its promises to its people: hospitals, housing, food, and schools for everyone.

The government's drive toward free education for everyone had made spectacular strides. In ten years, between 1950 and 1960, the number of primary schools had doubled (from 1,530 to 3,330). And the number of primary school students had also doubled (from 1.3 million to 2.6 million). Yet the momentum was slowing—partly for economic reasons, partly because of language. During the colonial period, Egypt's business was conducted in French or English, not in the indigenous language, Arabic. Hence thousands of teachers had to be trained to teach in their own native language.

Bob and I found that educated people did not want to speak Arabic with us but preferred to keep up their more fluent English and French (foreign languages, though currently out of fashion, could be useful in the long run). But since we both felt strongly about keeping up our Arabic, and improving it from our Iraqi days, we hired Sheikh Ali, who came twice a week to our apartment for tea and lessons.

"God be praised," Sheikh Ali would intone when he sat down in our apartment, slowly developing from five bare rooms with electric wires hanging from the ceiling into a kind of home. Winter, spring, or fall, Sheikh Ali requested politely that all our windows be closed, "because of the dangerous breezes," so we would shut the front windows reluctantly, the windows that looked out over the balcony, to the ganeena, where Laura Ann and then David, our newborn son, went each day for recreation, and across the cottonwood and casuarina trees to the limpid, gleaming Nile.

"The breeze brings disease," Sheikh Ali would explain, blowing his nose ceremoniously on a white handkerchief which he secreted somewhere inside his many layers of clothing: overcoat, suit coat, vest, shirt, and long underwear (the edges showed white outside his shirt cuffs). Whatever the season, he wore that underwear and the high black laced shoes of my grandfather's day. In winter he added a sweater, spring meant no overcoat, "but one had to be careful." All seasons, however, he wore what we would, in the past in America, have called a Shriner's hat, a red fez; here, he explained, it was called a tarboosh, and there were still special men in the markets who steamed and cleaned tarbooshes, Egyptian hatters who blocked the tarbooshes on tarboosh molds that looked like overturned flowerpots.

"The tarboosh is worn by the middle class," Sheikh Ali explained to us, and we realized he was speaking of the past. Few people wore the tarboosh anymore, that sign of Turkish days, when the Ottoman effendis or white-collar workers wore tarbooshes to indicate their government rank.

"True, young people no longer wear the tarboosh, but they do not deserve it," he would add, while he drank thirstily two or three cups of hot black tea with plenty of milk and sugar which Abbas provided for our "lessons."

We learned many things from Sheikh Ali, and we probably learned some Arabic, too, though his methods of teaching were, to say the least, unconventional, if not innovative. Faced, during his entire lifetime, by a stream of American and British missionaries who wished to be tutored in Arabic, Sheikh Ali had developed the parable approach. After his opening statements, blessing the occasion, remarking on changing times, he would launch into one or another of the parables in his repertory: Bible stories shared by Christians, Jews, and Muslims, stories from the Old Testament that could not ruffle the feelings of anyone but a Goliath supporter. We sat politely in our newly furnished study, closed to the view of the Nile, listening while Sheikh Ali told us the tale of Daniel in the lions' den; Samson and Delilah; Joseph and his many-colored coat. Each of the parables contained a wealth of new, if not always useful, vocabulary words: lion, bars, growl, green, yellow, scarlet, purple, pillars, temple, passion. We listened, and we asked questions, and he corrected our grammar between parables. But when the session was almost over, signaled by Sheikh Ali passing his hand over his eyes beneath his heavy horn-rimmed glasses to get a surreptitious look at his watch, Bob would leap into the pause and ask questions about Egypt of the past. Sheikh Ali would reply, reluctantly.

"In the old days, foreign people like you came to Egypt, too. But they stayed. Not here for one year, two years. The Vandersalls have been here twenty-five years. *Their* Arabic is excellent." (We felt properly humbled.)

"Then we knew each other, all peoples, Christians, Jews, Muslims. We believed in the same God, but we worshiped differently," he was going on. "Now Cairo is full of strangers, Russians, Japanese, people from Yugoslavia. Who are they? What are they doing here?"

Whatever we may have felt about Sheikh Ali's opinions, we were provoked enough to comb our Arabic dictionaries in search of the right words so we could answer him; for his great virtue—tarboosh, Bible stories, and all—was that he spoke no English. Or at least if he did, we never knew it.

We found ourselves putting together sentences in broken Arabic to explain Nasser's five-year plan to Sheikh Ali, describing economic development, agricultural cooperatives, the plans for the High Dam. In response to all of our eager attempts to describe what new things were happening, however, Sheikh Ali would simply nod, correct our verb endings, take another huge gulp of tea, and then, hands folded in his lap, launch into another Bible story. "The old ways," he said to us over and over, "are the best ways."

"But things are now improving for everyone," Bob insisted, "not just for a few."

We had really given him up as a hopeless reactionary until the occasion of Laura Ann's birthday, when, proud new mama that I was, I brought her out to show her off to Sheikh Ali. "Do you have daughters, Sheikh Ali?"

"Yes, thanks be to God," said Sheikh Ali, wiping an eye—was it a tear? And without further ado, he launched unexpectedly into a long, detailed story about his daughter, prefaced by "You are right, madame, things are changing in Egypt and it is for the better. *Today* I realize that! For the first time."

His young daughter Asma, it seemed, was engaged to be married. The man was a schoolteacher, not too old, of poor but morally upright parents, of whom Sheikh Ali approved. The daughter was not too excited about marrying the man, and had in fact protested, but her father had paid little attention. "I thought it was natural, she was a good girl and loved her home, probably did not want to leave it, but it was time for her to marry, that is our custom, you know, madame. This week, when I was supposed to come here for this lesson, for some reason I forgot and came on Tuesday instead of Wednesday. And when I was halfway here on the bus, I realized my mistake and I went back home. It was about three o'clock and my wife had gone to visit her mother, and I called up the stairs, 'Asma? Asma?' But she did not answer. I thought it was strange and I went up the stairs, and opened the door and there was my beautiful Asma and she was lighting a match to herself. And as her scarf flamed, I threw my arms around her and beat out the flames and cried, 'Why? Why?' And do you know what, madame? It was because she didn't want to marry!" Sheikh Ali looked quite surprised. "I said, 'My God, what have I done? What has the world done? This is not Islam.' And I said to Asma, 'Stay here, my darling, for the rest of your life, don't marry, why didn't you *tell* me?' And she said she did, but I wouldn't listen. My wife says I was set in the old ways, but I now see that if the old ways lead to something like that, they must be changed."

Bob and I had sat there silently, not knowing how to respond, but fortunately Laura Ann, a happy child, smiled and giggled, and Sheikh Ali smiled back at her, and the moment passed. "I would not have mentioned this," said Sheikh Ali, regaining his composure, "if the sight of your daughter (may God keep her safe) had not prompted me."

"Some things must change," suggested Bob, "perhaps some things may be better staying the same."

"No," said Sheikh Ali. "It is hard to change just one thing. Everything is changing in Egypt. Things will never be the same."

The American University, where Bob was teaching, was one of the institutions that mirrored change, resistance to change, and the lessons of the past. For it had only declared its commitment to secular rather than religious ideals a decade before and the atmosphere of a missionary school still hung over the university, as it did over the American Girls College, a preparatory school in Heliopolis, from where many of Bob's students had come. But the religious atmosphere seemed to bother us more than it did our Egyptian friends. "There young people learn good English and are preparing themselves for the Egypt of tomorrow," General Fahmy explained to us. "The Koran says, 'Educate your children for tomorrow,' and as Muslims, we feel our faith is strong enough to deal with the issues raised by other faiths."

As President Nasser's campaign for free public education gathered momentum, the Egyptian universities—Cairo, Ein Shams, Alexandria—increased dramatically in size. Some say that university attendance in Egypt jumped 500 percent in one generation. By 1960 over 100,000 students were enrolled in institutions of higher education; the total had tripled in a decade. Here, if one passed the government examinations at a sufficiently high level, one could obtain professional education (engineering, law, medicine) as well as the Ph.D.

(social science, science, humanities) at no cost whatsoever. These unprecedented opportunities were seized by thousands of bright young people whose parents would never have been able to afford to send them to college or university. And from these graduates, a new kind of elite was emerging, upwardly mobile, intelligent, and supportive of President Nasser's regime (after all, hadn't he been responsible for their success?). Young, hopeful, dedicated, they began to inject new enthusiasm into a tired bureaucracy, new ideas into an intellectual establishment devoted until recently to Europe and Europe alone, new forms into arts and letters, new plans into the architecture and public works of the city. Sawsan, one of our friends from Cairo University, came from a family of seven children whose father had been an assistant gardener at King Farouk's Abdine Palace. Ten years later, Sawsan had become an anthropologist, her sister a film producer for Cairo television, her four brothers an engineer, a librarian, a doctor, and a short story writer and reporter on one of Cairo's daily newspapers. Cairo University offered a system of competition based on merit, not only on family ties. It also offered coeducation. Cairo University was becoming the great leveler.

But coeducation meant something else in Egypt, which after all was an Islamic state. It meant a relaxation of the close supervision usually accorded to young women. Going to the university became not a duty but an honor, and a redefinition of women's role and place began to be attempted. No one in the middle and upper classes of Egyptian society had been veiled for years. That had disappeared in the 1920s, with the dramatic public unveiling by Hoda Sharawi and Seza Nabarawi and the subsequent formation of the Egyptian Women's Union. Though peasant women still wore long loose-fitting dresses and wrapped a black *milaya* around their heads and shoulders when they went out, middle-class and upper-class Egyptian city women wore Western dress. Yet dress of the West did not necessarily equal freedom of the West. Boys and girls did not date Western style, and marriages were arranged by families. Before 1952, the educational level of women was very low, no matter what they wore, and work laws and family laws still favored men. The opening of schools taught in Arabic and President Nasser's public statements about the duties of all citizens, men and women, in the new Egypt gave impetus to the participation of greater numbers of women in education and in the workplace than had ever been involved before.

But parents of a more conservative generation were often not ready to give their daughters the run of Cairo University, with its great mass of students from all parts of socialist Egypt; for them, the American University provided an acceptable alternative. Further, one did not have to pass government-administrated examinations at a high school to be admitted. One of President Nasser's own daughters, Hoda, had not done well on her exams, so he sent her to the American University, which admitted her on probation. Fairly small (1,500 students), fairly expensive (and thus beyond the reach of all but the well-to-do), the American University was reputable academically but its degrees were not yet accredited by the Egyptian Ministry of Education. Thus the American University, by default, directed its graduates to nongovernment jobs in what remained of private enterprise, in the worlds of banking, tourism, public relations, and private schools where good English or French was still as much an asset as a degree from the new national university. Thus the university, American missionary school though it may have been in the 1940s, had become a different place by 1960 with an international flavor (forty-eight nationalities), a kind of private-school cachet, and a more pluralistic even if more elitist student body than other educational institutions in the country.

Our two children grew and prospered in the Egyptian sunshine, in spite of the "noxious" breezes Sheikh Ali so abhorred. They prospered also in the Egyptian social climate, where children are universally desired, indulged, and adored. Several years later, in Cambridge, Massachusetts, Laura Ann came home from her first-grade class each day with a glum look on her face. "What's the matter, dear?"

"People are so mad here."

"What? What do you mean?"

"Well, nobody says hello. When I say hello, on the street, they just look mean at me."

Poor Laura Ann. It was difficult to explain to her that she was missing a whole attitude, a whole culture, that was hospitable and affectionate to all children, in a way that her own society was not. But I tried.

Then she said, "Even the ganeenas here aren't the same."

She was right. The parks in Cambridge were larger and greener and had far better play equipment than the small garden outside our house in Cairo, but the people were not as friendly. What I, brought up in America, found perfectly natural, Laura Ann, brought up in Egypt, found alien. The mothers and fathers in the park, good Bostonians, did not speak to all the children, and certainly did not bounce strange babies on their knees or comfort any passing toddler that was crying, as the good-hearted Egyptians in the ganeena did without thinking twice about it. "Our" ganeena in Cairo was a kind of school, though we did not realize it at the time, socializing children in the ways of play and affection and what could be expected from adults; socializing country girls, new servants for the newly well-to-do, in the ways of city nannies. The ganeena also served as an employment bureau for female servants, at a time when the old ways of hiring help (through relatives) were changing, and new families that needed and could afford servants had appeared alongside some of the old ones.

Parks. Public gardens. Ganeenas. They had existed in Cairo long before Nasser's time, but not in such profusion, and not without the restrictions of entrance fees. The new public gardens were free, another demonstration of Nasser's belief that Egypt belonged to all Egyptians. And he had appropriated more urban space for parks. Early in his presidency he had begun by leveling the British army barracks that had occupied a vast area beside the Nile. The old military parade ground was planted with trees and flowers, transformed into walkways and parks which led into the Corniche, a new tree-shaded esplanade that wound along the river from the Kasr al-Aini bridge in the south to the northern edge of Boulac district, allowing ample space for public picnicking, strolling, and just sitting beside the river. The private gardens of the aristocracy came next. Princess Fawzia's garden in Zamalek became a children's playground; the Manyal Palace, the Abdine Palace, and the King's summer palace at Ras al-Tin in Alexandria were made into public grounds and museums. Like all the other parks, the ganeena below our apartment was free, but not to everyone. Only women and children were admitted. This seemed strange to us at first, but eventually friends made it clear that this was a protection for women in a society where reputation was still crucial, and where being seen talking to a strange man could ruin a woman's reputation—and life—forever.

My own feelings about the ganeena were mixed, for although it looked like any children's playground anywhere in the world, it was not. The ganeena was really not for mothers and children to take the air; it was for nannies and children. When I had adjusted to the fact that the nannies in the ganeena were vaguely unfriendly when I spoke to them (after all, wasn't I letting the side down by not providing a job for one of them?), and when I decided that a good Egyptian nanny could both increase the amount of care and affection my own growing family would receive and give me some time to write, I departed from the ganeena forever. I occasionally observed the children from the balcony but I let Farida take Laura Ann and David to the park. Everything changes, Sheikh Ali had said—including us.

President Nasser returned from an international meeting of the nonaligned-bloc leaders. He was cheered by thousands as he rode through the streets, standing upright in an open car, smiling, waving his hands in recognition of the applause, the shouts of adulation—"*Ya Gamal! Ya Gamal!*"—that greeted his progress. "He has diabetes, you know," said an Egyptian colleague who stood with us above the crowds on the roof of the American University to comfortably watch the triumphant cavalcade pass. "He is not well. And I'm sure you've heard about Vice-President Abdul Hakim Amer. Corruption, the old story."

"But not Nasser himself?" asked Bob.

"No. No one criticizes him personally. But the people around him, that is another matter. The Helwan steel plant cost a lot, there were bids, contracts. You've heard the newest joke?"

"Which one?"

"The one about the vote and the man who makes up the jokes?"

"No. Tell."

"It seems Nasser heard all the jokes that are going around and he wanted to meet the man who was making them up. So they brought in this very old guy and Gamal says, 'Aha, you're the one.'

" 'Yes, Mr. President,' said the old guy.

" 'Did you make up the one about the price of meat?'

" 'Yes, sir.'

" 'And the one about Abdul Hakim Amer and Mustafa Kemal?'

" 'Yes, sir. I did.'

" 'And the one about my winning the presidency in the last free election by 99 44/100 percent of the vote?'

" 'No, sir,' says the old guy. '*You* made up that one.' "

By 1962 President Nasser had been in power for nearly ten years. The plans were familiar and promises were coming due. The industrialization program had been a moderate success: Egyptian textiles, furniture, plastic dishware, cosmetics, refrigerators, drugs, appeared in limited supply. The Egyptian-made small car, the Ramses, built in cooperation with Fiat of Italy, was seen on the streets. But food prices were rising, the agricultural reclamation program was lagging, and so many new college graduates were being turned out that Nasser was having to add staff to the already crowded offices of the government bureaucracy to keep his promise of a job for every young Egyptian B.A.

Yet the biggest promise of all, the key to future advances, was the High Dam, the oft-dreamed-of, constantly discussed engineering miracle that was meant to change the face of Egypt by providing more arable land, more hydroelectricity, and insurance against disastrous floods. The High Dam was the subject of newsreels at every local cinema, of gossip, of more jokes, of party chatter at every social gathering. Could Nasser pull it off?

Thumbing one's nose at the West and taking on the Soviet Union was no joke. And it was rumored that Nasser had mortgaged Egypt's cotton crop for many years to repay the Russian loans. It was a great, costly gamble and as the years passed the dam became more and more a symbol of Nasser's aspirations for a new Egypt, and of the snags that were developing in the plans.

For word had reached Cairo that many unforeseen problems had developed around the dam. It would take longer to finish than expected. Costs were mounting. The Russians were having trouble working in Upper Egypt's intense heat. And our friend Sawsan, whose brother was one of the Egyptian engineers employed on the dam, said there were "differences in temperament" between the Egyptians and the Russians. "The Russians are so serious," said Sawsan. "They won't listen to us. And my brother says they never laugh, except at silly things that aren't jokes at all. Very heavy-blooded, the Russians."

The dam had many implications. When the structure was complete, the backwaters would form a lake, flooding the Nile Valley south of Aswan into northern Sudan. Magnificent Pharaonic monuments, including the temple of Abu Simbel, stood in the path of the floodwaters. Their plight was attracting international attention. UNESCO appropriated funds for a giant project to save or to document all the monuments before they disappeared forever.

Omar, our Egyptologist friend, was delighted by the international attention. "My nation is finally being noticed again in the world of art and culture," he announced at a dinner given by his parents for a visiting French archaeologist. "Abu Simbel is a word known today around the world, Bob."

"What about the people who live near Abu Simbel?" asked Bob. It was a large dinner, elegantly presented and served, and most of the guests seemed to be concerned in one way or the other with the archaeological monuments of Egypt.

"Who? Oh, you mean the Nubians. Nasser," said Omar, "is making arrangements for them, too."

"He is?" Bob sounded interested.

"Yes. The government is taking care of it all, I think."

"Hmmm," murmured Bob, then, a bit louder, "I suppose they are but I've been wondering if anyone is interested in *their* life and culture. It would be interesting to find something out about the plans for the Nubians."

"Go to Dr. N. in the Ministry of Social Affairs," said Omar. "He will tell you."

Bob was staring intently at Omar. "Okay." Then to me, he said, "Don't let me forget his name, B.J. Dr. N. in the Ministry of Social Affairs."

I opened my mouth to ask the reason for this sudden interest in the Nubians when dessert arrived on an enormous silver tray. To judge by the hush that fell over the long lace-covered table, this dish was very special, a kind of cake or pudding festooned not with cream or icing but with crystallized sugar spun into golden threads, an edible transparent froth of sugar. *"Cheveux des anges* [angels' hair]!" breathed the French visitor appreciatively. "What a treat! No one has time to make it in Paris anymore."

Aziza's mother, a tall patrician lady with carefully arranged coils of black hair, smiled. "It's only sugar and eggs and almonds," she said. But cheveux des anges is a difficult dish and had probably taken her cook the entire day to make. It was obviously a triumph. Omar burst out spontaneously, "It is for you, monsieur! We are honored to have such distinguished scholars coming to Cairo to help in the international efforts to salvage our monuments."

"Hear! Hear!" Omar's father had joined in.

There was a slight pause, almost a sigh, as the guests sank their spoons into the shining dessert, a small masterpiece of culinary creativity, using, as Aziza's mother had said, "only sugar and eggs and almonds."

Professor G. was one of many archaeologists, Polish, Austrian, French, American, German, Japanese, Italian, who had accepted the Egyptian government's invitation to excavate and record the monuments of Nubia before the dam was finished.

"Salvage archaeology," I heard Bob say to Dr. Hani, the Egyptian representative from the Department of Antiquities. "Why not some salvage anthropology, too?" Bob was not about to drop the subject, it seemed.

Dr. Hani paused with his spoonful of cheveux des anges in midair, the loops and strands of spun sugar glistening in the candlelight. "Why not?" he returned.

"Why not indeed?" Bob was smiling to himself as he almost, but not quite, scraped his crystal dessert dish clean. I caught his eye. "Maybe as part of the Oriental Institute's effort?"

"What, Dr. Fernea?" Dr. Hani asked politely. He had finished his dessert, too, and laid down his spoon.

"Just thinking," said Bob, but he was still smiling. Although I did not realize it at that moment, the Nubian ethnological survey, on which we were to work for several years to come, had begun to take shape.

Bob took Omar at his word and went to the Ministry of Social Affairs to inquire about the Egyptian Nubians.

"Yes," said Dr. N., the official to whom he had been sent, "there are about fifty thousand Nubians south of Aswan. We are making plans for them."

"They'll all have to move?"

The ministry official nodded. "Of course. It is too bad, but that is the price of progress. Besides, they'll be better off in new homes."

"New homes? What new homes?"

The ministry official sighed. His desk, Bob said, was piled with folders, long folders of dusty rose, short folders of blue. He tapped one of the long rose folders. "This," he said, "this is an outline of our plan. We will resettle all Nubians."

"Where will they go?"

"Downstream. To Kom Ombo, north of Aswan, where a place will be made for them. Egypt today, Professor Fernea, assumes responsibility for all its citizens."

"Yes, I understand," Bob replied. "Thank you very much."

But no ethnographic research was planned before the move, the official admitted. It was too expensive. The foreign governments and UNESCO were paying for the documentation of the monuments, but no one had offered to take on a study of the present culture of the region.

"How is it that studying what people made is more important than studying the people themselves?" Bob asked.

"It's not that objects are more important," returned Dr. Laila Hamamsy, the vibrant cultural anthropologist who directed the Social Research Center of the American University. "It's just that they are easier to work with, my friend. Stones are more predictable. They don't complain, collect names on petitions, and so forth."

"Are the Nubians doing that?" asked Bob, surprised.

"Yes, yes," said Dr. Laila. "They are becoming very active on their own behalf, and the government has now promised to ask their advice before the resettlement, and so on."

"But we're talking about fifty thousand human beings," said Bob. "Hundreds of village communities are being torn from their native land, changed forever by the move, and no one is paying attention. Why doesn't UNESCO do something about living people?"

"Why don't *you* do something about it?" John Wilson, the late great Egyptologist, had said. "You're young and vigorous."

"Me?" Bob had gotten his Ph.D. only two years before. Cairo was, after all, his first teaching job.

"Why not?" John Wilson returned.

"We could do something through the center," suggested Dr. Laila.

John Hilliard, Ford Foundation representative in Cairo, came to share our concern for the Nubians. And so the Nubian project became a reality, a three-year ethnological survey before the High Dam was finished. Anthropologists, sociologists, geographers, architects, statisticians, a photographer, and research assistants became project members.

Americans and Egyptians worked together, recording the culture of the Nubian peoples and coordinating efforts, wherever possible, with the Egyptian Ministry of Social Affairs, which had been given the task of resettling the fifty thousand Nubian men, women, and children who were living in Egypt. About the same number of Nubians in the Sudan were being resettled by the Sudanese government, because of the rising High Dam reservoir.

Dr. Laila was right. The Nubians were already petitioning the ministry on their own behalf. A census was taken. Surveys were conducted. Did the Nubians want compensation for the loss of homes and land? No, they wanted new communities, with new houses and new land. Thus New Nubia was planned, a twenty-four-mile-long crescent of government housing north of Kom Ombo, to replace the string of villages along the Nile that would be drowned by the coming flood.

Nubia turned out to be a far more diverse region than we had at first realized. There were three separate social groups, to begin with, each speaking a different language. The Kenuzi in the north spoke one language; the Arabs in the central area spoke Arabic, and the people in the south, near Abu Simbel, spoke a third, Fadija.

Hassan Fathy, the celebrated Egyptian architect, recorded his own feelings of amazement when, with a group of artists and writers from the Ministry of Culture, he first visited this southernmost region of his own nation. "It was a new world for all of us, whole villages of houses, spacious, lovely, clean, harmonious. . . . Each village seemed to come from a dream country . . . from Atlantis itself it could have come. There was not a trace of the miserly huddle usually seen in Egyptian villages." But, as we came slowly to understand, this clean, sparkling, and dreamlike look of Nubia was due in part to the fact that the villages were not involved in the messy business of making a living: that was done largely by absent males working in Cairo and Alexandria, whose lives became another segment of the study.

Arrangements were made to have members of the project in each of the three language areas, and Bob settled in the south with two research assistants. I went down with Laura Ann, then two and a half years old, and David, then one and a half, for the winter of 1961–62. We lived in one of the villages of Ballana, near the Abu Simbel temple, and shared one of those spacious lovely Nubian houses with Saleh, his two wives Dahiba and Hanim Ali, and his niece Khadija.

The house, high on a sand dune, above the valuable arable land along the river, was indeed lovely and spacious and the scenery below us was marvelous, the river flowing past the green strips of cultivated land, and palm trees forming a verdant frame for the worn ancient table-topped mountains on the opposite bank.

But the living was not easy. Bob was excited about the research, but also tense with the responsibilities of three field camps, diverse assistants and colleagues, many of whom had never lived outside urban, comfortable Cairo before. I might have felt more adventurous if I had not been four months rather heavily pregnant with our third child, and had the responsibility for Laura Ann and David. On the other hand, though baby food, in fact all food, was a problem, rapport in the village was no problem at all. It was quite obvious that I was a woman in the family way and my sniffling children behaved no better and sometimes worse than Nubian children. This gave the Nubian matrons plenty of opportunity to observe, chide, and tease me for my permissive childrearing methods while at the same time expressing genuine kindness and helpfulness toward all of us.

"See," Khadija explained kindly to me, "if you just tie Davy's ankles together lightly, with a cloth, he will sit in one place longer and won't crawl into the dirt."

She demonstrated with her own son, Abdul Nasr, but I also noticed that Abdul Nasr's proud grandparents watched him fondly getting *out* of his ankle sling craftily, and applauded his cunning and strength. I could not bring myself to tie David's ankles. He wheezed and sniffled with asthma so badly that I was happy to see any movement on his part.

"Taking him to Nubia can't make the asthma any worse," my Cairo pediatrician had advised. "The dry air might improve it. The Nubians call it a blessed land, you know."

"Yes," I said. "I know."

But for us, Nubia did not seem a blessed land at all, at least at first. My feet and legs swelled ominously from so much plodding in the sand, Laura Ann's eyes swelled shut with eye infections from the flies, and David's asthma seemed to grow worse every day.

"Maybe you'd better go back to Cairo, B.J.," Bob said as David's breathing failed to improve. He smiled a little wryly. "Maybe it's because we're not Nubians. The benevolent spirits of this land are not with us."

"Sometimes I feel that way," I confessed. When the children were asleep, we would sit out on the mastaba or bench along the front of the wall of the house; the stars blazed in the quiet sky. "You know, Bob, Muhammad's mother,

Shemessa, really has it in for me, and for David. She doesn't want me down there giving Muhammad's twin sons those antibiotics. I hate to go."

"I know, I know," Bob said and sighed deeply. "But Muhammad is my best friend here. He asked me as a special favor to have you do that, because he says his mother doesn't believe in modern medicine and throws it away, and his wife is not strong enough to stand up to her."

"How can she?" I returned. "Nezla has to take care of all those children *and* iron Muhammad's beautiful galabias every day so he can march around and look impressive, and then she's supposed to stand up to his old mother too? Sometimes I think that old woman is a witch, putting a hex on me and poor David."

"B.J." Bob put his hand on my arm. "You're crazy. You probably should go back to Cairo. This life is hard on you, too."

I tentatively agreed to return, but then David came down with pneumonia and was too sick to move. For days we watched hopelessly beside his crib, and our friends brought things they said would help: *karkaday* herb tea; a kind of thick oily paste to rub on his chest; a blue bead to hang on his bed and ward off the evil eye. It was Nezla who proffered the blue bead and I took it as a good omen: she knew Shemessa's virulent moods and tempers better than anyone and I felt she was trying to thank me for caring about the twins. Shemessa did not come, and I was glad she stayed away. I did not want her around David's sickbed.

Our Nubian adventure had a happy ending. Either the spirits changed or I had been overanxious about Shemessa's influence in the blessed land, but one night after the crisis of the pneumonia, David suddenly began to breathe normally for the first time in months. He was cured—miraculously, it seemed. And the asthma never returned. Our pediatrician later confessed he didn't know why, but our friends believed they did.

"It was the karkaday," said Khadija.

"It was the blue bead I gave you against the evil eye," said Nezla.

"The antibiotics finally took hold," Bob stated.

Whatever had done it, it was done, and I thanked the gods—and Nubia—for our son's restored health.

When we returned to Cairo, Bob wrote a series of papers, based on the preliminary research, for the Ministry of Social Affairs. These papers dealt with the problems of resettlement from the Nubians' point of view and included some suggestions about how the problems might be solved and possible dangers to the community averted.

The Nubian project was an opportunity for us to become involved with a special group of people and their problems. We began to feel some sense of participation in Egyptian life, and we became unashamed partisans of the Nubian community and its interests.

The camaraderie of the project staff continued even after we had all left the field camps and come back to the city. Our third child, Laila, was born, and

Nubian as well as Egyptian friends came to call. I went to visit Dahiba, Saleh's wife, in the Kasr al-Aini hospital, where she was having a cataract operation. Then Sawsan became engaged and I had a bridal shower for her. Amina, one of the other research assistants, invited us for a weekend at her family's *ezba,* the country estate of her father, a member of the nineteenth-century landed gentry. Her brother took Bob around the farm and talked about some of the serious agricultural problems which had yet to be solved in Nasser's Egypt.

"It's not the land reform," he had said. "It's overirrigation, bad crop planning, village-to-market problems."

We were settling in to Egypt, and our parents, apparently deciding that we were there to stay for a while, came and visited. I began to write a book about our earlier experience in southern Iraq.

"Which did you like best, Egypt or Iraq?" Fadwa, one of the research assistants, would tease.

"You can't compare. They're different."

"Ah, but you don't want to," said Fadwa. "And you are really getting to be Egyptian anyway," she teased. "Pretty soon you and Bob will no longer qualify as Americans."

"They can't get over the way they look, though," Sawsan would put in. "So American. Though I must say, B.J., speaking as an old friend, you are a little more chic than you used to be."

"Egyptian friends have helped," I could not help admitting.

"How can you justify what your government is doing in Palestine?" Karim, who had worked with us in Ballana, would ask, and ask. Himself a Palestinian, he was more sensitive than most, but everyone asked that. "And why don't they invite Nasser to the White House?"

"America still thinks of Egypt as inferior, that's what it is," said Hassan, another research assistant. "A second-rate African country." He was laughing, but he was not joking.

They had touched a nerve and they knew it. We were good enough friends now that we could be teased about our behavior or U.S. foreign policy and be expected not to take offense. But we had become extremely sensitive on the issue of our country's record in the Arab world. It was becoming harder and harder to explain America's indifference and even hostility to the nonaligned bloc of nations, of which Nasser was a major leader. America, from our point of view, at least where we lived in Egypt, did not seem to be paying much attention to the new nations in Africa and the Arab world.

In 1962 Algeria's ten-year struggle for independence ended finally, with the departure of the defeated French. But this historic occasion did not seem to us to get enough attention in the American press. Yet it had been John Kennedy, while still a junior senator, who had been the first member of the U.S. Congress to raise the issue of French torture and imprisonment of Algerians. Although this action earned Kennedy the undying respect of the Middle Easterners, it was considered a real faux pas at the time by many Kennedy supporters. France was an old and trusted ally, after all, and Algeria only a North African colony (known in the American press for using so-called terrorist tactics against the French *colons*).

John Kennedy's popularity in Egypt at that time was apparent in every newspaper kiosk, where his photo could be bought for pennies, along with photos of local leaders like Nasser, and public figures such as the great singer Um Kulthum. When Kennedy was assassinated in 1963, strangers came up to us on the streets of Cairo, tears in their eyes, to shake our hands and offer condolences.

Like other Americans both at home and abroad, we were stunned by that event and had no more explanation for it than did our Egyptian friends. It just wasn't the sort of thing that happened in America—or was it?

Yet even though Kennedy had been widely admired as a person and a president, U.S. foreign policy, even under his presidency, was not. At best it was felt we were naïve, and being used by the Israelis and European powers for their, rather than America's, best interests. Hassan and Karim and Fadwa and Amina and Sawsan charitably conceded that American intentions were good, but our behavior was at odds not only with our own interests but with our expressed values. At the crux of the problem, they said, lay America's unwavering support for Israel, at no matter what cost—to the Arab world, and to America's long-term interests there.

"What are we doing here, anyway, B.J.?" Bob asked one night in late 1963, as we sat on our balcony enjoying the cool breeze from the Nile after dinner guests had departed. The children were soundly asleep, our cook Abbas had departed for the night, the ganeena was empty, we were finishing another year as strangers in Egypt.

"It's true we are strangers, always will be," I ventured, "but aren't we doing something that may be valuable in its way?"

"For Egypt? Or for ourselves?"

"Certainly mostly for ourselves, but surely your Nubian project benefits Egypt, or at least some Egyptians."

"I hope so," said Bob. "But I'm beginning to have doubts about living as an expatriate anywhere. What has to be done has to be done by the people who live here, the Egyptians. We're just freeloaders really."

"And lotus eaters? Adventurers? Copping out from the responsibilities of our own society?"

"Well, not exactly," worried Bob. "But it seems that America is changing fast, or faster than Egypt, and we should go back there before we become strangers there, too. And the children need some kind of roots. Laura Ann is four now."

"Yes, but wait until next year," I replied. "You have to finish your contract—"

"And teach in Alexandria."

Bob's mood suddenly shifted. "That should be interesting, talking to engineers about community development!" The Ford Foundation was sponsoring a graduate program in community development and the dean of the faculty at Alexandria Agricultural College had asked Bob to give a weekly seminar. His students would be the young Egyptian engineers and planners who would be working in the first tracts of reclaimed land to be opened to small farmers. He had enthusiastically agreed on the spot, even though he would teach in Arabic, imperfect as his still was. "Sheikh Ali will be shocked." Bob smiled. "I have no correct verbs—and no shame!"

The Nubians were moved north in several stages, and in 1965 we visited our friends in their new homes above Kom Ombo, barely one year after the final resettlement. It was a very painful experience. The government-issue cement-block houses were raw and ugly, some still unfinished. Many old people and children had died. Markets and schools were not yet operating. Lack of fodder had decimated the animal stock. And the sugarcane crops that the Egyptian government wanted the Nubians to raise were unfamiliar; the farm development was not proceeding as rapidly as expected at any level. Much of the agricultural land allotted to the Nubians was still unirrigated. And small family savings were dwindling in the new situation.

"We have to buy everything in the store, here," explained Khadija, "even sand, for the courtyard floors."

"But it's the river we miss the most," said her aunt, Hanim Ali, who still wore on her fingers, as she had in old Nubia, a number of strange and curious rings. "Look, B.J., there's no view at all. We brought some palm trees and planted them but it will be years before there is shade."

"We're making out, though," Muhammad told Bob. "It will get better. We'll fix up these awful houses. Give us time."

"Yes," Galal Moursy had said. "We'll do all right. The government is trying. And the lake is filling up. We'll go back when the lake reaches its new banks."

Many Nubians said that at the time, but most of the researchers on the project, though they nodded pleasantly, did not believe it was feasible.

"A dream, not practical," they said. "Much too difficult. The government will never give them permission to go back, even if they want to."

By 1964 people in Cairo were worried about the high prices of food and the growing authoritarianism of the regime. People spoke of the secret police, of the torture of dissidents, of long incarceration of political prisoners in faraway oasis prisons. The nonaligned bloc of nations did not seem to be developing into the influential force people expected. President Nasser's attempts at Pan-Arabism, his short-lived federation with Syria, his military adventures in the Yemen, had come to naught. But he apparently felt he held one trump card: the High Dam.

That summer the Nile rose and flooded the land, as it had done every summer for thousands of years. The farmers watched the precious silt pile up in the fields as the waters withdrew, and the television cameras recorded the occasion, which would soon, said the commentator, be an event of the past, a part of history. In his dark-blue business suit and sober striped tie, the commentator extolled the advantages of a new controlled Nile. But was it our imagination that his voice broke a little as he spoke? The Aswan Dam was rising, and when it was complete, the Nile would no longer flood the land. Was this a good thing or a bad thing?

President Nasser insisted in his speeches and on television that the dam was a marvelous thing for Egypt. Whatever drawbacks it might have would be more than compensated for by the new areas of land that could be farmed, by the electric power that would be generated to bring lights and television to every Egyptian village. Man could harness nature, Nasser asserted, to make it work for the good of all the people. His strong face stayed full in frame until the sequence faded and Abdul Halim Hafiz came on to sing the song of the sixties, "Sud al-Ali," the Song of the High Dam. An orchestra of drums and violins and flutes and ouds backed him onstage and the audience clapped enthusiastically until the music ended.

When we went home to the United States in 1965, the High Dam was still not finished. The structure, however, was growing higher and higher and the waters of the Nile had covered all of Egyptian Nubia except for the tops of the palm trees.

Comment

THE DOMESTICATION OF THE NILE

THE RELATIONSHIP between the Nile and the people of Egypt has radically changed since the completion of the High Dam in 1971. No longer is the river an unpredictable variable in the equation that determines the size of the harvests. Its waters now flow steadily all year long, and its slight rises and falls are easily accommodated to the agricultural cycle. The mighty Nile has become a large irrigation ditch.

Unquestionably, the High Dam has had positive effects. Two and a half million acres of land in Upper Egypt are now cultivated two or even three times a year; this is possible thanks to a system of irrigation ditches that have replaced the basin method of catching the floodwater behind a dam and then releasing it after the soil is soaked. Nearly 950,000 acres of formerly unusable desert land have also been reclaimed for agriculture (although there is little net gain owing to the loss of farmland through urban expansion and shoreline erosion along the Mediterranean). Turbines at the High Dam are producing 4 billion kilowatt-hours of electricity per year and are presumably able to produce again that much. This has permitted the electrification of most of Egypt's villages. With the population (44 million) at nearly double its size when the High Dam was completed, it is hard to imagine how Egypt could do without the dam.

Yet the radical transformation of the flow of the Nile has had many other effects on the lives of the people who depend so entirely on this river they now control. The Nile no longer contains itself within its banks but seeps constantly into the land around it, waterlogging and salinating the alluvial deposits its floods once carried to the sandy plains. In the past, though the untamed Nile would sweep away hundreds of acres of land from one bank, at the same time it deposited as much or more fresh soil somewhere else. Any living river does the same. In the past, farmers never knew which bank would come and which might go and thus riverside cultivation always held an element of chance. With the dam, that element of chance has been eliminated. But the constant presence of the water is slowly melting away the banks, dissolving the Nile's own container, and often requiring cement reinforcements, the costs of which are far beyond the means of the river users.

Further, the river can no longer keep itself clean. Before the dam checked its flow, the Nile scoured its own bottom, flushing excess mud into the alluvial fan it had deposited at its mouth on the Mediterranean Sea. Today the Nile carries nothing to the sea. Its old bed is full of mud islands near the shoreline, its waters used up in the irrigation ditches of the Delta. The Mediterranean, unchecked, is eroding the shoreline and threatens to break through the land which divides the sea from the freshwater lakes on the edge of the Delta. If this happens, it will be a disaster for local cultivation and for fishing.

In Upper Egypt, eight hundred miles to the south, the constant presence of the Nile waters has permitted the change from basin to ditch irrigation to take place, but the lack of free flow is becoming a dangerous convenience for farm families. Constant exposure to the standing ditch water, which is used for drinking, sanitation, laundry, and the washing of animals such as water buffalo, increases the possibility of infection by water-carried diseases, particularly the debilitating schistosomiasis. Before the High Dam, these diseases were generally only found in the Delta, where ditch irrigation had been customary for centuries. Today schistosomiasis and intestinal parasites threaten the health of the population which, before the dam, drew its water directly from the free-flowing Nile rather than from standing water. Projects to provide piped water for drinking purposes will help but will only partly reduce the human health risk from this new, more intimate involvement with the river.

In the millennia during which the Nile rose and fell according to the amount of rain several thousand miles away in the mountains of Kenya and Ethiopia, the Nile was the center of year-round attention among Egyptians, whether city dweller or farmer, rich or poor. The changing color of the river, the beginnings of its summer flood, the wonder at its power, or the mourning at its failure to rise was the subject of constant conversation, the reason for major ritual and economic activity. Among the ancient Egyptians, the Nile was a focus of religious attention. Around the river they wove a complex web of mythological expression based on their need to have this source of life, and to explain its unpredictable behavior. Indeed, the ancient Egyptians were so involved in the life of the Nile that they described rain, another unpredictable natural phenomenon, as an "inundation from heaven."

However, the end of Pharaonic ideology did not result in the loss of the material circumstance it reflected. Thus, throughout Egyptian history the Nile has remained central to a rich body of folklore and legend; it forms part of the proverbs and idioms in every Egyptian's vocabulary, and it is the object of local rituals, such as Sham el-Nessim, which have remained separate from the orthodoxy of the great modern religions.

Since 1971, the Nile has no longer provided the seasonal rhythm, the pulse of tension and release, which once animated Egyptian society. The color of the water stays more or less the same, the wild spaces of new floodland no longer appear. Egyptians still worry about the future of the Nile, but not, as in the past, in terms of the next cycle of seasons. They worry about an indefinite future in which this new tamed Nile, now part of the local economy, dominated by the imposing technology of the High Dam, will grow older and develop more problems with increasing age, like any one of us. There is no annual relief from this worry, and hence nothing to celebrate.

Egypt was the gift of the Nile. Its floods brought the alluvial soil which fertilized and renewed the agricultural land its waters irrigated. That gift was given on its own terms, however, and people had to manage as best they could. Now, as a domesticated resource, the Nile is dependent for its health as a river on those who use its waters. Like house plants or pets, the Nile can be no better than its owners. Soon the Sudan will be building dams and expecting its share of Nile water. Competitive needs and claims may arise and lead to new international quarrels.

But the Nile will not be able to settle international disputes any more than it can clean its own riverbed. The days when the Nile was a wild, unconquered part of nature already lie in the nostalgic past. Today the question is whether the Nile can survive its domesticity.

CHAPTER XI

Egypt and Nubia

1981

Our pallid Egypt
The sun scorches and scourges
with bitter-and-spite-laden arrows
and exhausts it with thirst and disease.
Our sweet Egypt
in a gay fair
gets drunk, forgets, and adorns itself, and rejoices
and scorns the tyrannical sun.

C. P. Cavafy
Sham el-Nessim

CAIRO, THE PRESENT capital of Egypt, lies on a site that has been continually inhabited for as long as historical records have existed. The ancient Egyptians called it Khere-ohe, "place of combat," because it stood on a legendary battle-ground where the god Horus, beloved son of Isis and Osiris, took on the god Seth, his wicked uncle, in order to avenge his father's murder. The myths are not clear on the outcome of the battle; some say the city of Cairo contained and absorbed that superhuman struggle, a struggle that supposedly still goes on to maintain a balance in the universe between the forces of good and evil.

The Greeks called the city Babylon, and it remained Babylon under Roman rule, when it served as headquarters for one of Augustus' legions. But when it was captured in A.D. 641 by the victorious Muslim army of Omar, the second Caliph, General Amr ibn al-As called his new city Fostat, literally "surrounded by trenches." The capital was extended, away from the old Greek and Roman fortress, toward the Nile, where the Nilometer was built to measure the annual flooding of the river, and north and east where the great mosque of Ibn Toulun was raised.

"Cairo" as a name came later, when the Fatimid Caliph took over in 969. While the cornerstone of the Caliph's new residence was being laid, the planet Mars—*Qahir* (Victorious) in Arabic—crossed the meridian of the new city.

"Call it Al-Qahira after the planet," the Caliph is supposed to have shouted, "for we are indeed victorious." And Al-Qahira is the name it bears to this day.

In 1981, when we returned to live again in Cairo, it was the old name of the city, Fostat, that was painted in dark blue letters on the white prow of our temporary home: the boat where Bob and I settled in on the edge of the Nile. The *Fostat* was an honorable if slightly run-down old *dahabiya,* a once-elegant passenger river steamer retired from its former duties as a Thomas Cook's tour boat in the twenties and thirties, and as a Nubian archæological expedition headquarters in the sixties and seventies. It now served as a hostel residence for the American Research Center in Egypt and housed fellowship students, the Library of Congress representative, and professorial nomads like ourselves. Outside the hectic bustle of the city center, yet close to the riverboat commuter stop in Giza, the *Fostat* was for us an ideal temporary residence.

Bob and I were alone, as we had been when we first arrived in Egypt in 1959. Our children were grown. Bob had support for further study and research in the region; I had a grant to make an educational documentary film about social and political change as seen from the local women's point of view. Part of my proposed film involved Palestinian women; another segment, I believed, should be shot in Cairo. Both Bob and I were traveling frequently in and out of the city, interviewing, meeting people. It did not seem feasible to set up housekeeping, gather cooking gear and furniture, hire a servant. We lived on the *Fostat* in one comfortable room with an adequate if quirky bath attached. Nescafé, eggs, and bread could be prepared in the downstairs galley kitchen; a meal of sorts was cooked each evening by a resident cook; and despite the cool winds of winter that blew from the Mediterranean, we had an unparalleled view of the Nile.

In the shelter and under the protection of the *Fostat* and other large boats moored along the riverbank lay smaller craft homes for the few independent fishermen that still plied their trade on the river. The *Fostat*'s permanent visitor was a small, dun-colored fishing boat belonging to a middle-aged man named Abdulla, and his wife Um Fethy. Abdulla and Um Fethy's humble quarters could scarcely compare with our comforts aboard the two-deck, many-roomed *Fostat,* but in some ways our lives were comparable. Their children too were grown; they had sold their small piece of land in the Delta and invested in the boat. As we were out in the city all day, they were on the river, spreading their nets for enough river fish to eat and a small surplus to sell. In the evenings, our boat harbored theirs, and we all rested at anchor in the clumps of reeds and bushes growing beside the stone wall that marked the *Fostat*'s designated moorage, a hundred feet from the two restaurant boats to the north, several hundred yards from a larger, unoccupied vessel to the south.

Um Fethy had stood up in their small boat and waved as Bob and I came aboard with our suitcases one morning in January.

"*Ahlan wusahlan!*" she had cried. "Welcome!" speaking like the lady of the house, as indeed she was, mistress of that solid if modest little boat. She wore a scarlet head scarf and a long full black dress tucked at the yoke, like the women in the Delta village where she had been born.

"Thank you!" I called back.

Our communications continued to be friendly but limited. Being tied together much of the time seemed to bridge our material differences enough for us to share greetings and friendly conversations from deck to deck.

Now, after a week in Cairo, I sat with Bob on the *Fostat*'s deck and tried to make sense of my violent and unexpected reactions to the new Egypt. I was appalled at how much the beautiful city I had so loved had changed. Cairo had a population of 12 million, more than double its size of 5 1/2 million when we had left in 1965. Every place, every institution, every part of the city, reflected that increase, and strained against it. The city was noisy, dirty, jammed with people.

The river below us, however, appeared serene and uncrowded. Um Fethy and Abdulla were presently rowing in to shore with the day's catch. They did not break their rhythm to wave as they passed; Um Fethy simply inclined her head and shouted out, "Good evening!"

"Good evening," I answered.

They seemed so calm, so unruffled, rowing steadily toward their little port. While we watched, Abdulla placed his oars in their locks and pulled up the nets, while Um Fethy continued to row, turning, turning the little boat. As they neared the bank, Abdulla leaped across to shore, secured the rope for the night, leaped back aboard. Um Fethy stowed *her* oars, stood up in the bow, and stretched her whole body, her arms held high above her head. It could have been an exercise or a prayer. Abdulla had already turned to evening chores, hauling up the rope of the blue-painted kerosene can they used for water. Um Fethy held out the battered kettle, and Abdulla poured. The Nile water ran from the blue can into the kettle in a glittering stream, the drops shining in the waning sun against the reddening sky. Their Primus stove sputtered softly; soon there would be tea.

The rhythm of that small domestic scene quieted the turbulence in my own heart, my reaction to Cairo revisited: a series of contradictory and debilitating moods: despair, euphoria, distaste, amusement. But tears always seemed very close to the surface, and I was beginning to wonder whether some sort of new midlife crisis was attacking me in my sojourn to far lands.

"It's natural what you feel, it will pass," Bob had counseled.

"Hope so." Where was my former enthusiasm for the filmmaking task that lay ahead? My delight at the film grant? My curiosity in what was happening here in one of the most ancient cities in the world?

"Can't help but be a shock, dear," Bob went on. "Talk about social change. This is it in its most *physical* sense. Too much of everything: cars, consumer goods, dust, smog, debris, even people. It'll take a while. The shock will pass. You'll see."

Bob had been in Cairo for four months already, and was now a seasoned visitor. He had even taken steps to conquer the transport problem in new Egypt and had bought himself an Indian bicycle with balloon tires. He kept it downstairs near our boatman's tiny bunk room at night, and by day he scorned the taxis and buses, pedaling his way triumphantly through the choked, stuttery traffic of a city that not only was spilling out over all of its boundaries but had difficulty moving through the streets that already existed. He seemed to like it.

"I hope this gloom or lady's vapors or whatever will soon get over with," I said. "I don't know what's wrong with me. I hate it!"

"What's wrong is that we lived here for six years and we loved it, or at least that's what we remember, and now we're back and it's not the same, that's what's wrong," answered Bob. "You have to look at Cairo for what it is now, the most enormous improbability. It's amazing that it runs at all. Don't look for it to be what it was."

He was right. Yes. He was absolutely right. I knew it. But the images kept running through my head, over and over. A mixture of old memories and new experiences like moving snapshots, black-and-white for the past, color for the present.

Garden City, for example. The image machine in my head stopped there, in that quiet quarter where we had lived for six years. I was standing, much younger, on the balcony of our comfortable apartment looking out toward the Nile, across the children's playground, the ganeena where baby Laura Ann (with nanny) jumped and shouted enthusiastically in her blue pram. *"Garagoz! Garagoz!"* cried the traveling puppeteer, who came into focus and began setting up his stage. Then bang, he was gone! And we had a slide of Garden City today, a building site. Houses had been turned into places of business and the streets were lined with small plastic billboards, advertisements mounted along the pavement, like stationary flags on flagpoles, testifying at every step to the new entrepreneurial purpose of Garden City. Clearly Sadat's open-door policy, after Nasser's tight controls, had attracted Western enterprise. Green and white and blue and red, those billboards proclaimed the desirability of HERTZ Rent A Car, AVIS (we try harder); KUWAIT AIRWAYS; the Egyptian American Bank; PATCO Incorporated; Tunny Supermarket; Barclays Bank. IBM was more discreet, as befitted a consumer product that was so eminently desirable; it needed no other advertising than the small polished-brass plate set into the gate of one of the loveliest old mansions in the district. Pasha N.'s heirs, owners of the house, had been given a fortune by IBM, we were told.

The image machine stopped, reversed. We were back in the black-and-white past: the daughters of Pasha N., in white frilly dresses, hair ribbons, and curls, came out of the mansion and got into an old black limousine. Past. Gone. Forward again.

Boom! Boom! The image machine had added sound to its repertoire: the sound of a technological marvel, a pile driver, that operated within a great gash in the earth, a block-square chasm of Technicolor mud and rocks that stood to the right of our old apartment building, on the edge of the ganeena. Boom! Boom! Boom! A makeshift fence around the chasm had been painted red, and a sign announced that an international business and recreational center would soon rise out of the chasm in the earth.

Click! We were back in the past. A black-and-white snapshot of a palace, the palace that had once stood in the chasm. An old stone mansion with a wrought-iron balcony on the top floor commanding, we supposed, a superior view of the Nile. When we sat on our own balcony across the ganeena, having tea in good weather, we would often observe activity on the palace balcony. A very old gentleman would be wheeled out. In a red fez, covered by a lap robe, he, too, would drink tea and look out, like us, at the marvel of changing colors on the river. The sun would go down suddenly, in tropical glory, and the flocks of kites would rise screeching and calling above the nearby rooftops before settling for the night in the branches of the cottonwood and casuarina trees in the ganeena beside the palace.

The image machine switched off. The palace disappeared into the hole.

Cairo friends assured us that sunsets these days were more dramatic than ever before, owing to the dust and smog on the horizon. But the old gentleman in the wheelchair was not there to see the panoply, and we had yet to find a proper spot to herald the new spectacle.

We visited our old apartment. Not for sentimental reasons, actually. We had been invited for cocktails by the assistant cultural attaché at the American Embassy, who just happened to live in our old building, though in a grander flat. The doorman greeted us as old friends; he was the same man we had known twenty years ago.

"How are you, Am Taher?" Bob and I shook his hand.

Am Taher, older, grayer, broader, turned to me. How were the children? Fine. How were his children? Fine. He reported that our old cook, Abbas, was in Kuwait, making "much money," and Farida, our nanny, was still in Cairo, but her health was not good.

"Please tell her I'm here," I said. "Where can I find her?" I had sent a letter ten years before that had been returned with an "unknown" notice stamped on the envelope. Am Taher shook his head. He did not know her address, but would tell her where to reach me if she came by.

A tall dark-haired boy in jeans and navy T-shirt appeared through the door which led to the building's bank of mailboxes. "My son," said Am Taher proudly. "He is in the university."

We shook hands again and smiled at each other. It was Am Taher who broke the impasse by striding up the wide marble stairs to open the elevator doors for us, as he had done hundreds of times in the past when we had come carrying flowers, groceries, presents, bearing the babies home from the hospital. The same elevator. We got in and closed the door and moved slowly upward. It was then that it happened, an entirely unexpected outburst. Tears. A flood of tears. Tears for what? For the past? For a vanished time in my own life? For children once small and lovable, now grown and gone? For youth? It was true that in the crowded bus we had taken from the other side of town, I had been surprised when an old man gave me his seat. Was I old? Of course not, but, yes, I was well into middle age, not *really* old though, I told myself.

What had triggered that tearful reaction? The smell of the elevator, perhaps, a good smell of wax and furniture polish, the same smell as long ago when we rode up in that elevator with one child or another, Laila in her stroller with the yellow sunshade, Laura Ann and David in their Port Said nursery school uniforms, those uniforms they were so proud of, a pink pinafore for Laura Ann, a blue coverall for David.

"We could just leave, B.J.," suggested Bob.

"Yes," I answered.

With great tact and understanding, he had simply pushed the elevator button and we had gone down again, in unspoken agreement to skip the cocktail party. Am Taher had gone back into his room behind the mailboxes, so we left unnoticed, a pair of middle-aged expatriates, at least one suffering from nostalgia, furtively wiping her eyes.

At that time I had been back in Cairo three days.

We had walked out toward the river, past the darkened ganeena. One corner of the garden now held a long rectangular building, the *hadana,* or nursery school, Am Taher had told Bob. Another corner held a different kind of nursery, where potted plants were raised for use in government offices.

"The plants help pay the salaries of the people who work in the ganeena," Am Taher had explained to Bob. "And the hadana is open to all kids. Mothers can leave them for six piasters a day. A great bargain." Indeed a great bargain. Low-cost daycare in pleasant surroundings.

End of tears then! Nostalgia begone, I told myself. A new era is dawning in Egypt, it is ridiculous to romanticize the past. Eight hours of childcare for six piasters, less than ten cents. Servants and idle mothers have had their day. Now it is the era of working mothers, most working not out of some need to fulfill themselves as individuals but to help put food on the table. Bread was subsidized heavily in Egypt, but meat now cost five dollars a pound.

We headed out to the Corniche, the broad tree-lined river walk that Gamal Abdul Nasser had presented to his people as a gift. It still stretched along the Nile, but we followed its meanderings with some difficulty, for parked cars filled the sidewalk, all the way from the Nile Hilton to the Meridien Hotel, near that great gash in the earth, where the palace had once stood. The pavement was buckling from the unaccustomed weight of the cars, and as we walked, the broken cement pointed upward and caught at our shoes, stockings, ankles.

A fine cloud of dust rose everywhere, settling on the buildings, then sifting down again to mist the streetlights and blow against the hundreds of yellow eyes of headlights on the automobiles rushing up and down the Corniche. The old Semiramis Hotel with its Victorian porch was gone, and in its place was another immense pit in the ground, where a sign on still another makeshift board fence announced that the new four-hundred-room Semiramis Hotel would open in

1981. But 1981 had already arrived and the new Semiramis was not even a shell of its projected grandiose self.

At the Kasr al-Nil bridge we dipped down below street level to the new pedestrian underpass that protected us from the many lanes of traffic entering and exiting over the bridge. On the other side, we could see that the bridge was still protected by its stone lions, shabbier now, encrusted with smog and dirt from the cars and buses that wound down and up and around the cloverleaf channeling the evening traffic toward Zamalek, Roda Island, Giza, the suburb of Maadi. The noise was deafening—insistent honking of horns which meant "Move over, move over," squealing of tires coming to sudden stops to avoid collisions and fender scrapings, backfiring of imperfectly tuned engines, and the thunder of the overloaded red buses, leaning dangerously to one side or the other depending on which side carried the most passengers as hangers-on.

"Giza!" Bob called, stepping out into the street to try to hail one of the passing taxis, the little black-and-white Fiats that used to ceremonially traverse all of Cairo's streets, carrying people to their destinations for what seemed to us at the time as a tiny price. Now, however, to make their struggle through traffic worth the effort, the taxis collected passengers en route and one hailed an on-coming cab by shouting out one's destination. This one, unaccountably, stopped, while Bob was shouting "Giza! Giza!" for the third time. It was empty. We climbed in gratefully, Bob took my hand, and another noise assaulted our ears, a well-remembered, not so unpleasant noise. The cries of street vendors.

For, in the storm of traffic, the street vendors had not stopped vending. On the contrary, because of the frequent traffic jams, vendors had an easier time, Bob pointed out, moving in and out between the rows of stalled cars. Through our taxi window, we were offered tissues, flowers, oranges, and bumper stickers for the popular Ali soccer team. The driver bought a plastic bag of bread rolls. He offered us one.

"Thank you, we just ate," replied Bob, which wasn't true, but the offer deserved a polite refusal. One of the marvels of the new Cairo was that people still seemed remarkably good-natured and helpful despite constant provocation and hassle.

"Amazing, isn't it?" Bob said, pointing to the policeman at the head of our line of cars, who had stepped out into the middle of the street and stopped us all so an old man in a galabia, with a cane, could cross the road against the red light. "Would you ever see that in New York? Or on the Houston freeways? They'd be scraping that old man off the street!"

We ate dinner in the Swissair restaurant in Giza, a new eatery where Sadat himself was rumored to dine on the cook's night out. His residential palace was only two blocks away. He ate upstairs, however, in the luxury establishment; we ate on the ground floor, where the good but unchanging table d'hôte menu attracted many middle-class Egyptians, as well as foreigners in business, the media, the diplomatic corps.

An old friend had suggested that my gloom might be due to coping with the empty-nest syndrome, a suggestion that Bob greeted with a hoot of laughter. "We're the ones who flew away," he said. "We left two of our children and the dog to take care of the house and came off by ourselves."

"You left—"

"The children are twenty-one and twenty-two years old," I hastily said to the shocked look on the Egyptian woman's face.

I did not really believe that the nostalgia I felt was for my years of motherhood that I had spent in Egypt, happy as they were. I liked my life now and would have found the old responsibilities tough to take on again. What I thought I was feeling was a much more general sense of regret and loss as I looked around, walked through, experienced life in Cairo in 1981. I could not convince myself that the thousands of new cars, luxury hotels, foreign banks, flashing neon lights and billboards, the flood of consumer goods, were an adequate exchange for clean air, leisurely crowds, lovers walking on the Corniche, and the poor-but-proud attitude which for a time was fashionable among Egyptians of *every* class.

We walked home along the Giza side of the Nile, away from President Sadat's heavily guarded palace, past huge new apartment buildings in the process of construction, where guards and workmen slept on pallets in the shadow of the scaffolds, past the Turkish Embassy, where police kept watch in their little closet-size black billets. Fewer cars raced beside us. It was nearly midnight. By the time we reached the *Fostat*, Um Fethy and Abdulla were asleep. We tried not to clatter unnecessarily on the gangplank so as not to rouse them from their bed on the floor of the boat, their bodies barely visible beneath a dark blanket and the remnant of a sail.

In 1981 the United States was heavily involved in Egypt's economic life, its struggle to come to terms with the modern industrial world, not only because President Sadat's open-door policy had made it possible for many American firms to invest in enterprises but also because the Camp David accords included large bundles of aid for both signing parties, Israel and Egypt. United States government aid to Egypt was estimated at a billion dollars a year, not including arms and military equipment. Most of the billion dollars was allocated for economic aid projects administered largely by Americans or American companies. The projects were initiated and approved by joint U.S.-Egyptian committees: agriculture, education, sewage, water, garbage disposal. An entire office building was devoted to the U.S. AID mission. By January of 1981, nearly five hundred Americans were associated with the official American presence in Egypt; they constituted the second largest U.S. mission, it was said, in the world. This was a far cry from the small community at the embassy that had existed during the sixties. By 1981 the embassy and the AID mission were both protected by walls, computers, electric eyes, and automatic doors as well by U.S. Marine guards and Egyptian police. The Iranian hostage crisis and revolution had sent shock waves all the way across the Persian Gulf and up the Nile. Our more pessimistic friends talked about Egypt as the next Iran. Sadat was not as popular in Egypt as he was in the United States. Things were not good. But both American and Egyptian businessmen were making millions from American AID contracts. Most Americans in Egypt seemed to feel that Sadat was immortal.

Sadat's *infitah,* or open-door policy, had indeed brought rapid wealth to many Egyptians, even some from the middle and lower classes. But its effects were uneven and the growing differences between the new rich and the still poor were very conspicuous in a crowded city where both groups constantly looked at each other.

For us personally, Egypt had also changed. Many of our friends were gone. General Fahmy had died. Sawsan, a Muslim, had married a Copt, to both families' dismay; the young couple had compromised by moving to Paris. Dr. Laila was working for the ILO in Geneva and several of our Egyptian co-workers on the Nubian project were teaching at universities in the United States. Omar had gone into the diplomatic service after the UNESCO documentation of Pharaonic monuments was finished; he now served as cultural attaché in an Eastern European capital. His sister Aziza was married but still living in Cairo, in her parents' apartment, in fact. She invited us for lunch to meet her husband, a pleasant middle-aged lawyer.

"Hello, Bob! Welcome back!" It was another Egyptian archaeologist, older than we, who had worked for the Department of Antiquities but was now retired. He and his wife were Aziza's other lunch guests.

"Do you find Egypt much changed?" asked his wife, Nawal, younger than her husband. She was not a close friend, but I remembered her well from parties at Aziza and Omar's, from lectures at the French Institute, the Italian Cultural Institute.

"Much," said Bob, dutifully stating the obvious. "There's more, more of everything, people, cars, problems."

"Yes, yes, yes," the archaeologist agreed. "The city is bursting, it is true, but don't you find it more luxurious than in Nasser's time?"

I could not hide my surprise. "Luxurious?"

"Ah, B.J.," said Nawal. "It is the outside of Cairo you are thinking about. Cairo was always shabby, more or less, on the outside. But you know people in Egypt care more about their *own* space, the inside, their homes." She gestured vaguely around the apartment, its antiques well kept and gleaming, the paintings in the dining room where we sat sporting tiny new spotlights.

The archaeologist's wife's gesture was eloquent. She was right, this house had not changed, had perhaps even improved; weren't the spotlights on the paintings new? In the collapse of the old upper class, Omar and Aziza's family had emerged as survivors. Education had helped. Omar was well placed in the diplomatic corps, his younger brother had gotten an engineering degree from a British university and now held a good job in an engineering firm owned by Sadat's brother-in-law.

"I have good memories of the old days in Cairo," I said. "I remember a marvelous cheveux des anges that we ate at this very table years ago. Weren't you here, too, Nawal?"

Nawal smiled and nodded and Aziza, serving the chicken tarragon, turned toward us, a bit plumper, graying slightly, but still smiling mischievously, as she had done in the past.

"The cheveux des anges!" Aziza laughed and looked at the archaeologist's wife. "She has the most amazing memory," she said lightly, with a sideways glance at me. "Cheveux des anges. Maybe she'll put us in one of her books, Nawal. Do you suppose?"

"Cheveux des anges," Nawal was reflecting. "What a wonderful dessert. I used to ask for it on my birthday when I was a little girl." She sighed. "No more. No cooks. The servants are all gone," she said to me.

"To the Gulf, I suppose," I said politely.

"Yes," said Aziza, "to do construction work. So we have simple food today. No frills."

We had heard that thousands of Egyptian workers had migrated to Saudi Arabia, where they earned several times the salary offered in Cairo or Alexandria.

"Our old cook is in Kuwait," I put in. "Earning hundreds of dollars a month."

Aziza nodded. "They get enormous salaries there. But some old family retainers have stayed on to help. Muhammad, for example, B.J., is still with us."

"That's because he's too old to migrate, my dear Aziza," said Nawal rather bitterly. "It's not because of loyalty. That's all gone the way of progress."

"All gone? Twenty years ago you said that would happen, Aziza."

She looked at me hard. Aziza, in a purple silk dress that became her matronly years. "That's true, I did. And it's happened. The people who run things in Egypt now, Sadat and his crowd, those are people we had never even heard of."

"But at least Sadat is so much more understanding, Aziza, than Nasser was," insisted Nawal. "He lets everyone keep more money. And there aren't all those horrid controls on travel and imports. These days"—she turned to me—"you can occasionally find quite nice foreign blouses and stockings, and cheese comes in from Europe regularly."

Aziza made a face. "Yes, but at what prices."

The conversation became general: prices, inflation, taxes.

"But you see, Bob, the government still subsidizes basic foods for the poor people," Aziza's husband was explaining seriously. "Tea, sugar, oil, meat, they can buy at the jamaiiyas, the government cooperative stores."

"And we buy there, too," put in Aziza.

"Yes, that's true, my dear," said her husband. "It is a good policy for everyone."

"At least the rich Saudis and Kuwaitis that come here for vacation don't go to the cooperatives," said Aziza crisply. "They have too much money, so they don't care."

"They spend it all in the nightclubs on the Pyramids road," added the archaeologist. "Those clubs really are something of a scandal. A bad influence on young people. They should be curbed."

Bob and I had noticed those nightclubs one night on our way to an Indian restaurant near the Pyramids. But the road was so crowded we decided we were on the wrong street, and had driven miles into the country before realizing our mistake. The old Pyramids road had become a major urban highway. It was no longer empty, as in the old days, a straight line in the middle of the alluvial plain, leading from Cairo to the mighty mausoleums in the desert that were one of the Seven Wonders of the Ancient World. Twenty years before, a few country houses hugged the sides of the Pyramids road, modest embellishments to the impressive vista of the looming Pyramids in the sand ahead. By 1981, that vista had disappeared behind rows of high-rise apartment houses, brightly lit Las Vegas–style gambling casinos, and sumptuous many-storied villas.

"How are the children?" We moved into the salon for coffee and I sat down with Nawal on a newly upholstered satin settee to exchange photos and bits of news about our grown and growing progeny.

"A friend of ours at the American University is living in your old apartment," said Nawal. "Would you like me to see whether you could go by and visit?"

"No. No, thank you." I answered, too quickly perhaps. "Best not. Things have changed so much," I added.

Nawal raised an eyebrow. *You* talk about how Cairo has changed. It's been our home all these years, but for us it's not the same, either. Things have happened so fast." She stopped.

"Yes, Nawal?" I prompted.

"Well . . ." She paused and looked across at Aziza. "Wouldn't you say it's since the '73 war that Egypt seems new, or different, somehow?"

Aziza nodded.

"Life isn't the same," went on Nawal. "It won't be the same for the children, I think. They'll have to deal with different problems than we did." Her voice held an edge of irritation.

"At least your daughter isn't covering her head with one of those awful scarves," said Aziza, "like Najat's girl at Cairo University. Be grateful for something, Nawal."

"Najat's daughter is wearing what they call Islamic dress?" I asked.

Nawal sniffed. "Islamic dress. What Islamic dress? The Koran does not prescribe a particular kind of *dress,* it says be modest, show respect."

"But many girls seem to think that covering up is the way to do it, at least that's what I've heard," I added quickly at the mounting hostility in the two well-dressed ladies' eyes.

"They are just frustrated, I think," said Aziza lightly, a little too lightly; "a neurotic reaction to traffic and so on. They want to hide from the world so they don't get pinched on the bus."

"Where?" said her husband.

"On the bus!" said Aziza sharply. Bob laughed.

She got up to pour the men more coffee from a beautiful old Meissen pot.

Lunch was splendid even if simple. We told Aziza truthfully that we had to go home and take a little nap, as in the old days. She and her husband smiled and bid us goodbye.

We walked home along the Nile. When we reached the *Fostat,* we found Abdulla and Um Fethy unexpectedly moored. They sat at opposite ends of their small boat, mending nets, each plying a needle strung with beige-colored string. The wide mesh, with its coral-colored plastic floats, was spread out between them, its edges trailing in the river.

"Good afternoon!" cried Um Fethy between stitches. "How are you?"

"Good afternoon!" I replied. "How are you?"

We smiled at each other and went on about our separate business.

The newspapers gave the 1981 International Book Fair all the attention due a spectacular public event, and indeed it seemed deserved, as we watched thousands of people streaming into the gates of the fairgrounds in Giza and lining up to enter the exhibit halls where ninety-seven nations, the handout said, had sent their printed wares, their records and audiovisual materials, to tempt an obviously eager population.

"Tell the story, Forest!" urged a large sign at the Asian United Front Movement desk; it turned out to be the title of a new book about ecology and conservation in Asia. A record accompanied the book, said the polite clerk, on which the forest's own song was sung. The French exhibit displayed new titles in semiotics and lavishly illustrated travel books about the Middle East. Special volumes for learning English were featured at the American table, and Dar al-Kutub, Dar al-Maaref, Al-Ahram Publishing Company, the major Egyptian presses, offered engineering and technical books in Arabic, newly translated from English, German, and French. The American University Press showed new English books on Egyptian social science. The Soviet bloc was represented, as were Western Europe, Asia, and Africa. And, in this post–Camp David era, there was an Israeli book exhibit. The Israeli exhibit had been moved to the great hall from its earlier placement outside, next to the Palestinian book exhibit. Not surprisingly, there was an "incident," avidly covered by American and Israeli television. Not by Egyptian TV, however. Much too inciteful to publicize locally.

The greatest crowds were milling about the specialized religious book exhibits from many different parts of the Islamic world: exhibits of Korans, editions of the hadith, philosophical essays. Mostly young, mostly neatly dressed, these young Egyptian Muslims were attired in a variety of what Aziza denied was "Islamic dress." The women wore head scarves, some in simple babushka style, others folded and tucked over their foreheads to cover every strand of hair. Some wore long flowing gowns and wimples like the nuns of an earlier age, though these gowns and wimples were not black and white but multicolored:

blue, green, yellow, plaids. Less dramatic were the simple toques and turbans; the skullcaps and beards of the men.

"Nobody dressed like that when we were here before," I volunteered. "At least I don't remember it. Do you, Bob?"

Bob shook his head. We had decided to eat lunch at one of the scores of picnic tables set out on the fairgrounds. Kebab, turnip pickles, and bread constituted the standard fast-food meal.

"There were some getups like that when I first got here in 1978," declared Tom Hartwell, a friend from Texas now living and working as a free-lance photographer in Cairo.

"New images," I mused. "For the film maybe. New self-images," I explained in answer to Bob's and Tom's questioning looks.

In the sixties, what was called "Islamic dress" was not apparent at all. At that time, more and more young women had been wearing Western dress, not only upper-middle-class and professional women like Aziza and Dr. Laila, but the new group of high school graduates who had gone out to work as shopgirls, secretaries, government employees, bank clerks. In 1965, traditional long, full gowns, tight head scarves, and wraparound milayas were worn by peasants and the more conservative so-called *baladi* or country women in the cities, particularly in poorer districts. Even in those areas, however, Western-style dress was often worn under the milayas and was a sign of upward mobility. The new 1981 style of Islamic dress bore little resemblance to the traditional baladi style. It was a most dramatic visual addition to the crowded streets of Cairo, to Alexandria, the new universities in the Delta. Bob said he had also seen it during his fall trip to Aswan.

"Are they counterparts of the Muslim Brotherhood, a kind of sisterhood?" I asked. As puritanical advocates of theocratic rule, the Muslim Brotherhood had constituted a political threat to many of Egypt's leaders, from the 1920s on, and Nasser had been no exception. In Nasser's time the Muslim Brotherhood had been suppressed, many jailed, some executed.

"No, no," said Bob. "It seems to be a much more inclusive statement of Islamic identity than that."

Tom looked unconvinced. "Come on, Bob. You know people say these guys —and girls—are really into politics." He indicated an especially pious-looking young man in a kind of Nehru jacket and trousers of unbleached cotton. "That costume is supposed to be a political protest against Sadat."

Against Sadat? Yes, said Tom. Lots of complaints against Sadat. Stories of corruption, of high living, of favoring the rich, of turning the gardens Nasser had opened to the public back into personal palaces, à la King Farouk. But, I said, in America we heard of Sadat as a brave political genius, at least in foreign affairs, who had taken the initiative in the Arab-Israeli dispute and maneuvered a peaceful settlement at last.

"You think Sadat gets brownie points with Egyptians because he made peace with Israel, B.J.?" Tom asked me incredulously. "You should know this country better than that."

"Yes, Tom," put in Bob. "I know they don't like Israel, but I get the feeling people are delighted to have peace. Last fall I talked with people all over the Delta and in Upper Egypt who told me they were not interested in going to war anymore."

"But do they have a choice?" interrupted Tom.

"They have to be considered," insisted Bob. "Any leader worth his salt will think twice before getting into more adventures. Really, Tom. Everybody I met had lost a son, a brother, or at least an uncle or some relative in the wars of '48, '56, '67, '73. Egyptians have taken the brunt of all the fighting and they're tired of being shot up. And besides, war is damned expensive. It has drained this country."

"But all the Arab world has pulled away from Egypt, Bob, Egypt that used to be its leader, and—"

Tom stopped himself. "Look over there," he said suddenly. Near us three young men occupied a table for ten while all around us the picnic tables were jammed. Good-looking, dark-haired, they wore fashionable jean suits. A television crew, obviously, by the equipment, the Nagra sound recorder and the booms, the camera with its peering, protruding lens. I had just spent two weeks in London looking over equipment like that.

"Why are they hogging the whole table?" asked Bob.

"Not their choice. It's an Israeli TV crew. Nobody will sit with them. Peace? Yeah. Maybe. No love lost on either side."

It was true. Two years after the Camp David accords had been signed, peace was still just the absence of war as far as most Egyptians were concerned. Double police details were stationed around the Israeli residence and the Israeli Embassy. Arab guests tended to leave parties unceremoniously when Israeli diplomats arrived. The Egyptian lawyers' syndicate had staged a protest rally on the anniversary of Camp David.

The situation was not improved by braless Israeli female tourists wearing T-shirts with "Shalom" written across their chests—not necessarily from a standpoint of decorum or morals (Egyptians have seen the worst as well as the best) but because of the implied contempt. Yet bus service had been instituted from Midan al-Tahrir for the eight-hour trip to Tel Aviv, and El Al planes flew regularly in and out of Egypt. No one reported any overtly unpleasant public incidents and many Egyptian merchants and hotelkeepers were very welcoming.

This was part of the setting in which Islam and the statement of Islamic belief was generating enthusiasm among all groups of people. Twenty years before, when we had lived in Egypt, Egypt called itself a Muslim state, but that identity was not so publicly demonstrated. Now the new style of dress for women and men was only one such kind of overt statement. Most taxicabs and private cars carried Korans in velvet cases on their dashboards rather than the Kewpie dolls and teddy bears of yore. Jewelers in the gold and silver markets had developed an entirely new range of medallions engraved with Koranic verses. And a large selection of religious magazines and books was to be found in every newspaper kiosk and bookstore. New mosques had opened all over the city and more were under construction. Some people, we had been told, had even gone so far as to "claim" unused land as places for community prayers. One of the most popular local programs on Cairo television was hosted by Sheikh Sharkawi, a religious authority who sometimes gave short talks on morals, sometimes presented formal sermons, but always answered the studio audience's questions about faith and practice.

When I visited the television building in connection with my forthcoming filming, I was surprised to see small areas set aside on each floor for employees to say their daily prayers.

"It's become a requirement," Bob said. "You'll find them in factories, ministries, offices, everywhere."

On Friday, the day of worship, the mosques were overflowing. For those who could not make it in to the mosque, the public address system broadcast the prayers and homilies over loudspeakers, and people came out of shops to pray on mats laid out on the public sidewalks, not just in the more traditional parts of town, but on the main streets of the city, even Kasr al-Nil and Sharia Talaat Harb, the focus of Westernized luxury shoppers in the 1960s. The public prayer in the streets was accepted and accommodated by the nonpraying passersby.

There had even been an upsurge of Islamic political activism two years before. A group that called itself Repentance and Holy Flight had plotted against Sadat, been uncovered, its members jailed, its leaders executed. But most of our Egyptian friends said that Repentance and Holy Flight was a fanatic exception to the general rule. It was not representative, not part of the general interest in Islam expressed by many Muslims, especially younger people.

"Does it surprise you, these 'born-again' Muslims?" Bob asked me. "It seems important to include in your film."

"Yes and yes," I answered. "It surprises me, and yes, it should be included in the film."

We sat on the deck of the *Fostat*, our refuge from the frantic activity of the city. The gleaming pewter-gray water of the river, rippling toward us and away, muted the noise of automobiles, buses, trucks, and people, buried the city dust in its moving depths, carried debris past us, north to the sea. On the opposite shore stood the new Salah al-Din Mosque, sand-colored by day, golden at sunset, when the muezzin's call to evening prayer marked the moment for scores of electric light bulbs to be flashed on, outlining the minaret and dome in a pulsing radiance, casting a glow over the entire edifice.

"Why are we surprised at this return to religion?" asked Bob. "It's even happening in America. Ask yourself why it's happening in America. Some of the same reasons may be here."

"I guess we thought Nasser was promoting secularism when we were here

before. People talked about Egypt in terms of nationalism, or maybe anticoloni-
alism and so on—not in religious terms so much."

"Yes. One thought of Saudi Arabia as religious, maybe, but Egypt—as what?
Progressive? Socialist? Too political, maybe?"

"Are the two contradictory?"

"Religion and politics?" Bob laughed ruefully. "We used to think so."

Many people used to think so. A quarter of a century earlier, when we had
first come to the Middle East, social scientists used to measure what they called
progress and what they called political maturity by the degree of separation
between church and state. Just as in America. Insofar as the Arab world appeared to be separating itself from its "outmoded religious attitudes," adopting
a more secularist, pluralistic Western-style stance, so then was it seen by such
scholars to be progressing, socially and politically preparing, at least, for economic development.

Below the *Fostat,* from his harbor in the reeds, Abdulla had heard the distant
muezzin's call, too, and was saying his prayers on one end of his boat. At the
other end, Um Fethy was taking a pot of food, still steaming, from the fire of the
Primus stove. She set the pot on the boat's shallow deck, with two spoons, and
two loaves of flat brown bread, the *aysh baladi* that was the principal food of the
majority of Egyptians. Abdulla made his final obeisance in the direction of
Mecca and joined Um Fethy for dinner.

From the prosperous and comfortable Zamalek dining room with its lace-
covered table and its spotlighted old masters where we had lunched with Aziza
and her new husband, it seemed a long way to the shrine of Sidi Ali, in the old
medieval city, where hundreds of working-class men and women went each
week to pay homage to the grandson of the Prophet Muhammad and were
joined by many thousands more during the annual *mulid* (birthday celebration).
Yet Aziza and her husband, along with Um Fethy and hers, would have agreed
that the people performing the hadra, or ecstatic ritual, in the court of Sidi Ali's
shrine, were all indeed Muslims like themselves. Though they might not have
entirely agreed on the best ways of expressing that fact, the basic principles of
their belief were the same.

Attendance at such religious ceremonies was growing. So said Valerie Hoff-
man, a University of Chicago graduate student who was doing research on
women's participation in Islamic practice. She had found that many of the
women wearing Islamic dress were making both intellectual and emotional expressions of their faith and were trying to learn more about their heritage. Study
groups for men and for women had sprung up all over the city, she said, in
mosques as well as in private homes. Further, more people than ever were
making regular *ziyaras* or ritual visits to the seven major shrines in Cairo. And in
all the shrines weekly hadras, or ritual devotional ceremonies, were held.

"Seven shrines in Cairo?" I found it hard to believe. In all our six years in

Egypt, I had learned nothing about ziyaras, ziyara days. Seven shrines? Like the seven shrines of Marrakech?

"When you were here before," Valerie suggested politely, "the people you knew didn't talk to you about them. And the shrines were supposedly only for the poor anyway. They say it's not so today. Would you like to go and see?"

We set off one cold February day on a preliminary visit, to inquire whether we would be welcome to attend the weekly hadra, which took place on Saturday afternoons. The shrine of Sidi Ali is not on any tourist map, but Valerie had found a reference in an old city atlas in the American Research Center library. We thought we knew more or less where we were going, following the tracks of the Maadi–Bab al-Loukh railway line until the street opened suddenly into a huge dusty square filled with bleating, baaing animals—goats, camels, sheep cavorting together. No fence enclosed the flocks, but they were hobbled, and the camels bore on their dun-colored backs the shocking-pink stamps of the government butchers. We were near the municipal slaughterhouse.

"Well, this seems right," Valerie reported, "but I don't see the shrine. It's supposed to be very close by."

We inquired of several people, who shook their heads, whether in refusal to answer or inability to understand our Arabic I could not tell. Valerie leaned down to a woman sitting on the sidewalk wearing a traditional long flowered dress and a black milaya about her head and shoulders. She held a covered basket on her lap, and a little boy in striped flannel pajamas sat beside her.

"Can you tell us where we can find the shrine of Sidi Ali?" Valerie asked. "It's supposed to be near the mosque of Zaynab Abdine."

The woman looked up, stared from Valerie to me, shook her head. "Don't know," she said. "I'm not from here."

Another, older woman, all in black, paused beside us. "Sidi Ali you want?" she inquired. "Look up! There it is!"

And there it was. The domes and minaret of a mosque-shrine rose above the row of houses and shops, opposite the square where the animals milled and cavorted before being led to the slaughter. We had kept our eyes down modestly and had missed the most impressive sight on the horizon.

"Look up once in a while, why don't you?" scolded the old woman, but in a friendly way.

We started, somewhat hesitantly, down a small street in the direction of the minaret; it seemed to dead-end. But suddenly a group of women came around the corner talking excitedly, wrapping and unwrapping their black milayas as they walked toward us. Obviously the street was not a dead end at all but a kind of false entrance, such as is found in old Islamic houses, a kind of architectural obstacle to keep the heart of house—and shrine—hidden from casual viewers.

As we rounded the "false" corner, the mosque-and-shrine complex unfolded before us slowly, a U-shaped arrangement of buildings enclosed within low walls. First came the two rooms where the guardian of the mosque (the *muqaddam*) apparently lived with his family, for laundry was hung to dry, and piles of bedding were visible within one of the rooms. Behind the laundry lines we could see a few whitewashed gravestones tipped in green, the Prophet's color. Surprisingly, there was a tea shop against the farthest wall, and to our right, bounded by the mosque itself and the saint's tomb, lay a good-sized open square (perhaps the space where the hadra was held). A somewhat scraggly little garden containing a single stone bench stood directly in front of the saint's tomb and we paused there. Two older women, rather poorly dressed, sat on the bench and we sat beside them for a moment, not sure whether we should ask permission before entering the shrine. The old women moved to the far end of the bench, as far away from us as they could manage. What was wrong? I looked at Valerie, she at me. Two or three newcomers came close to us and stared into our faces, rather aggressively, I thought. Then we both noticed, almost at the same time, that the shabby old women on the bench held tin bowls in their hands, and we realized we were occupying the space reserved for beggars. No wonder we had gotten such funny looks! We were treading on indigents' turf. For shame! We both rose hastily and at that moment the guardian of the shrine beckoned. We gave our shoes to the shoe man at the door and padded in on stocking feet along the whitewashed entrance passage. It was cold, a cold that penetrated through the floor mats from the stones paving the passage floor.

The shrine was nearly empty. We walked round the catafalque, the supposed resting place of Sidi Ali, which was covered with a crimson brocade *keswa* and bore a turban at its head, as is customary in the tombs of walis, or holy men, who are called friends of God. The fence of brass filigree surrounding the tomb had been polished till it shone like gold; it had been worn down in many places by the hands and lips of pilgrims, in the same way as the foot of the bronze statue of St. Peter in St. Peter's Basilica in Rome. While we made the ritual circle around the tomb, we noticed the muqaddam following us; coming closer, he proceeded to give us a whispering history of Sidi Ali.

"He's actually not buried here, but in Najaf, in Iraq. Only his spirit is with us," he said, extending his hands upward to embrace the cenotaph, the shrine, the world beyond.

"I haven't been to Najaf," I volunteered, rather shyly, "but I visited Kerbela, in southern Iraq, years ago. The shrine of Hussain, Ali's son."

"You did?" The muqaddam looked surprised, started to speak, cleared his throat, and finally said, "Hussain too is blessed." He patted me on the shoulder and ushered us into a high-ceilinged alcove, a room really, that looked through an open door toward the mausoleum and yet was separate from it. Several women were sitting on mats in the alcove; one had her eyes closed, presumably in prayer. We thanked the muqaddam, sat down quietly, and looked about us.

This was obviously the room for meditation and prayer. I did not feel much like praying. Instead, I thought of the strange set of circumstances that had brought me here, to the cenotaph of Ali, the Prophet Muhammad's son-in-law, nearly twenty-five years after I had made a pilgrimage to Ali's son's tomb, with my friends from the southern Iraqi village of Al-Nahra. That pilgrimage had been very different from this moment of meditation within the quiet shrine. The streets of Kerbela, tumultuous, crowded, had thronged with thousands of pious pilgrims from all over the Shi'a Islamic world, Pakistan, Iran, Iraq, Lebanon. Young men, in groups, passed in procession down the main avenue to the golden-domed shrine, ritually flagellating themselves, crying aloud in pain and loss over the death of the martyred Hussain, son of Ali and grandson of the Prophet Muhammad. The young men's sorrow had seemed real then, and fresh, even to me, the stranger, though Hussain had died nearly thirteen hundred years before, on the fields outside Kerbela, the city where I stood with my friends from Al-Nahra and watched the ceremonies. That ancient battle, over who was to lead the new Islamic community after the Prophet's death, had been a turning point in Islamic history. Afterward, the community split in two, between the Shi'a sect (followers of Hussain and Ali) and the Sunni sect (those who opposed them). Who was to be the leader, a blood relation and descendant (Ali, Hussain) or a man of proven merit (Omar)? The people of Egypt, where I now lived, were Sunni, not Shi'a. But Ali and Hussain were still the Prophet's relatives after all and thus also honored here, not in sorrowful flagellation but in quiet prayers and, we were told, devotional hadras on Saturdays: commemorative rituals of a different kind.

The names of God, Most Merciful, Most Compassionate, Most Generous, lettered in gold, formed a border around the ceiling of the whitewashed room where we sat. And an entire wall of the alcove was covered by an artist's rendering of the Prophet Muhammad's family tree. Valerie and I were too far away to make out individual names, but we could see many men's names inscribed on the leaves of the tree and many women's names inscribed on hearts (symbolic fruit of the tree).

Pilgrims came and went. First a young couple, hand in hand, the woman in black skirt and polka-dotted blouse, her head uncovered, the man in white shirt, dark pants. They stood together in the doorway for a moment gazing silently at the saint's symbolic tomb within its filigree fence before sitting down near us to pray. Then a young man in jeans entered, took off his wraparound sunglasses to look at us, looked away, put his sunglasses back on, and stood up straight, facing the cenotaph. He bowed his head. A woman carrying a small baby greeted each of us in turn, sat down, and gave her baby a cracker. Then she sighed deeply, passed her hand over her eyes, and audibly uttered a prayer. Valerie and I looked at each other and got up to leave. I handed a small offering to the muqaddam, who smiled and patted me on the shoulder again, a tip to the attendant at the door and to the beggar women whose business we had unwittingly interrupted.

The hadra, said the muqaddam, was indeed held on Saturday and we were most welcome to attend. "But be here early," he cautioned. "It fills up fast after three o'clock."

While we were tying laces on our sensible walking shoes, a woman selling incense hissed to the attendant, "Who are those foreigners?" "Americans," he answered. "Americans?" she repeated in astonishment, then to us, "They are interested in religion in America?" We nodded and wended our way out.

On Saturday, we took the muqaddam's advice and arrived at the square early for the hadra, a wise decision, since by three-fifteen the open space was entirely filled, from the shrine all the way to the tombstones. People even crowded in to sit on the doorstep of the muqaddam's apartment.

"Is everyone going to take part?" I asked an elderly woman, who, like us, sat on a chair in front of the tea shop and, also like us, was drinking steaming tea at a price high enough, it seemed, to include rental on the chair for the duration of the ceremony.

"Oh no, no," she answered. "Most people are here just to watch, to share in the baraka, the grace of God. Only the people in the middle there will do the hadra."

Hadra. The word literally means presence, but has come to mean, in religious usage, the acknowledgment, through a prescribed devotional ritual, of the presence of God in the world.

A modern sound system had been set up on a platform near the muqaddam's house, and the musicians took their places, three drummers, a piper, and a master of ceremonies who, we discovered later, was also the vocalist. Still another man, in a green turban, climbed up on the back of the stage and adjusted a pair of castanets in his hands, shaking down the sleeves of his white galabia as he did so. The castanet man was apparently the leader, for as the hadra "intentions" were announced by the master of ceremonies—"for the intention of Alwiya, daughter of Ali Mahmoud," and "for the intention of Ahmed Muhammad, son of Muhammad Abdul Karim"—the man with the castanets began to move slowly across the back of the stage, as though warming up, a slow, silent rhythmic movement. His castanets were held above his head, where, still soundless, they caught the winter sunlight that fell across the dome of the mosque, the old stone wall, the modest house of the muqaddam, the little group of tombstones in the corner.

"This is the hadra of Sayyid Ali," announced the master of ceremonies. "I have been asked to announce that the mulid of Sayyidna Hussain begins on Monday, and the mulid of Sayyidatna Nefissa will follow." Sayyid Ali, Sayyidna Hussain, Sayyidatna Nefissa: three of the seven holy figures sacred to the city of Cairo.

The participants took their places in the square, in formation, as for a group dance, a kind of quadrille. Each had a place, a space, thirty to forty men and women, most in galabias and traditional dress. One man supported himself on crutches. And there was also a woman in jeans and a long tunic. The leader, in his green turban, looked upward toward the sky, and, clicking his castanets lightly, began to turn. The people in the square followed his example. The leader looked upward, a pleasant smile on his face, and was turning quietly by the time the drummer struck up a beat. The singer adjusted the microphone, fiddled with the sound system, then came back to the center of the stage and began a song. The pipe followed his voice, and the dancers were already moving, slowly at first, in a regular pattern, sway, sway in place, a half turn, a full turn, a move slightly clockwise. The circle moved as the dancers progressed in measured beats, in measured steps, the sound of many feet striking the ground in unison covered by the drums, the pipe, the castanets, the song amplified by the electric system. The man on crutches turned, too, swayed with the group. One woman's scarf had slipped down and her hair flew out around her, like a wide, dark veil, as she turned, and the group turned. Faster. Faster. Stop!

"We'll take a break," announced the master of ceremonies.

Tea was being served in the tea shop. We bought another glass in order to hold on to our chairs. It was expensive tea, for we were paying for a good location; our two chairs were close enough to the square to observe the ritual, yet not too close to be intrusive.

During the break, a woman turned to us and asked who we were. Were we Muslims? No. Russians? No. We were Americans. Are you enjoying the hadra? she asked. Oh yes, we replied. "They are wonderful, aren't they?" she said, smiling a little to herself. "I go to the Hussain hadra on Friday, come here on Saturday, and to Sayyidatna Nefissa on Sunday. I don't dance. I watch. But my daughter does the hadra every week at Hussain."

For the second part of the hadra, even more people crowded into the square. How will the participants be able to move? But they do, each keeping his or her place, as before, following the beat, sway, sway, half turn, turn. The tight circle moves clockwise. The only person out of step is a man who sways and nearly falls, trips, catches himself. Is he in a trance? Perhaps. Perhaps not. The music is insistent, growing louder, more intense. The beat is faster, faster, the castanet man is whirling but the clicking is regular. The singer pronounces the name of Ali, in whose honor the hadra is being held, Ali, son-in-law of the Prophet, treacherously slain. Ali. A holy figure in the Shi'ite tradition. Revered here in Cairo, a Sunni city, but in a different way from in Shi'a cities, where the ceremonies approximate those of mourning for the dead. Here the ceremony is a ritual performed for the intention of loved ones both living and dead, like a prayer, a novena. And for some, like the old lady, it is wonderful, an uplifting experience.

"Do they have hadras like this in America?" asked the old lady. We had offered her tea before, but she had refused. Now she accepted our invitation.

"Not exactly, but things that are like it."

"Really?"

Valerie nodded. The woman smiled at us. "That's lucky for you," she said.

The clouds were turning pink in the sky above the wall containing the shrine, the mosque, the courtyard filled with moving figures who turned, swayed with the drums, the pipes, the song. "It's late," cried an old man behind us, shouting in the direction of the musicians. "Nearly time for the evening prayer." One of the drummers nodded but did not skip a beat. The sun was slowly sinking. Faster came the beat, faster the turning, swaying, turning, turning, the piping higher, close to the edge of the instrument's range. The singer's voice rose upward with the pipe, trilled with the drums, and suddenly it was finished. The hadra was over. In the brief silence the sun sank and was gone. The dancers dried their sweaty faces, adjusted their clothes, turbans, and scarves. The old man on crutches limped out of the arena. The woman in jeans tied her sash tighter around her tunic, pulled a pair of sunglasses out of her pocket, put them on, and walked away. Those faces that had appeared lost in motion, lost in time, resumed everyday expressions, and people, both dancers and viewers, streamed out as the call to evening prayers sounded from the minaret. Two hours from start to finish, including break.

"Will you come next week?" asked the old lady. "Or to the *mulid?*"

"Certainly to the *mulid,*" replied Valerie.

Even in the sixties, the annual mulids, or birthdays, of Sayyidna Hussain and Sayyidatna Zaynab were celebrated in Cairo, along with the mulid of the Prophet Muhammad himself. In old Cairo, near the Khan al-Khalili bazaar, lies the mosque that bears the name of Sayyidna Hussain, son of Ali, whose hadra Valerie and I had attended, and grandson of the Prophet. Here the activities of his mulid would take place, beginning with a parade of the Sufi brotherhoods, complete with flags and banners. The brotherhoods would then set up their tents in the shadow of the mosque, to receive members and guests from city and country. For several days the mosque would be filled with the faithful, praying and attending hadras. Singing and other entertainment went on far into the nights. The mulids were religiously based holidays that had, over the years, incorporated other functions, for they were in essence minipilgrimages, social and economic.

For the 1981 mulids, the crowds everywhere were greater than we remembered, not only at Sayyidna Hussain, but at the mulid of Sayyidatna Zaynab as well. Around both mosque shrines, the nearby shops and streets were festooned with colored lights, and the booksellers, the nut vendors, and the peddlers of balloons, cotton candy, and souvenirs thronged the neighborhoods. Was it that we were more conscious of the celebrations than before, more sensitized by published descriptions of the Islamic resurgence? No, friends both Egyptian and American assured us, more people *were* attending the mulids now. Not just the poor, for whom the mulids had always constituted great festivals, but also middle-class and professional people who had previously not taken part. Had the newer members of the middle class discovered, in their march forward toward modernity, that they did not need to leave behind their traditional religious practices? Had Egyptians decided to reject outdated Western measures of "modern" behavior? Was it a political expression? A personal search? We asked these questions and received a variety of answers. Yes, it was a search. No, it was not an anti-Western movement, for that would be seen as negative in tone, it was rather a positive pro-Muslim stance. Politics? Partly. Not just one reason, but several.

It was Nabila in the end who made that cliché phrase "Islamic resurgence" a reality for me. Nabila was a secretary for the Egyptian National Insurance Company, and I went to see her, in her place of work, to deliver a letter from a mutual friend and invite her to tea.

"You are interested in Islam? Tim wrote to me in his letter that you are," said Nabila in rather slow and stilted English. We sat in the garden of the American University, in old rattan chairs, drinking tea; it seemed a good compromise between Groppi's (Nabila would never go there, Tim had told me) and our houseboat, which was rather far from Nabila's office. She was a small girl, lovely, with huge dark eyes.

"Yes," I said. I explained about my plans for a film, about our previous years in Cairo.

I asked her about "Islamic dress," which she herself was wearing, a pleasant costume in tones of peach, a cream-colored scarf clasping her throat and fastened on each side, behind her ears, with small pearl-tipped hatpins.

"It is out of respect," she said gently, looking up at me with those great dark eyes, measuring me, I felt. She looked down at my book, at the cover, a drawing of the famous Egyptian singer Um Kulthum.

"You see, in your book, Um Kulthum too wore Islamic dress."

I made no objection, not wishing to begin an argument in our first five minutes of acquaintanceship. Um Kulthum, however, had taken off her head scarf and sung without it for years, though her dress was always modest.

"Respect for God or for others or for oneself?"

"It is all—together," said Nabila very gently, bringing her hands together and clasping them tightly. "Like this. You see?"

I nodded. We looked at each other once more. Nabila, I felt, was still measuring me, searching for whatever dark spots might lie upon my soul.

Nabila began again. "It is simple," she said. "This is the dress God says we should wear, and so we wear it." Her hand was raised again, in self-deprecation, but her smile belied the deprecating gesture. Nabila believed in God and in herself as well.

Two Egyptian students paused near our table, one in Western dress, one in a head scarf. They spoke to Nabila, and she asked them to sit down. A discussion began, in Arabic, a discussion from which I was not actually excluded, but the three of them talked around me, looking occasionally in my direction and nodding, as one does to a child who is not quite old enough to understand. They were discussing Islamic dress. The girl in Western dress asked detailed questions that I could not entirely follow; Nabila answered her carefully and slowly, quoting the Koran, chapter and verse, smiling gently.

Thus began a series of meetings that took me all over Cairo to witness the phenomenon of Islamic resurgence from Nabila's personal point of view. I visited Nabila at home, where her father, a government civil servant, told me how proud he was of his youngest daughter. We attended a women's study group in one of the newer city mosques. The subject that day was the validity of a particular hadith that had been long ago incorporated into sharia law. I attended an exhibition of handwork at the medical school on Kasr al-Aini Street, where I met several women medical students, each of whom was leading a study group. Proceeds of the exhibit were to go to help finance the new clinics for the poor. I was introduced to Dr. Zahira Abdine, medical director of the Giza children's hospital and the leader of the Muslim Women's Association.

"We speak of Islam and belief, but we also mean service," said Dr. Zahira carefully and slowly. "Service to others. We have many young women and men doctors volunteering their time in these clinics for the poor."

"Where are they?" I asked politely.

"They are in the big mosques in districts where medical care is unavailable. Nabila will take you, won't you, my dear?"

Nabila took me to a clinic at the Sayyidatna Zaynab mosque. She also took me to some Koranic schools that were modeled along "modern lines," she said. In one of these, Nabila herself was a volunteer teacher.

Dr. Zahira said she would be happy to help me in trying to present Islam to the West on film.

"For they have misunderstood Islam, I think," she said. We sat that day in her home in Zamalek, a luxurious apartment not too far from Aziza's house.

"The West, that is," she continued. "You think of Islam as restrictive, but it is actually flexible. This is an advantage and a disadvantage, as it can be pulled in many directions. But Islam is really for *people;* it should be an expression of the best of the human spirit."

I visited the five-story building of the Muslim Women's Association. The plump, kindly lady in charge showed me the dormitory for women students attending the university, the daycare center for students' children, the Koranic class for schoolchildren.

"And we help the girls," she said. "We have a cooperative, you know, like the government cooperatives. But ours is our own. The girls can borrow small sums of money for books, we help them with doctors; the cooperatives are all over Egypt now. It is very good, our work."

Nabila told me that Dr. Zahira was important in the lives of many young Egyptian women. "She is—like a—"

"A model?"

"Yes. This is what women in Islam should be."

"But what about politics?"

Nabila looked pained. "All Americans ask that. That is all you are interested in. Do you speak of Repentance and Holy Flight?"

I nodded.

"They did not understand the spirit of Islam. One must not put oneself above one's family, above other people, above one's duty to others. God does not want that. No, I am not with that group. That is not Islam."

I perhaps did not look convinced. "They say that in the West people believe our religion is bad, is that true, B.J.?" Those dark eyes searched mine again, testing for flaws, for bad intentions.

"No," I said firmly. "But—"

"Yes?" Her small, gentle face was troubled.

"But sometimes—sometimes we believe religion can be *used* by bad people for bad purposes."

Nabila smiled triumphantly. "But so can anything," she said passionately. "It is the *intention* that is important. You understand?"

"Yes, Nabila," I answered. "I understand. We will talk about all this in the film, and with Dr. Zahira, too."

"Oh yes." Nabila looked very pleased. "It is important to do that. When will your technicians come?" she asked.

"In May," I said. "We will need to prepare everything beforehand."

"I will do what I can," said Nabila.

Nubia. 1981

Once upon a time a great and good prince was beset by evil enemies. He had no recourse but to try to escape, and so, taking his sword, he fled north from caves and rocks deep in Africa. He began to run very fast, trailing his sword behind him. He turned this way and that, to avoid his enemies who were close behind him, and wherever he ran, wherever his sword touched the ground, the earth opened and a silver river flowed to protect him. When he reached the Mediterranean Sea, he disappeared. Many people have waited for the return of the good prince; but he has never been seen again. The river still remains. It is the Nile.

The old fairy tale about the creation of the river Nile is no longer told by Nubian mothers to their children. A man, Gamal Abdul Nasser, interrupted the natural course of the Nile. By 1971, the structure of earth, rocks, sand, clay, and cement known as the High Dam was finished. More than 2 miles wide and 130 feet high, the dam was changing the face of Egypt, molding its contours, filling its hollows in patterns not foreseen by the old storytellers. A huge lake covers the old "blessed land" of Nubia—Lake Nasser. We could see it from the plane that morning in February 1981 as we circled Aswan, on the way to visit our Nubian friends once more.

"The lake's supposed to have filled up long ago," said Bob, "but they didn't expect so much water to be lost through evaporation and seepage." He leaned across me in the seat to look down where before only a shining slit of river had been visible: now a wide expanse of silver water stretched below us, said to be at least three hundred miles long, six miles wide, and covering a total area of three thousand square miles.

"It doesn't look like a lake, it looks like an enormous uneven leaf," I protested.

"What did you think, it would be round, like a pool? It's bound to be uneven.

It's backed up into all the wadis that used to cut into the river from the desert. Lots of water surface; the shoreline varies from place to place."

"How can it?"

"Well, the water slides away from the desert, half a mile or more in some places, when the water level falls in the winter and spring."

Now, below us, the water shimmered in the early afternoon sun and lapped gently out in all directions, as though deliberately pushing out for new banks, propelled by forces deep beneath the earth. Wherever the water came to rest on the land, a fringe of green was visible, the new foliage tracing boundaries of fertility, suggesting possible new areas of cultivation. Had this eventuality been predicted by the Russian engineers of the dam, the Egyptian planners? I asked Bob.

"Yes, of course," he answered. "They always counted on the shores of Lake Nasser to offer new agricultural land. And you've heard the stories. Nubians are actually already going back."

"They knew before everyone else that the land would be good?"

"No, not really. But some of the Nubians have always wanted to go back. And now they've gotten permission from the government. They're there. Four settlements! I've visited them. Pioneers, they call themselves."

"Is the land as good as it looks there, on the green banks?"

"Yes. It's amazing really. The only thing is they can't cultivate much when the water level falls. They need more pumps." We were circling north now, and the outline of the giant leaf-shaped lake was disappearing from the edges of our vision as we approached the city of Aswan and the great earth-fill dam south of town.

"The government's helping the Nubians move back? Someone in Cairo said that."

"Not much, really. They started a couple of settlements near Aswan but the wells dried up. They've financed some house construction farther south near Abu Simbel, where the tourist planes come and go. Actually, it's close to where we used to live. But across the river, above what was Adindan in old Nubia, other Nubians have built their own homes. Traditional style. They're independent. No government assistance there."

The government settlements north of the High Dam in Kom Ombo had been much improved since that sad time in 1965, said Bob, just after the move. He had been down earlier in the year, to see the land allotted to the Nubians by the Egyptian government. They were growing sugarcane, as the government wanted them to do, but with Upper Egyptians to help with its cultivation, something the Nubians had never done themselves. Often women were supervising the farms, since many men were working abroad, as migrant laborers.

"They can make more money in the Gulf, I suppose," I said.

"Yes," said Bob. "Labor migrants, like before. And there are lots of educated Nubians now, teachers and engineers as well as cooks and waiters. They're making big bucks and sending it home to brighten up the home villages. You'll see."

"Mmm."

"And they're anxious to see you, B.J."

"In Cairo, people said many of our friends were dead. Saleh, his wife Dahiba. And the midwife, Aisha, who wanted to deliver Laila, long ago."

"True, but many are still there. The only thing they won't understand is why we didn't bring the children," he said. "I explained to Muhammad, though, that we couldn't afford both education *and* air fare for expensive trips. Muhammad understands, everybody understands the high costs of educating and raising children these days."

"I just dread seeing his mother, Shemessa," I finally brought out. "She used to scare me really, when David was so sick and she'd glare at me in that evil way when I went down to dose the twins."

"You still think about that after all these years?" asked Bob. "I don't believe it."

"Well, not all the time, obviously," I said defensively, "but—" and I subsided in a fit of coughing. We both had bad colds.

"Fasten your seat belts, please!" The Egyptair stewardess repeated her admonition in Arabic and French.

Bob blew his nose as we landed. "Maybe the dry air will be as good for our old chests as it was for David's," he said hopefully.

And, coughing and sniffling, we filed out of the plane onto the tarmac. We were in the new boom town of Egypt—Aswan.

The effects of the High Dam and the great silvery Lake Nasser were not much in evidence on the ground, among the rocks and dusty dunes beside the road from the airport to the center of the city. But there was a great traffic circle on the outskirts, and colorful signs proclaiming the benefits of the dam. "Peace," the signs said, and "Prosperity."

"There's also a new soccer stadium, and many more schools, and lots of luxury shops along the Corniche. Plus new first-class hotels. They say it has a hundred thousand people."

"Aswan?" I remembered Aswan as a small sleepy town in a beautiful riverside setting. On my first trip down with the children in 1961, we had had to wait several hours between the time the train from Cairo deposited us at the railroad station and the time the Sudan Railways post boat left Shellal for the two-day trip to Ballana.

"Why not take the children on a carriage trip around the city?" Susan had suggested brightly. Susan Spectorsky, our good friend, had devoted her winter vacation from the American University in Cairo to coming to Nubia and helping me get settled with the children in the village.

"Horse!" Laura Ann had cried delightedly, and we climbed up into the old-fashioned black *arabiya,* or horse-drawn carriage.

I had expected the ride to be good for a diversion of at least an hour, but we seemed to cover the entire city in ten minutes of slow clop-clopping around, after which we simply trotted back and forth along the short riverfront, Susan entertaining two-year-old Laura Ann by counting the beautiful lateen-sailed feluccas that were moving up and down the river. Aswan, now a city of a hundred thousand people with a soccer stadium and luxury shops? It seemed impossible.

Bob's old friend Muhammad was waiting for us at the airlines terminal. I had known him, of course, when we lived in Ballana in 1961 and 1962, but I had seen more of his wife and mother than of him. Thus I was somewhat surprised, though not displeased, to be engulfed in an enthusiastic bear hug.

"Well, you're like a member of the family, B.J.," announced Muhammad, almost as though he were surprised at himself. He drew back, and there he stood, impressive and dignified as ever, in a flowing immaculate blue galabia (who ironed it today? I wondered), a wide white turban, and fashionable black sunglasses.

"Welcome back to Nubia!" he said in English. We shook hands and exchanged news of our respective children. Our David had been very ill and near death in Nubia, Muhammad remembered. His twin sons had been very ill and had died in Nubia, I remembered.

He took off his sunglasses to wipe his eyes and I could see that he now had an unmoving, artificial eye, his own lost from infection. Handsome Muhammad, who was once the best hunter, the best tambura player in southern Nubia. What was he doing these days? He managed his new sugarcane land, he said, and he had plans for a Nubian cultural center in Aswan. He had also, Bob had told me, been one of the forces behind the pioneer settlements, pushing the requests to the government, to President Sadat himself, that had finally resulted in permission being granted for the settlements to legally exist. He had become a well-known spokesman for his people.

"And your mother, Muhammad?"

"She's fine. She went to Mecca."

"Wonderful."

"But she's old now, B.J."

We looked at each other, standing there in the road, Muhammad, Bob, and I.

"You're staying at the Cataract Hotel?"

"No," said Bob, "at the old Social Research Center apartment."

There was a slight pause. "Let's go to the Cataract, though, and have some tea," suggested Bob. "We can talk there."

"We're going back to old Nubia," announced Muhammad, swinging in step along with us up the steep hill where the Old Cataract Hotel, built during the days of British rule, commanded the best view of the river. "Did Bob tell you?"

"Yes, he did," I answered. "And I also read about it in the New York *Times*, a big American paper."

Muhammad looked pleased. "It's important to go to the old blessed land," he said. "But it's really hard getting started. Hard going." He turned to Bob. "You saw it, Bob. It doesn't pay for itself yet. But it will."

We were nearly at the top, the river swirling down on our right, new buildings rising on our left.

"My son is in New Nubia, B.J.," added Muhammad.

"You must be very proud of him."

"I am. And David? Bob says he's working in the Texas oilfields. Why?"

"He says he's taking time off from the university until he figures out what he wants to do."

"Ah." Muhammad nodded. "Here we are not so lucky. The students, particularly the Nubian students, must work extra hard to make high marks on the government exams the first time so they can go to college at all. Then it's free."

"Well, it isn't free in America," put in Bob. "It gets more expensive all the time."

"People in Cairo say the Nubians have done very well in the new schools, Muhammad."

"Yes, they have. We hired tutors for the boys and girls so they could do well on the exams. The schools are really too crowded. It's the only way to be sure they get an education these days."

College educations on the one hand, and on the other a movement back to a faraway agricultural settlement on the banks of Lake Nasser. The two efforts seemed contradictory. But the Nubians had always selected well from what was available to them, fitting bits and pieces into their own plans wherever possible, discarding what would not work.

"Here we are." We came out on the open terrace of the Old Cataract, the splendid setting for the film of Agatha Christie's *Death on the Nile*. The Victorian verandah's Moorish-style carved pillars framed a magnificent view of the Nile, of ancient Elephantine Island, of the sailboats on the water, the tomb of the Aga Khan glistening white, high on the opposite bank. The cataract for which the hotel was named tumbled over the rocks below.

The tea came. Heavy white ironstone china, lemon, sugar, an extra pot of hot water. Scotch shortbread on a plate. The English habits lingered on.

"You see all kinds of tourists in Aswan these days," offered Muhammad conversationally as he poured hot milk into his tea, an old Nubian custom. Half milk. Half tea. Nutritious, Khadija had explained to me. "Mostly French and German, but some Israelis, too."

He sipped his tea, became serious. "We can get tourists to come to the Nubian cultural center when it opens."

"When it opens." Bob smiled appreciatively at his friend's audacity. "Here you have just designed postcards to raise money for the center and you're already talking about opening it to tourists?"

"Why not?" asked Muhammad. "We'll have baskets and things for sale, Nubian music and dances. The tourists will learn something. You have to think this way, Bob. I'm serious."

"Okay, Muhammad, okay." Bob paused and then went on. "They say Aswan was an important city thousands of years ago. Maybe it's becoming one again, thanks to Gamal Abdul Nasser and the Aswan Dam. And John Foster Dulles," he added mischievously.

Muhammad was indignant. "Dulles. The American. What did he do?"

"Made Nasser so mad he signed the contract with the Russians and got the dam built."

"Okay, Bob, okay."

The three of us were silent for a moment.

The view from the Victorian-Moorish terrace encouraged musings, silences, contemplations on the past, on fate. Perhaps because it was so unexpectedly and wildly beautiful, the dark rocks flung down into the gleaming Nile, the river water bubbling and boiling up around them, first light and then dark, as the legendary river must have bubbled up to protect the legendary prince from harm. And then, just in front of us, the river became calm again, and the feluccas in full sail, like heavy wide-winged swans, moved silently with the wind, up, down, and around the islands.

Muhammad broke the silence. "Nasser did the dam, you're right, Bob, but he didn't live to see it finished. Sadat opened it in 1971. And he's the one who has given us money for a new pump down in the pioneer settlements."

"Who will want to live in the settlements, Muhammad?" I asked. "Other than the pioneers," I added hastily, and Muhammad turned and faced me. "I mean, with all the young people doing so well in school, and all . . ." I finished lamely.

"They will," asserted Muhammad with conviction. "At least some of them. The good ones. We'll have modern farms down there, owned and run by Nubians. We will raise vegetables for the Aswan market." He gestured with his teacup. "Tomatoes, eggplant, okra." He set down his cup carefully in the saucer. "But though the farms will be modern, we will all speak Nubian together. And we will have Nubian houses."

Nubian houses. Those beautiful structures that Hassan Fathy had described as pristine and dreamlike were very different from the government-issue houses we had visited in New Nubia in 1965. Cement-block structures, a small court open to the broiling sun, an animal shelter and a toilet side by side in the court, leaving little room for the human occupants.

"The houses in Kom Ombo weren't very nice in the beginning, I grant you," Bob said.

Muhammad nodded vigorously, his wide white turban teetering slightly. He adjusted it carefully and said, "We've fixed those houses up properly. You'll see when you come to us, B.J."

Bob looked at his watch, then out to the river, where the sky was filling with dusky color. "We should get to the apartment before dark," he said. "We can come back here again and look at the view."

The hill beside the Cataract had been landscaped into a public park set with benches and chairs where several young couples sat decorously drinking Coca-

Cola and munching cookies. At their feet small birds with black-and-white faces hopped about hoping for crumbs. The sky had become a clear, glorious red.

Bob turned to Muhammad. "We didn't see young people holding hands in public in the old days."

"They are not Nubians," said Muhammad rather crisply. "Nubian women don't hang around like that. Or Nubian men either. Our girls go to school, but then they come home and help their mothers."

"Your girls are all in school?" Muhammad, for all of his interest in the outside world, had never been too interested, I thought, in allowing his own daughters or his wife much share in it.

"Two are. The others are needed at home," he said, then added, almost gratuitously, "My mother, Shemessa, is very old now, you know, B.J."

Hmm, I thought to myself.

"Many teachers are women," went on Muhammad as if in answer to our unspoken question. "And you know, Bob, Mekki's daughter is running his shop in Aswan now. She inherited it from her father."

"Come on, B.J.," urged Bob. "You know how fast the sun sets here. We have to get to the apartment before dark so we can turn on the water and electricity. It's been so long; I'm not sure I even remember where the place is."

"Oh, I do," said Muhammad airily.

Dark was coming, dulling the sky as we turned in from the river, toward the large government housing block where Bob had rented an apartment years ago for the Nubian project. Twelve Egyptian pounds per month, for four rooms, bath, and kitchen. Headquarters for the project staff who had taken part in the initial three years of fieldwork and the follow-up studies after resettlement. The Social Research Center had kept the lease all these years.

It was here that we would stay at night while we spent our days in New Nubia. Fourth floor. Walking up the outside cement stairs. Opening up the door. The first time in a long time. The air inside was stuffy. I moved forward to open windows. Bob turned on the bright unshaded overhead bulbs. The quick tropical darkness had come down upon us, as he had predicted.

"When will you come to Ballana? Tomorrow?" asked Muhammad. "Everyone wants to see you, B.J. They've already seen Bob." He laughed.

"The day after tomorrow," said Bob. "We're both tired and have bad colds. You know Cairo these days. Everyone has colds. We need a day just to rest."

"Fine, okay." Muhammad nodded. "I'll see you then on Friday for lunch."

The door shut. Bob and I were alone in the old apartment. Neatly piled sheets, towels, blankets, were covered against the dust with yellowing newspapers, copies of *Al-Ahram* nearly two years old. The windows had been blocked with paper to discourage the desert dust that blew hard during the khamsin, the sandstorm season. The furniture was simple but adequate; we had bought some of it ourselves. New beds, refrigerators, cupboards, all made in Egypt, the first fruits of the ambitious industrialization program of Gamal Abdul Nasser. "Keep Egypt independent," he had urged, and he had pushed for the manufacture of consumer goods for the new Egyptian middle class. "Ideal" was the proud Egyptian brand name. And here still were the old Ideal refrigerator, the metal Ideal cupboards, and beds. The refrigerator still worked well, and it began to hum when I turned it on. Bob was moving through the rooms, opening windows, folding papers. In one metal cupboard lay mimeographed interview schedules in English and Arabic: name, age, number of children. The little balcony that gave onto the river was just wide enough to hold laundry lines. Its view of the Nile was cut in half by the corner of the apartment block in front of us.

Nineteen eighty-one. I had not been to Aswan since 1965. Sixteen years. Why did the apartment seem so familiar to me, so loaded with memory. It was plainly furnished for working, not for leisure. I had stayed here only briefly, twice. Yet when I opened the dining room cupboard and laid out the teacups—a gray-and-white calico pattern with a pink rose overlay—my heart thumped strangely. All the clichés about remembrance of things past rushed into my head. It was not the length of time we had stayed here, perhaps, but the quality of that time for us, for our Nubian friends. And although we had changed, the apartment had remained the same. I could almost hear the voices. Nineteen sixty-five. With some of the research assistants, we were getting ready to spend the day in New Nubia, our first visit after resettlement.

"Are you going to take Laila?" It was Fadwa al-Guindi, who had worked in the Kenuzi villages.

"Well." It was myself, younger, more worried, more uncertain. "I don't know. Farida wants to keep her here." Laila was only three then, and Farida was our nanny, whom we had brought with us on this brief trip to Aswan.

"No, no, Fadwa." It was Hassan, one of the research assistants. "Leave Laila here with Farida."

"They could both come for the day," suggested Fadwa.

Hassan made an inarticulate sound of annoyance. "Fadwa," he said, "you *know* that wouldn't work. Nubian women don't work for other people as nannies. They would be rude to Farida."

"But everyone will want to see Laila," insisted Fadwa. "You were pregnant with her when you lived in the village, B.J.!"

"Take a picture of her!" Bob, younger, brusque, in a hurry. "No discussion, it's a waste of time. Leave Laila here. Come *on*, B.J., aren't the other children ready yet?"

"Bob . . ." It was Fadwa again, laughing. She had a wonderful laugh that often successfully masked other emotions. "Remember that old Egyptian saying, words are like whips! Give us a break. We're coming."

The calico cups with roses. Farida was gently pulling those cups out of Laila's fat little fingers. . . .

"B.J., you're too quiet," said Bob. "You're thinking sentimental thoughts about the past, right?"

"Right."

"Good times those. Bad times too. We nearly lost David, but think what the Nubians lost."

"Yes, I know. Everything."

"But just think," said Bob, "what life was like in those doomed villages, people doing what they'd always done, all the while knowing that in a few months everything would be covered with water."

"They didn't really believe it, though," I answered. "The women told me they thought it would never happen."

Our open window showed a strip of Nile, darkened, new lampposts lighting the Corniche, along which people walked and cars drove. A much larger Corniche, widened since 1965.

"And when it did happen," Bob continued, "when the boats came and took the people away, they say everyone cried and some old people actually died of shock."

"Now *you're* talking about the past, Bob."

He nodded. "But still, we know all this, but we didn't actually live it. It has to be lived and suffered through, I think, to—"

"Bob."

He stood up. "You're right, we're run down from bad colds. We need to sleep, not moon about the old days."

"We weren't mooning exactly. We were trying to put it all together. It's strange, coming back like this."

"Good night, dear."

We fell down on our Ideal beds and slept. And I dreamed of the past, of Fadwa and Hassan and Farida and Laila and Laura Ann and David and of Shemessa, Muhammad's mother. Old Shemessa in her traditional *gargara,* the full black pleated dress that trailed behind her in the sand when she walked, appeared and reappeared in the dream, snatching a cup out of my hand. Shemessa who glared at me when I appeared at her house with the bottle of medicine for the twins. "Babies that are meant to live, live," she had said to me then. "It is God's will." "Yes, Shemessa, but sometimes God helps those who help themselves." "Ha! And isn't your own son sick?" "Yes, he is." "And do you give him that medicine?" "No, but his sickness is different." "Ha!" Shemessa's face seemed to become the calico cup, growing larger and larger to the edges of the dream.

Then Muhammad's wife appeared. Nezla, kind, pleasant, pretty, not up to the iron backbone of her mother-in-law. Nezla smiled at me in the dream and told me she was pregnant. And I woke up, shouting, "It's Muhammad's fault! It's his fault."

Bob called out, irritated. "B.J., wake up, you're talking in your sleep. What, for heaven's sake, is Muhammad's fault?"

"I was dreaming."

"But what was his fault? Now I'm awake, you might as well answer the question."

"Well, in the dream Nezla got pregnant, so how could she expect to nurse the new baby *and* the sick twins, of course they would die. And so that is why . . ."

". . . it was all Muhammad's fault? Well, it takes two to tango, as they say. Now go back to sleep."

Bob was snoring in a moment. After tossing and turning, I got up and went into the dining room and sat at the table in the dark. The calico cups were back in the cupboard behind me. The shutter on the riverfront window was half open and I walked toward it, toward the tiny laundry balcony. The Nile, that part of it I could see around the neighboring apartment house, was black and still, the streets below me empty. All sensible people were asleep.

Never go back, the poets said. It is not the same. It is never the same. Well, I don't want it to be the same, I said to the anonymous poets. But there is something to settle with Shemessa. Some vague dark frightening feeling. It is better to see her, to banish the unreasonable nightmare fancies in which she occurs and recurs as nemesis.

Our sentimental journey to New Nubia began with the muezzin's call to Friday prayers. We set off in a rented taxi, in order to reach Ballana by lunchtime. The taxi driver, an old man, had his wife beside him and a Koran on the dashboard, as we had often seen in Cairo. He said he would like to turn on the religious station and listen to the prayers celebrating the holy day of Friday and the recitations from the Koran which would follow.

The chant rose and fell through the cracked speaker of the taxi as we passed by the older Kenuzi villages, settled in the 1930s after the first Aswan dam was heightened by the British. A man in a white galabia, his beard as white as his garment, was climbing up the rocks on our right, toward the little mosque at the top of his village. The walls of the barrel-roofed Kenuzi houses were painted with flowers and animals, but the mosque was pristine white. The rim of the road was shaded by heavy old acacia trees, and clay *zirs* or water coolers, hung from them, like giant Christmas tree ornaments.

"Ah yes." The wife of the taxi driver turned around in answer to my question. "The *zirs* are *bénéfices,* in thanks to God for a vow, or a wish granted." She used the French word for a good deed, but I wondered who would drink from the clay containers so suspended among the nodding leaves of the tree. Birds? Djinns, the spirits of the trees, the earth, the river?

The narrow fingers of land between the road and the river, and between the road and the rocks upon which the village lay, had been plowed and planted. It was winter wheat, Bob said, and alfalfa. Makeshift scarecrows, rags on crossed sticks, stood in the rows of onions, the fields of rounding gray-green cabbages. A gasoline truck roared ominously behind us, and the old taxi pulled over onto the road shoulder to let it pass.

"You have friends in Ballana?" asked the driver politely.

"Yes," said Bob. "We lived in Ballana long ago before the water covered everything."

The old lady turned around to look at us. "The land was beautiful there," she said. "The river was beautiful, too."

"Yes," I answered. "Where are you from?"

"We are from Kalabsha," she said. "The big temple. It is gone, too."

We talked about our children, about the farming. "They want us to grow sugarcane," said the old man. He spat out the window. "Who knows how to grow sugarcane? We rented our land to some Sa'idis. They know how."

"And our son is in the Gulf. He sends us money," added the old lady. She turned around full in her seat and smiled a gap-toothed but contented smile below her black head scarf. "He is a good son," she said.

"Yes, we do all right," said the old man.

In the south, the river's banks had disappeared under Lake Nasser, but here, below the dam, they seemed much the same as in the past. The river still served as a main transport route. A huge flat barge was chugging slowly along on our left carrying, of all things, sand, to the north. The river thronged with feluccas, large, small, one close enough so we could see its striped mast of orange and green, its banded boxes and cartons piled above decks. Acacias and cottonwoods edged the tiny fields, giving shade, and a few date palms had been planted among them. The donkeys being driven along the side of the road by small boys carried wide loads of dried palm fronds. The Nubians were cultivating their beloved date palms again. We had seen hundreds of palm shoots from the trees of old Nubia lining the banks of the Nile in 1963, shrouded in their own fibrous netting, waiting to be transported to Kom Ombo by government boats. Other trees had been brought to the new settlement by the Nubians themselves, to plant near their new homes. The actual fruit of the tree, the date, was only one of the many products of the palm that were used in everyday life. Dried palm fronds like those loading the donkeys beside the taxi could be woven into roofs for the courts of the new houses, into fences for the animal shelters, and into mats for the floors. The bits and pieces could be used for fuel, and thin strands of the fiber served as the base material for Nubian baskets and plates. The fronds were more valuable now than ever before, since the old stands of date palms lay under water, and the new trees were just beginning to bear fruit.

"I believe in peace," said the taxi driver suddenly. "That's why I bought this dove for my taxi; peace is what the Koran says is best. Nubia was always a land of peace. That's why it was blessed."

The old man was right. There had been practically no crime in old Nubia. When the government policemen assigned to Ballana Province had occasionally stopped by our house there, they complained of boredom. Bob served them tea and discussed the ways of the world with these homesick men from Cairo who were at a loss to explain the total absence of crimes of violence.

"Of course there is a little smuggling, we know that." The policeman had smiled knowingly at Bob.

"Of course," Bob would answer. Everybody knew about the smuggling of tea and cigarettes from the Sudan. A lot of people were in on it, too, including, some said, the police. But petty smuggling was accepted; nobody considered that a crime. Even a policeman liked Italian sunglasses.

"Well," Bob had added, "there's bad feeling between some families, but the only crime I ever heard of was a man last year who went stark raving mad and started running through a northern village with a butcher knife. He had to be taken to a mental hospital in Cairo."

"I remember the case," said the policeman. "But, you know, he didn't hurt anyone!"

There must be some dark places in Nubian culture, I had argued with Bob and the other research assistants. Circumcision. Yes, everyone had agreed that female circumcision, which was still practiced in the area, did not fit into the idealized picture of peace, contentment, and love that was the local cultural ideal. And here the radical, or Pharaonic, circumcision was common. Not only did the operation cause physical pain and long-term discomfort to women in their sex life and in childbirth, it also caused frustration and concern among the men, Muhammad had confided to Bob. Where did it come from, this seemingly bizarre and cruel act? How did it fit into the picture? No one seemed able to answer except to explain that it made women "more feminine," that it had "always been done."

Bob and the driver were speaking. "We have another hour to go," Bob said to me. "We should be turning off soon, away from the river."

I hoped the sweets I had brought as a present to Muhammad's family were adequate, appropriate. But why was I worrying? They were old friends.

"The candy should be given to his mother, Shemessa, I think," said Bob. "We'll be having lunch with them."

"Shemessa?"

"Yes," he said firmly. "And stop being so silly about the poor old lady."

We turned east, away from the river. A clear empty sky. An empty landscape of hills. Bits of broken grass tufts rolled toward us, against the car, like tumbleweeds. This was the moment we had dreaded in 1965, leaving the riverside. Over a ridge, the villages appeared, rows of houses, boxlike as before, but now as we came closer, we could see that the cement had been covered with smooth sand-colored plaster, the fronts of the houses had been adorned with mud-brick benches, or mastabas, and the walls and the doors of the houses were ornamented as the old Nubian houses had been, with geometric designs in white, with flowers picked out in red and green and blue on the smooth matte surfaces. An occasional wall was illustrated with scenes of everyday life, of travels. A donkey carried a load of grain, a taxi returned from Mecca, a plane was bound for London. The scenes were meticulously painted and signed, with the name of the house owner. The women had done the painting in old Nubia; was it the same in New Nubia?

"Here we are!" The taxi came to a stop beside a gas station. A school building rose behind it. We got out and I shook hands with the driver's wife through the open car window. Bob paid our fare and we said goodbye.

"See, B.J., doesn't it look better?" Bob had taken my arm and we walked down the streets, swept clean of trash, decorated with great mud-brick tubs in which small palm trees flourished. Soon they would be big enough to replant in the fields. Potted palms, no less! I smiled. The children running ahead, behind, and to each side of us gave one reason to smile. They looked much stronger and healthier than the children I remembered in old Nubia. Their eyes were clear, too, of the suppurating infections that had been the bane of the old villages, that had caused our own children so much trouble and had cost Muhammad his eye.

"Ahlan wusahlan! Why didn't you tell me you were getting off at the gas station? I would have come to meet you." It was Muhammad, greeting us warmly and literally propelling us down the street to his house, into the salon where the center table was covered with a white cloth and the new television set was turned on immediately for our pleasure.

"Where are Nezla and your mother?" I asked politely, after we had watched an Egyptian soap opera for about five minutes. The old pictures were on the wall again, the picture of Muhammad with his tambura, photographed by a French newsman before the temple of Abu Simbel. I felt as though I should get up and go into the women's quarters myself, but it seemed more polite to inquire, in case they were not ready to receive visitors.

"Come, B.J., they're out here." Muhammad opened the door of the guest room and Bob handed me the big box of candy, mouthing as he did so, "Shemessa."

There she was, all in black, the center of my recent nightmares, Muhammad's mother. "Ah! Ah! *Ahlan wusahlan!"* That high cracked voice was the same, a little thinner perhaps but still the same tentative welcome—"Ah . . . Ah" came first, as though signaling that she was not quite sure she *wanted* to welcome me. I shook myself inwardly and remembered my promise to Bob not to be silly.

"Sit down then, will you," Shemessa said, and I did so, while she eased herself down beside me, on a mattress covered with a green spread and carefully placed in the shade in the coolest corner of the courtyard.

"Soraya! Pillows!" she shouted and a young daughter came running, a flowered pillow in each hand.

I presented my box of sweets. Shemessa looked at it, cleared her throat, whether in disdain or pleasure I could not tell, and gave it to Soraya to whisk off into another room.

"Ah!" said Shemessa. She did not seem nearly so malevolent in person as I had conjured her up in my dreams. She was a feeble, very old lady, her eyes milky with cataracts. Could she see me? Did she even know who I was? Her hair, the bit that peeped out from her tightly tied black head scarf, was sparse, the gray mixed with the bright orange tint of henna.

"Ah!" repeated Shemessa, clearing her throat once more, loudly, and pushing her scarf back a little, loosening it slightly, scratching her head. After all, she was at home, she could relax. Then she enunciated, finally, the traditional greeting of welcome in the Fadija language.

"*Mascagna!*"

"*Mascagna!*" I replied. "And how are you, Shemessa?"

"Not bad, nah, not bad." A clearing of the throat again, and she stretched out her old legs on the mattress, grunting with the exertion as she did so. "It's my knees," she said. "Ahh!"

"*Mascagna!*" It was Nezla, Muhammad's wife, who had come forward to shake hands, older, plumper, but still smiling, gently, kindly, wearing a flowered print housedress without the old fashioned Nubian black overdress, the gargara.

"*Mascagna!*" I answered. "How are you, Nezla?"

She nodded, a kind of *comme-ci, comme-ça* reply.

"You have a lot of work, can I help?"

"No, you are a guest. But come and see my new stove. And our house. We have fixed it up."

She gave me a tour, proud of it all: six rooms around the wide half-roofed courtyard: the guest room where Bob and Muhammad and several other men were presumably still watching the Cairo soap opera, a kitchen with a white enamel gas stove, two bedrooms, a storeroom, and an immaculate toilet off in a far corner, where the sun beat down fiercely, "to kill off the smell," she explained.

"We put a wall in here, B.J.," she pointed out, "see, so the animals stay on the other side, can you imagine such a filthy thing, who would put animals in a house with people? I've been in Cairo and I never saw *that.*"

It was true that many farmhouses in rural Egyptian villages had animals stabled in them, but the government architect who had designed these houses for the Nubians probably had never been south to see the beautiful old Nubian homes. Even if he had, it was unlikely that the government would have been able to afford to build such spacious residences for the resettled people.

"We have a washing machine, too," said Nezla proudly, and she demonstrated. "First we got the washing machine, then the television. Next, I hope, a refrigerator. Ah, I fought with Muhammad to get the washing machine first, he wanted the television. We got both."

The little girl, Soraya, hanging on to Nezla's skirts, smiled at me.

"Soraya was born here in New Nubia," said Nezla. "So were Mona, and Latifa. I have all girls except the oldest, the boy."

"Your son is at the new settlement?"

"Yes," said Nezla. "It's better for him. He doesn't get on with his father. And Hanim, you remember her, is married." She smiled. "She has two children. She's coming to see you after lunch."

"And the others?"

Nezla turned from me, gracefully folding back her sleeve to stir the stew on the stove.

"They died," she said shortly. "The twins died first, then the little boy that was born after, when I was pregnant and you were pregnant with Laila in old Nubia. And my daughter with the growth. You remember, you came to see us in the hospital in Cairo."

I remembered. The little girl had lain on a cot in a dim hospital ward, her body bloated out of shape. An inoperable tumor. And Nezla had bedded down beside her on a mat. The child did not suffer alone. Nor die alone. The hospital was scarcely the Mayo Clinic, but the small patient at least had her mother to comfort her.

"Ha! Nezla! Beeja!" It was Shemessa calling us from the mattress in the shade.

"Go sit with her, B.J.," said Nezla. "She's old now."

"But still strong, I think," I offered tentatively.

"Yes, God knows," she replied, the daughter-in-law, and turned back to her pot.

"Nezla needs to get her eyes fixed," said Shemessa shortly when I had settled myself beside her again. "She's getting old."

"Nezla?"

"She's got a skin over the eyes, like me." Shemessa demonstrated, pulling up her eyelid so I could see where a grayish milky cloud was forming over the lens, the cornea. It was a cataract. I wondered again whether she could see me at all, but the other eye looked a bit less affected. "In the hospital in Aswan they do it in two days, peel it off like a grape. Ha!" She smiled a toothless smile. I didn't remember ever having seen her smile in old Nubia.

"Soraya! The whisk!" Soraya came running with a horsehair fly whisk and Shemessa began to apply it lightly, back and forth across her shoulders.

"Flies! Flies!" Shemessa flicked the whisk over her shoulders. Slap. Slap. "We put the wall between the animals and us, the girls scrub the toilet every day, but still there are bad flies."

"Where?" I almost asked, but then stopped, realizing there were more flies in Shemessa's old mind than in the sunny well-kept courtyard where we sat. Muhammad had hired workmen to plaster the court, creating different levels, increasing the sense of space if not its actuality. The water jars of traditional clay had bright-green plastic drip buckets below them so no water was wasted. Three finely woven plates from old Nubia, in shades of purple and orange and mauve, hung on the gray wall, points of color tastefully applied, as a decorator might have said.

"Ah! Ah!" Shemessa was flicking the nonexistent flies away. Her feet, stuck straight out in front of her, were seamed and wrinkled, and the skin, decorated with patches of healing henna, was shrinking inward, creating hollows around each instep.

"I've been to Mecca, Beeja," she said. "You can call me *hajjiya* now!"

"Congratulations," I said. "That's wonderful, Shemessa!"

"I went with Hanim Ali."

Hanim Ali had been childless. She was famous for her many strange finger rings, magic rings, people said. She had told me during David's illness that she would pray for him. It was Hanim Ali who had fought to unite the two marriageable children of her family, her nephew, Jabbar, and her grandniece, Naima. It had taken her years, but she had succeeded. Her husband, Saleh, in whose house we had lived, was dead. His other wife, Dahiba, was also dead. But Hanim Ali was triumphantly alive and had made the pilgrimage, the fifth duty of all good Muslims who could afford it.

"We went on the plane, that was great," said Shemessa. "But it was very hot in Arabia. We went around Mount Arafat, like the Prophet says we must do, around and around, from the morning prayer until the afternoon prayer. We prayed all the time. We were half dead but it was wonderful! And now I'm a hajjiya!"

Slap. Slap. The whisk went back and forth. Shemessa, my nemesis all these years, was obviously not a witch at all, but only a very old woman who had done her duty as she had seen it, all her life. Crotchety perhaps and certainly domineering but hardly a witch. Perhaps she and I had become the objects of each other's anxieties back in old Nubia.

For I had been very insecure in those days, worried about the children, worried about the baby I was carrying, worried about my fatigue, my feet swelling as I plodded over the sand, worried about the progress of Bob's project. Worry that could not be assuaged, as Shemessa's worry about the twin boys could not be assuaged. And we had therefore fixed on each other as the focus of our discontents. I was an obvious target for Shemessa's antagonism, a stranger bringing unknown medicine, doing things to the babies that she did not understand, an instrument of possible harm to her family.

"Hanim Ali will tell you she stayed a month in Mecca," went on Shemessa. "Don't believe her. She only stayed three weeks. I stayed a month. But then, that's Hanim Ali, always pretending she's better than she is. Can't trust her. Look at the way she carried on over Naima's wedding."

Naima's wedding was the occasion for which Hanim Ali had fought, had bargained for special dates, first-quality henna, for extraspecial music, good fat lamb, and for dancing. The dancing had been memorable. She had danced herself, at the end, Hanim Ali, with all the other Nubian women, young and old, celebrating the joining of two families, the strengthening of the community.

". . . and just because the Begum gave money for a present, that was all Hanim Ali was interested in. . . ."

Old grievances. Shemessa had been spiteful then, and was now.

"Oh, I don't think so, really, Shemessa. She always wanted Naima and Jabbar to marry. It wasn't just the money the Begum gave—"

"It's always money," interrupted Shemessa. "Or maybe God. We had both in Mecca . . . thanks be to Him." She pointed the whisk at me. "Hanim Ali never bore any children of her own, you know, that's what was wrong with her. . . ."

The whisk went back over the old shoulder, covered in two layers of black,

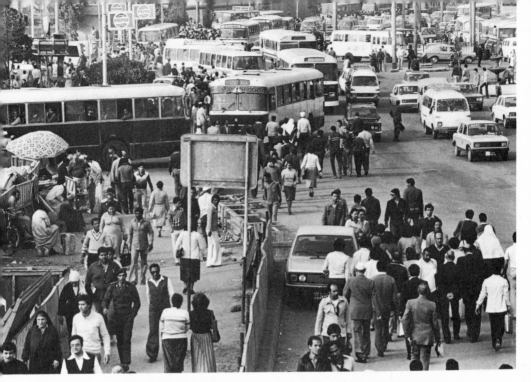

Cairo traffic. The city now has a population of 12 million.

A modern Egyptian farmer and his assistant.

A prospective Berber bride in the Atlas
mountains of Morocco.

Primary schoo

Moroccan youngsters head to school
through a market street.

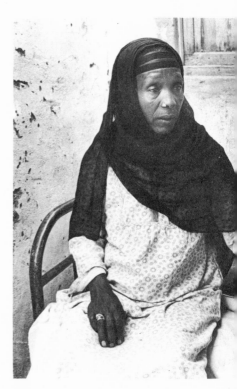

Nubian women in Kom Ombo

...assroom, Cairo.

Egyptian family group at an
outdoor restaurant near Cairo.

...orth Aswan, preparing a meal.

A Moroccan mother and baby.

Palestinian women learn to machine-weave at a training school on the West Bank, near Jerusalem.

A Palestinian home in front of an Israeli settlement in East Jerusalem.

like the shoulders of all good Nubian elderly ladies. "Well, we leased our land," she said. "The boy is working in the south . . . we make it. . . ."

Looking around the courtyard, at the pattern of pleasant dappled shade cast on the neatly swept plastered floor, Nezla bustling back and forth between her storeroom and her kitchen with its new gas stove, hearing the television blaring in the guest room, where Bob and Muhammad were now listening to the soccer match, I thought, yes, they are making it. And now they are returning to the old land, trying to make it there, too. The material comforts offered by the new settlements—washing machines, flyless courtyards, television sets, schools, clinics—were not quite enough, it seemed. Other things were important: pride, sentiment, independence.

"Praise be to Him," muttered old Shemessa, half to herself. Slap. Slap. I was being lulled into half sleep when the old woman suddenly sat up straight and said, sharply, clearly, in another, younger voice, directly into my ear. "They died. The twins died! Your son lived, but the twins died. And it was *you* that brought the medicine when they were sick. You. You . . ." The rest of her sentence was unintelligible, but the intent of those words was not benevolent. Could she be cursing me? Something seemed to flash through the clouds of those whitening eyes. I had never been cursed before. And my heart chilled, as it had years ago in Nubia, when David, aged one, lay in a high fever, rasping and coughing, and old Shemessa had hissed, "Your son is no better, is he? Who knows where the evil eye hides, hey?"

"Come and eat, B.J." Bob and Muhammad were standing before us in the court, Bob greeting Shemessa, who barely replied, other men's voices audible from the guest room, where the television still blared.

I got up quickly from my place on the mattress.

"Please, Bob," I said in English, "let me eat out here with the women." I did not want to leave Shemessa at that moment. I wanted to work out, if at all possible, whatever remained unfinished between us. Her outburst had been so unexpected, so vindictive, after our earlier, peaceful conversation about old Nubia, Mecca.

Bob shook his head. "Muhammad says if you eat with us it's easier on his wife. She won't have to serve formally twice. Also I think the men would like a look at you. Jalal and Ahmed are here. Jalal came especially from Aswan."

I looked back at Nezla, standing at her kitchen door, Soraya by her side, at Shemessa, who was flicking her whisk again, not even looking at me. Nezla gestured me toward the salon. "We'll have tea later," she said.

The television was turned off as I walked into the room, "in your honor," whispered Bob. "Be pleasant." I went around, shaking hands with Jalal, with Ahmed, an older man whom I did not know but who had come back to Nubia to retire after living in Paris for many years. It was strange to shift so quickly to this formal gathering of men, from the courtyard where old Shemessa flicked the flies and little Soraya ran about to do her grandmother's bidding. Although men and women had never been strictly segregated in Nubia, as in Iraq, women tended to spend more time together since their tasks were different from men's. Bob had visited like this, in the formal guesthouses; but I had sat with the women and did not know Jalal and Ahmed except as appendages to their wives and children.

"How is your family?"

"They are fine, thanks be to God."

"Laura Ann? David? The baby Laila?"

"The baby is in college." (Laughter.) "Laura Ann, too. David is working on an oil rig in north Texas." (Expressions of interest, respect.)

"Isn't it dangerous?"

"Living is dangerous—fatal, in fact," said Bob.

"Right," agreed Jalal.

"And how is my old neighbor Khadija?"

"She is expecting you after lunch."

Formal inquiries. Formal replies. Bob's conversation was quite different, joking, relating with the men on a very different basis, a very different history. Muhammad served the meal, taking the tray from Nezla at the door. Soup flavored with cumin, roast lamb. "We killed a sheep, Bob," laughed Muhammad. "No, we didn't, we bought the meat at the store." Yes, the markets were working well now, the men said. They had the jamaiiyas, the cooperatives, just like in Cairo, for oil, tea, rice.

"There is even a cloth jamaiiya," said Jalal. "Where a couple about to be married can buy sheeting and toweling for half price."

Shemessa cursing me. Why? After all these years?

"B.J., you're not listening," Bob chided me. "Jalal was asking you about the Nubian club in London."

"Sorry." I talked about the meeting I had attended in a hotel in Earl's Court, about the speech of the president. Jalal's nephew, whose picture was in Bob's book, was a member of the club. They had sent more than 150 English pounds to help found the pioneer settlements. The conversation moved around and past the London club, the children, the price of meat. But in a little corner of my mind, Shemessa's vindictive face with the cloudy eyes remained. And the two moments of malevolence came together—the one long ago when David was so sick, the one today. What were my children doing at the moment? Was David all right on that oil rig? I hadn't had any news for a month.

"You must go visit your other friends," Muhammad was saying, picking up our empty plates and loading them on the tray. "Khadija and Hanim Ali will be mad at me for monopolizing you, B.J."

So off we went, down the street. Wherever we stopped, I found myself enfolded in the voluminous black garments the women wore, garments redolent of the marvelous odor of sandalwood.

"*Mascagna.*" An embrace, a kiss, three times lightly on each cheek.

"*Mascagna,*" I replied and was embraced again.

"Come have tea, B.J." "How is baby Laila?" "Why didn't you bring the children?" "We are so sorry to hear your mother died." "Your hair is still short, why?"

"Mascagna!"

"Mascagna!"

I was unreasonably glad to see everyone, Hanim, her children, Naima, Naima's sister from the other bank. It was reassuring, after Shemessa.

"Abdul Nasr is going to be an engineer," announced Khadija proudly. Abdul Nasr was the same age as David. In old Nubia, they had played together, but Abdul Nasr was stronger, healthier, than my son, able to work his way easily out of the restraining sling his mother and his doting grandaunts had tied around his ankles.

"And David?"

"He's fine." (Was he fine?) "Working on an oil rig in Texas. His father wants him to go back to school."

Khadija nodded sagely over our cups of hot chocolate. "Fathers," she said. "Sons! Thank God my husband is working in Khartoum."

"How do you like my salon, B.J.? I did it myself, but Hanim Ali gave me lots of advice." She giggled. "You know Hanim Ali!"

The salon was painted light blue, with a border of darker blue simulating a panel two thirds of the way up the wall. The ceiling was white and the floor covered with a new imitation Persian rug. "An elegant room, Khadija," I said.

We smiled at each other, then my hostess covered her mouth in embarrassment. She had lost her two front teeth but otherwise was still the village beauty, plumper and with a new hairstyle, frizzy curls framing her face all round her head scarf.

"It's like an Afro," she said, touching the front curls. "We see those American Afro hairdos on TV. And the tiny braids all over the head. Just like the little girls used to wear in Nubia, remember?"

I nodded. "Your hair is different, but you're still wearing the gargara, like in the old days, Khadija. I thought you might have taken up the new style I see in Aswan—"

"B.J., you wouldn't believe the things the young people are wearing," she answered. "I can't wear them. I'm too old for that. But the girls now, the dresses are so short you can see their legs up to their knees. They say if they have their hair in braids they don't even need a head scarf!"

But her tone of censure was belied by a pleasant half giggle. She didn't disapprove too much. I used to wonder idly about her and Muhammad. People had liked to gossip about them in old Nubia, with Khadija's husband away and Muhammad obviously not relishing spending too much time in his own house, where the children were always sick and his mother always hollered at him and his sweet wife did her best, but ineffectively. I had often said to Bob, with some bitterness, that I wished Muhammad, rather than I, had been the chosen emissary of modern medicine to his household. Perhaps he had trouble standing up to Shemessa, too.

Khadija put her hand on my arm. "If we don't go to Hanim Ali's," she said, "she'll kill me. Naima and the others will come there."

Hanim Ali looked much the same, more dried up and wrinkled, perhaps, but henna had been more artfully applied to her wings of hair escaping from her head scarf, so it didn't have the bizarre orange-and-gray look of Shemessa's. And when she embraced me in a cloud of sandalwood, her old strangely wrought rings pressed into my arm. I kissed her, in the Nubian way, lightly three times on each cheek, and the evil memory of Shemessa faded.

"Did Shemessa tell you she went to Mecca and stayed a month?"

"Yes."

Hanim Ali shook her head. "Don't believe what Shemessa says. She's getting old. We both stayed three weeks."

Yes, I thought. That's it. I must look at this whole situation from the proper perspective. She's getting old. Doesn't mean what she says. Doesn't know what she says.

"This year we watched the Hajj on television," said Hanim Ali proudly. "It's wonderful, television. In that little box we see Africa and America and London and Egypt and Syria and Saudi Arabia. We see wild animals. We see people. And we see that the cows in America are fat and *white*. Tell me, do you make good yogurt out of those white cows' milk?"

"Yes," I said. "It makes good yogurt, but you can buy yogurt in the stores in little containers now."

Hanim Ali sniffed. "You can buy it in Aswan like that," she said scornfully. "But it's not like what we make at home. In America I believe you have machines do everything."

"No. Not everything."

"Well, sometimes machines are *better* than people, they make life easier. Do you remember how we used to wash clothes? Look at my hands."

I looked at those old, scarred cracked hands, and I remembered well how they used to wash clothes; the women first had to haul water up the steep dunes from the river, in cans gracefully balanced on their heads. A picturesque ethnic sight for photographers, but hardly pleasant for the women who had to haul those heavy cans of water once, twice, sometimes three times a day.

"So it's better here," I offered.

"Some things are better, some worse," allowed Hanim Ali. "The water comes out of the tap, that's wonderful. But you know, in the beginning many died, many animals died, many people, many children—"

"I know, Hanim Ali, I am sorry." Her own husband was dead, her co-wife, and the three children of Muhammad.

"And Aisha, our midwife, Abdulla's mother, you know, she lasted longer than poor Fatima, her daughter-in-law. Fatima sickened, she was such a strong woman no one could figure out why. Remember Aisha wanted to bring your baby Laila?"

Yes. Aisha the midwife had offered to wash her hands in warm water and give me a special price for Laila's delivery.

"Abdulla still gives the call to prayer. He has become very religious."

"But he always was." Abdulla and Fatima had joined the Sufi Nakshabandi sect while we were still all living in Ballana. They had not remodeled their house in New Nubia; Fatima had explained to me in 1965 that one must accept one's fate. Money, time, and energy should go to God, not man.

"Oh, Beeja." Hanim Ali smiled suddenly. "Have you seen Elias, our nephew? You and Bahiga went to see him in the hospital in Cairo, when he had his cataract operation."

"No, I haven't seen him."

"He's a mulla, Beeja." Hanim Ali smiled all over her wrinkled face. "Isn't it wonderful? We are so proud of him. Abdul Nasr an engineer, Elias a mulla. And David?"

I explained again what David was doing.

"He's working on those towers I have seen on the television? That is very dangerous, Beeja."

"Yes, but—"

"He's your only son."

"Airplanes are dangerous too, Hanim Ali. Even flying like you did to go to Mecca was dangerous."

"Ah!" She raised her hand, the fingers covered with the odd rings. "But on pilgrimage we are protected by God's grace, and if we die on pilgrimage we go straight to heaven. That's what I told Shemessa on the plane, because she got scared."

"Shemessa *scared?*"

Hanim Ali almost laughed. "Shemessa gets scared when she's not in charge. She needs to do more good deeds, that woman, or she'll never get to heaven. And who protects your son on that high tower?"

"God protects him, too," I said firmly.

"Beeja." Hanim Ali was bringing me back from the Texas oil rig. "We saw on the television a program about the black people in America, and we see that there is trouble between whites and blacks in your country. Why?"

"It is better now, Hanim Ali," I began, "but . . ."

I was rescued from having to explain the history of racial conflict in America by the others who came in, Naima, Hanim, and the grown-up children whom I did not recognize but who recognized me. They wandered in smiling, to shake hands, ask after the children. What had I been dreading? That Nubia would be dying, that people would be sick, some dead? Some were dead. Times had been bad. But things were better now than they had been in 1965. The Nubians had taken what was offered—a government house, a piece of land, help in moving— and had made it into a base for something better. Many men had gone to work in the Gulf, just as they had left Nubia in the past to work in Cairo, Khartoum. In their absence, the womenfolk had leased the land to Sa'idis from Upper

Egypt, who farmed it as sharecroppers. The men told Bob that at first they made up to six hundred dollars or more a month as migrant laborers, but now they got less, since the migrant population in the Gulf had increased and wages had fallen somewhat. In Nubia itself, the women said, it was possible to live well for a hundred dollars a month. The children were almost all in school, many, like Abdul Nasr and Elias, going on to universities.

The high wages for migrant labor in the Gulf had helped the communities through the bad early days of resettlement, paying for architectural changes and additions to the houses, for consumer goods. But it was the Nubians' own hard work and enterprise that had helped them do consistently well in government examinations, in competing for bureaucratic posts from which they helped their fellow Nubians rise as well. It was not a completely rosy picture. Families were still separated for long periods. But it was better than it had been in 1965, and many said better than in old Nubia.

The warmth of our reception, the hopefulness of our friends, cheered us both. I decided again I had been imagining things with Shemessa and made a point of asking for her especially when we went back to Muhammad's house to say goodbye.

"Shemessa's taking a nap, B.J.," said Nezla. "She's tired out."

"Nonsense," Muhammad replied, and strode into the bedroom. He came out again more quietly, and closed the door softly. "I'm sorry, B.J. She *is* asleep. You know how mothers are, Bob," he joked, with a sidelong glance at me. "She's getting old. You must forgive her. She still has bad memories of old Nubia."

"Yes, Muhammad," I said. "I understand."

I thought I did understand. The work of Bob and his colleagues, the many publications that had resulted from the Nubian project, was important to the Nubians, for it documented and recorded their heritage. Bob had contributed to their community as they had contributed to the success of his career. But my relations with the Nubians and theirs with me were a much more personal matter. Shemessa and I, full of anxiety as we both were in those days in 1961 and 1962, had become the personifications of each other's problems. Time had not changed that.

All reasonable discussion with Bob not withstanding, I was not surprised when we got back to Cairo to find a letter from Laura Ann. "Don't worry, Mama. The worst is over. David had a bad accident on the rig, the pipe slipped. It weighed about a ton, so he was lucky not to lose his hand when the pipe came down. His hand is broken and swollen up like a boxing glove, but the doctor says they can save his fingers. He says to send his love."

The heavy pipe came crashing down on David's hand that last week in February, when we were in New Nubia. The day that Shemessa cursed me? Astrologers and psychic readers and fortune-tellers make much of the confluence of good and evil vibrations. I discounted such ideas, rational Westerner that I was. So did Bob. But I could not forget Shemessa, the flash from those clouded eyes.

The dark corners of the human heart have yet to be explained away; they are there. Violence. Passion. Hate. And all can be activated when unbearable situations arise in which the protagonists feel powerless. Whatever I might feel, Shemessa felt greater grief, greater hate. For my son David was alive. Her three grandsons were dead. And in her bitterness, she struck out, she still blamed me for their deaths.

"Coincidence is the gadfly of the imagination," was all that Bob would say.

Before we had left for Cairo, Muhammad came to Aswan bearing a proposal for a Nubian cultural center in Aswan. "Do you think the Ford Foundation would finance it?" he asked. "They supported your project."

"Why not try?" said Bob. He took the proposal back to Cairo and gave it to John Gerhart at the foundation. Muhammad himself came two weeks later for an interview and discussion. Bob in his denim suit, Muhammad in blue galabia, and Jalal in a new brown safari suit made up the delegation.

"We can have the main center in Aswan," said Muhammad, "and then maybe a branch at Abu Simbel, where the pioneer settlements are."

"Wait a minute, Muhammad, you'd better get the first one started before doing anything else," cautioned Bob, then translated again for the others at the meeting.

"We have already designed some postcards and we're collecting old Nubian art treasures for a museum," Muhammad went on, and Bob continued to translate.

John Gerhart looked at Bob. "I think we could help them get started," he said. "It's a great idea: their preservation of their own cultural heritage. Don't you want to be involved?"

Bob laughed. "Thanks, but I won't be here. Anyway, I think you'll be surprised at how quickly Muhammad and his friends will get things under way."

Twenty years ago Muhammad and Jalal had been surprised when President Nasser had addressed them on the radio as "Nubians" for the first time. Then it was not their name for themselves. Now being Nubian was something to be proud of. The proposed center would be an expression of their new ethnic identity.

The grant was awarded in the fall of 1981, to help develop "a Nubian center that will allow all peoples the opportunity to view the best of Nubian culture." By the summer of 1983 the foundations of the building had been laid. Muhammad and Jalal had launched a drive for more funds to complete the construction.

We returned to Cairo from Nubia on a calm, clear March afternoon, to be told at the *Fostat* that we had lucked out by missing a nasty out-of-season sandstorm, and to see that Um Fethy and Abdulla were celebrating the return of good weather by holding a family picnic.

"Good afternoon!" called Um Fethy, as we came down the gangplank. She sat not in her usual place on the boat but on a flowered comforter laid out on the rocky riverbank above the reeds. A younger woman and a man sat there with their children, a little girl and two medium-size boys holding balloons very carefully. Abdulla raised his head and nodded perfunctorily to us. He was peeling a hard-boiled egg for one of the little boys, whose head was closely shaved and who wore a striped red sweater.

"Good afternoon!" I answered, and Bob waved, following Abdulla's example.

"Did you have a nice time in Aswan?" queried Um Fethy.

"Yes, thank you. And how are things with you?"

"Fine. *Ahlan wusahlan!* Welcome!" Um Fethy indicated the flowered comforter on the rocks, the lunch of bread and eggs and tomatoes laid out on a small cloth, the ever-present teakettle poised on the primus stove, set on a flat rock to one side of the blanket. The younger woman also called out, *"Ahlan wusahlan!"*

"Thank you," I answered. "We've been traveling and are tired."

This was only partly true, for I would actually have loved some tea. The invitation was ritualized but also real. If we had stepped down from the gangplank and tiptoed over the rocks to the blanket, the children, their mother, and their father would have huddled together and made room for us on that tiny bit of private space. Hospitality is a way of life in the Arab world; the hard-boiled eggs, perhaps one for each person on the flowered comforter, would have been divided up into smaller pieces so that we, as guests, would have a larger share. It seemed best for us to stay home.

So we made tea for ourselves and sat upon our own deck. Before we had finished, the picnic on the bank came to an end. Abdulla, with a glance at the sky, got up, shook hands with his visitors, bent down to rinse his hands and face in the water, and headed back to the boat. Um Fethy followed, after farewell hugs of the boys and the younger woman (the little girl turned up her face to be kissed). Before the sun had set, the boat had shoved off. A good time for the fish to bite, Bob pointed out, and especially after a storm. Rowing hard and steadily downstream, they were soon near the center of the river. While we watched, Um Fethy stood up to cast out the nets onto the glistening water.

The visiting family sat on the bank a bit longer, the little boys playing with their balloons, the little girl sitting close to her mother, the man stretched out on the flowered comforter smoking a cigarette. Then they, too, packed the remains of their lunch, folded up the comforter, and disappeared into the evening traffic that was beginning to crowd Giza Street above us.

Long after we left Nubia, I remembered Hanim Ali's description of "that little box," the television set where she had seen Africa, America, Asia, and white cows cavorting on a distant green pasture. Egyptian television was just beginning in the 1960s. Now more than half of all Egyptian families owned their own television sets, and nearly two thirds of the entire population watched television regularly, either at home or in the local coffee shop. As the advertising copy writers might have phrased it, Egyptian mass media had made a quantum leap forward. The National Television Corporation occupied an entire building along the Nile, near the center of Cairo, a ten-minute walk from the Hilton. From that single giant twelve-story building emanated the news, the soap operas, the talk shows, the religious and educational programs that filled the Egyptian television screens for at least eight hours every day.

Sheikh Sharkawi dispensed homilies and religious advice; schoolteachers offered special tutoring sessions in mathematics and science, to compensate for the crowded classrooms where individualized instruction was not possible; Egyptian playwrights, poets, and filmmakers were interviewed, their latest works discussed. The soap operas, or "family serials," enthralled viewers with daytime romance and tragedy (the handsome young doctor falls in love with a poor patient in the hospital and deserts the rich and socially prominent girl his parents have chosen for him; a child ill with an incurable disease brings estranged members of his family together before death); President Sadat opened many news broadcasts with a long "chat with the people"; and the news was also presented in English and French. Then there were the imported shows: "Roots" and "Little House on the Prairie," the Monte Carlo entertainment show from France; "Edward and Mrs. Simpson" from Britain; and finally, the most popular of all, "Dallas."

"Dallas" was the one phenomenon that in 1981 brought traffic virtually to a standstill in downtown Cairo for the hour of its transmission; it kept children from their homework and ruined the conversations of many dinner parties. Money, sex, and power. Ingredients to appeal to any society; the Dallas combination had the added titillation of being foreign, Western.

"I must say I like to look at the decor, the sofas and the curtains," said one Cairo matron. "And of course Sue Ellen's clothes."

"It shows our people what they must avoid in the West," said an earnest young painter. "It is instructive to watch an evil man like J.R. and see that he is the *real* American, not like the ones we have romanticized in the past."

"I don't agree," said an Egyptian army officer with whom I sat at dinner. "I do not let my children watch it. It sets a *bad* example for them."

"You don't watch 'Dallas'?" I asked, amazed. I had yet to meet an Egyptian who did not.

The army officer smiled, shrugged. "Well, yes, I watch it myself. By myself. But my children"—he raised his finger and wagged it at me—"never!"

The television management, canny and public-minded, chose to put their most important public service announcements close to "Dallas." And these included spots promoting family planning.

Family planning, barely being discussed in the sixties, was now in. President Nasser's 1962 broadcast urging family planning had been seen as a landmark. Now President Sadat also backed family planning, though not as enthusiastically as his wife. Still, a vigorous and expensive government campaign was in progress, backed by U.S. AID and other foundations, and promotion was attempted not only on television but on radio, on billboards, and in hundreds of clinics through the country. By 1970 there were three thousand family planning centers in the twenty-five governorates of Egypt. Their effectiveness, however, was less impressive than their numbers. Even after ten years of the campaign, contraceptive use remained as low as 2 percent in some rural areas.

For the segment of the film I was making in Egypt, I thought it vital to document not simply the government's efforts at family planning but women's and men's personal and individual reactions to what could be viewed as an attempt to regulate the most private aspects of their lives. This was a society, after all, where children were universally desired and admired, as our own son and daughters had happily learned during their years in Egypt. Here neither men nor women were considered mature adults until they had produced children, children who were a source not only of pride and affection, but of economic assistance, insurance for parents' old age, and, last but not least, a continuation of the family line.

The Cairo Family Planning Association and the Media Campaign Personnel were very hospitable, and I was invited to several clinics, both in the city and in the country. In one Delta village an impressive experimental program was in progress, based on a cooperative effort between the overworked woman doctor at the government clinic and Sadika Mahmoud, a local woman, described in the experimental program brochure as the "volunteer village leader."

"I can't imagine anybody not wanting children," said Sadika, a warmhearted, intelligent mother of three, wife of the local elementary school principal. "Everyone wants them. But these days you know, times are changing. Many women tell me that they don't really want more than three or four. They can't afford to feed them."

She spoke as though this were a new idea, and in some sense it was. She wanted sincerely to help women limit their families to a more manageable number, and her work was showing results. In her village, thanks to the cooperative program, the number of women using contraceptives had risen from 3 to 30 percent in two years. A hopeful sign locally, but it would have to happen nationally—and fast—if it was to make any difference. Though the average number of births per woman was falling slightly, the downturn could not overcome the inevitable cycle of multiplying births that had begun a half century earlier. Egypt's population was growing at a staggering annual rate of 3 percent per year, and the projected population for 1985 was 50 million.

"We can only try," said Sadika, when I talked about the national figures. "Three or four children in a family is better than it used to be."

She was right. In 1965, for example, women in one rural area averaged thirteen pregnancies each, but only five of those children survived. The death rate had declined since then, but the memories of an earlier generation were still fresh. Fear of loss of children led to larger families, much larger than the total of three or four that Sadika was trying to promote in her village. And even though half of Egypt's people had become city dwellers, and hence children were not needed as laborers on the farms, they could still work in the cities. More children could mean more incomes, however small those incomes might be.

The only way to deal with the growing population was to increase the productivity of the nation, President Nasser had said, and President Sadat had concurred. The two leaders had gone about it in different ways, Nasser opting for control and central organization, Sadat trying out free trade and encouraging foreign investment and private business. And over the years since 1959, the gross national product had increased. The industrial plant was also impressive, but the results had not been as glorious as had been hoped. In fact, after initial early improvements, the overall economic situation had slowly worsened. The Egypt that could feed itself in 1964 was by 1981 importing 60 percent of all its food. And the 1981 trade deficit was estimated at $4.8 billion. Of course, there were signs of prosperity everywhere—the cars, the consumer goods, the well-dressed Egyptians in foreign banks and luxury hotels. But this was deceptive, if only because it was seen just in those places most frequented by foreigners. Millions of Egyptians were no better off than they had been when we had first come a quarter of a century before. The Egyptian economy seemed to have come to a standstill, like the apartment blocks and luxury hotels that stood unfinished throughout Cairo, waiting for a new injection of capital so building could begin again.

In 1983, when we returned for a brief visit, Egypt, on the surface, did not seem to have changed much since 1981, except for another great chasm in the earth, this time right in the center of town. Midan al-Tahrir, the traffic circle that commemorated Nasser's time, was being excavated to make way for a modern subway! The traffic was still frantic, but efforts had been made to improve the flow with the completion of several new overpasses and cloverleafs. Even the pedestrian walkways were painted in bright greens and blues. Painters and builders had been at work in downtown Cairo refurbishing stores and buildings, in defiance of the dust that still settled everywhere, like a fine film of decay that disappeared at the first light wind, only to settle somewhere else. The television had kept its nightly audience, but the annual birth rate had dropped slightly, from 3 to 2.9 percent. Islamic dress was still evident on the streets, among both men and women. Whatever the excesses of the fundamentalists who declared their responsibility for Sadat's assassination, the majority of Egyptians had separated that act from the other, more personal aspects of Muslim identity. And more mosques had been illuminated, many with green neon lights that shone brightly in the dark quarters of Cairo's new suburbs.

President Sadat had been dead for nearly two years, and the shock of his assassination had subsided. Hosni Mubarak, his successor, was a different kind of man: low-keyed, quiet, almost self-effacing. But he began his term of office by dealing firmly and effectively with the young army officers who had killed Sadat, an act that some saw as a bizarre and twisted replay of the Free Officers' Revolt in 1952. President Mubarak had attacked corruption, bringing to trial Sadat's own brother. These were highly visible actions, much approved by the general populace, it seemed. The economy, sluggish and slow, was tackled next. Mubarak cut back on imports, particularly cars, by increasing import taxes. And he reduced government subsidies of many food items, such as imported cheese, olive oil, and beer, which had been consumed principally by more prosperous citizens. But he did not advocate checks on free enterprise, either in industry or in any other private sector, and this included agriculture. Indeed, by 1983, the government was offering generous subsidies in both spheres, rather than direct government control as in Nasser's time.

Government subsidies were helping many people, including, to our surprise, Sharif, a young college-educated friend of Tom Hartwell's who had worked for CBS in 1981. Sharif, a handsome and eminently urban young man, had resigned from CBS and gone back to the land.

"The farm is a lot more interesting than television journalism," he said, laughing a little. And when Bob and I looked slightly skeptical, he invited us to come to his ezba and see for ourselves.

"An ezba?" I repeated, remembering other visits to other ezbas in bygone days, the large estates of Amina's family, of Dr. Laila's family.

Sharif nodded. "Yes, I guess it's an ezba, but not like the old pashas'. It's our family place, but we hardly ever lived there. My father had an overseer who lived on the place, grew animal fodder, had water buffalo, sold the milk. But my father never was interested in changing things."

"How does he feel about your taking it over?"

Sharif drew back slightly. "Well, he's not giving it to me, Bob, I've leased it from him. I'll either make it or I won't. I'm raising chickens for the Cairo market; they buy them from me the minute they're ready to cook."

"Big population. Big appetite," said Bob.

Sharif nodded. "And I'm working on improving the milk yield from the water buffalo, the *jamoosa.* They're a lot of trouble, jamoosas." He paused, and his handsome face lit up. "But what characters. I'd really miss them if I had to get rid of them. They don't bring in as much as the chickens. Come see."

"We'd love to come," said Bob.

Sharif came to collect us one morning in his old Toyota, on the way to the farm with some refrigerated serum against Newcastle disease, a common malady of chickens raised in chicken houses rather than in chicken yards. Sharif was being cautious with this batch of five thousand chicks, he said, because the last time had been a disaster. One thousand young chicks had died in an hour in a heat wave, halfway through their six-week growing cycle. Chickens were profitable, he said, but chancy; if all went well he could expect to clear $2,500.

"Not bad for six weeks' work," commented Bob.

"Yes, *if* all goes well. But heat or disease can wipe out my profits and leave me with interest that has to be paid. Poor people can't take the risk!"

The government subsidies helped the larger farmers most, he said, subsidies for chicken feed and fertilizer and price supports when the chickens were marketed.

"Economies of scale."

"What, Bob?"

"The bigger the operation, the greater the profit and loss margins."

Sharif nodded absently, swerving quickly to avoid a bicyclist balancing a large box on his head, who had veered suddenly in front of us.

For an hour we pushed through the heavy morning city traffic heading east toward Heliopolis, once the center of religious life for the ancient Egyptians, now a middle-class residential suburb that gave way to housing projects and to textile factories on the north, military training schools and barracks at the northeast. The international airport lay straight ahead.

Sharif pointed out a complex of condominiums ahead of us as we turned off the main Cairo road. "One of Nasser's last promises," said Sharif. "*Alif sukaan.* The project of a thousand houses. Still not quite finished. Like a lot of his plans. But, you know, Bob, he was a good president. He really tried. Mubarak's trying, too, with private enterprise, like in America. That's how I got my loans, he's opened things up."

"But will it be enough?" asked Bob. "Can you raise enough food?"

Sharif shrugged. "Maybe not. But what else can we do but try?"

We had suddenly left urban life behind. After the blare of automobile horns and the roar of buses, the noises of the countryside were like a balm, a release from irritation: the bray of a donkey, the whine of an occasional mechanical water wheel, and the gentle twittering of small birds dipping down and rising above the fields. The green land, stretching away on each side of the road, was marked off by banana trees that rustled in the morning breeze, by stands of palms, heavy now with clusters of dates in different shades—yellow, red, and brown—waiting to be harvested. A cart ahead of us, its wheels creaking, and donkeys, loaded with baskets of newly picked dates for the village markets, moved over for our Toyota to pass.

"Why do they have to have the date market exactly where it's always been, right in the middle of the bridge?" Sharif asked testily as he maneuvered around the approach to the narrow bridge, where scores of men and women sat close together offering baskets of dates for sale. The road spanned a large feeder canal, the focus of the village, and here the harvested dates were everywhere.

"Beautiful! Look at that!" I murmured, looking down as we crossed the canal, where enormous clumps of violet flowers grew outward from the grassy banks and stood in the water.

"You may think they're beautiful, B.J. Not me!" said Sharif. "They choke up the canal and cut down on the flow of water we get for the crops. And nobody wants to clean them out. They're like elastic or something. I clean my part, but the others won't cooperate. It's a real headache."

"Problems, problems," said Bob lightly, eyeing the new Sharif, who until recently had appeared to be a dedicated playboy and who now worried about water hyacinths and canal cleaning.

Sharif laughed. "Well, it *is* more interesting than working for television," he said. "And I can still go to Cairo on Fridays and see my friends."

Tomato plants were sprouting in the field nearest us. The fall wheat was coming up, row upon row of green shoots, and yellow mustard burgeoned in the fallow furrows. In the distance one field seemed to be dotted with white blossoms, but as we came closer I saw they were rows of small white birds pecking at the earth.

"Ibis? The sacred ibis?"

"No, B.J. They're something else, I can't remember the English word. We call them the 'friend of the fellah'; they eat bad bugs. Maybe you've seen them on TV, sitting on the water buffalo's backs and eating the fleas? Egrets," he brought out triumphantly, "that's what you call them!"

To our left, a large rambling house was visible, shaded by thick trees, protected by high walls.

"Nahas Pasha's house. Muhammad Naguib has been there for years, under government supervision. His son is there too. But Naguib is sick, in and out of the hospital."

"Naguib? I thought Nasser had let him stay in town."

"Maybe," said Sharif. "I don't know. But anyway Mubarak is different. Naguib is an old, old man. He probably likes the country better. Nicer here than in Cairo now."

"Yes," I answered.

Still, it seemed ironic that General Muhammad Naguib, leader of the 1952 Free Officers' Revolt that unseated King Farouk and such leaders of Parliament as Nahas Pasha, should now live out his days in the country retreat of his former political enemy.

Sharif turned a corner quickly into a driveway, with a yellow stone house and a garden on one side, and a farm compound on the other.

"Here we are!" he said. "And there's Ahmed. He helps with the chickens. Now we all have to work fast to get the serum into them. Do you want to help?"

We said we would be glad to help.

In the new, modern chicken house, screened and airy, Ahmed and Sharif mixed the vials of serum into the barrels of water, and then each of us, bearing tin cups, began to fill the water trays, narrow rims along the red plastic cone-shaped trays that hung like lanterns in rows from the ceiling. One by one, we lowered the trays after they had filled, so the chickens could drink, five thousand of them, half grown, softly chirping and peeping and following us or rushing from us in waves of moving white feathers as we walked across the newly cleaned floor.

"Don't let it down too low, B.J.," cautioned Sharif.

"It's so they can drink more easily."

"Yes, I know, but that's what I'm trying to *avoid*. I want them to work a little," he said, "stand up straight, stretch a bit to eat and drink. That strengthens their legs, gives them a bit of muscle, improves their appetite."

"So they gain more weight and you can sell them for more?"

"Exactly."

"What kind of chickens are they, Sharif? My aunt Mary used to raise white Leghorns. These look like them."

Sharif, tall, dark, and handsome, answered, "Don't know. They're French, they're white, and the Ministry of Agriculture is pushing them this season."

Five thousand chickens stretched their legs to drink, pecked at the scientifically mixed food that Ahmed and Sharif put in the feeders for them.

"They're thirty days along in their forty-five-day growing time," said Sharif, pleased with himself, "gaining weight and feathers, as you can see," and he picked up one white cheeping example to show us the fattening thighs.

This was obviously another kind of ezba. Another kind of farmer. No need for ritualized entertainment of guests (leisurely coffee, then luncheon served by old family retainers, followed by a tour of the grounds). Nothing embarrassing about honest work; you and your guests rush to the chicken coops together and administer serum to five thousand chirping, cheeping half-grown white fowl.

It was a pleasant estate house, utilitarian and comfortable. A workmanlike compound, stable, barns, housing for the hired men. And a small mosque, newly built so that the doors and windows looked not inward to the stable yards but outward, to the fields, where bright blue morning glories spilled over the mud-brick walls.

"It was my duty to build a mosque here, Bob, for our help," Sharif explained.

We did have a tour of the grounds, however, for Sharif wanted to show off his much prized water buffalo, all twenty-eight of them, who gave the richest milk in the neighborhood, Sharif said proudly.

"They're a big investment, two thousand dollars *each*. And they're strong. Independent. You have to have one man to stake out and work with every three buffalo. And I have to pay each of the men at least $120 per month. In the old days around here, we'd pay fifteen cents a day."

"There they are!" He raised his arm and pointed to the fields beside the farm road, where the great beasts stood, their curving horns vaguely reminiscent of Texas longhorn cattle, though these animals were heavier, broader in the beam. They were staked out on long ropes, but one (at two or three tons of weight) had already managed to pull up her stake and wandered forward, nuzzling into the earth for choice bits of grass, and pausing occasionally to raise her head and stare at us as we walked slowly down the dirt road, separated from the beasts in the field only by a narrow irrigation canal, where the troublesome but beautiful water hyacinths grew.

"We didn't own a lot of land, my father's family, I mean," explained Sharif. "My grandfather had a little land in Zagazig, but he was a judge there. When my father came to Cairo, during Nasser's time, he sold the Zagazig spread and bought this."

"It's lovely here, Sharif," I said. "Nicer than Cairo in many ways."

He nodded. "I'd like to stay on, I think. But now my father wants to sell at least part of this land to developers."

"Developers. Here?"

"Yes, they're already on their way. See those houses over there? See that fence? All that land has already been sold, and the plots marked out for houses."

"People who would work in Cairo and commute here?" from Bob.

"Exactly. But I say to my father, what will they live *on* if all the land is used for houses? They're already scraping the loam off up along the river, and making it into bricks," Sharif said bitterly. "Spending millions to reclaim land up north and here they're burning up the best soil. People are crazy."

"But that's illegal, to use the farmland like that."

"Yes, sure, but they do it anyway. The workers come back from Saudi Arabia with money and they want good brick houses. Houses are more important than food? What're they thinking about?"

He had walked to the end of the road, through the dappled shade of morning cast by the cottonwoods and palms, and now turned back.

"It's called progress, I believe," said Bob.

"Mmm." Sharif did not answer. After a bit, he said, "This land still belongs to my father. He can sell it if he wants to. I have to make a good enough profit on the chickens and the jamoosas together so I can buy some land myself, and convince him it makes more sense to farm than sell."

"The jamoosas aren't profitable?"

"Oh yes, I make about a thousand dollars per month from the milk, but the profits aren't as much or as quick as chickens. Jamoosa profits are like jamoosas look: sure, steady—and slow."

Ahmed came out of the chicken house to wave goodbye. We set out for Cairo, past the date market, more crowded than before.

"If I could build a milk-processing plant here," Sharif was saying, "I could do a lot better on the jamoosas. I'm trying to get Ali to go in with me. Then I could pay back my loans to the Agricultural Bank and buy a lot of land before it's gone forever."

Bob said, "Why not?"

Sharif sighed. "There may not be time," he said. "There aren't many people like me out here. Most people say to hell with it and sell out to the developers. It's easier. You don't have to work, you don't have to mess with the government, this office, that form. I had one guy who put pressure on me just last month to do a scam on the Ministry of Agriculture—"

"And—?" said Bob.

"And of course I refused. I'm not into that. But I had to refuse very carefully, because I still have to do business with that guy all the time."

"Corruption even in the chicken business?" asked Bob.

"You said it," answered Sharif. "Not me."

We drove on, through orange groves, past fig trees, grape arbors, planted in full sun.

"But you know, Bob, all that propaganda about people going hungry in Egypt. That's not true. There's enough here. Look at this beautiful land. But it has to be used right." He paused. "They should sell it to me, not to the developers. The developers aren't developing it, they're destroying it. It's the *farmers* that develop the land, that make it work."

"Yes."

Sharif laughed shortly. "Sounds like I think I'm important, doesn't it? I don't. I like what I'm doing. It's interesting, and I'm making good money. But I'm Egyptian, too, you know, and I think the land is important. If it goes, so does Egypt."

We had reached the crossroads beside the unfinished thousand houses. Behind us lay the ezba, the fig trees, the lemon and orange groves, the stands of date palms laden with ripe fruit, and the newly planted fertile fields where the small white egrets presumably still sat and quietly ate insects. Was it possible that such land could really disappear, be scraped up and burned, and its remains filled in with asphalt so that a few hundred more cars and a few hundred more houses could be fitted in where the tomatoes and wheat were now growing?

"It's possible," said Sharif.

Sharif's optimism, the busy country date market, the lush fertility of the countryside around his ezba, were difficult to reconcile with the dismal statements about Egypt's economic condition published in the foreign press and in academic journals. According to these analysts, Egypt was an economic disaster area that would collapse if outside aid from Saudi Arabia or the United States should cease.

Yet Egypt did not look as if she was teetering on the edge of disaster. With all the overcrowding in Cairo, the barely adequate public facilities, great strides forward had been taken in improving basic services such as electrification and piped water. New overpasses and bridges had begun to relieve some of the worst bottlenecks in Cairo traffic by 1983. Cairo still had one of the lowest crime rates in the world. To us, and to many more privileged Egyptians and resident foreigners, the decline in the quality of life—pollution, lack of services—was a sign of decay. Yet there was another side. In 1983 some Egyptians who had begun life as poor as many of their fellow countrymen were making money and enjoying material comforts. Asian labor was actually being imported into Egypt, as Egyptians found better jobs abroad. Even if upward mobility was still exceptional, if only one out of twenty Egyptians had been able to buy cars and TV sets and approach the "good life" so explicitly depicted on local TV soaps, the example served to encourage hundreds of thousands of others.

Egypt has tried state socialism and free enterprise and, under President Mubarak, a more careful mixture of both. It has experienced foreign rule and foreign patronage under the Turks, French, British, Russians, and now the

Americans. "Can we survive the Americans?" one of our older and more sanguine Egyptian friends asked at a dinner one night.

"You mean because of the peace treaty with Israel?" an American student asked.

"No," he said. "I mean because of the corruption, the money being made from AID contracts, the get-rich-fast attitudes."

But not all the money flowing into the pockets of Egyptians comes from American assistance; most of this aid, under U.S. law, must be used to buy American goods and services in any case. By 1983 over $3 billion of hard currency was estimated to be coming into Egypt each year from migrant workers, an amount greater than any other source of foreign exchange. Although the male migration rate was leveling off, the female migration rate was rising, as the demand for teachers, nurses, and maids in the oil-rich countries increased. This unexpected injection of wealth had the added virtue of bypassing governments and going directly into the pockets of the people who earned the money. The resourcefulness and ingenuity of Egyptians has always made a difference in the unfavorable ratio between the resources of the country and the needs of its people. Of course, the inevitable result of labor migration spending, labor shortages, and higher wages is inflation. Millions of Egyptians are hard pressed to maintain minimum standards of living and as a result depend on government subsidies of basic food as well as on their own arduous efforts to keep whole families at work, often at several jobs at once. A slight rise in the price of bread resulted in rioting in Cairo in 1977 with the burning of nightclubs and other symbols of wealth. The specter of uncontrollable disorder was clearly presented to Sadat's government and its American security advisers. Thus it seems doubtful that a rise in basic food prices will be permitted again.

American patronage has been a limited success so far, providing capital for joint business ventures, foreign job openings, opportunities of making money in foreign banks, and a limited range of other possibilities in the local economy's Westernized sector. But Egypt is not a Western country and never will be. In mosques and private homes, hundreds of thousands of young men and women look with disfavor on what they regard as the moral corruption associated with Western-inspired prosperity. They regard peace with Israel as a betrayal of Muslim brotherhood, and they see the Israeli presence as a return to infidel colonialism, with only token differences. The mild optimism we sensed among working- and lower-middle-class Egyptians we knew, as well as among the younger, educated men like Sharif, could quickly disappear, given a loss of job opportunities abroad, a decline in Egypt's current limited prosperity.

The Islamic advocates of radical reform, of return to government based on Islamic principles, are waiting in the background for an opportunity to press their case. Whether their outlook is practical or hopelessly utopian has yet to be determined. But their case is not unappealing to the majority of their fellow citizens. For in many ways, the Egyptian community is a classic example of human strengths and limitations. Hard as they might try to expand their economy (and they have tried with the High Dam, with the renovation of the Suez Canal), Egyptians have limited national resources. In the modern era of great power struggles and international market systems, Egypt as a country has little control over its fate. A drop in international oil prices, for example, would send Egyptian workers home, a prospect that looked possible by the summer of 1983.

But Egypt, after all, is not only rocks and sand and fertile fields. Egypt is its people, who are, one official quipped, the burden of Egypt as well as the bearers of that burden. However, the Egyptians whom we had known in the sixties, whom we had seen again in the eighties, did not seem to have fallen into despair when contemplating their own personal futures. They were all—Omar, Aziza, Sharif, Muhammad, Nabila, Dr. Laila, Sadika, Abdulla, and Um Fethy—doing their best to survive creatively in circumstances not of their own making. In 1983 Egyptians were still finding places in the crowded city to have family picnics by the river, they were still telling ironic jokes about themselves and their leaders, they were still trying to achieve a stable and pleasant life for themselves and their families. Perhaps this personal hope bodes well for the nation.

Yet Egyptians as individuals can only do so much, and they know it. As Nabila once said to me, "We are all guests of God on this earth," and guests have responsibilities as well as privileges, not only to their hosts but to each other. Nabila and many others of her fellow citizens are beginning to wonder whether those responsibilities are being fulfilled as class differences increase in modern Egypt.

Comment

RELIGIOUS FUNDAMENTALISM

"FUNDAMENTALISM" has been a term much used recently, applied by our media (with considerable abandon) to religious phenomena in both the Middle East and the United States. Indeed, there do seem to be some basic similarities between the born-again Christians, modestly attired, and the born-again Muslims, bearded or veiled. Both are attempting to return to their own versions of God's truth, based on what is felt to be a literal acceptance of His word, whether in the Bible or the Koran. Thus, whether in Egypt or in America, this means the rejection of certain behavior felt to be contrary to God's will and the injection of a religious consciousness into many areas of daily life previously regarded as secular or even profane. Is there not something analogous between the American boy who says he lifts weights for God and the Egyptian girl who studies engineering veiled, gloved, and totally robed? Are not both a form of fundamentalist behavior?

Such apparently similar styles of behavior must be related to the contexts in which they occur. For while we cannot examine the inner states of mind which accompany such forms of piety, it is reasonable to ask what significance such acts may have as a form of social communication. What do the conspicuous signs of godliness mean to those who adopt them and those who in daily life observe them?

In the United States, signs of godliness are announcements of preference for a more conservative pattern of social behavior. At least among high school and college students this is very important. A person who is "born again" cannot be teased or ridiculed because he or she drinks little or no alcohol, smokes no pot, and refuses to engage in sexual intercourse after a couple of dates. Indeed, such behavior, seen as evidence of newly important religious faith, earns respect and support, even from many sinners. The nonbelievers find it prudent to keep their cynicism to themselves. Fundamentalism provides a high road through the new and uncharted frontiers of post-Pill sexuality and street-corner pharmacopoeias. It's a way to say no and it is the basis for warm friendship among fellow believers.

For the young Middle Eastern man or woman the contemporary social scene is also new and unprecedented if compared with that of parents and grandparents.

In Cairo, scene of perhaps the strongest Arab Islamic fundamentalist movements, the middle-class standing to which ever larger numbers of Egyptians
aspire certainly cannot be obtained or sustained without wage-earning by wife as
well as husband. In the last thirty years this has meant the assumption of Western
dress by both men and women and the association of male and female employees who are unrelated to each other. Brotherly and sisterly terms of address are
often used in work situations, suggesting that forms of mutual respect may be
developing between men and women. But riding the bus and walking the
crowded streets mean constant and often very close contact with strangers. One
has only to observe the respect with which the modestly dressed working
woman is treated in Cairo today to know how rewarding this must be after a few
(or many) experiences of her being shoved, pushed, and often manhandled in
short skirts, Western style.

So, insofar as conservative dress is concerned, it is the public situation which is
changing for the better for women in a city like Cairo. In the United States, it is
more the problems of private relations in private settings which are made less
complicated for the young, unmarried woman by the new fundamentalism. In
neither case are born-again Christians or conservatively dressed or veiled Muslim women returning to some old-fashioned, traditional form of behavior. For
many of the grandmothers (and even some of the mothers) of the middle-class
working women in Cairo today would not have appeared in the street in the
past, veiled or otherwise. Nor would many of the great-grandmothers (or
grandmothers) of American girls have been allowed to party with boys without
benefit of chaperones. At least for many Egyptian and American women, signs
of religion solve two quite different sets of problems, one public, the other
private.

But this is only one aspect of Christian and Muslim fundamentalism today.
The movements involve both sexes and speak to wider issues. Recently, in
Dalhart, Texas, we watched a well-produced TV program in which two ministers, one white and one black, calmly explained why films such as *E.T.* and
Poltergeist were to be avoided by good Christians. Why? Not because evil spirits,
demons, and other nonhuman creatures such as are portrayed in such films do
not exist. Indeed, they do exist, the ministers insisted, and they cited passages in
the Bible to support this contention. Such films are satanic because they show
extraterrestrial Muppet-like beings curing wounds with a touch of their inhuman
(and ungodly) fingers, while mediums and other spiritualists (rather than the
ministers of God) are shown driving out demons.

The restatement of orthodoxy has, of course, been extended to schoolbooks
and libraries as well as films. For those who do not share the sense of what is
godly and what is not, such attempts to order the world are most unwelcome:
we cannot accept the religious significance which some but by no means all
fundamentalists would attach to forms of entertainment and intellectual interest.

In the Middle Eastern context the more militant forms of Islamic fundamentalism carry a far different set of concerns. Basic to those concerns is an overall

criticism of the socioeconomic status quo from what has historically been an irreproachable position: religious faith. It is not the poor of Egypt who adopt, on religious grounds, a critical stance toward the rich and powerful. Rather it is the men and women of the fledgling middle class (women in modest dress, men in beards and white robes) who implicitly and explicitly condemn the excesses of the Western-style nouveaux riches.

For Americans who have not lived in Egypt, it is difficult to appreciate the overwhelming quality of the Western presence, especially the American presence. The American Embassy in Cairo is one of the largest in the world; the total American population in Egypt is close to ten thousand. Along with our technology go our sales techniques, administrative methods, ideas about investment and economic growth. Accompanying these methods and ideas are rock music, bars and nightclubs full of alcohol and fashionably dressed women and men. In the more European areas of the city, high-priced prostitution flourishes. To the fundamentalist Muslim (and many other Muslims, it must be emphasized) this general pattern of behavior is not only sinful, it is seen as the herald of a new phase of Western domination. And it also signals the loss of Egyptian, Arab, and/or Muslim ways of life—a shameful loss of independence, respectability, and honor itself.

If the militant fundamentalists in America share a concern for the "right" way of life, it is essential to understand that in the United States this means imposing on one another forms of orthodoxy about which there is no agreement but about which our differences of opinion are as old as American society. The "right" way of life is seen here as one that existed in our own historical past and to which we must return. In the Middle East the concern is somewhat different: many Islamic fundamentalists see their enemy as Western in origin, a force from outside their society, one as alien as the weapons for their armies and the episodes of "Dallas" on their television screens. And it is this alien force that needs to be criticized, even fought against, so the "right" way of life may be reestablished, so that honor and independence may be restored.

CHAPTER XII

Hail, Saudi Arabia

1983

> How often, when the country is barren and dry,
> The people are more generous than nature,
> Not scorning, coldly, their fellow man,
> But giving, as naturally as the wind blows.
> Among our lineage, our ancestors, we see
> How hospitable were the old ones of the tribe—
> We come from a tradition of generosity,
> Of riches, nobility and greatness.
>
> Labid
> *Mu'allaqa*

THE REAL ARABIA, for romantic Westerners and travelers since the Middle Ages, lies in the deserts of the region and among the nomadic Bedouin, who are believed to wander about in those deserts living in tents and raising camels. Even within the Middle Eastern world, the Bedouin has a special place in the hearts and minds of Arabs themselves, for the word still symbolizes a purity and courage associated with right living and right thinking. The city is the seat of corruption, but the desert is seen as the place where morality is a natural outcome of a life-style free of laxity brought about by material comforts and self-indulgence. The Prophet Muhammad was a city man, from the important mercantile center of Mecca in the Arabian Peninsula. But, like many men of the period, he had spent time with nomads as a child and in middle life he retreated to the desert again to hear the words of God.

Yet the attitude of today's settled Arabs toward the nomads is ambivalent. Generally, nomads and their life-style are seen as having no place in modern society. Old resentments also rankle, memories of the days when desert uprisings made travel risky and when Bedouin raids on towns and villages were common occurrences. Townspeople, in some contexts, also characterize Bedouin as ignorant, indifferent in the practice of Islam, and generally unreliable. Thus the logic follows that nomads, for their own good, must be encouraged to leave their historic ways and settle down in one place—preferably as farmers. Like the forest outlaws of medieval England, nomads may be unequivocally admired in the Middle East only when they no longer exist.

The movement to settle the nomads in the Middle East coincided with the end of the Western colonial period in countries such as Iraq and Egypt. Tribes had always played a role in the area's politics, but the Western-educated Arab urbanites who took control of the new nationalist governments viewed with dismay and distaste the special interest and attention given to nomad tribes by colonial administrators, travelers, and writers. During the mandate period, English and French administrators had officially recognized sheikhs as tribal representatives in some countries, and eventually appointed them members of Parliament. Customary tribal law was also recognized in the legal codes of the time. "Tribes are a primitive form of social organization," said one Iraqi government official, and another said to Bob in 1957, "What did the British think we Arabs were, American Indians?" In the newly independent countries of the fifties and sixties, the official, publicly stated view of the tribal Bedouin was that they were a remnant of a primitive past and must be settled as soon as possible.

Today, in most countries of the Middle East, the percentage of nomadic Bedouin is small, about 2 percent in Egypt, for example. But in Saudi Arabia, despite twenty-five years of gradual sedentarization, the nomads still constitute a significant segment of the population, nearly 20 percent. That percentage was considerably larger in 1964, when Bob went out to Saudi Arabia to conduct a brief socioeconomic survey of the newly settled Bedouin in the Wadi Serhan, a valley in the northern part of the kingdom, between Sakaka and Al-Qurayat. An American engineering firm had contracted with the Saudi government to evaluate the first efforts at government-sponsored Bedouin settlement in the valley. At that time, a six-year drought had reduced the available natural pasture to almost nothing, and thus the animal-dependent nomads were welcoming an opportunity to shift to sedentary cultivation. Government policy at the time seemed to coincide with Bedouin needs and desires.

The early results looked promising. The valley of the Wadi Serhan had, only fifteen years before, in 1950, produced nothing but "dates and a few tomatoes for the market," Bob wrote. But by 1964, the area under cultivation in Sakaka oasis alone had doubled, thanks to the opening of new lands by the central government. The government had also provided funds for irrigation, and for administrative personnel from the nation's capital, to help launch new agricultural activity and encourage further settlement. Though a few nomad Bedouin remained in the area in 1964, their plight was pathetic. Bob wrote, "Their flocks are barely enough to keep them alive and several [of the men] said that their children, women and animals had died in the past few years and that they had been reduced to catching rabbits, birds, even rats in order to eat. Most of the people I talked to say they would like to settle down."

Everything seemed poised for the move from nomadic pastoralism to sedentary agriculture. But there were problems. Successful farming in Wadi Serhan depended on the development of new water sources, specifically the new wells with engine-powered pumps, for the water of the oases' ancient artesian wells was already fully used by the settled Arabs of the oases. The government had foreseen the need and had supplied the wells and pumps. But the farmers were inexperienced and pumped too much water onto the oasis land, drowning the spring plants and causing large areas to become so saline that no crops would grow at all. Even some of the date palms, staple plants of the oasis, were dying. Everywhere Bob and his companions were shown broken pumps whose owners were unable to find spare parts or mechanics to repair them.

Finally, not enough land could be made available to take care of all the nomads who wished to settle down. These early problems led many farmers to hold on to their animals against the possibility of crop failure. Bob noted that most of the farmers in the valley settlements, from Jawf to Sakaka, kept a few sheep and goats near their new houses, and in some cases had farmed out more animals to their kinsmen who were still nomads.

Thus efforts to settle the nomads in the sixties did not fail because of Bedouin resistance. Drought and loss of pasture were breaking down the old preferences for a pastoral existence. Many Bedouin were already settled and others interviewed by Bob in the sixties expressed hope that they would soon be able to do the same. The problem was that in 1962 the Saudi government simply could not afford to pay the infrastructural costs of a complete changeover. Pumps and land were not enough; support services such as market roads and agricultural extension assistance, as well as pump parts and repair services, were vital, too.

In 1983, Bob returned to Saudi Arabia, again to do a demographic and economic survey of Bedouin, this time in the province or emirate of Hail, southeast of the Wadi Serhan, where he had worked nearly twenty years before. As part of his 1963 report, he had written that "development schemes are only worthwhile if they are economically feasible in the specific social and cultural setting of the people they are intended to benefit." The post-OPEC Saudi Arabian government of the 1980s could afford to take such advice seriously and had accordingly hired an American planning and engineering firm to provide a long-range program of economic development for the Hail Emirate. The plan was to take into account the specific characteristics of the Hail population, whether nomadic, agricultural, or urban, and try to forecast the population's needs over the next twenty years. Bob's particular assignment in the spring and summer of 1983 was to survey the condition of the nomadic Bedouin in the area and to try to contribute some information concerning the economic and demographic aspects of nomadic life to the overall planning process. The Bedouin population of Hail fluctuates according to the time of the year and the weather conditions, but it was generally considered to consist of from 10 to 20 percent of the total population. Between the Hail Emirate and the valley of Wadi Serhan lies the Great Nafud desert, heart of historic nomad life in the Nejd. Through this great desert the Bedouin used to travel by foot and camel each year in search of water and pasture. Bob set off in a Jeep to look for them.

"Things look much better than when I was here before," Bob wrote in one of his first letters.

It is not the stick of famine but the carrot of land grants, generous loans, and subsidies for machinery, housing, and crops that makes farming not only a more attractive but a more secure venture than it was in 1965. And what a wonderful difference to see no more ragged tents, thin people and animals, real dust bowl scenes. People show every sign of prosperity. Now I have to start traveling around in the area to see if my initial impressions can be justified by hard data from interviews.

The Great Nafud Desert
July 12, 1983, 1:50 P.M.

Dear B.J., At this moment my Jeep is stuck in the top of a sand dune. I am filthy dirty because I had a flat tire an hour ago and had to crawl around in the hot sand to change it; my hands are still scorched from that experience. Lucky I am in good shape or I would have had a heart attack, it was so hot and the tires were so damn heavy. As to my present situation, a Bedu tent with a truck is visible on the horizon about two miles ahead and I think I am on a main track so it seems unlikely I will perish here. The wheels of the Jeep are in sand up to the hubcaps and there is nothing I can do but sit in the cab out of the sun and hope some truck will eventually pass by and pull me out. I am more ashamed than frightened for having driven so badly, particularly because I said I did not want the driver to come along. So goeth pride. However, I intend to stay out here for five days interviewing nomads and I did not want the driver on my hands. Besides, when a native speaker of Arabic is with me all the conversation flows in his direction and no one tries to understand me because of my bad pronunciation of the local Arabic dialect.

Fortunately, I do have a lot of water with me—supposedly enough for the whole trip. It is so hot here (120° F., I suppose) that I can hardly touch the steering wheel. I'll need to drink a lot. I guess I do feel a kind of panic. Though I know I will be found eventually, the space around me is so vast and so fearsomely hot that it is frightening. I think of some of Paul Bowles' stories and get a tightness in my stomach.

One bad thing is that this is the *Id,* the second day of the big holiday after Ramadan, and all right-minded people are celebrating with their friends and families. I wish I were.

It is very annoying to be within a few feet of solid ground but still unable to move. It happened to me once on the beach in Oregon. I was worried about the tide then, but not as much as I'm worried about the heat here. I also hate the idea of having to confront strangers with my stupidity.

I don't like being here at all, soaking wet, sweat running down my face. I am getting too old for this sort of thing. My heart is racing, just sitting here. I don't feel like writing anymore.

2:15, same afternoon

I doubt I have ever shared such feelings with you, but I have always thought that deserts can provide a particularly horrible kind of death. The idea of hell must come from bad experiences on deserts like this, from stories that big Bedouin tell little Bedouin as warnings against getting stuck out here. The Nubians hated the desert. Their houses faced the Nile, the palm groves, and gardens along the riverbanks. Somehow, when I was living there on the edge of the Sahara, I never thought of the desert behind me unless I walked to the end of the village and noticed the sand which was gradually blowing over the deserted houses there. No way to stop the blowing sand. The Nubians never went out behind the villages except to bury their dead. They felt the desert was full of unfriendly creatures, and since they used to be regularly raided by the nomads, they were right.

At this moment the silence really seems deafening. It seems to hum in my ears. Behind me is sand. Below and ahead of me as far as I can see are rolling hills of sand with widely scattered tufts of brown grass, scrubby shrubs, and that one distant black tent. I am glad that tent is there. If by night no one has come by I will flash my headlights and perhaps the people in that tent will drive over to see what is up—or down. Nobody expects me, nobody is worrying about me, so if I must stay here all night no one will be concerned, except me, that is. I have an orange and half a sandwich. I am beginning to feel better. Perhaps I will just continue to write. We never pay much attention to what anyone is saying but ourselves, so why should letter-writing be regarded as a chore? Too much of a commitment, I suppose. Anyway, I don't feel very wise or smart just now, only dirty and worried.

The desert is still empty. Perhaps I am the only damn fool in these parts who would try to cross the Nafud in the middle of the day. I was here once before but I wasn't driving and you can't get the hang of sand driving without doing it.

Turaba, the town I was heading for when I got stuck, looks like a teardrop on the relief map. It is a flat basin which has remained uncovered by sand because its position is in the lee of a small clump of mountains. The wind blows the sand around the mountains and leaves this clear space. Turaba has no agriculture. It is a service center for the Bedouin. They come in to buy supplies and get their pickup trucks gassed up. When I was here before and stayed overnight with the Emir of Turaba, he struck me as a very tough gentleman. He is the voice of the government here and I guess it must have to be a loud one; all the tribesmen I saw last time were armed.

The wind has picked up. The sudden gusts which whip around the Jeep have the effect of voices, indistinct and blurred like those of a crowd which are blown in from a long way away. A single gust comes across like the muffled voice of an announcer at some distant game. I have to leave the windows open or I'd be cooked, but the air burns my neck as it blows through the Jeep. I hope I can get out of this mess without having some kind of rescue mission. I can just hear the authorities asking, "Why did you let him go out here alone?" "Because he is fifty-one years old and we thought he knew what he was doing." I should have taken a lower track over this dune. I should have switched into four-wheel drive sooner. Oh well. Too late now. If I sleep here will a truck come over the hill and run into me in the dark? Should I sleep in the sand? Will a scorpion bite me? A viper? I'd better sign off again. Such nonsense.

3:30 P.M.

Now I am a bit more worried because I just saw a pickup traveling about half a mile to my left. I realize I must have swung out quite a long distance to the right of the main track. I thought I was much nearer the main road. But I've seen many tire tracks around here. I suppose someone will come this way eventually.

4 P.M.

I have just taken steps. I have put long strands of white toilet paper on the top of my radio antenna—a bit of "papering" in hopes that someone will see me. I now realize that my Jeep is almost out of sight from the main track since I've heard at least five or six pickups going by and apparently no one has seen the Jeep. (Did you know that you can hear wind in the distance, before it arrives?) One thing I will not do is leave this Jeep. I may get awfully hungry but I can last for at least four or five days with the water I have. I can't believe I won't get help before then.

A car or truck has just stopped on the main road. I think they have seen me. They can't get over to me from where they are but at least someone knows I am here. How glad I am and how embarrassed will I be. However, I won't leave this Jeep to walk to the tent, even at night. You really can't tell how far away something like that is. Anyway, the lights would probably go off when I got halfway there. It would be crazy.

I can still hear the truck in the distance. Perhaps it will try to find a way to get here—or perhaps it will report me to someone else? The truck is out of earshot now. Just the rustle of toilet paper in the breeze. I think I will try to use my side-view mirrors to flash the sunlight on the main road.

July 13, 6 A.M.

About 6 P.M. yesterday a Toyota pickup turned off and came down my side track. By that time I was standing on top of the Jeep, waving a rag I had found half buried in the sand; it looked like a woman's head scarf. There must have been a Bedouin encampment on the dune a long time ago. The driver roared up this dune at about 60 mph and didn't slow down till he hit firm sand about twenty yards from my Jeep. He got out of his Toyota, walked over, asked if I had four-wheel drive (I did), shook his head at the mess I had made (front wheels turned, in the sand down to the axle). I got half under the Jeep and dug out the transmission while he dug out the wheels a bit; we were both working with our hands, of course. Then he got in, straightened out the wheels, and proceeded to back out of the hole I was in! Said I should have power steering! But he seemed to take the situation pretty much for granted, as if I wasn't the first damn fool to get stuck like this. He really knew how to drive on the sand. I think I know more about it now too, but I was terrified every time I hit soft sand on the rest of the drive to Turaba and it is going to take a while before I get over that feeling.

I reached the residence of the Emir of Turaba last night about 7:30 P.M. and had a rather cool reception. He was leaving for Hail early next morning, he said. Why had I come alone, what was I doing? Luckily I had brought some photos of him from the last trip and that warmed things up a bit. After finishing some business (settling a quarrel of some kind, as near as I could tell), he took me to a small gathering at the other end of the village where we met several other men. The emir seated me with a tribal sheikh, on the same rug outside the sheikh's house. We all turned out to be the same age, fifty-one; they said I looked at least fifty-five; I think that was a compliment. I guess I should have said they looked sixty but it didn't occur to me.

The roast lamb and rice were excellent and my companions became very friendly. The big surprise, however, was that one of them knew Sheikh Hamid, our host in Iraq long ago. He said he probably visited the village in Iraq at the same time we were there. Twenty-five years ago his tribal group used to travel from here northeast across the rest of the Nafud desert and over the border into southern Iraq. There they could graze their animals near the Euphrates River. Not far from where we were living. He said they don't make the trip anymore (seven days by camel) in search of pasture for their animals. No need to, even when they have a dry year here, since the government subsidizes barley for feed. They knew Sheikh Hamid well, he said. "Head of the Al-Agra confederation," they said, "wasn't he?" I nodded. "Lived in Al-Nahra. A big sheikh." The tribes here are part of the Shammar tribal confederation, just like the Al-Eshadda with whom we lived. The sheikh and I realized that we must have been in Al-Nahra about the same time, and here we were, sitting together twenty-five years later, in Saudi Arabia, two men the same age from different parts of the world, and mutual friends of the same man. The coincidence was quite amazing, and we both realized it, I think. It put me on a quite different footing with my new acquaintances.

It's now early in the morning and I am writing this while waiting for my host to get out of bed. He's one of the local tribal emirs. The Turaba district emir turned me over to him last night and has gone off to Hail, as he said he would. There are many kinds of emirs here just as there are many kinds of sheikhs in other parts of the Arab world. The most important is the district emir, who is appointed by the King. He's the one I contacted last night. However, the government also appoints tribal emirs, who are the official intermediaries between the government and the sections of the tribe. The tribal emirs have a lot of clout since they must stamp all the official papers of their tribesmen, loans, birth certificates, things like that.

I slept outside last night and got badly bitten by mosquitoes. Not surprising, since I've seen standing pools at the big hot spring in the middle of this settlement where the tribesmen fill their trucks with water for their herds. I hope I can start interviewing soon, before the temperature gets up above boiling again. From the conversation last night, it sounded as if my host is supposed to help me. It all depends on what the big emir said before he left. He'll be gone two or three days in Hail. It would be good to finish my thirty interviews before he gets back. *Inshallah.* My stomach feels like it has a brick in it. Oh well. The conversation last night, the coincidence of meeting the sheikh who knew our friend in Iraq, was really great. For a while I felt as though I was back with Sheikh Hamid in the *mudhif* [guesthouse] in Al-Nahra.

3:45 P.M.

I did twelve interviews. My voice is sort of raw but I really learned a lot. I started at six-thirty after my host got up. We went out to interview camel herders who water at the big cement troughs set up for them on the edge of the oasis. They had over a hundred camels there. It was very hard to talk with them. I had a tremendous sense of distance from them. Men who still live with their camels on the high desert, without pickup trucks, without interest in selling their animals at the market, are really the last of the traditionalists out here. Their Arabic is unlike even that of the people I sat with last night; some ancient desert dialect, perhaps, uncorrupted by transistors and Egyptian schoolteachers! Last night there was always someone in the group who understood what I was saying in my mixture of Egyptian and Iraqi dialects, and I had no trouble communicating most of the time today with the goat and sheep herders. With the camel herdsmen I might as well have been speaking English and I needed a lot of help from my host-and-guide, the tribal emir. My host got into the act early in the day and started asking the questions, but finally got bored with the same subjects. Can he drive, though! My God, he just flew across the desert in my Jeep. Each time we started out he broke into loud song, like a war cry, as he pushed his foot down on the gas, far down, let me say. The first time he took over the Jeep and put that foot down on the accelerator, I decided it would only be a few minutes before we rolled over. But then I got caught up in his mood and didn't care if we rolled over or not. In comparison, I drive like an old cow.

We are now taking a midday break. I have my galabia on and he is smoking his water pipe. All is tranquil. In a moment I will try to nap. Today seems like a week, a month, from yesterday. It is so eventful, so full of life and people. We have driven miles from tent to tent to visit people who live by and for their goats, sheep, and camels. There is only animal husbandry here; no agriculture for miles and miles. Only the desert, the Great Nafud.

July 14, 12:30 P.M.

I am sitting under a goat-hair tent awning attached to the tent of a group of goat and sheep nomads. Just finished lunch, consisting of many fistfuls of rice and some lamb covered with tomato sauce. It's been quite a while since I ate with my hand so I was pretty messy but had a lot to eat. There were twelve other men for lunch, although when we first stopped, only a small boy and his mother were here and she was on the other side of the tent partition. Then one after another Toyota pickups rolled up and suddenly there was a feast in front of us. It seems like a lot of visiting takes place at all the tents but maybe it is more these days since it is the end of the big holiday following Ramadan. We are still on the Nafud, about ten kilometers from Troba. My host/guide who drives so well has brought me here. He sometimes complains a bit but seems to be having a good time traveling with me and introducing me around. There is general conversation now—gossip which is hard to follow. I did eight interviews but it was hard to keep attention and get questions taken seriously: they don't think about their herds in quantitative terms, nor do they keep family accounts. No surprise, of course. However, since they buy their supplies in large quantities (fifty-kilo sacks of rice, sugar, etc.) it is possible to get some idea of what is spent for what. From tent to tent there are variations but lots of similarities.

I may have to leave tomorrow as my host also wants to go to Hail and I have no alternative guide in sight. I am not too disappointed. After getting up at 5:30 A.M. and working till late at night I am pretty tired. I am also filthy dirty and very bitten by mosquitoes and last night I was also attacked by ants. But I could manage to stay another day or two, if it works out. Will have to see what develops. It's good to speak nothing but Arabic. A lot of dusty old vocabulary seems to be creeping back into the active zone of my brain. I find myself saying things that amaze me.

The floor of the tent where I am sitting now is covered with a Persian rug. The tent itself is set on reddish sand full of dried sheep droppings. The sides of the tent are up, and in the "room," thirty by thirty feet perhaps, are several oriental rugs, machine made. At the center of the U shape made by the rugs on which we are sitting is a fire pit. An incense burner was carried around after our meal. We pulled our head scarves forward and made a kind of tent for our faces and body in order to get a good scenting; it's very refreshing to take deep breaths of the incense. Rose water was also sprinkled on us every once in a while from a small container that looked like an oil-can. We had the local coffee-and-cardamom brew in small porcelain cups and then tea in little glasses. The other furnishings? There are a set of coffeepots of graduated sizes, a teakettle, three storage boxes, brightly colored padded boxes on the rugs beside us to lean against as we sit cross-legged.

We've left the tent with the rugs and are in a neighboring tent. You can't pass by a tent without stopping for a long hello and some tea and coffee. These people are doing all right, I think. For fuel, they use dead wood from the low shrubs or trees around here. The wood falls off as green branches grow in at the top of the plant. The wood is gnarled, twisted, and very dry. Looks like it takes a long time to accumulate. When the grass is consumed and the wood is finished nearby, the people move their tents but still stay within trucking distance of Turaba. There they fill their water bag once or twice a day, depending on the heat and the number of their animals. Some men have to make three trips a day. The bag is a sort of canvas bladder that takes up the entire bed of a pickup truck. Of course, if you are well off, you may have a real water truck to haul water for your herd of goats and sheep—and camels, too. You haul the water to your herds rather than bringing them to the water. It is quite a system. And when you couple this with subsidized barley you can see that these nomads are doing all right; if they get fifty sheep to market they can afford to buy a new Toyota!

3:45 P.M.

Same day. We are back at my host's home—where it seems like paradise. It is hot under those goat-hair awnings with the glare of the sand and the scorching wind. Everyone says it is not as bad as yesterday, which was *hot*. Yes indeed.

July 16. Hail.

I am back home—at least, back to my own room, with the door shut, the fan and the air conditioning on. A different world from the desert. Today is Friday so the day is mine. I got home yesterday afternoon, with twenty interviews complete plus a pricing of commodities from a little survey I did at the weekly market in Turaba. The trip to Turaba took ten and a half hours, what with the two flat tires and the five hours I spent in the sand dune, but the return trip was only three hours: I hit the right roads (or tracks) and had no mishaps. When I first got home, I was very "high" on my successful adventure but developed a bad headache (dehydration, I think) and sort of collapsed and slept very fitfully all afternoon and night. But I feel fine now. Drank gallons of water. I did have some strange dreams, one in which I was looking for my watch and the hands fell off.

The Turaba trip was quite an experience. It is strange to plunge into another culture like that: everything changes, language, food, ways of relating to people, clothes, even toilet habits. Hard as it was in some ways, both physically and emotionally, I find I am looking forward now to the rest of the summer far more than before this trip. I feel I can handle both the interviewing and the getting about by myself. The hard part is being always a guest, having to drink thirty coffees and teas a day and eat more food than one wants. Twenty interviews meant at least twice that many visits. Sitting and sleeping on the ground also takes some getting used to, though it will be easier next time.

Throughout the whole intense trip I had a very strong sense of *déjà vu*. Indeed, I was often in the same situations as I had been in twenty-five years ago in Iraq when I traveled out of Al-Nahra with the sheikh's son and visited the different tribal settlements. The people here are far better off than the people in Iraq in those days. However, there is also the same unevenness in their knowledge (from our viewpoint, at least). For instance, in one tent, after a vigorous and critical discussion of American foreign policy ("How long do you Americans think you can be friends of two enemies at the same time?"), I ended up moderating an argument about whether or not the world is round. This was between two men who had more knowledge of U.S. foreign policy than most of our friends in Texas. The teenaged son of our host, who was sitting in the fire pit handling the coffee service, offered the accepted scientific opinion about the shape of the earth but was not taken very seriously. The boy and I exchanged glances as the argument moved on to the citation of Koranic verses. But after that same night they asked me to point in the direction of Troba, which way the town lay. I said truthfully I had no idea. They then proceeded to show me how to read the stars and navigate at night, laughing kindly at my ignorance. That is the way it is out here.

More later.

Love,
Bob

In the months that followed Bob's first trip into the Great Nafud, he traveled extensively throughout the Hail Emirate, an area the size of Oregon. Sometimes he was out for several days at a time, interviewing Bedouin as he found them in their widely scattered campsites.

Historically, the Hail region in north central Saudi Arabia was the independent domain of tribal groups led by the Rashid emirs, allies of the Ottoman Turks. At the end of World War I, as Ottoman power was waning, Abdul Aziz ibn Saud, founder of the present dynasty that rules Saudi Arabia, was engaged in unifying the Arabian Peninsula. The British encouraged him to include the Hail region, which would further reduce Turkish influence. In 1921 Hail surrendered, and the Emir of Riyadh, Abdul Aziz, gave himself a new title, Sultan of Nejd, and sealed a peace treaty with the Rashid tribe by marrying one of the widows of the tribe. Today the son of Abdul Aziz and the Rashid widow, Fahada, is the head of the Saudi National Guard and second deputy premier of the nation. Long before the peninsula was united under Ibn Saud, Charles Doughty visited Hail. In his classic nineteenth-century *Travels in Arabia Deserta,* he describes the escarpments of Hail, which could be seen from a great distance, the jagged mountains which rise, as Doughty says, from "the extreme barrenness of the desert plain, barren as a sea-strand and lifeless as the dust of our streets; and yet therein are hamlets and villages, upon veins of groundwater. It is a mountain ground where almost nothing may spring of itself, but irrigated it will yield barley and wheat and other Nejd grains." A little overdone as a description, according to Bob, since this "extreme barrenness" where "almost nothing" grows, may, depending on seasonal rainfall, support thousands of goats and sheep, as well as camels, on its natural pastures.

Doughty then found what is now Hail City, a large town with "some high buildings with battled towers. These well-built and stately Nejd turrets of clay-brick are shaped like [English] lighthouses." Palm groves, walled then, surrounded the town, which contained a small market souk, some houses, and the palace of the Rashid emirs. Today, the town is a city of around two hundred thousand. The palm groves have diminished in size in favor of tree-lined, paved streets, modern shopping districts as well as a more traditional souk, hospitals, clinics, administration buildings, and an industrial zone. Bob jogged on a synthetic-fibered four-hundred-meter track in the recently completed large sports center. It stands amid the modern villas which have replaced nearly all the mud-brick homes. The "stately Nejd turrets" are now national monuments, some of the older buildings which have been preserved. The Saudi government is attempting to use its oil wealth to benefit all the provinces of the kingdom, including Hail, home of the once fiercely independent al-Rashid dynasty.

Outside the modern city of Hail hundreds of villages of various size still line the "veins of groundwater" of which Doughty spoke, while on the desert plain around these villages are the tents of the nomads, widely scattered over the area. The herds still graze on the wild grasses and browse on the low shrubs and trees which grow in this arid environment. As Bob traveled about the region it became clear, however, that the old patterns of nomadism had changed somewhat. No longer are animals produced only for nomadic consumption and limited exchange. The majority of the Bedouin are becoming increasingly market-oriented and are raising their animals with the expectation of selling them to urban consumers. A large animal market exists in Hail along with government-controlled slaughterhouses. Even the proud camel, raised in the past for its own sake and valued so highly as to be eaten only under special circumstances—great feasts or dire emergencies, for instance—now may be seen awaiting the butcher's knife. The demise of the camel was offensive to Bob's romantic soul but he explained it as a pragmatic answer to the national shortage of meat. Saudi Arabia now imports around half of the meat it consumes. The Hail development plans were to include schemes for increasing meat production among the Bedouin.

He soon found, however, that there were many differences between the Bedouin in terms of life-style and standard of living. Tent dwellers near the city of Hail were "suburban tent dwellers," Bob felt. They often had jobs in the city or went to school there. In fact many Bedouin families stayed within pickup-truck distance of villages and towns where their children could regularly attend the local schools. Others had agricultural land or hoped to acquire land through land-grant programs. So semi-nomadism was common throughout most of the region south of the Great Nafud.

Not until his last trip in mid-September of 1983 did he go back into the Nafud, where full-scale nomadism was most commonly practiced. This region had actually fared better than the desert plains to the south during the rain-short years of 1981 and 1982, since the desert plants with their large root systems managed to grow on the water which was stored under the surface. As his first letter suggests, the Nafud was a formidable environment for the inexperienced traveler. The British explorer William Gifford Palgrave also thought so in 1876:

We were now traversing an immense ocean of loose reddish sands [he wrote], unlimited to the eye, and heaped up in enormous ridges running parallel to each other from north to south, undulation after undulation, each swell two or three hundred feet in average height, with slant sides and rounded crests furrowed in every direction by the capricious gales of the desert. In the depths between the traveller finds himself as it were imprisoned in a suffocating sand-pit, hemmed in by burning walls on every side; while at other times, while labouring up the slope, he overlooks what seems a vast sea of fire, swelling under a heavy monsoon wind, and ruffled by a cross-blast into the little red-hot waves. Neither shelter nor rest for eye or limb amid torrents of light and heat poured from above on an answering glare reflected below.

Bob found this an accurate as well as poetic description but was determined to go back to the Great Nafud desert, not only because of the requirements of his job but also to conquer the fears he had brought back from his first trip. If the travelers of yore had made it on foot and camelback, why couldn't he do it in a Jeep?

September 16, 1983
Jubba, Hail Province, Saudi Arabia

Dear B.J., I'm off in the Great Nafud again, once more alone, and with a much greater distance between me and Hail than the last time in Turaba. I got stuck again this time, too. The graded road (a paved one is being constructed) came to an abrupt stop at the bottom of a sand dune and so did I. I didn't feel so bad, though, because several other Jeeps were stuck in the same place; you lose your momentum and that's what happens. Another guardian spirit, robed and scented, took charge and let half the air out of my already low tires. After that I could drive myself out. Just hope these tires make it over the rocky parts of this track. You should see me on the sand these days, floorboarding the gas pedal in second gear. Suspend all driving rules and keep it at 40 mph no matter whether you can see over the next dune or not. That's the way you do it!

I made it here to Jubba oasis in about four hours, so it wasn't a bad trip. Just now I've had lunch with the very cordial district emir, who has sent for a tribal emir to help me find the tents in the dunes around here. Jubba is the first place I've seen in Saudi Arabia that comes anywhere near the storybook image of an oasis. Green trees on a white plain right in the middle of red sand dunes. We seem to be on the floor of an ancient lake. This area, maybe two or three miles square, lies in the lee of a mountain, like Turaba, so it doesn't get covered with sand of the Nafud. The sand blows around rather than over the basin. The village is strung out—no cosy cluster of houses nestling among the palm trees. And it is dusty, fine white powdery dust from the gypsum soil. There are lots of cement-block houses built and under construction, replacing the old mud-brick ones. A lot of Bedouin stay here in the winter, the emir told me. It gets very cold; remember the Iraqi winters?

Speaking of Iraq, I'm back among tribesmen of the Shammar confederation, like our hosts in Al-Nahra. But they don't have memories of Sheikh Hamid because they travel north toward Jawf oasis and Jordan from here, not northeast toward Iraq like the Shammar in Troba used to do. In fact, Jubba is on the old desert trail along which people used to make the trip to Amman and Jerusalem; it took five days by camel. Today you can get to the border in seven hours by Jeep, if you know what you are doing; trucks can't make it through the dunes, however. They are too slow and heavy and sink in. But there will be a paved road through here one day soon. Much talk of it in Hail and the road is already partly finished from there to here. It will make Hail the major gateway to the north.

What with all the construction work going on—a new secondary school and clinic in addition to the houses—the village is full of migrant workers from Egypt, India, and Pakistan, just as in Hail and the other villages I've visited. Labor migration isn't limited to the cities of Saudi Arabia by any means. My host has rather contradictory attitudes toward these foreign workers: he feels that Saudis should learn to do the work and not rely on others. But he thinks the country is benefitting from them too. He seems to be saying, "We shouldn't have them but we can't get along just now without them."

At the moment, it seems I've been stood up. One of the two tribal emirs (at my host the district emir's suggestion) was supposed to send his son to act as my guide. No show. That explains why I am writing to you now, sitting under an arcade in my host's courtyard, where he does his business in the summer. My host finally got mad and sent a man to see what happened to my proposed guide. The deputy, he said, was to convey the message that I'm here on official business and must be looked after. It's obvious that I'm regarded as a nuisance (which I am) and my mission (to ask the Bedouin questions about their animals) of no great importance. But I have acquired good thick skin over the years; I will outlast their polite indifference.

4 P.M.

After a bit, the father emir turned up at my host's majlis, in answer to the emissary. He didn't know what happened to his son who was supposed to pick me up, he said. He didn't seem particularly angry, but he offered to take me out. I could stay with him, he said, and go out to the tents from his place on the edge of the oasis. Our first excursion over the nearby sand dunes produced nothing except views of old campsites. The father didn't drive my Jeep with quite the verve of the younger men, but he did damn well for a man in his fifties or older, who had probably not started to drive until ten or fifteen years ago, when Jeeps began to be common out here. In fact, he said that when he was a young man he would travel by camel with his father to Riyadh to collect their *ma'ash* (living) from the King; the trip took fifteen days. Today, it seems the ma'ash comes here, with the land grants, the feed subsidies, and the other money the government is spending on the people in the provinces. After a fifteen-day slow camel trip, Jeep travel must seem luxurious, but it's very tiring to bounce around so much. And Jeeps last only two years, the emir said, "before they begin to eat you up in repair costs."

The tribal emir and I finally visited two tents belonging to Bedouin families who are building blockhouses below the dune where the campsite lies on the edge of the oasis plain. They are among the ninety-five families to whom the emir distributed land. He says two thirds of the Bedouin families are still trying to farm; it didn't seem that many to me. Egyptian farmers were working with both the families we visited, trying to get crops started in the sandy soil. When the Egyptians heard me speak Egyptian Arabic, one looked up and we exchanged greetings. He said he was from Beni Suef and would be staying another year to complete a two-year contract. The emir himself has six Egyptian farmers working for him, he said. He also owns a cement factory that is supplying cement blocks for a new school and a new clinic that are under construction. The emir is probably very wealthy, but nothing in his personal style indicates it.

September 16, evening
The tribal emir's house

It is now settled that I will stay in the tribal emir's house for two days and go out from here to interview the nearby Bedouin. His house is much like that of my earlier host, the district emir in Jubba. An arcade, shaded, facing a pleasant courtyard with plots of tomatoes and other vegetables. The wall at the end of the arcade, behind the fireplace, is papered with a ten-by-fifteen-foot beach scene—waving palms, ocean, but no people. At the moment I've been left alone with an Egyptian worker, maybe thirty-five, who comes from Sharqiya Governorate in the Delta. He acted very "tough" at first, but after some conversation, became very affable. He wants me to interview him as I'm interviewing the Bedouin, and I'm trying to explain why that is of no use (do you produce animals for the market, etc.?—he obviously doesn't, but is here, like other Egyptian workers, to help the Saudis get their farms started).

A videocassette has been turned on for our entertainment. It's an Egyptian feature film, vintage 1963–65, I'd say. Fantastic, really, after just coming from crowded Egypt, to see the streets of downtown Cairo so empty, and the people dressed exactly as they were when we lived there. Only Sa'id, the Egyptian migrant laborer, and I seem interested in the film. The family men have gone into the house.

9:30 P.M.

The men have come back out and we are sitting around informally. Two young Saudi boys, looking like dandies, are sharing their impressions of Cairo with Sa'id and me. They were not impressed and complained about the crowds and the dirt like any other fastidious tourists. One wants to come to the United States to study, but he doesn't speak a word of English. I'm tired. But I can't sleep, with the video on and the conversation as well. But the electricity goes off at 11 P.M., so I should be able to sleep then.

September 17, 7:45 A.M.

Well, the electricity didn't go off till midnight. I watched a super-duper Indian melodrama with no Arabic or English subtitles, which kept a couple of Arab boys fascinated for two hours and a half! This tells me more about Indian-Arab cultural relations than I had ever even considered before. I found the films intensely boring, full of all the old tricks of fades and time extensions. One minute the lovers floated like scarves across the grass toward each other for a long, loving look deep in the eyes; the next moment Indian cowboy types were galloping madly after a train. If I could understand why I found it such a bore and why they liked it so much I could write a fine article. Are film styles a one-way street? Is melodramatic exaggeration now forever hopelessly corny? I should add that technically speaking the Indian film was fully up to Hollywood standards. And the color was good.

I slept in the majlis where we watched the Indian film. This morning a veiled lady came in, built the fire, and as I rose from my mattress told me to help myself to coffee. I took the coffeepot out of the hot coals left from the small wood fire she had made. She had left some flat bread and canned cheese. Now the emir has come in and is eating with me. No camel milk here; no camels! I didn't sleep well—mosquitoes and sand flies and it was too hot under the arcade, no breeze. It did cool off around 4 A.M., and I slept a few hours. Now if I can just do my interviewing. One son (of the two young men from last night) has disappeared and the second one is supposed to take me around the Bedouin tents in the area. The emir just asked me if he had shown up yet and I told him he hadn't. The father went out to look for his son. Where is parental authority? He doesn't seem to have much more than I do! The emir says he has a brother studying in America. Although he has been there five years, the emir doesn't know the name of the place where he lives. (I am clearly still a nuisance and it isn't certain to me that I will ever get taken out to the tents. As in Turaba, up here in the Nafud I have to have a guide as I can't find anything by myself in the sand dunes. They all look the same to me.)

September 17, 11:30 A.M.

The emir took me out, and we spent three hours traveling up one dune and down the next. I only did three interviews in four hours, but the trip was spectacular—fantastic desert landscape—a real calendar scene with sharp-edged dunes and rolling hills of sand. Some sparse vegetation, clumps of green grass and low bushes. Didn't find many people, because the camel nomads have gone north toward Jawf in search of better pasture. Jawf is four hours over a desert trail from here, outside the Hail region of the Nafud, where I must stay.

The new road they're talking about will make a big difference, for it will open up a new stretch of desert to the goat and sheep herders. Now they can't camp more than ten kilometers away from Jubba, because they have to haul water to their herds twice a day in summer, and they can't manage more than forty kilometers per day over these dunes. The trip is just too tough; tires last only six months, for instance. But still, as I wrote earlier, this breakneck cruising over the sand is a real trip. Perhaps the emir threw in a bit of dash this time for my benefit, but I wasn't scared. Lapsed into another state of mind. A real trip.

Water is a problem in this area. But there is plenty of it underground, people say, and as the land is distributed to new farmers, lots of wells are being dug. The government is interested in developing agriculture here and has opened up the area to possible private investment. Government subsidies are also pouring in. The farming development schemes seem to be working.

When we got to the house, the young men were back: the son who was to meet me here this morning says he got here by eight-thirty. But his father and I were here then, and he wasn't. Could it be that the younger generation is going to hell here too? (Like all younger generations, of course.) The errant son has asked the servant if his father is mad at him. The servant boy seems to be a bit feebleminded, somehow not normal. They tease him but he loves it. The video is back on—another Egyptian film. This time a sixties comedy. The family has quite a collection of cassettes. Electricity is on for part of the day since the town has several generators.

It turns out that Abdulla, the son, was in Cairo not as a rich tourist but on business to arrange for five Egyptians to come here to work for his father. One of them is Sa'id, with whom I talked last night. The son volunteered that Egyptians are liars and thieves.

Four men from Jubba are studying in the States now. The emir's brother is in Kansas, according to Abdulla.

September 17, 9 P.M.

Tonight the Indian migrant laborers have come to the emir's arcade to watch an Indian film on the video machine. He invites them every week, I'm told, which is very nice of him as there doesn't seem to be much else to do for entertainment. I've found out that there are Egyptian and Palestinian school-teachers working here. And just up the street are Pakistani dressmakers. They were working late the last two nights, finishing up some fancy ladies' dresses: I saw fifteen or twenty dresses, rather conservative Victorian style, hanging on racks behind the old-fashioned treadle sewing machines, waiting to be picked up.

September 18, 4 P.M.

I've been bumping over sand dunes all morning and have just come back to the emir's house. I've finished fifteen interviews, an excellent sample of all the camp-situation types stretching as far as eleven kilometers from Jubba. But I'm exhausted, and my body feels like something heavy has rolled over it several times. The Bedouin I interviewed today varied enormously. Some had already cashed in on government assistance programs; others had never had any help from the government and hadn't thought of asking. The ones who lived farthest from Jubba looked worn out; they said they went back and forth all day hauling water to their herds. It sounds good to be using trucks for herding and hauling water, but it's in many ways much harder than the old way, when the traditional nomads had to settle for whatever water they could walk to. Today's nomad is working harder—here, at least. Pastoralism is becoming not so much a way of living as a way of earning a living.

In these intense days, I have been getting to know the tribal emir's sons—there are twelve of them—and like them very much. They are really good sons and help their father a lot, it turns out. Every one of the boys is either involved with his father's interests or in school. Even the one that didn't show up to take me out, as he was supposed to, was apparently out in his truck collecting firewood, nearly a hundred kilometers away.

This tribal emir has a lot of responsibilities beyond his economic interests. The whole family has to help. Like the old sheikhs of Iraq (which is more or less what they are, it seems to me), the emirs have to be ready to receive people all day long, make and serve coffee, tea, and meals, provide lodging for travelers, and look after unexpected problems like myself. My host is very lucky! His strong sons are essential factors in his prosperity.

One of the boys told me that he spent five years in the desert with his father before the emir settled down here in Jubba. He says that the Bedu are *jahal*, literally pre-Islamic, though the word also means kind of naïve, unsophisticated. But he still admires them. "Why is a young Bedu so much stronger than three boys from Hail, even if the Bedu is smaller?" he asked me. "How do you account for their confidence?" He is very ambiguous about them. I said, "You'll never forget those five years with the Bedu." He said, "Yes, you are right. When I went to Egypt and saw all the people crowded together there, I thought about the Bedu out here." But he thinks that in a few years, no Bedouin will be left. "They go to school and then it's all finished," he said.

September 18, evening

I've finished my interviews. We traveled about seventy kilometers today, around the edge of the oasis. It felt like seven hundred in some ways, but there were good moments. I feel I have made some new friends here. Literally. Today suddenly the emir and his sons and I seemed to be on much more personal terms. The older boys are twenty, twenty-two, and twenty-three, but there are younger boys, half brothers, since the emir has had three wives. I really like this family, and only wish I had met more people like them during my months in Saudi Arabia.

The job is nearly done. I will be leaving Saudi Arabia soon to meet you in Cairo. This is my last trip on the desert, the last session of interviews. A good trip to end with, I think. Last night I had a good sleep in the sand, parked high on a dune, and when I woke, from a distance Jubba looked more like a storybook illustration than ever. The construction and farm developments weren't visible, only the palm trees, which seemed to be floating in a bluish white mist (really the dust of the settlement). The people have been hospitable and friendly; they have that reputation, but it was more than I had hoped for or expected. It is an old settlement, Jubba, some say three thousand years.

The rocks are covered with pictographs from prehistoric times, so people must have been here even longer than that. The new paved road from Hail is due to reach Jubba in a few months. When the city of Hail itself has changed so much so fast, one can only hazard a guess about how Jubba oasis will change in the coming years. And I wonder how my friend the emir and his twelve fine sons will survive and manage, in such a different future. If the circumstances of their lives change as drastically as they seem likely to do, I wonder whether they will or can continue to be what they are—hardworking, generous, hospitable, the real inheritors of an ancient and proud tradition.

Comment

THE ANTHROPOLOGIST IN THE FIELD

CULTURAL ANTHROPOLOGY is distinguished from all other social sciences by the practice of fieldwork, a period of study spent by the anthropologist in a cultural setting other than his or her own. The ideas and concepts which are developed by anthropologists quickly find their way into the work of other social scientists, and anthropologists are just as free about picking up creative contributions from other disciplines. But it is the anthropologist's fieldwork, the research in unfamiliar cultural contexts, which sets the discipline apart from other social sciences. This research in the field, the observations and experiences organized and interpreted, results in theories or models about human thought and behavior. That is the standard view. As a member of a discipline which is concerned with the unique properties of each human culture but yet is devoted to the notion that there are fundamental similarities between them which bridge cultural differences, the anthropologist is faced with contradictory intellectual expectations. Fieldwork is a unique experience, but it must be understood according to some general pattern of interpretation which will permit comparisons. For this reason, no matter how unique and adventurous or mundane and familiar the experiences of fieldwork may be, they must constantly be subject to reflection so that the experiences will find a place within the discourse of anthropology, the conversation of the discipline.

Fieldwork is participant observation. Anthropologists are both actors and spectators in the field. Although this is what is said about the experience, it is not that the anthropologist is sometimes the participant and at other times the observer. From the moment one arrives in a village or suburb, a tribal guesthouse or a local bar, one becomes part of the social scene, whether one likes it or not. In a foreign setting this can be very difficult to manage, not from one's reluctance to take part in the local scene, but rather because one's participation (as a stranger) is potentially so disturbing. No matter how well one learns the language and local customs, the difference between the anthropologist and his or her hosts remains—a plus as well as a minus, for it is within the context of one's strangeness that one observes.

As a human being, however, the anthropologist consciously or unconsciously tries to transcend the participant-observer opposition, however impossible this may be. Such moments come closest to taking place during conversation. Not the ritualistic forms of conversation in which the exchange is more or less predetermined, but the kind of conversation in which both parties, the anthropologist and the other person, are struggling to come to a common understanding about a particular subject. In the areas where I have been fortunate enough to do fieldwork—Iraq, Egyptian Nubia, Morocco, Saudi Arabia, Afghanistan—there has been someone in the fieldwork setting who has been particularly adept not only at understanding my limited speech but also at understanding what I am talking about, what the questions I am asking "really mean." At moments in conversation with such persons the participant-observer opposition collapses and I have felt myself become a person interacting with another within a framework of shared understandings. That is what "really mean" means, of course, not an ultimate truth but a conceptual agreement. In this regard, I have never felt comfortable in another culture about ending a serious conversation when I felt I knew something the other person did not understand. My best informants—and my best friends—in the field have always seemed to share that attitude. They have been at least as stubborn as I am.

Anthropological fieldwork takes place in different cultural contexts and can have very different intellectual objectives. The latter are usually determined both by the history of research in the particular region of the world where one works and by the intellectual paradigms currently in favor. Just as the problems and approaches which are popular one decade may change to something very different the next ("culture and personality" studies have been out in the past few years while "structuralism" and "symbolic analysis" have been in), so too do the fieldwork situations to which one must adapt change radically from one region of the world to the next. Since fieldwork requires constant involvement in the local scene and a willingness to become part of social events to one degree or another, it is hard to understand how it could be undertaken by a person who really dislikes the situation, the setting, the people. Thus anthropologists generally stay in their regions of special interest with some degree of emotional enthusiasm for the one of their choice. This is not to say that anthropologists, like everyone else, never have negative feelings about people and living conditions. But the general style of life, of personal interaction, cannot be too irritating or upsetting. The Middle East, for instance, is no place for American men who have trouble being touched by other men, any more than Mexican villages are suitable for male researchers who can't hold their pulque. As a poor drinker, I've always been glad that alcohol is generally not part of the Middle Eastern village scene. And I have not felt threatened when a friend takes my hand. In fact, the measured rituals of traditional hospitality serve to ease the preliminary introductions to a Middle Eastern setting (tribal, village, or urban). Someone is always there to receive strangers, including the anthropologist, and this initial welcome provides an opportunity to make one's business known. The ritual of hospitality, however, requires participation. There is the pleasant obligation, on the part of the guest, to drink tea or coffee and often share a meal; I was astounded once when an anthropologist friend told me he never accepted tea in a field setting out of concern for infections. But he explained that in Africa, where he did his research, such customs did not prevail. The Middle East was definitely not to his taste, it seemed.

Most anthropological fieldwork has been done among people who are on the lower end of living standards, however measured. Why? Because such people are less well understood? Because they are in need of study in order to be helped? Because they are like the majority of people in the world? Because they are the way we all were, in some sense, before the industrial revolution made some of us middle-class? Perhaps all of these reasons motivate some anthropological research. Yet my esteemed colleague Laura Nader has rightfully chided us, her colleagues, for not "studying up," for not looking more closely at the behavior of the rich, the capitalists, the establishment, the upper classes, who call the shots in other societies, as well as our own. It is a point well taken and today, within the profession, Professor Nader and others are making efforts to "study up." However, the rich in all societies are very difficult to reach. One cannot walk into a village of millionaires and watch them conduct their business; the settings within which they carry on their daily lives are carefully protected from outsiders, including anthropologists. Thus, somewhat by default, the anthropologist often has no choice but to study the poor, the oppressed, the mistreated, the powerless, the neglected people of the world, the ones who are at best manipulated by the rich and powerful. In such studies, the behavior of the rich and powerful remains a matter of inference. Anthropologists also study the poor in part because the poor are less able to resist us, less able to tell us to mind our own business and get out. We try to think this is not the case, to discount the possibility and excuse our behavior in various ways, but we have to face the fact that we also benefit from the privileges of class and country, however modest our claims, however noble our intentions.

The difference in class and status, in power base, between the anthropologist and his or her subjects of study in the field leads to charges of exploitation. Anthropologists are deriving personal benefit from their researches, it is said, and are aiding the dominant political and economic forces by contributing to their knowledge of the subject populations. On the other hand, anthropologists are also accused of sentimentality, of wanting to preserve a state of affairs, a culture, which is outmoded, of trying to hold back progress to the detriment of the people they profess to admire. Both charges have elaborate ideological underpinnings. The first implies that we, as individuals, are no more than agents of our class, and the second assumes that a single measure of progress exists. I do not agree with either view. However, it is true that until recently much anthropological research has assumed that the group being studied exists in a kind of isolation, a never-never land of self-containment, which was misleading both for the anthropologist and for those who read the anthropologist's work. If anything of significance has resulted from the controversies mentioned above, it is the recognition that villages, tribes, and urban groups are part of a larger political and economic system, a system which intrudes upon and reshapes the local community wherever it may be. It is the anthropologist's responsibility to convey this reality to his or her students and colleagues.

Edward Said, in *Orientalism,* has illustrated how, in the discourse of scholarship, we describe and analyze other cultures, like the Middle East, with signs of our own historic creation. He suggests that the signs of such scholarship over the last two hundred years have been shaped by the dominant position of Europe vis-à-vis the Middle East and he wonders whether the superior economic and political position of the West is not still inevitably embedded in our contemporary studies of non-Western countries. So it is that terms like "lineage," "tribe," "veil," "peasant," "Islam," acquire meanings of their own in the West and resist our attempts to see beyond them to the "real" subject of our inquiry.

Certainly the anthropologist, like the literary critic, the economist, the historian, or the political scientist, has his or her own baggage of theories and categories, the intellectual tools of the discipline. But in the field, in the communities and the homes of others, the anthropologist, vulnerable both personally and intellectually, finds him- or herself in an inferior position. He or she is dependent on the help and goodwill or the tolerance of those "others" for information, friends. This position at least offers an existential basis for the development of a new perspective. For though the anthropologist, like other scholars, cannot escape historic intellectual theories and cultural categories, the fieldwork situation forces him or her to reflect on those theories and categories, to look at them more carefully, to rethink their implications, in personal as well as scholarly terms.

Today, fewer and fewer countries are open to anthropological research. Governments of the left accuse us of being imperialists, while those of the right see us as radicals and troublemakers. Fieldwork in other cultures may eventually disappear, along with cultural anthropology as we have known it. This will be doubly unfortunate, for the same authoritarianism which would eliminate this form of disciplined human concern would also put an end to the splendid human diversity which anthropologists have tried to describe.

CHAPTER XIII

The West Bank, Israel

1983

When words stop, the sword begins to speak.

Arab proverb

JERUSALEM. JERUSALEM. In twenty-seven years of travel and residence in the Middle East, I had never journeyed to Jerusalem. Bob had, in 1964, before the face of the city was changed by the 1967 war. Laura Ann, our older daughter, had come to Jerusalem from Damascus, as part of her ten-day visit to Israel in 1978. And in 1961, my mother and my aunt Mary had made a pilgrimage to the holy places of Christendom on their way back to the United States from a visit to us in Egypt. But now we were here. October 1983. Bob and I had come at the invitation of Bir Zeit University, one of four Palestinian universities on the West Bank, for a conference on rural society in the Middle East, a conference sponsored jointly by the University of Durham in England and the University of Amsterdam.

One of the oldest cities in the Middle East, inhabited continuously for perhaps six thousand years, Jerusalem is the home of the sacred shrines of Judaism, of Christianity, and of Islam. For Jews and Christians, Jerusalem is the city of beginnings; so is it also for Muslims, for whom it is the most holy city after Mecca and Medina. The Dome of the Rock is where the Prophet Muhammad is said to have visited during his lifetime, and the place where in a vision, many believe, he ascended from earth to heaven. The caliph Omar prayed on this spot in A.D. 638, after capturing Jerusalem from the Byzantine Empire. The Dome of the Rock was pictured on many of the posters we found pasted on the walls of buildings in the Palestinian quarters of Beirut, next to the posters of the martyrs. I saw the same posters in the houses of the refugees in Rashadiya, where I had filmed in 1981, as well as posters depicting the Church of the Holy Sepulcher, sacred to Christians and also to Muslims. A calendar bearing a small colored likeness of the golden Dome of the Rock hung in the living room of my friend Um Zhivago. Jerusalem was the city to which the people of Rashadiya longed to return. But they could not, for Israelis rule Jerusalem now. Three and a half million Jews from all parts of the world live in Jerusalem and in the surrounding cities and towns of the State of Israel, many of them refugees from the inhuman Holocaust of the Hitler years. Um Zhivago knows that, of course. But she also knows what we did not fully realize until recently: nearly 2 million Palestinians also live in or near the sacred city of Jerusalem, five hundred thousand within Israel itself, and 1.3 million on the West Bank of the Jordan River and in the Gaza Strip, which stretches along the sea from Israel to Egypt.

Jerusalem. The sound of the word vibrates in the mind and the heart of every person who has ever attended a church, a synagogue, a mosque, who has read a collection of literature, recited poetry, sung sacred songs, grown up within one of the three great monotheistic religions of the world: Judaism, Christianity, Islam. Western roots lie here, in the East. And the beauty of the city, its unexpected and dramatic setting, its austere majesty, makes its own statement. Stones quarried hundreds of years ago, stained over time with blood and anointed with oil, prayed over by bishops and archimandrites and rabbis and qadis, fought over by knights and barons, by sultans and emperors, pave the roads that wind through the enclosed city. Groves of olive trees rise, gray green against the sandy-colored soil, on the seven hills that are part of, that encircle, the city. (An olive tree, once rooted, will bear for generations, we were told. Some of the olive trees in Jerusalem are said to date from Roman times.)

The people of Jerusalem, many wearing Western dress, some wearing the distinctive dress of orthodox Judaism, orthodox Christianity, orthodox Islam, walk along the narrow cobblestoned streets of the old walled city, wait for buses on the streets of the new town, shop for tomatoes and bread in the traditional souks, for frozen foods in the modern supermarkets. We were shown the pool of the Greek Orthodox patriarch, the khan or inn which belongs to the Coptic Church. The massive stone walls which protect the city were completed in 1542 by Suliman the Magnificent, ruler of the Ottoman Empire. There are the remains of a real moat, and a drawbridge which was still operating in the early part of this century. This is the spot where the commander of the British Expeditionary Force in Egypt, Field Marshal Allenby, stood after capturing Jerusalem from the Turks in 1917. "Saladin, we are back!" he is supposed to have shouted, thus bringing to a triumphant end the Crusades begun eight hundred years before. Today Muslim and Christian conquerors have been put aside; Jewish conquerors rule the city. But whoever rules, Jerusalem within the walls remains an urban site of multiple religious enclaves: four distinct quarters, Muslim, Jewish, Christian, and a special Armenian quarter. Within these are numerous convents, hostels, offices, and delegations of various sects, watched over by religious congregations in all parts of the world. Jerusalem belongs, both literally and metaphorically, to millions of people who will never visit, much less live in, the city. And the stones, the streets, the buildings, the very niches within the buildings are charged with multiple meanings, with memories, with the history of many different groups, many different beliefs about the rule of God on earth, about truth, about justice.

Bir Zeit University, to which we were headed, is a relatively new institution of higher learning (1972) which has evolved from an older secondary school. Walled, pleasantly laid out with courts and flowering shrubs, it lies about fifteen miles north of Jerusalem, near Ramallah, a largely Christian town; about two hundred faculty teach two thousand students. While the conference was in session on the campus, the students went back and forth to class, sat on the low benches in the courtyard in the sunlight, talking, laughing, reading aloud to each other. In their jeans and sweaters, their boots and tennis shoes, they looked much like students in an American university. But here the situation differs vastly from that on an American campus.

Bir Zeit (the Arabic words mean literally "well of [olive] oil"), the town and the university, lies on the West Bank of the Jordan River, the area taken by Israel in the war of 1967 and since that time administered by a military government. Seventeen years is a long time for so many people to live under occupation. The people of the West Bank to whom we spoke chafed under the military regime, and we remembered reading about the incidents resulting from such alien rule which were reported in the Western media. Stones are thrown at military Jeeps. A Jewish settler is killed in the West Bank city of Hebron. Demonstrations are held at Bethlehem University, which is partly supported by the Vatican and has an American vice-president. Bir Zeit has been closed by the Israeli military authorities seven times between 1973 and 1982, for periods ranging from a few days to three months. The charge: political activities. The four West Bank universities—Bir Zeit, Bethlehem, Al-Naja, and Hebron—together constitute one of the better university systems in the Middle East. Developed since 1967 under Israeli occupation, the universities in the past have been allowed relative freedom to raise funds outside Israel—particularly in Jordan and other parts of the Arab world. Today the Israeli authorities are apparently having second thoughts about the autonomy of the Palestinian universities. Faculty and staff at Bir Zeit told us that a number of military orders have been issued; these orders, if implemented, could severely restrict the universities' hiring and firing policies and the contents of their curricula.

To us, in October of 1983, the West Bank looked outwardly serene, as did Jerusalem. Many of the houses, the domes and spires and towers within the walls of the old city were built of a distinctive local stone, which casts a faint rosy glow into the clear, golden light of the highland fall. The Jordan Valley, where we traveled to visit agricultural settlements, was lush with autumn planting near Jericho, where we lunched in an open-air restaurant under grape arbors, on a local Palestinian specialty: *mussakhan,* chicken grilled with onions and sumac. In the south toward Hebron, the famous grapes of the area, purple and dusky gold, were being harvested from the stone terraces and offered for sale in lean-tos along the roadside by women in the colorfully embroidered dresses and flowing head scarves of their villages. Bob was scheduled to present a paper at the conference about Saudi Arabia. I had agreed to show my documentary film about the lives of Palestinian women in the Rashadiya refugee camp.

We could not view the West Bank and Jerusalem and Bir Zeit in a neutral light. Like other Americans involved with the Middle East over the past twenty-five years, we had come to be concerned about the Arab-Israeli conflict, about the growth of the State of Israel, about the situation of the Palestinians, both in Israel and on the West Bank and Gaza. The controversy, bitter and long-standing, about rights to the land and to the city of Jerusalem, looked to us in 1983, as we talked with people on both sides, at least as far from settlement as it had looked in 1967 at the end of the war when Israel occupied the West Bank.

Yet everyday life proceeds in Jerusalem and on the West Bank. People, both Israeli and Palestinian, would describe, politely and pleasantly, their lives to us, lives that to middle-class Americans like ourselves seemed unreal. The Israelis in the more than one hundred legally contested new settlements which are rising around Jerusalem and on the West Bank live in totally segregated communities, in huge, self-contained white-painted housing developments that ring the villages and hills around Jerusalem like fortresses, modern stockades of cement and stone. A Swedish filmmaker whom we met in the American Colony Hotel told us that in some of the settlement apartments a single button closes all windows and doors automatically and that the location of the crucial button is taught very early to Israeli children. We ask Israeli acquaintances against whom the windows and doors are closed automatically and the reply is, "The enemy."

One of the representatives of an international welfare foundation, a British friend of ours, says he feels obliged to present his "solution" to anyone who will listen. Of all peoples in the world, his lecture goes, the Jews and the Arabs would seem the most likely groups to be able to live together in some kind of harmony. Says Hugh, "They have so much in common. They share roots in the same religion, in the same language family, they value the family tie greatly, they have a rich tradition of folklore and literature."

However, there are few social meetings between Arabs and Jews under present circumstances. Instead, these groups of people so divided, so shut off from each other, live together, uneasily and full of mutual distrust, on the same small piece of historically contested ground, and talk about the violation of the ideals of their forefathers.

Israelis explained to us, again patiently and politely, that ideologically Palestinians do not belong in Israel, whether they are Muslim or Christian. Why? They are not Jewish, and Israel is a Jewish state. But they are there, nearly 2 million, and half of them are under fifteen years of age. Since the great flight of Palestinians from their home in 1948, fewer and fewer have left Israel, partly because of the strict laws which stipulate that any Arab who chooses to emigrate must formally renounce the right to return. Given the close family ties among Arabs in Israel, such a decision is very difficult. More West Bank Arabs leave, to study or work abroad, but even so, only 3 to 4 percent are lost through emigration each year. The lack of employment opportunities for educated Arabs is a problem, however. As a group, the West Bank people have one of the highest levels of formal education in the Middle East.

"What do they think of us in America?" a high school girl at the East Jerusalem YWCA, where we were housed for the conference, asked me. She was a student in one of the classes offered at the YWCA for girls who wish to obtain vocational training after finishing secondary school.

I answered that many people in America, I thought, had sympathy for the Palestinians and hoped that a solution could be found for their problems.

She was about sixteen, dark-haired, plump. She simply stared at me. "I can't believe that," she said.

"Why not?"

"Because everyone says, in the newspapers and magazines, that the Americans think of us all as terrorists, *beasts*. Who has sympathy for *beasts?*"

I started to explain how Americans might get that idea, the way the media referred to the PLO and saw all of its behavior as the acts of terrorists. She heard me out, polite to the end, but I could see she did not believe me. "Thank you," she said, and that was the end of the conversation.

Many Israelis expressed their concern about government policy on the West Bank. "The old consensus in Israel has fallen apart on this issue," said a well-known Israeli professor, a friend of friends. "In the old days, when we came here, we all thought we were dedicated to a common goal, developing a free state, a symbol for the world. It's not true anymore."

"But perhaps that's to be expected," I temporized, "given the growth of the state, the differing backgrounds of the people who have emigrated to Israel over the years."

He was an old man with white hair, a lame leg. He shook his head. "I understand what you are saying, the values of a pluralistic society, and so on. But in a pluralistic society people can criticize, complain, have the power to change things. We can still do that here. This is a democracy still. We have a free press, you know."

"Yes," I said. "We've noticed the kiosks—all kinds of newspapers, in English, Hebrew, Arabic, expressing all kinds of differing opinions, presumably. Very heartening—and important."

The older man pointed a finger at me. "But it is only the Israelis that really have that freedom, you know. People on the West Bank do not."

"So what you are saying about the consensus falling apart here has to do with the government policy toward the West Bank—"

"Toward the Palestinians generally. How can we, supposedly one of the most idealistic societies in the world—we *were*, you know—"

I nodded.

"—how can we support the policies that do not let another group of people live useful, free lives, live in peace—"

"Do they let *us* live in peace?" angrily, from a younger man. "Isn't that the crux of the issue?"

"Have either of us tried?" asked the old man of his younger colleague.

Peace, everyone says on both sides of the divided city, is what everyone wants. Peace would bring an end to the devastating cost of arms, the draining wars; peace would bring relief to the economy, which, despite years of hard work by Israelis, is not even close to self-sufficient. But the atmosphere of Jerusalem, of the West Bank, is not conducive to peace. Israeli soldiers turn up unexpectedly in the markets, as they did when Bob and I were shopping in the Old City, pushing people and goods aside with their weapons. Traffic police may choose to search an entire car that has been stopped for a minor violation, as happened on the Gaza road when we were traveling with our friend Hugh. Life is expensive in Israel, and inflation continues to rise. An automobile, after import duties and taxes, costs three times what it would in the United States. The government subsidizes basic foods, such as bread, but the flat Arab bread is not subsidized. Cars registered on the West Bank bear blue license plates to distinguish them from Israeli cars (yellow license plates). To make it even more confusing, Palestinian cars in East Jerusalem also have yellow license plates. But in Gaza, where more than four hundred thousand people, the majority refugees, are jammed together on a narrow strip of land and where trouble is reported to be frequent, the license plates of the cars are silvery gray so they can be more quickly distinguished by the police, people told us.

In general, however, any action that is taken by Israeli officials or police must be justified legally, we were told by both Palestinians and Israelis. The courts regularly hear lawsuits brought by both Israelis and Palestinians. Recently, a Palestinian woman scientist submitted a petition to the faculty of the Hebrew University, where she was then teaching, to obtain permission to publish a scientific journal in Arabic, since none now exists. This petition, supported by many Israeli faculty groups, ended up in the courts and was denied in late 1983. The woman also lost her job. Permits must be obtained to grow tomatoes, to buy land, to get a telephone, to travel, to build a house, to register a company, to stay overnight in Israel proper (if you are from Gaza), to plant olive trees or grow plums. (You need not get a permit to plant grapevines or grow plums if you have a deed to your property which has been accepted by an Israeli court as valid or if the grapes or plums are for personal consumption and the plants do not exceed twenty in number.) People on the West Bank must carry their identification cards with them at all times; Jews as well as Arabs who are stopped by police are expected to show their cards of identity.

Westerners in Jerusalem and on the West Bank to whom we spoke exhibited a wide range of reactions to the present situation. For tourists, very little out-of-the-ordinary activity is noticeable, other than the presence of many armed soldiers on the streets. For Americans and Europeans stationed in the area as staff members of the many volunteer organizations, it is a different story. Such organizations would not be there if they did not regard the Palestinians to some degree as war victims, and thus in need of special help. In addition to the UN agency UNRWA, at least seventeen voluntary organizations operate on the West Bank, in Gaza, and in Jerusalem; they include CARE, Save the Children, Catholic Charities, Oxfam, the Friends Service Committee, American Near East Refugee Aid, German Aid, AMIDEAST.

What do the agencies do? They provide supplies for schools in the refugee camps in Gaza, they dispense grants for piped water, improved drainage, agricultural cooperatives, scholarships for Palestinian students to go on to the university. The voluntary organizations fall into two distinct categories, we were told: those that cooperate with the Israeli government and help the Palestinians on the West Bank by supplying what amounts to welfare services (food allotments, for instance), and those such as American Near East Refugee Aid that try to promote independent development among the Palestinians. The latter groups often wait for months, even years, for permission to implement their projects.

"We're here to help, in whatever way we can," said one representative. "I would rather work with the Israeli government because then I know it will be done."

Henry Selz, the representative of American Near East Refugee Aid, disagrees with that position. "The only way we can help the Palestinians is to let them rely on *themselves,*" he stated. "And the way to do that is give them the means to achieve some economic independence."

Mr. Selz is not always able to fulfill his aims. In the last three years many ANERA projects have not been approved by the military government.

"That's because the early ones were too successful," he argues. White-haired, lean, rangy, restless, he has been working for the American Friends Service Committee and other peace-promoting organizations for most of his life. "The Palestinians are good businessmen and excellent farmers. They organize well. Look at the olive oil cooperative in Tarqumiya, one of the poorest areas on the West Bank. It has twelve hundred members, representing people in fifteen villages. They're marketing the oil. It's working. And the same with the chicken and egg cooperatives in Ramallah. But those products compete against Israeli products in the market."

"And then what happens?" asked Bob.

"They're not allowed to sell the chickens or the eggs or the olive oil outside a small, specified area. Actually, that's not quite true," Henry corrected himself. "They must get a permit. But of course the permit isn't granted."

Henry Selz took us to see the new construction in many parts of the West Bank, to view small industries financed and run by Palestinians. "Look at that," he said, as we rounded a curve on the road south. A factory complex of some sort lay in the valley below us. It was empty, closed.

"What is it?" asked Bob.

"A cement factory. Doing very well," answered Henry. "Too well, in fact. So the military government passed an order, required the owners to buy their raw materials at retail rather than wholesale prices. That put them out of business rather quickly."

The situation in Israel and on the West Bank becomes more complex the more one travels, the more one sees, the more people one meets. Not all Palestinians are destitute, nor are all Israelis rich. The diversity in the Israeli population was expected; we had read about the different groups of people, from every class and every country, that constituted the new state. But we had not read as much about the Palestinians, even during our years in the Arab world. The Palestinians we met were as various as would be found in any sizable population, and 2 million is obviously a sizable population. Poor farmers, rich landowners, college professors, small-scale artisans, unskilled workers. The Palestinians are divided in other ways: geographically, between Israel proper, the West Bank, the Gaza Strip, and the Hashemite Kingdom of Jordan, just across the eastern border of the West Bank, two hours' drive from Jerusalem. Palestinians are also divided on the means to deal with occupation—militant, passive, opportunist, collaborationist. We visited a settlement in the Jordan Valley where the village leader explained to us in Arabic that he preferred to go along with the military government so he could obtain the things his village needed: electricity, a school. "You understand?" he asked anxiously.

We said that yes, we understood.

Hebron, a West Bank town of forty thousand southwest of Jerusalem, is a different story altogether. Hebron is sacred both to Jews and to Muslims as the site of Abraham and Sarah's tomb, and it is called Al-Khalil in Arabic, that is, "friend of [God, or Abraham]." The foundations of the city predate its biblical mention. A sizable Jewish community always lived in Hebron until 1929, a time of strife throughout Palestine, when four to five thousand Jews and Arabs lost their lives. Jews were killed by Muslims and most Jews left the area. Today a small group of Jewish families has come back to Hebron. After first settling outside the town of mostly Sunni Muslims, they are now moving inside the old city, praying in the old Ibrahimi Mosque, which developed from a Byzantine church. The joint prayers in the building proceed according to an agreement reached between Muslim and Jewish leaders. However, said Muslims, the Jews who come to pray still refuse to take off their shoes as a mark of respect to the mosque space.

We were sitting in the American Colony Hotel with a Western journalist when this tale was recounted to us. The journalist retorted, "Familiar kind of situation. Nothing new. Garden-variety colonial problems."

The garden-variety colonial problems looked more ominous when we drove to Hebron, past the outskirts of the town where the potters still produce the flowered painted plates that the Crusaders presumably took home as souvenirs in the Middle Ages, just as the German tour group pouring out of the bus paused on the road was preparing to do. In the center of town, across from the partially destroyed old market area, stands a military outpost, an armed camp surrounded by a high barbed-wire fence and floodlights. An Israeli flag has been planted in the middle of the parade ground, behind the barbed-wire fence.

What is happening in Hebron?

"Fanatics from the Muslim side and the Jewish side," asserted an Israeli professor of history. "The Jewish fanatics are all Americans. Why don't you keep your citizens at home?" Then he laughed. "I am only teasing," he added. "But you see what happens. A Jewish settler was killed. Then in retaliation you have that terrible attack on Hebron University, where three Muslim students were killed and many wounded, up to fifty, they say."

The wife of Rabbi Levinger, who heads the new Hebron Jewish community, was interviewed by a Jerusalem *Post* reporter for a feature on life in Hebron, which appeared on October 5, 1983. Asked whether she was upset by living in a hostile environment, she replied, "Not at all. We had the same problem in New York. There we were in danger, too, from blacks and Puerto Ricans. Here at least we are guarded by Jewish rather than Christian police."

We left Hebron and headed back to Jerusalem. "Would you like to live in Hebron?" asked Henry Selz. "It gives me the shudders whenever I come here these days."

Bob and I said that we would certainly not care to live in the city of Hebron.

Jerusalem has been the symbolic site of power struggles for centuries, not only between Muslim empires and Judaic leaders, but also between Christian groups, between the Egyptian Coptic Christian Church and the Ethiopian Christian Church, between the Russian Orthodox Church and the Greek Orthodox Church, between the Vatican and the Austro-Hungarian Empire. Today it is still a symbolic site, an ancient walled city, governed by Israel, yet fragmented into many small segments that are controlled by Christian, Jewish, Muslim groups. And outside the ancient city lie two other cities. To the west the new modern Israeli Jerusalem stands, with efficient buses, Western shops, art galleries, antique stores, pizza parlors, film clubs offering the newest American and European films. To the north and east of the walls, past the Damascus Gate, morning assembly point for Arab day laborers, lies the Arab city, officially considered part of the occupied territories, and under military occupation. The line seemed vague to us, and we asked people how they could tell where one section (legal) ended and the other (illegal) began. The Palestinians to whom we addressed this question looked at us incredulously.

"You *know*," they answered. "And you carry your identification cards all the time, everywhere. The Jews do, too. It's that kind of place."

As occupied territory, the West Bank is not a country, it is a non-nation, just a place, publicized on Western television by the incidents, the rock-throwing, the demonstrations, the weeping women. How do more than a million people go on living in such a situation?

"We don't all throw rocks," said one Bir Zeit student, rather defensively. "But that's all you hear about us in America."

"It's true," said Henry Selz. "Given the provocation under which these people live, I am constantly astounded at how peaceful they are."

"The small amount of violence constantly amazes me," agreed another voluntary agency official.

"We are *samid*," said a Palestinian professor.

"Agreed," said his wife. "It means *steadfast* in English. We are that."

Many Palestinians told us they were samid, steadfast. "It is a policy," they said, a stand, a way to survive with dignity. Samid means, "I will stay firm. I will not move."

But samid, as a stance, did not appear to be as passive in practice as we had expected.

Standing firm also involves standing by one's principles, expressing one's identity. Ibrahim Daqqaq, the elderly chairman of the Engineering Association of the West Bank, heads the Arab Thought Forum, an informal group established after other ethnically based organizations were declared illegal. "In old Palestine, we had problems, too," he said, "the individualism of our peasant farmers versus the communal ideal of the society. Here we must think about these kinds of problems, too."

The forum holds regular meetings with speakers; it has established a library. Members are academics, students, and, as Mr. Daqqaq describes them, "more practical persons." Part of the purpose of the Arab Thought Forum, he said, is to "make life bearable under unbearable conditions, to help create identity, cultural ties, combat a sense of despair and nihilism among our people."

The Israelis have talked about expelling or encouraging the emigration of Palestinians, according to Mr. Daqqaq. "But," he said, "getting rid of Palestinians is not an easy job. We try to help our people in the short term and in the long term, too, by protecting and developing Palestinian indigenous institutions."

Samiha al-Khalil, a vigorous dark-haired widow, views samid in another way. She is the founder and director of In'ash al-Usra, the society for the preservation of the family, which she sees as the most important indigenous Palestinian institution of all. With a study-tour group of American YMCA representatives, I visited Mrs. Khalil's educational and training center for girls. One hundred and fifty girls a year graduate from the society's programs in sewing, secretarial skills, hairdressing. She has organized support on the West Bank and abroad for children orphaned by the conflict and runs a nursery for working mothers. Mrs. Khalil has been jailed by the military government five times, we were told. When I asked her about her imprisonment, she brushed the question aside. "We want only to live in peace," she said. "Let them live. Let us live. We just want to stay on our land."

As we were leaving the center, waiting to shake hands and thank Mrs. Khalil for showing us the workshops, one of the American representatives of the Young Men's Christian Association of New York State said to me, "Isn't it wonderful to have a Christian woman in a place like this? She can do so much good with her faith, here in this Muslim land."

I turned and looked at the woman, pleasant-faced, gray-haired, well dressed. "But Mrs. Khalil is a Muslim," I said.

"Oh no," said her husband. "She can't be. She speaks about peace."

"You don't think the Muslims want peace too?" I asked.

The man and his wife looked slightly embarrassed. By now we had expressed our thanks and were standing outside in the midmorning sunshine, in front of the whitewashed building that housed Samiha al-Khalil's Institute for the Preservation of the Family.

The man said, "Well, that's not what we hear at home, is it?"

I found myself suddenly angry. "But you're *here,* not at home," I said, and at my tone two or three other members of the group of Christian leaders looked around curiously.

The pleasant-faced wife looked at her husband, at me. She fumbled with the brochure.

"Shall we go back and ask her whether she is a Muslim?" I finally got out, but the couple were already turning away, heading toward the tour bus.

"No, no," they murmured.

And I was left in the street feeling foolish, but still annoyed.

Abdurahman Natsche is the director of the University Graduates Union, a kind of student union building/night school/cultural center for Palestinians in Hebron; surely a difficult place these days, we thought, to practice the stance of samid.

"Oh no." Dr. Abdurahman smiled. "It is important. We must stay here. The building provides a recreation area for the youth of this town. We had the first library in the area."

"You've been here a long time?" asked Bob.

"Since 1953. We now administer the secondary school examinations of Jordan. We have adapted our institute program to the Israeli public school system here, which lacks history, geography, any sense of local culture, and so on."

"You fill in, in other words?" Bob said.

"Yes," said Dr. Abdurahman, a middle-aged man, heavily built, with a soft voice and a pleasant smile. "We give courses, fill in the gap between the local public school and a good education. A good education equals a good citizen. We try to connect this generation to its roots."

Law in the Service of Man is another kind of samid approach, a legal research and information unit, rather like the American Legal Aid Society, which occupies three small rooms on the upper floor of a small office building in downtown Ramallah. Begun in 1980 by two Palestinian lawyers, Jonathan Kuttab and Raja Shehada, to observe and report on the way in which international law is administered on the West Bank, the unit now has the support of the International Juridical Association. Leaflets, written in simple language, have been prepared by the unit on such subjects as what to do when you are arrested and what to do if the military government tries to take your land. It was Raja Shehada's moving book *The Third Way: A Journal of Life on the West Bank* that was being widely discussed in October, that was sold out in all the bookstores in both the Israeli section and the Arab section of Jerusalem. Shehada's account opens with an epigraph which, he says, is "from the wisdom of the Treblinka concentration camp: Faced with two alternatives, always choose the third. Between mute submission and blind hate—I choose the third way. I am Samid." Steadfast.

Two nights before leaving Israel we had dinner in a small Arab restaurant in East Jerusalem, around the corner from the National Hotel and its nearby tourist bazaars offering brass ashtrays, olive-wood carvings, crucifixes, Arab headdresses, and postcards of the holy shrines. We were a curious party: Bob and I; our photographer friend Tom Hartwell; the Swedish filmmaker; the British director of Oxfam Middle East; and an Israeli army officer who was active in the Israeli Committee for Solidarity with Bir Zeit University. I had noticed him at some of the sessions of the conference, tall, imposing, the biggest person in the room.

Human rights. The discussion was of human rights, East and West, of Israeli and Palestinian films and filmmakers—Jud Ne'eman, Michel Khleifi, Avram Gitai—of groups within Israel which protest regularly and loudly against the policies of the government toward the West Bank and Gaza. Peace Now. Israel Left. Committee for Solidarity with Bir Zeit University. Israel Association for Civil Rights. Oz VeShalom (Religious Zionists for Strength and Peace). There Is a Limit (Army Officers Who Refuse to Serve in Lebanon). The evening had begun in a series of somewhat wary interchanges, since at first we did not all know each other well and Bob and I and Tom had not even been introduced to the Israeli army officer, who was, it turned out, also a member of There Is a Limit. But the evening developed slowly into a serious discussion of serious subjects. We ate and drank—shish kebab, stuffed zucchini with yogurt sauce, lamb and vegetables, beer made in Israel from a Dutch recipe, wine from a local Christian monastery—though the Israeli army officer ate only bread and salad, I noticed, and drank a glass of water.

"What you don't realize," said the filmmaker, who had covered Vietnam for Swedish television, "is that the West has screwed both Israel *and* the Arabs."

The Israeli army officer was wearing a red shirt and blue denim overalls. He sat back in his chair, his thumbs under his overall straps. "Easy for you to say," he offered mildly. "Sweden has never taken a position on anything."

"Oh, come now," said the Briton, as the Swede opened his mouth to reply. "Let's not blame everything on the British and the Americans again."

"Why not?" said Bob. "Who bears more responsibility? Billions of dollars in U.S. aid means involvement *and* responsibility."

"Yeah, looks that way," chimed in Tom.

"I agree," said the Israeli officer. "But it has become more complex these days. It is an issue *here,* for *us,* in Israel." He banged his finger on the table to emphasize his words. "A moral issue. *We* must solve it, not *you.*"

"The Palestinians must also be involved in solving it," put in Bob.

"They already are involved," said the Israeli.

We stood on the street outside the restaurant, exchanging names and addresses. The Israeli was talking about the latest officer to be jailed for refusing to serve in Lebanon.

"But *you're* not in jail," said the Swede suddenly. "Why not?"

The Israeli looked down at the Swede. "I am a famous war hero," he replied. "It would embarrass the government to put me in jail."

We left the West Bank feeling that most of the Palestinians there were no longer convinced that a military solution to their occupation was possible; they seemed ready for a settlement which would involve their neutrality and independence. Clearly, the present polarized situation, the split society, benefits no one, neither Israelis nor the Arabs.

Rabbi Ovadia Yosef, chief Sephardic rabbi in Israel, said in 1979, "Under Jewish law, it is forbidden to give back even the smallest parcel of the Land of Israel, [but] if there is any question of life and death, if there is any danger whatever of a war involving bloodshed, for example, then it is surely permitted to hand back areas of the Land of Israel and arrive at territorial compromise anywhere including Judea and Samaria. . . . I am of the opinion that Israel should negotiate with all moderate Arab Palestinians who recognize Israel and accept UN resolutions 242 and 338."

And Raja Shehada had written in 1982, "It is the faces on the West Bank and in Israel that I love, admire, am proud to know, that have pushed aside my nightmare visions. . . . Our struggle is not senseless: it is not yet proven that good never wins the day."

A compromise on the West Bank could reduce the polarization, and improve the lives of everyone in this ancient region where Christian, Jew, and Muslim have fought for centuries over land they all love passionately. But what of the refugees outside the West Bank and Israel, three hundred thousand still in Lebanon alone? Where will they go? Who will concern themselves about them?

Thirty years of conflict, of violence, of rhetoric, have created a fog that, however dense, still cannot mask the two basic facts. The Jewish people were disenfranchised and suppressed in the brutal events of the Holocaust. The Palestinian people were disenfranchised and are being suppressed in the actions of the West to atone to the Jews for the great injustice done *them*. But the Arabs were not responsible for the Holocaust and do not see why they should suffer for the sins of Western civilization. Today both Jews and Arabs suffer.

Comment

ARAB LEADERSHIP

AMERICANS WHO notice are often surprised, even bewildered, by political leadership in the Arab world. How is it that a rather grubby-looking, unshaven man like Arafat has enjoyed so much loyalty while an attractive and well-groomed gentleman like Anwar Sadat turns off his former followers? In our media-oriented country, where makeup and hair dye are as much a part of the politician's image as proud parents and adoring wives (or attentive husbands), a man like Arafat, who speaks to the United Nations in fatigues and five-o'clock shadow, makes little sense to us.

Of course, one cannot very well generalize about all Arab leaders, ranging as they do from the President of a country of 44 million people (Egypt) to the reigning Emir of a small principality of 370,000 in the Persian Gulf (Bahrain). But it is reasonable to talk about some of the features of Arab leadership which, at all levels and in all places, seem to contrast with patterns of leadership in the United States and Western Europe.

High office in the United States is associated with celebrity; we want and expect glamour from our politicians, whether mayor or president. There must be a bit of excitement attached to the pressing of the flesh in a campaign tour. Even if bulletproof Plexiglas and tough-looking escorts with bulging suit coats keep us at a safe distance from the star, a public appearance remains an occasion, an event, and the more hoopla associated with it, the better. Indeed, many a political appearance is preceded by warm-up entertainment, like any other first-class act.

In the Arab world, it is still necessary that the leader be approachable. While modern measures of security may make this more difficult, the poorest and most obscure Arab man or woman expects to be able to call the leader's name and ask for his help. This is especially true if the person has been the victim of injustice. The King of Saudi Arabia still holds court regularly, open to all Saudis, in which petitions may be presented and where the King often acts directly to solve the problems. A big smile and a shake of the hand will not do; in fact such hype is largely missing and would be regarded with considerable suspicion. On his visits to Egyptian villages, the late President Anwar Sadat was expected to sit down and talk with the villagers about their problems; total authority means total responsibility, and Middle Eastern rulers must act on the most local issues if these are brought to their attention. Recently, President Hosni Mubarak of Egypt, accompanied by the foreign press corps, visited the Sinai Desert to open a new development project. Arab Bedouin, herders of sheep and goats, interrupted his public address to shout out complaints about the way in which their interests had been overlooked. The President of Egypt promptly asked the press corps to leave the assembly, which then became an open hour-long discussion between Mubarak and the outspoken herdsmen. At the conclusion of the private session the press, heels well cooled, was asked to return.

If this quality of personal concern for personal problems is successfully projected in the Middle Eastern political scene, other issues having to do with foreign and domestic policies are likely to be of far less general interest to people than is true in the States. At least this has long been the case so far as villagers and herdsmen are concerned. The Egyptian urban public is generally more sophisticated these days, however, and the growing middle class of high school– and college–educated Arabs is certainly no longer so easily satisfied as in the past.

Along with the quality of personal concern for his subjects, the Arab leader is expected to exemplify, albeit in somewhat grander form, the values and traditions of the people he leads. Thus the ceremonialism of the court or presidential residence is seen as only a more elaborate form of the hospitality expected of any household head in the Arab world. And, like their followers, leaders are expected to appear regularly at the public mosque to participate in the Friday prayers. Although today these appearances are surrounded by security precautions, they are expected nonetheless.

Middle Eastern leaders also do well not to move too far from the personal styles of their followers, or to do so in a most discreet fashion. King Hassan of Morocco keeps luxurious homes in France and Switzerland where, it is rumored, all kinds of goings-on take place. In Morocco, however, he behaves like the saint-king he is supposed to be. President Nasser always appeared in the uniform of his fellow officers, or in a modest business suit. Libya's President Qadhafi is seen in uniform or simple leisure suits. King Hussain of Jordan also favors the military uniform of his army, the major source of his political strength. In the absence of personal popularity, it will not do to become enamored of the extravagant trappings of royal rule, as the deposed King Farouk (and the late Shah of Iran) discovered.

An Arab leader is still perceived, by many followers, as a kind of superpatron, and the patron-client relationship can continue indefinitely, as long as the necessary duties are performed. (In much the same way an American senator is kept in office through satisfying his constituents.) Thus Arabs have traditionally felt quite comfortable having their leaders remain in office for as long as they exhibit basic competence, proper conduct, and what is perceived to be concern for the needs of their subjects. Age and wisdom are still considered to be related and experience is highly valued. The Americans' regular shift of presidents, on the other hand, is an alien idea to Middle Easterners, who find the rationale difficult to understand. Why does an American president have to leave office after four or eight years? Doesn't he learn anything? These are the kinds of questions Arab friends have asked us over the years.

Today Arab central governments are far stronger than was true at the end of the colonial era and the leaders are accordingly more powerful than before. At the same time, the state (and its leader) is now obliged to perform more duties than any leader in the past. This is also true in terms of the American presidency, where the responsibilities of that office have surely outgrown the mental capacities of any single person, leaving us to wonder who actually makes the decisions.

As the nation-states of the Middle East grow older, the styles of leadership will change and diversify in response to local conditions and expectations. However, many elements of traditional forms of leadership still remain, and those elements are very different from leadership qualities in other parts of the Third World, such as Latin America.

In the eighties, it seems less likely that a single head of state will speak to and for most of the Arab world as, for a time, Nasser seemed to do. Still, the length of tenure in office of a number of current leaders (Hussain, Hassan, Bourguiba, Qadhafi) is noteworthy, as is their domestic popularity, relatively speaking. Though not subject to popular recall, these leaders still seem to be fulfilling the expectations of the majority of their followers in the ways that count. Occasional abuses of power, such as the Iraqi government bombing of its own Shi'a village of Dujaila, are a familiar part of history in the Middle East and less surprising to Arabs than Americans. However, Egyptians, Tunisians, and Moroccans all took to the streets in recent years to protest violently when their leaders, pushed by international lending agencies, it is said, tried to raise the price of subsidized bread by a cent or two. Arab people have never failed to express disapproval when the issue at hand was deemed important enough or the leader incompetent enough. The question is what form those expressions of approval and disapproval will be able to take in the years ahead.

CHAPTER XIV

Baghdad and Al-Nahra, Iraq

1956, 1983

> O Iraq!
> O Iraq! I can almost glimpse, across the raging seas,
> At every turn, in every street and road and alley,
> Beyond the ports and highways
> Smiling faces that say: "The Tartars have fled,
> God has returned to the mosques with the break of day,
> A day on which the sun shall never set."
>
> Badr Shakir al-Sayyab
> *An Ode to Revolutionary Iraq*

IT WAS NOVEMBER 1956. Bob and I were in Baghdad. The pastries we were nibbling were crescent-shaped, stuffed to bursting with finely chopped nuts, sugar which seemed to have crystallized in the baking process, and plenty of cardamom. Delicious. The tea was strong. We sat gratefully around the Aladdin kerosene space heater on which the kettle hissed and steamed, for outside, along the partly paved streets and between the unfinished houses of this new part of Baghdad, the winter wind from the desert moved, rattling the windowpanes and pushing against the freshly stuccoed camel-colored walls in sharp gusts.

The Kirtikars' house, where I had taken a room while Bob traveled through southern Iraq, searching for a hospitable village in which to conduct his anthropological research, was new and drafty. The thick Persian carpets and the green and wine velvet upholstery on the furniture did not totally absorb the wind, nor the dank, bone-creeping cold that came up through the cement floors, directly from the chill, damp ground.

Bob had rejoined me in Baghdad for the weekend. "And why did you come to Iraq, sir?" asked the young man with sandy hair and a sandy sweater under his British tweed jacket. (In those days, the old Spinney's stores sold tweed jackets and Marks and Spencer underwear in addition to canned brussels sprouts and English biscuits—provisions for the ex–colonial civil servants who still lingered behind in the employ of King Faisal, and for the American Point Four assistance families who had arrived, it seemed, to take their place.)

"I came here to learn," said Bob. "It's part of my studies in anthropology, to do research in the field."

The young man looked at Bob with a mixture of astonishment and pity. But then we already knew that Baghdadis thought we were crazy. Anyone who would voluntarily go off to live in southern Iraq, much of which was without electricity and running water, half the time cut off from the rest of the world by impassable muddy roads, anyone who would do that had to be mad. And to be interested in tribesmen . . . there were no tribes in Iraq anymore, not according to the newly rewritten British laws, anyway. But then, everyone had ulterior motives. "It's very strange," said the young sandy-haired man, nibbling at his pastry. "All of us"—looking around at the Kirtikar family—"all of us have been here too long. We would like to leave, and you come all the way from America. I don't understand."

Bob began to explain, about the important relationships between America and the West and the Middle East, about reclamation of new lands, about technical assistance and international cooperation. He spoke eloquently and I was quite impressed. Not so the Kirtikars, nor their visitor, the sandy-haired young man, invited to meet us at this afternoon tea honoring Bob's weekend visit to the big city. (The cardamom crescent-shaped pastries were for Bob, Mrs. Kirtikar had shyly explained to me.)

The two Kirtikar girls, one pretty, one plain, listened to Bob and turned to each other and giggled. Their mother gave them a sharp look and they subsided. Mr. Kirtikar looked as though he might speak but decided against it. Our naïveté or our ignorance or our own duplicity was apparently too boundless to contemplate.

"Sir, I beg your pardon," said the sandy-haired young man. "There is nothing here. You don't seem to understand. The Middle East, all of this, this is nothing." He gestured around the new living room and toward the window, where we could see a half-finished house, obscured in the fading winter light by a haze of blowing sand.

"The Middle East," he said, firmly taking another crescent, "is just a corridor, a pass-through for great powers. Always has been. Throughout history. Even more now."

"But the Golden Age," I protested. "The Arabian Nights."

"That was centuries ago." The young man laughed disdainfully. "Do you see any magnificent palaces in Baghdad today?"

"Where are you from, please?" I asked politely, trying to head off what seemed to be developing into an unnecessarily unpleasant afternoon.

"Me? I am a Christian from Syria originally, but my family has lived here for about a hundred years. Mr. Kirtikar is from India, but his wife is a cousin of mine, from Damascus."

"But surely if people come from Damascus and all the way from India to Baghdad, there must be something here to come for," Bob observed. "Otherwise, why bother?"

Mr. Kirtikar set down his biscuit-filled plate. "Ah, Sami," he said to the sandy-haired young man. "You're not being fair to our guests. We are all here, my friend, because there is work to be found. What you mean, my dear Sami, most probably, is that you do not see a long-range future for yourself here in Baghdad."

"Why?" asked Bob. "Is it politics? Religious discrimination against Christians? East-West tensions? The Arab-Israeli conflict?" Bob came out with it. The company looked slightly embarrassed. Mrs. Kirtikar offered more tea. There were more cardamom crescents and also large round thick cookies with whole almonds pressed into their centers.

Sami nodded. He had apparently decided to take this strange American seriously. "All of those things," he replied. "Yes. I would like to go to America. Maybe you could give me a list of places where there are scholarships available? Because," he rushed on, "well, in addition to all of those things you mentioned you must remember that this is a poor area, a poor country. Without resources such as you are accustomed to taking for granted." He laughed, bitterly, I thought. "Nomads. The desert. Living off of goats' milk. You have surely heard of all that, even in rich America."

"But what about oil?" Bob asked. "You have plenty of that."

Mr. Kirtikar sniffed. "The British take most of it. Iraq gets only a small share. But you see the British made a great investment and they are the ones who brought the technology that made it possible for Iraq to exploit their oil. So they deserve the largest share."

Was he serious? I stared at him. He was, and he was not finished talking. "And the Arab-Israeli conflict, that is not such a problem. It will pass with time." He sounded a bit as though he were reciting a lesson.

"Mr. Kirtikar," Bob said, "you've just built a new house. Why, if there is no future here . . ."

Mr. Kirtikar shifted in his overstuffed chair and looked uncomfortable. "One must live as well as one can in the present circumstances that are open to one," he said stiffly.

"What about Mr. S. across the street?" pressed Bob. "The Iraqi UNESCO officer who has come home and built that big house, the one with the Ping-Pong table on the porch?"

A look passed among the company.

"Well, of course," said Sami. "He is a Muslim."

Mr. Kirtikar sat forward. "That is not the only thing, Sami. Being a Muslim is important, but he also has a degree from Oxford and a lot of money. His servant is a Muslim, too, but there is no future for him except as a servant. Just like us. We live in a poor area," he repeated, "a poor country."

In our freezing-cold cement room later, Bob and I discussed that conversation and could not decide what to make of it. What the Kirtikars and Sami were saying simply did not make sense to us. The Baghdad Pact had tied several nations together in a protective alliance against Russian encroachment. With the advice of English and American experts the Iraq Development Board was pumping millions of dollars from Iraq's small but growing oil revenues into irrigation projects, drainage schemes, land-reclamation projects. New homes were being built all around Baghdad, new hotels were under construction downtown. The political discontent among some of the intellectuals we had met was hard to take too seriously. They all seemed prosperous enough, well dressed, and with good jobs. It was true that the Parliament was hand-picked by the Prime Minister, and democratic elections were still not established. But they were surely on the way; it was only a matter of education. What could our landlord possibly mean, that this was a poor area and there was no future here?

But while we huddled in our cold little room in Baghdad, events had already been set in motion that would transform the Middle East and change the relationship between the West and the Middle East forever. After centuries of wooing and fighting, like old lovers, the West and the Muslim world were about to part again. But Bob and I were too close to see what was happening, just as were the Kirtikars and the tribespeople in the south and Sami the Syrian and Mr. S. of UNESCO. We all had our own rather myopic points of view.

Bob's and my meeting in Baghdad that November of 1956 was a kind of reunion for us, as the October rioting that followed the Suez war had separated us from each other and from the rest of the world for several days. Bob had been in Diwaniya, a small southern Iraqi town, and the local irrigation official, fearing for his safety—or perhaps because of orders—had confined Bob to the government rest house for his protection. There were demonstrations in the city streets, guns fired and stones thrown, protesting the Israeli, French, and British attack on Egypt, in an attempt to retake the Suez Canal. No matter that Bob was an American and America was trying to call off the troops; one Westerner looked like another, said the irrigation officer bluntly. For several days Bob's only contact with the outside world had been the rest house guard-servant, Ali, who brought him food and bits of news with each meal. "Russia has bombed New York," was one of Ali's first cheerful messages, making his subsequent report that it was only the American *Embassy* in *Baghdad* which had been burned, a welcome relief. Ali was full of news which was a mixture of radio broadcasts and street talk. Fortunately most of what he reported to Bob was pure imagination—or wishful thinking.

After five days, Bob managed to get to the public phone in the Diwaniya post office and call me at the Baghdad YWCA, where I was living until the Kirtikars' room was finished. Our conversation was full of mutual concern. Who had worried the most? I reported rather tearfully that I, with several other foreign ladies, had stayed in the YWCA building and its walled garden. We had been cautioned not to go out. We had been told that the tribes of the south were rising against the government. Bob had heard that Baghdad was in flames. Now that the situation was settling down, he promised to try and join me as soon as possible.

Ali had been Bob's source of knowledge during the troubles; I had had the YWCA director, a slender Englishwoman of uncertain age. The noise of gunfire plus the shouts of marching mobs which reached us occasionally from nearby streets apparently stimulated her to reminisce in graphic terms about the terrible events in Africa during the Mau Mau rebellions, which she had witnessed.

"The natives went quite berserk," she had reported cheerfully, in a high, thin voice. Her audience—me, two Sabena airlines secretaries, a German nurse, and an Iraqi woman teacher—listened without comment. "We could do nothing to stem the evil tide," she continued. "But we drank tea every afternoon. Kept up the routine, just as we are doing now, ladies." Her smile seemed slightly superior.

In fact, it was Bob and I who felt superior. After all, President Eisenhower was taking a firm stand against the British as well as the French and Israelis. It was infuriating to be identified with the English and their repression of African rebellions, as if America were also to blame! By helping Egypt, America, we thought, was now being true to its own origins as a once beleaguered colony.

The curbing of Israel and the old colonial powers in the Suez war, with U.S. help, seemed very significant to us at that time, marking the beginning of a new era in the region, the true end of foreign domination. Egypt under Nasser seemed to be setting a new pattern of independence and self-determination. While the remnants of British authority were still to be found in Aden and the small Gulf States, it was clearly only a matter of time till this would end. To us, the United States now seemed solidly on the correct side, supporting national independence for countries which had once been colonies, just like ours.

Even the Arab-Israeli conflict did not seem so far from solution in the late 1950s, nor did America's role in the Arab-Israeli conflict seem particularly important. Of course, many Palestinians had been displaced. We had seen the Palestinian refugee camps in Lebanon. But we had also met many prosperous middle-class Palestinians in Baghdad, doctors, teachers, and government civil servants. We supposed that in time both groups would merge with the local populations as the need for jobs and the possibilities of intermarriage completed peacefully the migration which the Israelis had begun by force. The Israelis would become more "reasonable," perhaps, offering compensation for the lands they had seized, so that both sides could become reconciled to the status quo and learn to live and let live.

Of course, what the United States had done to the Palestinians by helping the Zionists wasn't right, but one had to be realistic about such things. After all, what our ancestors had done to the American Indians wasn't right either. All we could do now was to push the Israelis to provide compensation, and our government had stated its support of this principle. Surely anyone could see the need for that; after all, Israel was an isolated country whose people were greatly outnumbered by the surrounding Arab populations. It had to make peace with the Arabs for the sake of its own survival.

The tense five days in Iraq during the Suez fighting was only part of a "transition" period, we felt, a slight danger for us as our life in Iraq began, but a clear sign to the Western world that a new era had begun in the Middle East. The demonstrations by the Iraqi people had been a statement to Iraq's Prime Minister Nuri Sa'id and his British advisers that a pro-Western policy in Iraq could not proceed in the face of Western aggression in other parts of the Arab world. This was a sign of Arab nationalism, the spirit of the times.

We were exhilarated by our own involvement in this event and felt slightly heroic, just to be Americans, on the right side. Bob as an anthropologist was devoted to the idea of cultural relativism, and we felt this included the right of each nation to set its own course and develop in its own way. But dearest among our unspoken assumptions was the belief that democracy would be the ultimate choice.

How then could the Kirtikars and Sami say there was no future in the Middle East? Coming from abroad, we had a clearer perspective. We could see that the future held a great potential indeed for the West, the East, for Arabs, Israelis, for everyone. The dark colonial period had passed, economic development was under way, and America was involved in improving the lives of the people who had been colonialized. Baghdad had been the center of a great Golden Age of civilization a thousand years ago. Another Golden Age, we firmly believed, was about to begin.

Bob settled finally in Al-Nahra, a village near Diwaniya in southern Iraq. The sheikh of the major tribe in the area, the Al-Eshadda, lived on the edge of the village and had offered us a small mud-brick house to live in; we accepted his hospitality with pleasure. I bade goodbye to the Kirtikars and set off, with Bob, one winter evening in December of 1956. For the next two years we lived in Al-Nahra as the guests of the sheikh. Sheikh Hamid traced his ancestry to the Shammar, the groups of nomadic tribes of the northern Arabian peninsula; his tribe had been settled in southern Iraq for nearly a hundred years. In the 1930s the Al-Eshadda and the other tribes who formed the Al-Agra confederation had been the last groups to surrender to British troops engaged in the "pacification" of the Iraqi countryside. The dissident confederation had held out until the heat of midsummer, when the British cut off their irrigation-canal water and bombed their villages. (The average temperature was over 100° F. in the shade.) While we lived there, from 1956 to 1958, the women I knew still spoke of that incident, though it had happened twenty years before our arrival.

"I dream that I go down to the irrigation canal," said my friend Laila, the niece of Sheikh Hamid. "And the canal is dry. In my dream I am very thirsty, but there is nothing to do about it. I sit there on the banks of the canal, but the water doesn't come back."

Bob's research, for his doctorate in anthropology from the University of Chicago, was a study of the relationship between irrigation and central authority; he was interested in the idea that "oriental despotism" had arisen from the need to create a bureaucracy to organize and direct water use on the farmland. He traveled with the men of the tribe, interviewed in the village market, and talked with the central government administrators in town.

My life was different, spent almost entirely with the women of the tribe and of the town, for Al-Nahra then was still a sexually segregated society. Honeymooning in a mud-brick house in a remote village of Iraq was not something I had exactly anticipated, and it was not easy in the beginning: the isolation, the difficulty in learning Arabic, and the need to wear the local ladies' garment, the abbaya, to cover up whenever I went out. We settled gradually in our little house with its walled, wild garden, a house that the sheikh had built for his youngest and fourth wife, Selma. Selma the beautiful, I used to call her, and she became a good friend to me, someone to whom I turned for help in those years. For I was often lonely at first.

Bob, as a Western man involved in research for a foreign university or government, was a reasonably familiar figure in the area, for he looked much like the British colonial civil servants who had administered the Diwaniya region until very recently. But I was an oddity, a Western woman who did not sit in the sheikh's guesthouse, the mudhif, with the men, as Gertrude Bell had done when she visited Al-Nahra in the twenties. And yet I had none of the personal or social attributes an Iraqi woman was supposed to have: no children, no gold jewelry, no women relatives as company, no skills as a housewife. I was a sad figure by local standards, and if it had not been for the kindhearted ladies who took pity on me, I might had led a miserable life, or simply left the field, decamped to Baghdad, and waited for Bob to finish his work. The women of Al-Nahra felt sorry for me and took me in; they taught me how to cook rice; how to embroider my pillowcases with the proper Arabic proverbs; how to improve my halting and broken Arabic. They took me on a pilgrimage, taught me poems, and tried to introduce me to a new world. They taught me by their example that there are many ways of organizing one's life, one's society, and that the diversity of human life in this world is one of its strengths rather than one of its weaknesses.

In many ways we were privileged in those years, though we were not really aware of it at the time. Privileged to witness a system that was coming to an end, a system that for better or for worse had served the peoples of southern Iraq since long before the British mandate began in 1920. The settled farmers, the town merchants, the government administrators, and the tribal nomads had lived in a relationship that was probably thousands of years old, since human beings first began to settle in Mesopotamia, the legendary site of the Garden of Eden. Al-Nahra was close to that site, which, according to myth, lay near the confluence of the Tigris and Euphrates rivers.

Bob's closest friend in Al-Nahra was Jamal, the irrigation engineer, a tribal boy himself who had gone to the university and risen through the new bureaucracy instituted by Nuri Sa'id, who ruled Iraq then under King Faisal II and the consultancy of the British government. Jamal appreciated the old tribal system, but he felt it had to go—and would go—in the new democratic Iraq that would arise from the revolution, a revolution, he said, that was just around the corner. Here we were much closer to Iraqi everyday life than we had been among the members of the foreign community in Baghdad, and we could see that the system as it stood had serious flaws. Life was hard, and people were hungry despite the highly publicized development board schemes that were supposedly transforming Iraq from a subsistence agrarian society to a more prosperous industrial nation. After the revolution, Jamal said, farmers would own their own land rather than be in constant fiefdom or sharecropping debt to the sheikhs, and the government would take on the task of cleaning and desalinating the land as well as distributing the new centrally pumped irrigation water. More equal laws would be passed, and women and men would work together in the new Iraq, Jamal added. He enlisted us to help his sister, who kept house for him, adjust to the new Western mode, in which unrelated men and women would sit together socially, without the veil or the all-enveloping black abbaya. In those days, all women of Al-Nahra covered themselves in public, and I had followed their example.

One month after we left Iraq, in July 1958, the revolution did take place, as Jamal had predicted, toppling the monarchy and the regime of Nuri Sa'id. Abdul Karim Kassem became Premier; the King was executed; Parliament was dissolved; sheikhs were outlawed. Our host Sheikh Hamid was clapped into jail for a brief period but soon released upon the intercession of one of his own sons, Hadhi, who had demonstrated against the Nuri Sa'id government in 1957 and 1958, while a student at the university. Hadhi himself had been jailed while we were living in Al-Nahra, and released through his father's intercession. But Sheikh Hamid had at that time refused to support his rebellious son at the university any longer. It was Hadhi's mother, my friend Bahiga, who had sold her gold jewelry so that Hadhi could continue his studies. Now the political tables had been turned. Hadhi eventually received a generous fellowship to do graduate work in chemistry in the United States.

Bob returned in 1964 to Al-Nahra, where he was received, as he said, "as though I had been absent six months rather than six years." By that time I had borne three children and the women of the sheikh's family sent back a present to my youngest child, Laila, a gold charm set with tiny turquoises such as children in the village wore to protect them from the evil eye. The village had benefitted from the revolutionary government's development programs, with improved roads and a new intermediate school. Sheikh Hamid was back in the village, receiving guests in the mudhif, and all seemed, in the village at least, much as it had been before. Construction had resumed on the nearby Mussayyib Irrigation and Drainage Scheme, a project begun in the fifties that was to benefit the entire southern alluvial plain eventually. The soil was to be leached and thus desalinated, the canals were to be cleared of the dread schistosomiasis-bearing snails, and water would be delivered on a regular basis to the farms. For the big difference in the area was that the large estates of the sheikhs had been broken up under the new land reform laws, and thousands of acres distributed, under government supervision, to small farmers.

Abdul Karim Kassem had fallen. Another central government took over the administration of the new Iraq. In 1967 Bob stopped in Baghdad on his way to Afghanistan. He did not have time to go down to the village, but his good friend Noor, Sheikh Hamid's oldest son, came to Baghdad to see him. People were still farming in the Al-Nahra region, Noor said, though many other agricultural areas were almost deserted, as hundreds of farmers had left the countryside for Baghdad in search of urban jobs. The situation generally was not good. The Mussayyib project had been stopped again. Sheikh Hamid had died of a heart attack while police guards stood outside his hospital room, for he had been accused of unpatriotic activities, unspecified, relating to his years as a member of Parliament in the old Nuri Sa'id government. "But he was well treated," said Noor, "in spite of everything." Bob felt that Noor's visit to see him was taken at some personal risk, the political situation being so volatile in those years, and both of us felt some reluctance to correspond with our friends for a time, in case their connection with us, as Americans, placed them in difficulty.

Thus we were more than pleased when Hadhi called us from California one day in 1973. He was nearly finished with his Ph.D. and had heard, he said, that I was scheduled to lecture at a nearby university. "Bob," he said, "I know you don't want your wife staying alone in a hotel room, it wouldn't be proper, so I've arranged for her to stay with a good Iraqi family. Don't worry about her at all. I'll be staying in the same house. I will meet her at the airport and take her back when she leaves."

At first I was somewhat taken aback. I had not seen Hadhi for years and had indeed scarcely known him in Iraq, though I had known his mother and sisters well. I had been rather looking forward to the privacy of a California hotel room for a day or two. But then I remembered that to my friends in Al-Nahra, the greatest misfortune that could befall any person was to be alone, without kin, and among strangers. And I was moved and touched that, after all these years, Hadhi still considered me enough like a member of his family so that he had gone out of his way to make my stay more comfortable and more respectable.

The Iraqi family welcomed me warmly. The lecture went well; I asked Hadhi to make a few comments about his own experience, and he did so with grace and charm. The day I was to leave he invited me to visit his laboratory, where his thesis was in preparation. I protested that I knew nothing of chemistry, but he insisted. When we got to the laboratory, I saw why. Instead of demonstrating the complicated experimental equipment he had set up for his thesis, he showed me photographs. Dozens of photographs of the family and the tribe—the children that had been born since we had left in 1958, the new wives and husbands, the sons and daughters who had graduated from high school and college. One of Hadhi's own sisters, the sheikh's daughter, was teaching in a boys' school in Diwaniya, something that would have been unthinkable when we were living in Al-Nahra. At that time girls of the sheikh's family had only been attending the village school for five or six years. It had been Selma, beautiful Selma, herself a secondary school graduate, who had encouraged her husband, Sheikh Hamid, to send the girls to school.

"The revolution had many good effects," said Hadhi. "If we look outside of politics, we can see that. Lots of schools. The girls are really becoming independent."

"And do they marry outside the tribe?" I asked, remembering Laila's long-ago explanation of tribal purity. The reluctance of the lineage to give its daughters in marriage to strangers outside the clan meant that many girls of the Al-Eshadda did not marry in those years. For the boys had started school before the girls; many had gone on to college and often did not wish to marry their illiterate cousins.

"Well . . ." Hadhi temporized. He paused, took off his glasses, wiped his eyes. He was tall and dark, with a look of his mother, but with the height and breadth of his father—a big man. He had the high cheekbones and aquiline features of the desert Arab. "Not yet," he said, put on his glasses, smiled at me. "Maybe I will arrange for one of my younger sisters to be the pioneer."

"*Inshallah* [God willing]," I replied, rather mechanically. Things hadn't changed too radically in Al-Nahra, at least not yet, I thought.

When I left, I thanked Hadhi profusely for his help and chided him for not visiting us in Austin. "You must come before you go back to Iraq," I said, "or it will be great *ayb* [shame], on our house if not on yours. What will people think if you spent all this time in America and we never had you in our home?"

Hadhi shook hands with me, nodded, rather formally. Had I not insisted enough? It had been fifteen years then since I had lived in Al-Nahra. Perhaps I had forgotten my Al-Nahra manners.

"We would really like you to come," I said again. "And my husband Bob would like to see you."

Hadhi inclined his head slightly.

"Have you ever stayed with an American family?" I tried another tack.

"No," he replied.

"Well, then, Hadhi," I said firmly, "you must come. That's terrible. What kind of idea of Iraq would we have had if we had only stayed in Baghdad and talked to Americans?" I rushed on, "And you must meet our children so you can report back to your mother that I'm really okay. She and Selma and Kulthum were so good to me when I was there, and felt so sorry for me because I was childless."

Hadhi smiled then and nodded, much less formally this time. "I will try, B.J.," he said. "Though I cannot promise," he added, "that I will convey your news *personally* to Selma. I think my mother still does not like her very much."

"Yes," I said. Yes, I thought. Selma was the fourth wife, very beautiful, replacing Bahiga in Sheikh Hamid's affections. How could she like her very much?

Hadhi spent a week with us in Austin. It was a good time. Returning, even briefly, the hospitality that had been offered us so generously years ago by Hadhi's father was a great pleasure. Having someone from Al-Nahra see us in America, in our own setting, somehow completed something, closed a circle we could never quite complete while we had been in Iraq.

As a guest in our house, Hadhi was able to talk about those times with us, the role of Nuri Sa'id and the King, the prerevolutionary demonstrations, the imprisonments, his father's displeasure and anger. Time had softened his own resentment of his father and all he represented. "But still, I was not wrong, Bob," said Hadhi, "in opposing the system then. It was a bad system. They tell me that the Ba'ath party is really improving things in Iraq now. That's good, if true. I'm looking forward to going home—"

"But—" Bob interrupted.

"But what?"

"What about politics?" Bob asked. "You were always into politics, Hadhi. It sounds like it might be dangerous these days."

Hadhi set his jaw. "I have resolved not to meddle in politics," he declared, "but only do my research and teach at the university."

"And will you marry?" I asked.

"Yes," said Hadhi, and, suddenly turning to Bob, "I will not behave toward my wife in the macho way many American men do."

"Macho way . . . ?" Bob looked surprised. "Compared to Iraq in the old days?"

"Yes!" said Hadhi vehemently. "Why even you, Bob, are . . . somewhat that . . . way. . . ." He trailed off and looked anxiously at Bob. "Don't be upset, it's just—"

"I'm not," said Bob, "I'm just surprised, that's all."

"You see," said Hadhi, "when you were in Iraq studying us, we were studying you, too, you know. And we watched you very carefully to see how you acted."

"You did, did you?" Bob said, half smiling.

"Yes. We learned that some things in the West are good, and some things are not."

"Like . . ."

"Like marriage and relations with women and so on. Your system is a good one, but you do not take marriage very seriously. Marriage, I believe, is to found a family," he said.

"Well." Bob gestured around our house. "That's what we tried to do, wasn't it, B.J.?"

"Yes," I answered.

Hadhi nodded. "But there are some things that you could improve, Bob, in the way you *treat* your family. That's all I mean."

"You're right, I'm sure, Hadhi," said Bob, a bit stiffly. Then, "But did your father treat your own mother so well, marrying Selma and all?"

"That was the system at the time," Hadhi said. "Unjust. Your own system in the West seems to me to be more just to women and men. But it differs from one person to another. It can be abused. But I think it can be wonderful, if one works hard at it."

"Yes," I said. "Now let's have dinner."

We took Hadhi to San Antonio, into the Hill Country around Austin, and down to the LBJ Ranch, which he wanted to see. He was particularly fascinated by the contrast between the tiny house where President Johnson was born and the great sprawling house of the ranch itself.

"And the big house belonged to his mother's brother, not his father's family?"

"That's correct."

"And he grew up here, in this little house, seeing that big house, all the time, and knowing that it wasn't his?"

"Yes," said Bob.

"Now I see," said Hadhi, quite seriously, "what drove Mr. Johnson to his ambitions. He wanted his uncle's house and had to get rich enough to buy it. He couldn't inherit it, right?"

"Right," said Bob, without hesitation.

We have not heard directly from our friends in Iraq since Hadhi left Austin in 1974, on his way home. And we have not written, being advised by Iraqi friends in England, Egypt, and the United States that it is better not to draw attention, these days, to individuals of the Shi'a sect. The Iraq-Iran war, which has been in progress since 1980, has disrupted civil life in Iraq, for it has drawn attention to the historic religious differences which have always divided the country, between Sunni Muslims in the north and Shi'a Muslims in the south. The Shi'as of southern Iraq have been in contact with the Shi'as of Iran for centuries, through trade and more especially through pilgrimage—as men and women traveled back and forth across the borders to visit the Shi'a shrines in Iraq (Najaf, Kerbela, Kadhimain) and in Iran (Meshed, Shiraz). The Ottoman Turks, who were Sunni, encouraged the Shi'a-Sunni split, as did the British administration which followed, using tactics of divide-and-conquer as a means of more easily controlling a subject population. In general, it has been Sunnis who have ruled Iraq. But after the 1958 revolution, efforts were made to heal the traditional breach, and Shi'as as well as Sunni figures were named to Cabinet posts and other positions of importance in the new revolutionary hierarchy. That entente has been eroded by the current war.

In the struggle against Iran, a Shi'a country, Iraqis of Shi'a persuasion are under considerable pressure to demonstrate that their primary loyalty is to their nation, rather than to their religious sect. Some Iraqi soldiers have apparently actually defected to the Iranian side, stating that their Shi'a ties were stronger than their ties to the nation of Iraq. The situation has become more and more complex. Shi'a families, say Iraqi friends in the West, have been persecuted, jailed, some even deported on the justification that not only are they Shi'a, but they are registered as Iranian citizens!

These allegations are made on the basis of documents of the pre–World War I period, when the Ottoman Turks, recruiting men to fight against the British, went from house to house in Iraq asking the men, "Are you Turkish or Persian?" In those days, answering "Persian" meant one was not under Turkish rule and hence not subject to military service; "Turk" meant instant induction into the Ottoman army. Many Shi'as, understandably, declared themselves Persians (they are now called Iranians) in order to avoid conscription. One of our Shi'a friends remembers that, at the time of the Turkish census, his grandfather was one of ten sons; eight were of military age, two were past fifty. The older men told the census taker they were Turks, the younger insisted they were Persian. It is the descendants of the eight younger brothers that have been persecuted by the Sunni government of Iraq today. In recent months, we have been told, this movement of arrests and deportation has stopped. But we have had no opportunity to find out for ourselves, for we have not been able to return to Iraq.

In 1981, Bob was invited to present an academic paper at a conference at the University of Basra; as his wife, I was included in the invitation. We were delighted at the prospect of seeing once more the land where we had begun our long sojourn in and relationship with the Arab world. We hoped also to see some of our old friends. We were in Cairo at the time, and telex messages reached us regularly from Baghdad, informing us that our visitors' visas were waiting for us at the Iraqi Embassy. Accordingly, we went to the Iraqi Embassy in Cairo, no longer an embassy exactly since Iraq and Egypt have no diplomatic relations at present, but an "interests section," under the Spanish flag, which performs the routine business of processing workers' visas and issuing passports. We stood in line with migrant Egyptian workers, who were waiting for their permissions to arrive so they could accept contracts for construction work and farming in Iraq. The Iraqi officials were polite, pleasant, offered us tea. Most of the migrant workers eventually received their permissions. Our visas never came.

Despite the tensions between Shi'a and Sunni, all of our sources, including both Iraqi friends and American archaeologists who have spent part of each year in Iraq for the past twenty years, insist that great economic improvement has taken place throughout the country. The new Iraqi antiquities museum in Baghdad is described as a jewel among museums. Slum sections of the capital have been torn down and public housing erected. Villas, luxury hotels, and modern public buildings surround the new public squares. In preparation for the conference of nonaligned countries scheduled to be held in Baghdad in 1981, a full-scale urban renewal program was launched. A convention hall was built, parks landscaped, high-rise housing for conference delegates begun. Labor was being done by Iraqis in cooperation with migrant workers from Turkey, Egypt, Korea, Pakistan, and India.

And although the government may be questioning the loyalty of its Shi'a citizens in the south, at the same time it has been spending a great deal of money to improve the area. The Mussayyib irrigation development scheme is almost complete. Diwaniya, a sleepy provincial capital in 1958, now boasts an automobile tire factory, a plant which produces heavy metal machinery, and several brick factories. Industrial smog hangs over the roofs of the town. Al-Nahra itself, where we lived in our mud-brick house, has tripled in size. The market is larger and the mosque has been refurbished. Fewer women wear the abbaya and veil than in the past. Today many foreigners live in the village, since migrant workers from Egypt, Turkey, Pakistan, are present even there, two hundred miles from the capital.

The tribal system officially ended in 1958 with the revolution, but some of the trappings and traditions of the system apparently still survive. Another sheikh from the Al-Eshadda lineage succeeded Sheikh Hamid after his death, and the mudhif, or tribal guesthouse, where Bob spent so much of his time in the years we lived in Al-Nahra still stands, on its slight rise, near the outskirts of the village. Modern brick houses have been built next to the mudhif, friends say, but they are dwarfed by the majestic proportions of the mudhif, constructed of reeds and mats in a distinctive arched style reminiscent of ancient Sumerian temples.

A new railroad is under construction from north to south Iraq, and an eight-lane highway, the autobahn of the Fertile Crescent, is being laid from Jordan to Kuwait. When finished it will pass within two miles of Al-Nahra, ending whatever remnants of isolation the village might have had.

Before the 1958 revolution, Badr Shakir al-Sayyab, one of the great Arab poets of his time, wrote:

> In Iraq there is hunger.
> At the time of the harvest the crop is winnowed
> So crows and greedy locusts will be fed.
> But the people still stand in the harvested fields,
> And the mill grinds them with the gleanings and the stones.

That stain of poverty has been erased. People in Iraq are not hungry anymore. Thanks to OPEC, the country's oil revenues have risen far beyond any limits that our old friend Mr. Kirtikar could have imagined, twenty-five years ago when we sat in the drafty living room of his new Baghdadi house. Actually, few Western or Arab observers predicted the extent of the oil wealth that was to change the Middle East in one generation from a backwater, a corridor between continents, into an area of major importance in international affairs. A goodly portion of Iraqi oil revenues has been used, as was promised by one revolutionary government after another, for capital improvements, for development of human resources.

But all the urban renewal, the construction of railways, highways, and irrigation projects, has come to a standstill in recent months. The war between Iraq and Iran has changed everything. Fears of bombing caused the nonaligned nations conference to be canceled. The economy is being drained, to the point, friends report, that women have been asked to contribute their gold jewelry to the national cause. Battle casualties are rising. The war drags on, a conflict not so much an outcome of colonialism as one which goes back much further, to the ancient rivalries between Persian and Arab, which were expressed later in the differences between Shi'a and Sunni Islam. Oil revenues today are being used to buy munitions and food.

Iraqi friends in Cairo, exiles from the current regime, spoke glumly about the situation in 1981.

"Sometimes I feel that the spirit of human dignity has been violated in Iraq," said Mme. R., passionately. "It breaks my heart. There were so many possibilities, so much potential."

"Yes," said Bob.

"You remember, both of you, you were there," went on Mme. R. "And I, I was young, newly educated, full of enthusiasm for the new nation. I was one of the first women in Iraq to become an engineer."

We nodded, remembering that time.

Dr. R. spoke up. "Then we thought all we had to do was bring down the bad regime of Nuri Sa'id, get rid of the British, and everything would be fine."

"Not that simple," said Bob.

"No," Dr. R. replied. The midafternoon light, coming through the window of the Swissair restaurant where we were lunching, shone harshly on his face, showing the deep lines of disillusionment, fatigue.

"We were too young, too naïve," he said. "We didn't take seriously the differences between us. You can't change a society overnight, educate a people in one generation."

"But really, Adnan," put in his wife, "we were doing it, really, until the war."

Dr. R. shook his head. He smiled at his wife. "Ideals. You have always had ideals, my dear. And that is wonderful. But ideals are not enough. You need experience. And attitudes between people, between men and women, must change, too."

I nodded, vigorously. "Yes," I said. "I remember that President Kassem changed the law after the revolution so men and women could inherit equally. Then when he fell, the next government changed the law right back to the old way—men getting twice what women get."

Bob stared at me. "I'd forgotten that."

Dr. R. smiled again, this time at Bob. "Women don't forget those things, Bob. Why should they? It's attitudes she's talking about. And let's not forget history. You in the West have had many years to develop your governments, your industry. We are just beginning."

"It's true," said Bob. "Even the tyrannical old sheikhs on the Tigris kept the food coming from their estates to the market. Who's farming now?"

"You can scarcely find a local onion to buy in the city," said Mme. R. "And a lunch like this"—she gestured toward the remains of the excellent fish and rice which still lay on our plates—"fish costs up to twenty-five dollars per *fish,* if you can find one."

"Something went wrong," said her husband. "The ideals went sour. And now we are killing and being killed. For what?"

Clearly, no new golden age can begin in Iraq as long as conflict, such as the Iran-Iraq war, continues. At the end of 1983, prospects for peace looked brighter. And Iraq was making overtures to American companies once more. Perhaps the time is coming when we will be able to return to Iraq, and visit, without risk to them or to ourselves, the old friends there who taught us so much about the world of the Middle East when we were still young.

CONCLUSION

As WE WRITE, several conflicts are in progress in the Middle East. Lebanon continues to be the site of intermittent fighting, though mediation efforts between the leaders of the different political groups are at least under way. Algeria and Morocco have still not solved their border differences, and the quarrel over the fate of the Western Sahara is not yet concluded. Iraq and Iran are involved in a dangerous war that began in 1980 as "a brief battle of a few weeks" and still shows no sign of conclusion. No breakthrough seems imminent in the thirty-six-year-old Arab-Israeli conflict, with the result that the Palestinian question remains unresolved, and thousands of people, both inside and outside Israel, remain in an unsettled state. Factionalism within the Palestinian revolutionary movement has complicated the situation, as have Jewish settlements on the Arab West Bank. Beyond the scope of this book, in Iran and Afghanistan, other struggles go on. Muslim guerrilla fighters badger the Russian-dominated government in Afghanistan, and Iran is having difficulty keeping the peace inside its own boundaries.

No single explanation can be found for the recent violence, which seems to be a combination of old animosities and new pressures. Certainly, since the fifties, when we first went to the Arab world, the traditional systems of political order have been undermined. In the old days, one of the factors that kept potential conflict in check was the ability of the old elites within the Middle East to control their own people and to conclude alliances with other groups out of a sense of common interest. Now, after the colonial experience and the growth of centralized government, these arrangements often no longer work. A further destabilizing factor has been the policies of foreign powers, both East and West, who provide enormous amounts of money for arms, frequently in cynical actions that seem to contradict their own statements of intention and ideology. Arms dealers in many countries have made many millions of dollars from Middle Eastern conflicts.

In our early years in the Middle East, all of these factors were present, but with a crucial difference. The level of outside arms support was less great and the power of central governments to make wars less strong than is the case today. Further, in the past a sense of outside security existed, left over from colonial days. If things got too bad in the Middle East, we felt (as did many of our Arab friends), "other forces, other powers," i.e., the West, whether it be America, Britain, or France, would come in and put it right. This happened in 1956 when Israel, Britain, and France launched their attack on Egypt during the Suez crisis, and the United States intervened to stop the attack and restore peace. But what worked in 1956 obviously does not work in 1984, as the disastrous U.S. intervention in Lebanon indicates.

As the old alliances and power hierarchies have disintegrated, new leaders have stepped into the vacuum, backed by loyal followers, combinations of relatives and true believers. For example, the village of Tikrit, in northern Iraq, actually runs the country through its favorite son, Saddam Hussain; in Syria, President Hafed al-Assad is the favorite son of the Alawites, a small Muslim minority sect. The Muslims in Lebanon, who feel they have been kept from the growing wealth and power of their country, battle against the Christian Arabs, who are struggling to maintain their crumbling ascendancy, backed by the West. In Iraq, a largely middle-class struggle is underway between Sunnis and Shi'as. Sunnis, who have traditionally run the country but are nationally a minority, are taking advantage of the war with Shi'a Iran to undermine the position of the Iraqi Shi'as, who have always been a challenge to the Sunni leaders and to the Baghdadi government. The most recent evidence of the attempt to suppress the Shi'as is a law supposedly already on the books: under this law, any Sunni man with a Shi'a wife is awarded a prize of ten thousand Iraqi pounds if he divorces her. In times of conflict, old scores are settled under new guises.

The respect for the United States in the Arab world has plummeted in the past generation. In the fifties, America still seemed somewhat anticolonialist. Not only did Eisenhower back the Egyptian right to nationalize the Suez Canal, but Supreme Court Justice William O. Douglas made special visits to the Moroccan nationalists who were in jail for defying the French. Senator John F. Kennedy spoke up in the U.S. Senate against the inhuman methods used by our long-standing ally France in trying to suppress the independence movement in Algeria. But the continually broken promises about attempting to resolve the Arab-Israeli conflict have gradually eroded any sense that America could be counted on to keep its word. We have tried to explain to Arabs over the years that American foreign policy, especially in the Middle East, is dictated more by domestic politics and interest groups than by realpolitik; but that makes the policies no more popular with our Arab friends.

"You're saying that America doesn't operate on the basis of its international self-interest?" asked an Egyptian friend, incredulously.

"Of course not," we answered. "We call it 'domestic realism' and every politician up for election understands it very well."

In our most recent visit to the Arab world in October 1983, no one suggested that America might be a friend of the Arabs anymore, or that America even represented, to the slightest degree, the ideals of independence and self-determination which we were thought to stand for in the fifties. We sensed disappointment, and embarrassment for us, as Americans, among many old friends; among new acquaintances, a good deal of politely suppressed hostility.

But it is not only America which has lost prestige in the Arab world. The Soviet Union has suffered as well. In the late fifties, when Russia picked up the financing of the High Dam at Aswan, which John Foster Dulles had arbitrarily shot down, political analysts spoke about the birth of Soviet influence in the area and predicted that Russian strength would grow in the Middle East. That expectation remains largely unfulfilled. President Sadat threw the Soviet technicians and advisers out of Egypt after their job was done. The Soviet system has little appeal for Arabs; the rich countries find no return for capital investments in Russia and they worry about communist subversion at home. In poor as well as rich countries, Russia's atheist doctrine is ideologically repellent to the majority of Muslims. Troubles within the Russian domestic economy are not lost on the Arab world, which receives regular satellite radio and television broadcast news about Eastern as well as Western Europe. The coup de grace for any overall Russian entente in the area was the Russian invasion of Afghanistan. There atheist Russians are attempting to subdue Muslim rebels, a fact that is obvious to Muslim communities everywhere.

Thus both great powers have failed in their efforts to dominate the area politically. Russia and the United States are at a far lower point of influence in the eyes of Middle Eastern leaders and their people than they were twenty-five years ago.

Still, even if the region as a whole is not a partisan of either East or West, its involvement in the international economic system is greater than in the fifties and sixties. This has domestic repercussions. The largest country, Egypt, has American banks and firms of every variety, while North Africa and Lebanon have French and English financial enterprises. Labor migration affects almost every country. Throughout the area a new middle class with European tastes and life-styles confronts conservative groups concerned about more traditional standards of conduct. Beneath these ideological differences lie questions of economic and political hegemony: which sections of the society are to enjoy it?

Not surprisingly, reactions and counterreactions are stronger than ever. Muslim groups are pulling more to the conservative side in countries such as Sudan, where alcohol has been newly outlawed and the Koranic punishment of amputating the hands of thieves has been imposed. In Saudi Arabia, a decade of growth and development in the women's universities seems to be slowing down, with the transfer of authority from the women administrators of the universities to a high council composed only of men. Egypt's new family law of 1979, hailed as a new reform, still does not prohibit polygyny (the goal of progressive women's and men's groups for years), though the law does place certain restrictions on its practice. At the same time, President Hosni Mubarak will not permit religiously based parties to participate in the country's proclaimed "new democracy," a policy he shares with the late leader of Turkey, Mustapha Kemal Atatürk. It was Atatürk who stated fifty years ago that only a secular government could achieve real democracy.

On the other hand, there are also some important indications of growing stability. Algeria and Morocco, despite the worrisome issue of the Sahara, are removing themselves from other internecine quarrels and assuming the role of mediators. It was Algeria, after all, which helped resolve the Iranian hostage crisis with the United States. Morocco seems to view itself as a potential mediator in the Arab-Israeli dispute; King Hassan II convened the Fez conference of Muslim nations in 1983 with this purpose in mind. Morocco still has a large resident Jewish population and the King himself has invited any Moroccan Jews who emigrated to Israel to return. Some have done so. Little progress seems to have been made, however, despite King Hassan's efforts. People asked us whether we thought Israel was going to continue to seek its security through military superiority or was willing to try to negotiate the demands of a population that still considers itself disenfranchised: some provision for a Palestinian homeland, some self-government for the Palestinians. For many thoughtful Arabs, that seems to be the key question. The new wave of American Jewish immigration to Israel for largely religious reasons alarms thoughtful Arabs, who see in this militant Judaism a religious irredentism that is even less tolerant of other groups than the older Israeli society. Their expressed ambitions to regain ancient Judea and Samaria (i.e., the West Bank of the Jordan) bodes ill for any resolution of the Palestinian population's hope for self-government there.

The 1984 Egyptian elections are an extremely hopeful sign, the first relatively free national elections in more than a generation. Elections are not new in Egypt, but they have been mostly pro forma. The governments of Nasser and Sadat seldom allowed opposition to develop. But in the 1984 election, four parties fielded candidates against President Mubarak's ruling National Democratic Party. The outcome seemed fairly certain, and it is true that the President's own party took 87.6 percent of the vote. But 12.3 percent of the seats in the 438-member Egyptian Parliament will be filled by opposition candidates, the largest number since the days of King Farouk and his British commissioners. Even more promising was the countrywide interest in the election, the seriousness with which the process was taken, the press coverage, the candidates' speeches, and the television appearances which accompanied the campaign. President Mubarak has apparently allowed much more freedom of the press than either of his predecessors. Since Egypt has the largest and most densely settled population in the Arab world, and is also considered the cultural center of the region, its example is watched, discussed, and often imitated.

A new development that seems irreversible is the rise of a new middle class, emerging in all countries, thanks to changes in the economy, the rise of education, the improvement in health conditions, and the growth of the media. This group of people has aims and expectations, demands and needs, which are different from those of their parents and grandparents; and its members will be the most important group to watch in the future.

Another new development in recent years has been the resurgence of interest in Islam. The West tends to view Islam as a regressive force, as a return to the Middle Ages. This is partly because of our own stereotypes of Islam, and partly because of our still-disputed constitutional separation of church and state.

Religious movements in the Middle East, however, like religious movements in Europe before the rise of secularism in the eighteenth century, have historically been either reactionary or reformist. For example, the Spanish Inquisition is considered reactionary, the Protestant movement reformist. On a different scale, the Muslim Brotherhood in Egypt is considered a reaction, the religious movements against colonialism a kind of reform. Religion provides as good an ideological basis for revolt as secular political movements, it is clear. Thus, initially positive statements of Muslim identity may evolve into reactions against the West. Militant groups such as Repentance and Holy Flight in Egypt are, as one Arab friend succinctly put it, "politics in a religious package."

Yet today the personal return to religion is more important to the people of the region than any political dimension. This return is evident in every country in the area, reflected by modest dress among women, increased piety, and new questioning of theological and legal issues among young middle-class Muslims. Women's movements (which in the Middle East are composed of many men as well as women) are also emerging, promoting legal reform (Jordan, Morocco, Algeria, Egypt) and abolition of female circumcision (Sudan, Egypt). In Egypt's Parliament, during the past three years, women members from all parties have developed a united front on issues which affect women, such as equal pay for equal work, pension and health benefits, and provisions for childcare in the workplace. And books such as *The Year of the Elephant* by Laila Abouzeid of Morocco are beginning to appear, defining a new approach to feminism, with indigenous rather than Western roots.

The independence following the end of the colonial period is now more than a generation old. Serious problems remain, and many of our Arab friends are saying that they need to be left alone to have time and space to develop their own solutions. Whether that will be possible in the interdependent world of the 1980s is another matter.

Finally, a more personal note. The current history we have been discussing has affected our old friends and new friends, some tragically, some more positively.

Hadhi, the son of the sheikh with whom we lived in Iraq from 1956 to 1958, received his doctorate in botany from the United States and visited us in Austin in the mid-seventies. Since then, he has disappeared from his teaching position at the University of Basra and has not been heard from. Iraqi exiles suggest that he is another casualty in the wave of anti-Shi'a feeling in southern Iraq.

The Palestinian refugee camp of Rashadiya, where we filmed in June 1981, was overrun and partially destroyed one year later, during the 1982 Israeli invasion of Lebanon, and what remains is still under Israeli control. We have heard nothing directly from Um Zhivago and her family, although relief agency personnel reported that Abu Zhivago was a prisoner in the Ansar camp but had been released. The whereabouts of the family is now unknown to us. Colonel Azmi, the PLO commandant of South Lebanon, guest at our end-of-filming dinner party in Rashadiya in 1981, has also disappeared and is presumed dead.

Mona al-Shafei, our old friend the poet, came to the United States in 1983 to escape the new wave of bombing and strife in Lebanon. She stayed less than six months, and just before returning to Beirut she called us. "I can't write here, my friends," she said. "It is not my place."

The Western press for a time discussed King Hussain of Jordan as the possible negotiator for the Palestinian cause. But King Hussain did not accept the option. His Queen, Noor, has borne two children since we were invited to tea at the palace on a rainy day in January 1981.

The American University in Cairo, once a bastion of the liberal arts, is shifting toward commerce. Over half the students are majoring in business administration, a reflection of what is happening in the Egyptian economy as well as in American education.

Abdulla and Um Fethy have retired from their small fishing enterprise on the Nile and are working as resident caretakers on the *Fostat*, the houseboat of the American Research Center in Egypt. Um Fethy says she is too old to sleep outside anymore.

Muhammad, our friend from Egyptian Nubia, is running his own Nubian project these days, with help from the Ford Foundation and from members of the Nubian community in Egypt and abroad. We hear that the Nubian cultural center is rising in Aswan, near the Cataract Hotel; Muhammad recently visited other African countries to get ideas for promoting his new center.

Omar, our friend in Marrakech, is indeed building a luxurious "villa" in the palm gardens outside the city, though his mother insists she will never leave the comfort and convenience of her house in the medina.

Aisha is recovering from her grief over her daughter's death, but she is worried about her two younger sons, who as of this date are without full-time employment. Her oldest son is teaching French in a secondary school in one of the new suburbs of Marrakech, where he has just received a merit promotion. He is married and has a son, who is currently the delight of Aisha's life. She cares for her small grandson while her son and daughter-in-law both work. "That," she explained, "is the modern way and I like it." Then she added wistfully, "I do wish they would have more children, though. At least one more. Who knows what's going to happen tomorrow?"

June 1984
Austin, Texas

INDEX